UNDERSTANDING
AND MANAGING
PUBLIC ORGANIZATIONS

UNDERSTANDING AND MANAGING PUBLIC ORGANIZATIONS

SECOND EDITION

Hal G. Rainey

Jossey-Bass Publishers
San Francisco

Jossey-Bass books and products are available through most bookstores. To contact Jossey-Bass directly, call (888) 378-2537, fax to (800) 605-2665, or visit our website at www.josseybass.com.

Substantial discounts on bulk quantities of Jossey-Bass books are available to corporations, professional associations, and other organizations. For details and discount information, contact the special sales department at Jossey-Bass.

Manufactured in the United States of America.

Library of Congress Cataloging-in-Publication Data

Rainey, Hal G. (Hal Griffin), date.
   Understanding and managing public organizations / Hal G. Rainey. — 2nd ed.
      p.   cm. — (The Jossey-Bass public administration series)
   Includes bibliographical references and index.
   ISBN 0-7879-0251-9
   1. Public administration.   I. Title.   II. Series.
JF1351.R27   1996
   350—dc20   96-25383

HB Printing   10 9 8 7 6 5 4   SECOND EDITION

THE JOSSEY-BASS NONPROFIT

AND PUBLIC MANAGEMENT SERIES

CONTENTS

PART ONE: THE DYNAMIC CONTEXT OF PUBLIC ORGANIZATIONS

PART TWO: KEY DIMENSIONS OF ORGANIZING AND MANAGING

PART THREE: STRATEGIES FOR MANAGING AND IMPROVING PUBLIC ORGANIZATIONS

FIGURES AND TABLES

Figures

Tables

PREFACE

The first edition of this book provided a review of the literature on management and organization theory and addressed applications for the public sector grounded in evidence from research on public organizations and their members. It was intended to be valuable to practicing managers, scholars, and students in the field. It has served primarily as a text in courses for master of public administration students and in seminars for doctoral students in public administration, seeing wide use for a book of this type. The revisions in this edition seek to enhance the book's usefulness in such courses.

Reviewers who critiqued the proposal for this edition mentioned that the book needed more learning aids of the sort most textbooks use, such as tables, figures, and examples. This edition includes numerous new tables and figures and some additional examples to flesh out the discussion of some of its topics.

The reviewers also suggested greater integration among the chapters and the addition of an organizing framework for the material. The first chapter presents a conceptual framework that links the chapters and topics in the book. That framework emphasizes a fundamental challenge for leaders and members of organizations, that of integrating and coordinating the components and domains of their organization, including its environment, its strategy- and decision-making processes, its goals and values, its culture, its structure, its authority and power relationships, its tasks, its communication processes, and, of course, its people—its leaders, teams, and groups, and their individual motivations, work attitudes, and behaviors. As this book illustrates, the management field has developed no comprehensive theory or scientific solution that achieves this integration. Yet the chapters in this book describe concepts and insights from the organization and management literature that support leaders' and managers' efforts to think and act comprehensively, to integrate the myriad topics and issues that they face that are addressed in this book. The final chapter illustrates how to use the framework in approaching various management challenges, such as managing privatization of public services and managing volunteer programs, in an integrative, comprehensive fashion.

The conceptual framework is fleshed out in the chapters that review the theory, research, and practice associated with major topics in the field of organization management. As Chapter One describes, the rapid development of the field of public management and leadership has continued since the first edition was published. Accordingly, many chapters and topics in this edition have been expanded to cover new material and new developments in the field. For example, the chapters on motivation (Chapters Nine and Ten) and leadership (Chapter Eleven) include more coverage of recent research and thought on those topics, such as the theory of goal setting as a motivational procedure. The discussion of organizational culture and the role of leaders within it has also been greatly expanded. This edition also covers new research on such topics as how public managers lead and behave, excellence and high performance in government agencies, public service networks and "third-party" government, the nature of public service motivation, organizational commitment in public organizations, differences between public and private managers' perceptions of the personnel systems they work with, organizational culture in public organizations, and many other topics.

In addition, this edition adds coverage of some important new developments in general management and public management. These include Total Quality Management and the influence of the best-selling book *Reinventing Government* (Osborne and Gaebler, 1992) on public management (including the federal government's National Performance Review, the management of privatization and volunteer programs, and other topics).

These latter topics receive the greatest attention in the final chapter of the book, which brings up a fundamental issue about the book, about management and organization, and about the book's audience. The fundamental issue concerns comprehensive thinking about organizing and managing and the value of the earlier chapters for support of such thinking. The last chapter of the first edition had a final section that provided exhortations and advice to public managers, including aphoristic sayings or prescriptions such as "know the system" and "make management matter." These points of advice were intended to be like others that have been popular in the management literature, such as those included in Peters and Waterman's *In Search of Excellence* (1982), which exhorts managers to "stick to the knitting" and "stay close to the customer," or those that inform the basic approach to quality management advanced by Deming (1986; described in Chapter Fourteen)—"learn the new philosophy" and "drive out fear." But some reviewers of the first edition complained that the proverbial advice given in the final chapter sounded simplistic and provided little useful guidance to managers. Actually, like Peters and Waterman's and Deming's simple-sounding aphorisms, that advice was elaborated upon and supported by the previous discussions in the book and by the discussions that accompanied them.

That final section is gone from this book. Its banishment not only responds to the criticisms of colleagues but also reflects a new decision about the nature of the book and about how to help students consider challenges in management and administration. The management literature has resounded with the sorts of aphorisms and glib points mentioned above. One could describe the trend as the *Reader's Digest* approach to leadership and management. *Reader's Digest* often carries articles that offer advice on personal matters that is condensed into snappy lists of simple prescriptions, such as "put fun into your exercise program" (for losing weight) or "put fun into your child's study periods" (to improve your child's grades). Such lists can be useful. Given the limited time they have to read and the brief periods they spend in training programs, managers often value crisp, stimulating, memorable bits of advice. As the literature on management points out (and this book affirms), clear, concise expression of values, principles, and priorities can have great value in organizations.

At the same time, however, this book emphasizes the importance of a well-informed, long-term, integrative approach to the management of organizations. The best advice I can provide is that leaders and managers should not seek quick advice from a person like myself, especially advice given in glib bursts. They should carefully develop their own approaches to management.

We can draw an example of this point from the 1991 Gulf War. Whether or not one supported the Bush administration's decision to use military force in the Persian Gulf, the Gulf War certainly involved practical management and leadership challenges. Observers described the U.S. forces as probably the best-educated, most intellectually talented military body ever put into the field. The members of that force reportedly did a lot of reading; one of the most popular books was Clausewitz's classic military treatise *On War* (1986). Clausewitz essentially takes the position that he cannot advise an individual commander on how to conduct a specific campaign, since such situations are so highly varied and contingent. Rather, he aims to provide general perspective and insight on how to conceive the nature and enterprise of war. The Gulf War was a successful campaign, in some ways supremely successful. Even persons who loathe military force and military analogies might accept the point that the Gulf War illustrates how people facing practical challenges often profit from general understanding and insight as much as from detailed prescriptions.

This edition provides a lot of useful guidance for those faced with practical leadership and management challenges, including guidance on managing relations with the media (Chapter Five), managing and leading organizational culture (Chapter Eleven), leading organizational change (Chapter Thirteen), motivating employees (Chapter Ten), managing conflict (Chapter Twelve), enhancing one's power and authority (Chapter Seven), and other topics. At various points this edition provides examples of the use of these insights and concepts in the field. For example, Chapter Thirteen provides examples of how strategies for leading organizational change have led to successful large-scale change in government agencies and how not applying such strategies has led to failure in other instances. Chapter Ten points out that many of the efforts to reform pay systems in government would have been much more effective if they had been better informed by a clear understanding of the motivation theories it discusses. Ultimately, the book pursues the theme that effective leadership involves a well-informed, thoughtful, integrative use of a variety of management concepts and points rather than the hot pursuit of catchy phrases and glib advice.

Audience

This edition of *Understanding and Managing Public Organizations* is intended primarily for graduate students and scholars interested in public management and applications of organization theory to the public sector. Reviewers of the first edition said that practitioners would be unlikely to delve into the detailed reviews of research and theory it provided. I concede this point, but begrudgingly. This assumption underestimates many practicing leaders and managers—certainly many of those that I have encountered. Many of them, given the time and opportunity, are among the most thoughtful and reflective students of leadership and management. They may dislike abstruse and ponderous academic discourse, because they are inclined to action and practical results. They may find quick advice and bright ideas attractive, because they do not have a great deal of time to read. They do not spend long periods in management courses but rather receive shorter doses of training and consultation that they use to search for new ideas and solutions. Yet practicing managers enrolled in long courses in academic settings often lead their classes in insight and in interest in new concepts and broad perspectives. They often spurn war stories and how-to manuals.

As the last paragraph suggests, the line between practicing managers, students, and management scholars is often blurred. Sometimes practicing managers seek degrees in long-term academic programs and play the role of student. Often they teach courses or help to do so. My colleague Larry O'Toole points out that many academics act as practitioners or quasi practitioners in their service on commissions and their research and consulting activities. Thus, although its primary goal is to serve students and scholars interested in research and theory, the book can also serve practicing managers and leaders. I therefore cling to the belief that this book can provide a reference for busy managers who want a review of basic topics in the field, who might find the conceptual framework useful, or who might value the book in other ways.

Organization

The best overview of the organization of the book comes from reviewing the table of contents. Part One covers the dynamic context of public organizations. Its five chapters introduce the basic objectives and assumptions of the book and the conceptual framework mentioned above. Chapter One introduces the book by discussing the current context of public management in practice and in scholarship and the challenges this raises for developing the application of organization and management theory to public organizations. Chapter Two provides a summary of the history of organization and management theory, describing the development of some of the most important concepts and issues in this field, developed further in later chapters. In addition, this historical review shows that most of the prominent organization and management theorists have been concerned with developing the general theory of organizations and not particularly interested in public organizations as a category. Their disinterest in public organizations justifies the effort in this book to apply organization theory to public organizations and illustrates the challenges involved. Chapter Three defines public organizations and distinguishes them from private ones. It also provides an introductory overview of the assertions about the nature of public organizations made in later chapters. Chapters Four and Five review the literature on organizational environments, particularly the political and institutional environments of public organizations.

Part Two focuses on key dimensions of organizing and managing. These chapters concentrate on major topics in organization theory and management, including goals and effectiveness, power, strategy, decision making, structure and design, and the people in organizations (including discussions of values, motivation, work-related behaviors and attitudes, leadership, organizational culture, teams and groups, communication, and conflict). They describe current research on these topics and discuss how they apply to public organizations.

Part Three covers strategies for managing and improving public organizations. Chapter Thirteen covers organizational change and development. The last chapter of the book, as mentioned above, covers ideas about achieving organizational excellence in the public sector, including recent developments such as the total quality movement, increased privatization, and greater attention to volunteer programs.

Finally, the chapter illustrates how the conceptual framework may be used to pursue a comprehensive management strategy that addresses both new initiatives and long-standing challenges.

Acknowledgments

I owe thanks to all the people mentioned in the first edition, and the list has grown even longer. It defies enumeration here. Despite my concern about leaving out anyone, I must leave out a great many anyway. I offer thanks to all the people who have discussed the book with me, made suggestions, or otherwise provided support or insight. These include Bob Backoff, Kathy Boyd, Barry Bozeman, Linda DeLeon, Santa Falcone, Bob Golembiewski, Ed Kellough, Tom Lauth, Jerry Legge, Rosemary O'Leary, Dorothy Olshfski, Larry O'Toole, Sanjay Pandey, and Jim Perry. I wish to thank Jeff Brudney, Patricia Ingraham, and Bart Wechsler for providing valuable, rigorous reviews of the proposal for the second edition. I appreciate the help of my colleague and research assistant, Rex Facer, in preparing the manuscript.

Like the first edition, this book is dedicated to my son, Willis, and my daughter, Nancy. My wife, Lucy, contending with a serious long-term illness, has taught me more about courage, without ever mentioning the word, than anyone I have known. She has made the travails of book writing seem trivial.

The assumptions and arguments made in each edition of this book amount to an acknowledgment of the contributions of numerous authors, both those I have cited and those I was unable to draw in due to time and space limitations. These arguments include the assertion that most public organizations are important institutions that provide crucial services. They currently face a measure of public scorn, pressures to perform better with less money, and increasing demands for an elaborate array of functions and services. These pressures are aggravated by misunderstandings, oversimplifications, myths, and outright lies about the nature and performance of public organizations and employees in the United States and many other countries. Public organizations are often highly effective, well-managed entities with hardworking, high-performing employees. Yet public organizations do face distinctive pressures and constraints in addition to the typical challenges all organizations face, and these constraints can lead to dysfunction and poor performance. The review of insights and concepts about organizations and management provided here seeks to support those who strive to maintain and advance the effective management of public organizations. The book thus acknowledges all those who strive with sincerity to provide public, social, or altruistic service.

August 1996   Hal G. Rainey
                                                                      Athens, Georgia

THE AUTHOR

Hal G. Rainey is professor of political science at the University of Georgia. He has published numerous articles on management in the public sector, with an emphasis on leadership, incentives, organizational change, organizational culture and performance, and the comparison of organization and management in the public and private sectors.

The first edition of *Understanding and Managing Public Organizations* won the Best Book Award of the Public and Nonprofit Sectors Division of the Academy of Management in 1992. In 1995 Rainey received the Charles H. Levine Award for Excellence in Research, Teaching, and Service, conferred jointly by the American Society for Public Administration and the National Association of Schools of Public Affairs and Administration. He has served as chair of the Public and Nonprofit Sectors Division of the Academy of Management and as chair of the Public Administration Section of the American Political Science Association. He received his B.A. degree (1968) in English from the University of North Carolina at Chapel Hill and his M.A. degree (1973) in psychology and Ph.D. degree (1977) in public administration from the Ohio State University.

In 1991, Rainey served on the Governor's Commission on Effectiveness and Economy in Government of the State of Georgia. As a commissioner, he served on the Task Force on Privatization. In 1995 he served on the Athens–Clarke County Consolidation Charter Overview Commission of Athens–Clarke County, Georgia. Before entering university teaching and research, Rainey served as an officer in the U.S. Navy and as a VISTA volunteer.

UNDERSTANDING AND MANAGING PUBLIC ORGANIZATIONS

PART ONE

THE DYNAMIC CONTEXT OF PUBLIC ORGANIZATIONS

CHAPTER ONE

THE CHALLENGE OF EXCELLENCE IN PUBLIC MANAGEMENT

Using Theory and Research to Improve Practice

All nations face decisions about the roles of their government and private institutions in their society. An antigovernment trend around the world during the last several decades has spawned a movement in many countries to curtail government authority and replace it with greater private activity.

This skepticism about government implies that there are sharp differences between government and privately managed organizations, but numerous writers argue that we have too little sound analysis of such differences. They contend that the elaborate body of knowledge we have on management and organizations pays too little attention to the public sector. At the same time, the large body of scholarship in political science and economics concerned with government bureaucracy has too little to say about managing that bureaucracy. This critique has elicited a wave of research and writing on public management and public organization theory, in which experts and researchers have been working to provide more careful analyses of organizational and managerial issues in government.

This chapter elaborates on these points to develop a central theme of this book: we face a dilemma in combining our legitimate skepticism about public organizations with the recognition that they play indispensable roles in society. We need to maintain and improve their effectiveness. We can profit by studying major topics from general management and organization theory and examining the rapidly increasing evidence of their successful application in the public sector. That evidence indicates that the governmental context strongly influences organization and management, often sharply constraining performance. Just as often, however, governmental organizations and managers perform much better than is commonly acknowledged. Examples of effective public management abound. These examples usually reflect the efforts of managers in government who combine managerial skill with effective knowledge of the public sector context. Experts continue to research and debate the nature of this combination, however, as more evidence appears rapidly and in diverse places. This book seeks to base its analysis of public management and organizations on the most careful and current review of this evidence to date.

Recent Ambivalence and Hostility Toward Government

During the last several decades, nations around the world have pursued privatization, selling state-owned enterprises to private operators. Antigovernment sentiment has also swept the United States. Opinion surveys reveal seething resentment of taxes and the widespread conviction that government operates in wasteful and ineffective ways. Tax reduction referenda have appeared on ballots in many states. Angry criticisms have focused on the government with such intensity that the term *bureaucrat bashing* came into use. Jimmy Carter and Ronald Reagan attacked the federal bureaucracy in their election campaigns. President Carter pressed for deregulation of industry, reduction of federal red tape, and major civil service reforms to combat alleged sloth and inefficiency among federal employees. President Reagan more aggressively impugned government and sought reductions in funding and authority for many federal programs and agencies.

Various writers and officials have touted an American version of the privatization movement. Some have proposed that all levels of government should increase contracts with the private sector for provision of services, charge more user fees, and adopt voucher systems whereby clients could choose among providers. Privatization of state and local government functions has increased dramatically (Chi, 1994; Council of State Governments, 1993).

More recently, when Bill Clinton won the presidency from George Bush, the change suggested some weakening of the antigovernment trend, since Clinton was the more liberal and progovernment of the two candidates. Nevertheless, President Clinton initiated the National Performance Review (NPR), a major review of the operations of the federal government, claiming that the federal government worked poorly and needed a drastic overhaul. In addition to many presidential directives and congressional actions aimed at achieving such reforms (described in Chapter Fourteen), the NPR involved aggressive efforts to cut employment in the federal work force by about 11 percent.

Then the 1994 elections brought into Congress the first Republican majority in recent history. These Republicans were led by a group of conservatives who took over powerful positions in Congress and proclaimed their intention to reduce the size of the federal government and its intrusiveness in the lives of U.S. citizens. Among other actions, they mounted a drive to balance the federal budget through sharp cuts in federal spending and reductions in federal programs. President Clinton announced his own plan to balance the budget through spending cuts. Thus the president and congressional leaders clashed not over whether the budget should be balanced but over how fast this should happen and what the specific cuts should be. A dramatic illustration of one of the central themes of this book—that management and organizational behavior in public organizations are significantly influenced by the political environment—is provided by the impasses between the president and the congressional leadership in their negotiations over the budget in 1995 and 1996. During these stalemates, much federal government activity had to be halted due to lack of funds, and many federal workers had to be furloughed.

These developments reflect the assumptions noted above, that government activities differ from those of the private sector and are performed less effectively and efficiently. In the United States, these beliefs serve as fundamental principles of the political economy. Many political ideologues and economic theorists treat them as truisms. Surveys find that the majority of citizens accept them.

Americans regard government with more ambivalence than hostility, however. Government in the United States, at all levels, stands as one of the great achievements of the nation and one of the most significant institutions in human history. No major nation operates without a large, influential public sector. Government in the United States accounts for a smaller proportion of the gross national product than do governments in most of the other major nations of the world, including economically successful ones. Taxes in the United States are low by international standards; as a percentage of the gross domestic product, the taxes levied by governments in the United States are among the lowest of the major industrialized nations. The contention that government in the United States is a massively ineffective, expensive, wasteful, overweening institution is not very well supported by international comparisons.

Americans show an implicit recognition of this fact. The same surveys that find waning faith in government also find fundamental support for a strong governmental role (Lipset and Schneider, 1987; Katz, Gutek, Kahn, and Barton, 1975). Even as the antigovernment trend described above was playing out, demands for a strong and active government continued. During the Bush administration, the nation launched Operation Desert Storm in the Persian Gulf. Popular support was overwhelming for this massive federal effort, which involved not just the Department of Defense but many additional federal agencies in moving a huge military force to Saudi Arabia. Critics of the action who urged caution were castigated by supporters of the war. Significantly, in relation to the theme of this book, critics had lambasted the U.S. military ever since the Vietnam War as being ineffective and poorly managed and led. In the months before the Gulf War commentators further worried that American weapons would malfunction in the desert and that American losses would be severe. But whether one supported the military action or not, it is clear that it was supremely successful by any reasonable standard. It crippled the Iraqi army, with American losses kept at such a low level that, while each lost life was tragic, the result bordered on the miraculous. The Gulf War illustrates Americans' tendency to sharply criticize their government even as they strongly support it in certain ways—and even though it often performs very well.

The struggle between President Clinton and the Republican leaders in Congress over the budget deficit during 1995 and 1996 is an example of the American public's paradoxical demand for both reduced government and for large government programs. In the debates over what part of the federal budget to cut, both sides omitted defense programs and Social Security from any serious consideration. Much of the debate centered on Medicare spending, and even that part of the debate was complicated by the findings of some surveys that a majority of Americans opposed cuts in this program as well. In the 1995 budget, defense spending, Social Security, Medicare, and interest on the federal debt accounted for slightly more than two-thirds of all federal expenditures. The budget cutters faced the chronic problem raised by Americans' penchant for complaining about taxes and big government even as they demand extensive government programs and services.

Hirschman (1982) has argued that sentiments for and against government activity wax and wane cyclically in the United States and other countries. That may be true of the predominant sentiments and actions at a given time. The situations just described, however, suggest that Americans often support both positions simultaneously. Americans have continued to play out the time-honored paradox of conferring massive funding and responsibility on government agencies and officials even as they castigate and ridicule them (Whorton and Worthley, 1981; Sharkansky, 1989). The book *Reinventing Government* (Osborne and Gaebler, 1992), which became a highly influential best-seller and exerted a major influence on the Clinton administration's National Performance Review, actually embraced both the positive and negative side of this paradox at the same time. The authors called for many reforms aimed at reinventing government (see Chapter Fourteen and below) because, they said, government was failing in many ways. Yet they also insisted that government performs crucial functions and that this makes effective public management essential. Significantly, they drew almost all of their proposals for reforms and effective practices from their observations of excellent and innovative practices already under way in many government agencies around the nation.

This pattern of ambivalence reveals an added dimension to the basic beliefs about government and business mentioned earlier: although Americans tend to regard government as different from and less efficient and effective than business, many of them also regard government as crucial. Thus, the United States struggles with a more complex version of the dilemma faced by all nations. We know that both government and private activities have strengths and weaknesses. The challenge lies in designing the proper mix and balance of the two and doing what we can to attain effective management of both (Lindblom, 1977).

General Management and Public Management

To begin our analysis of public organizations, we need to clarify which areas of research and expert opinion this book draws upon. The historical review in Chapter Three and the discussion in later chapters will show that scholars in sociology, psychology, and business administration have developed an elaborate body of knowledge in the fields of organizational behavior and organization theory.

Organizational Behavior, Organization Theory, and Management

The study of organizational behavior had its primary origins in industrial and social psychology. Researchers of organizational behavior typically concentrate on individual and group behaviors in organizations, analyzing motivation, work satisfaction, leadership, work-group dynamics, and the attitudes and behaviors of the members of organizations. Organization theory, on the other hand, is based more in sociology. It focuses on topics that concern the organization as a whole, such as organizational environments, goals and effectiveness, strategy and decision making, change and innovation, and structure and design. Some writers treat organizational behavior as a subfield of organization theory. The distinction is primarily a matter of specialization among researchers; it is reflected in the relative emphasis each topic receives in specific textbooks (Daft, 1995; Hellriegel, Slocum, and Woodman, 1995) and in divisions of professional associations.

Organization theory and organizational behavior are covered in every reputable, accredited program of business administration, public administration, educational administration, or other form of administration, because they are considered relevant to management. The term *management* is used in widely diverse ways, and the study of this field includes the use of sources outside typical academic research, such as government reports, books on applied management, and observations of practicing managers about their work. While many elements play crucial roles in effective management—finance, information systems, inventory, purchasing, production processes, and others—this book concentrates on organizational behavior and theory. We can further define this concentration as the analysis and practice of such functions as leading, organizing, motivating, planning and strategy making, evaluating effectiveness, and communicating.

A strong tradition, hereafter called the "generic tradition," pervades organization theory, organizational behavior, and general management. As discussed in Chapters Two and Three, most of the major figures in this field, both classical and contemporary, apply their theories and insights to all types of organizations. They have worked to build a general body of knowledge about organizations and management. Some pointedly reject any distinctions between public and private organizations as crude stereotypes. Many current texts on organization theory and management contain applications to public, private, and nonprofit organizations (Daft, 1995).

In addition, management researchers and consultants frequently work with public organizations and use the same concepts and techniques they use with private businesses. They argue that their theories and frameworks apply to public organizations and managers since management and organization in government, nonprofit, and private business settings face similar challenges and follow generally similar patterns.

Public Administration, Economics, and Political Science

The generic tradition offers many valuable insights and concepts, as this book will illustrate repeatedly. Nevertheless, we do have a body of knowledge specific to public organizations and management. We have a huge government, and it entails an immense amount of managerial activity. City managers, for example, have become highly professionalized. We have a huge body of literature and knowledge on public administration. Economists have developed theories of public bureaucracy (Downs, 1967). Political scientists have written extensively about it (Hill, 1992; Meier, 1993; Stillman, 1996). These political scientists and economists usually depict the public bureaucracy as quite different from private business. Political scientists concentrate on the political role of public organizations and their relationships with legislators, courts, chief executives, and interest groups. Economists analyzing the public bureaucracy emphasize the absence of economic markets for its outputs. They have usually concluded that this absence of markets makes public organizations more bureaucratic, inefficient, change-resistant, and susceptible to political influence than private firms (Barton, 1980; Breton and Wintrobe, 1982; Dahl and Lindblom, 1953; Downs, 1967; Niskanen, 1971; Tullock, 1965).

In the 1970s, authors began to point out the divergence between the generic management literature and that on the public bureaucracy and to call for better integration of these topics (Allison, 1983; Bozeman, 1987; Hood and Dunsire, 1981; Lynn, 1981; Meyer, 1979; Perry and Kraemer, 1983; Pitt and Smith, 1981; Rainey, Backoff, and Levine, 1976; Wamsley and Zald, 1973; Warwick, 1975). These authors noted that organization theory and the organizational behavior literature offer elaborate models and concepts for analyzing organizational structure, change, decisions, strategy, environments, motivation, leadership, and other important topics. In addition, researchers had tested these frameworks in empirical research. Because of their generic approach, however, they paid too little attention to the issues raised by political scientists and economists concerning public organizations. For instance, they virtually ignored the internationally significant issue of whether government ownership and economic market exposure make a difference for management and organization.

Critics also faulted the writings in political science and public administration for too much anecdotal description and too little theory and systematic research (Perry and Kraemer, 1983; Pitt and Smith, 1981). Scholars in public administration generally disparaged as inadequate the research and theory in that field (McCurdy and Cleary, 1984; Kraemer and Perry, 1989; White and Adams, 1994). In a national survey of research projects on public management, Garson and Overman (1981, 1982) found relatively little funded research on general public management and concluded that the research that did exist was highly fragmented and diverse.

Neither the political science nor the economics literature on public bureaucracy paid as much attention to internal management—designing the structure of the organization, motivating and leading employees, developing internal communications and teamwork—as did the organization theory and general management literature. From the perspective of organization theory, many of the general observations of political scientists and economists about motivation, structure, and other aspects of the public bureaucracy appeared oversimplified.

Issues in Education and Practice

Concerns about the practice of public management and about educating people for it also fueled the debate about public sector organization theory and management. In the wake of the upsurge in government activity during the 1960s, graduate programs in public administration spread among universities around the country. The National Association of Schools of Public Affairs and Administration began to accredit these programs. Among other criteria, this process required master of public administration (M.P.A.) programs to emphasize management skills and technical knowledge rather than to provide a modified master's program in political science. This implied the importance of identifying how M.P.A. programs compare to master of business administration (M.B.A.) programs in preparing people for management positions. At the same time, it raised the question of how public management differs from business management.

These developments coincided with expressions of concern about the adequacy of our knowledge of public management. In 1979 the U.S. Office of Personnel Management (1980) organized a prestigious conference at the Brookings Institution. The conference featured statements by prominent academics and government officials about the need for research on public management. It sought to address a widespread concern among both practitioners and researchers about "the lack of depth of knowledge in this field" (p. 7). At around the same time, various authors produced a stream of articles and books arguing that public sector management involves relatively distinct issues and approaches. They also complained, however, that too little research and theory and too few case exercises directly addressed the practice of active, effective public management (Allison, 1983; Chase and Reveal, 1983; Lynn, 1981, 1987).

Ineffective Public Management?

Recurrent complaints about inadequacies in the practice of public management have also fueled interest in the field. We generally recognize that large bureaucracies—especially government bureaucracies—have a pervasive influence on our lives (Chackerian and Abcarian, 1984). They often blunder, and they can harm and oppress people, both inside the organizations and without (Denhardt, 1984; Hummel, 1994). We face severe challenges in ensuring both their effective operation and our control over them through democratic processes. Some analysts contend that our efforts to maintain this balance of effective operation and democratic control often create disincentives and constraints that prevent many public administrators from assuming the managerial roles that managers in industry typically play (Warwick, 1975; Lynn, 1981; National Academy of Public Administration, 1986; Ban, 1995; Gore, 1993; Thompson, 1993). Some of these authors argue that too many public managers fail to seriously engage the challenges of motivating their subordinates, effectively designing their organizations and work processes, and otherwise actively managing their responsibilities. Both elected and politically appointed officials face short terms in office, complex laws and rules that constrain the changes they can make, intense external political pressures, and sometimes their own amateurishness. Many concentrate on pressing public policy issues and, at their worst, exhibit political showmanship and pay little attention to the internal management of agencies and programs under their authority.

Middle managers and career civil servants, constrained by central rules, have little authority or incentive to manage.

Experts also complain that too often elected officials charged with overseeing public organizations show too little concern with effectively managing them. Elected officials have little political incentive to attend to "good government" issues, such as effective management of agencies. Some have little managerial background, and some tend to interpret managerial issues in ways that would be considered outmoded by management experts. Many legislators and politically elected or appointed executives adhere to an "administrative orthodoxy" (Warwick, 1975; Knott and Miller, 1987). They believe that sound management requires a strict hierarchy of accountability in government agencies, strict accounting and control, elaborate reporting requirements, and tightly specified procedures. This orientation conflicts sharply with contemporary management thought and the practices of many of the most successful business firms.

The Dilemmas of Improving Public Management

The task of trying to control the federal bureaucracy in an environment of prevailing public hostility toward government requires better analyses of how external political processes influence organizations and management in government. The constant struggle for political control of the bureaucracy has often led to negative, control-oriented approaches that backfire.

Having attacked the federal bureaucracy in their election campaigns, Presidents Carter and Reagan moved to control and curtail it. Carter administration officials developed the Civil Service Reform Act of 1978 as a management-improvement initiative. Its provisions included steps to make it easier to discipline federal employees, to base pay more directly on performance, and to make it easier for politically appointed agency heads to select and transfer the career civil service managers who work under them. Yet administration officials saw little political support for a "good government" initiative. They found that they could mobilize support most effectively by stressing the difficulty of firing lazy, incompetent civil servants. Newspapers seized on this angle enthusiastically (Kettl, 1989). Later, surveys found that the act had resulted in high levels of insecurity and discouragement among federal managers.

President Reagan attacked federal agencies even more aggressively and worked for cuts in their authority, funding, and staffing. Reagan administration officials sought to increase the president's authority over federal agencies and to squelch resistance to his initiatives from career civil servants. These officials increased the number of political appointees to high levels within federal agencies.

In effect this demoted career civil servants by placing administration loyalists in positions above them (Volcker Commission, 1989). In addition, aggressive funding cutbacks disrupted many agencies (Rubin, 1985). Some agencies floundered when politically appointed executives were indicted for illegal actions.

Experienced observers began to warn of a crisis in the public service and a need for revitalization (Volcker Commission, 1989; Thompson, 1993; Denhardt and Jennings, 1987). Surveys found serious morale problems, with large percentages of career managers reporting that they intended to leave government and that they would advise their own children against a career in federal service. Other surveys found that students showed little interest in public service careers. Paul Volcker, who had chaired the Federal Reserve Board during the Carter and Reagan administrations, served as chair of the National Commission on the Public Service (1989), which brought together a panel of distinguished public servants to direct an analysis of the crisis and recommend remedies. The commission's report recommended steps to improve public support for public service; to improve pay, performance, recruiting, and training; and to improve relations between political appointees and career civil servants.

Numerous incidents suggested that the pressures on the public sector and public agencies seriously affected their performance. For example, the explosion of the space shuttle *Challenger* in 1986 was the greatest disaster to befall the American space program. Analysts blamed the catastrophe in part on political pressures on the National Aeronautics and Space Administration (NASA) that overpowered professional criteria in the agency's decision-making processes (Romzek and Dubnick, 1987). Engineers for the private contractor that built the shuttle (its construction had been privatized) warned NASA officials of potential problems with the craft's booster rocket seals in cold weather. Yet NASA officials, concerned about bad publicity due to delays and about possible budget cuts as political pressures on the agency mounted, resisted the warnings and demanded very strong justifications for delaying the launch. Executives for the contractor, perhaps concerned about losing their large contract with NASA, may not have pressed the warnings firmly enough (Kettl, 1988, p. 143).

Ironically, this and other examples illustrate how constraining government managers and diminishing their authority, although touted as a way of controlling the bungling federal bureaucracy, actually demonstrates the essential role those career bureaucrats play. The problems cited above stem from many causes besides the Carter, Reagan, and Bush administrations and reflect ongoing dilemmas in controlling and managing public organizations. Later chapters describe a variety of management reforms in government that have come and gone with dubious results. They raise the question of whether government organizations inherently resist effective management.

Excellence in Public Management

On the other hand, the sharp attacks on government and government agencies and employees evoked a counterattack from authors who argued that public bureaucracies perform better than is commonly acknowledged (Doig and Hargrove, 1987; Downs and Larkey, 1986; Goodsell, 1994; Milward and Rainey, 1983; Tierney, 1988). Others describe successful governmental innovations and policies (Poister, 1988b; Schwartz, 1983). Wamsley and his colleagues (1990) call for increasing recognition that the administrative branches of governments in the United States play as essential and legitimate a role as the other branches of government. Many of these authors point to evidence of excellent performance by many government organizations and officials and the difficulty of proving that the private sector performs better. Attacks on government agencies often misplace the blame, targeting the public bureaucracy for problems that arise from legislative or interest-group pressures. In addition, government bureaucracy serves as an easy target because of public stereotypes and misunderstanding. A Roper poll asked a representative sample of Americans how much of every $100 spent on the Social Security program goes to administrative costs. The median estimate was about $50; the actual figure is about $1.30 (Milward and Rainey, 1983).

In response to this concern as well as those described earlier about the adequacy of the literature and our knowledge about effective public management, the literature has continued to burgeon in the 1990s. Numerous books and articles continue to appear that describe and analyze effective leadership, management, and organizational practices in government agencies (Ban, 1995; Barzelay, 1992; Behn, 1991; Cohen and Eimicke, 1995; Cooper and Wright, 1992; Denhardt, 1993; Doig and Hargrove, 1987; Hargrove and Glidewell, 1990; Osborne and Gaebler, 1992; Riccucci, 1995; Thompson and Jones, 1994).

In addition, illustrating the need for continued careful research and analysis, researchers have produced provocative empirical findings about the characteristics of public organizations and managers. For example, studies have found that if there has been the crisis in the public service described above and lamented by the Volcker Commission, it is not easy to interpret (Lewis, 1991). Steel and Warner (1990) found that job satisfaction among younger employees is higher in the public sector than in the private sector. Other studies have found that the quality of people entering the work force is higher in the public sector than in the private sector (Crewson, 1995a). These findings do not necessarily negate the concerns about the public service that various commissions and experts have raised, but they do illustrate the complexity of public service and issues pertaining to it, and the need for sustained analysis.

The Challenge: Sustained, Serious Attention and Analysis

The controversies described above reflect the fundamental complexities of the American political and economic system. That system has always subjected the administrative branch of government to conflicting pressures over who should control and how, whose interests should be served, and what values should predominate (Waldo, [1947] 1984). Management involves paradoxes that require organizations and managers to balance conflicting objectives and priorities. Public management often involves particularly complex objectives and especially difficult conflicts among them.

In this debate over the performance of the public bureaucracy and whether the public sector represents a unique or a generic management context, both sides are correct, in a sense. General management and organizational concepts can have valuable applications in government; however, unique aspects of the government context must often be taken into account. In fact, the examples of effective public management given in later chapters show that there is often a necessity for both. Managers in public agencies can effectively apply generic management procedures, but they must also skillfully negotiate external political pressures and administrative constraints to create a context in which they can manage effectively. The real challenge involves identifying how much we know about this process and when, where, how, and why it applies. As the Volcker Commission and many of the authors cited in this book have said, we need researchers, practitioners, officials, and citizens to devote sustained, serious attention to developing our knowledge of and support for effective public management.

This book also proceeds on another assumption that may be more debatable among students and scholars in this field. Later chapters will describe many of the calls for reform and improved practices in public management. It will also argue that many exciting ideas about new ways of doing the business of government, such as those in Osborne and Gaebler's *Reinventing Government* (1992), can be improved by a better grounding in basic management topics. Sometimes proposals for new approaches offer new ideas without a clear sense of how to bring them about. They raise very basic issues: How do you exert effective leadership? How do you develop strategy? How do you lead successful change processes? How do you motivate employees? How do you approach the general problem of getting organized? How do you design an organization? How do you deal with external elements, such as the press and the legislative branch? How do you develop effective communication processes and manage conflicts? No book can provide completely conclusive answers for these questions, but this one contributes to the work of scholars, practicing managers, officials, students, and citizens who remain committed to developing answers.

This book provides a review and analysis of some important topics: what we know about distinguishing public organizations from other types of organizations, what we can draw from the major topics in research and theory on management and organizations, and what we know about the public sector context and its implications for those topics. This effort raises challenges of its own. Research and writing on public management have been appearing rapidly in many different places, and this book covers as much of the new evidence as possible. The body of potentially relevant material is overwhelming and beyond the scope of any one volume. The public and private sectors involve myriad variations in organizational levels, types, and settings, and we have not yet developed systematic frameworks for all of them. For each of the topics or variables covered in this book—power, political processes, motivation, leadership, organizational structure, and others—there exists an extensive, diverse body of research that is filled with controversies and is in some ways inconclusive. Yet these challenges represent realities we must confront, just as we must confront the inescapable paradoxes and conflicts inherent in public management.

Organizations: A Definition and a Conceptual Framework

At this point it is useful to clarify the meaning of basic concepts about organizations and to develop a framework to guide the sustained analysis this book will provide. Figure 1.1 presents a framework for this purpose. Figure 1.2 elaborates on some of the basic components of this framework, providing more detail about organizational structures, processes, and people.

Writers on organization theory and management have argued for a long time over how best to define what an organization is, reaching little consensus. It is not a good use of time to worry over a precise definition, so here is a provisional one that employs elements of Figure 1.1. This statement is too long to serve as a precise definition; it actually amounts to more of a perspective on organizations than a simple definition:

> An organization is a group of people who work together to pursue a *goal*. They do so by attaining resources from their *environment*. They seek to transform those resources by accomplishing *tasks* and applying *technologies* to achieve effective *performance* of their goals, thereby attaining additional resources. They deal with the many uncertainties and vagaries associated with these processes by *organizing* their activities. Organizing involves *leadership* processes, through which leaders guide the development of *strategies* for achieving goals and the establishment of structures and processes to support those strategies. *Structures* are the relatively stable, observable assignments and divisions of responsibility within

FIGURE 1.1. A FRAMEWORK FOR ORGANIZATIONAL ANALYSIS.

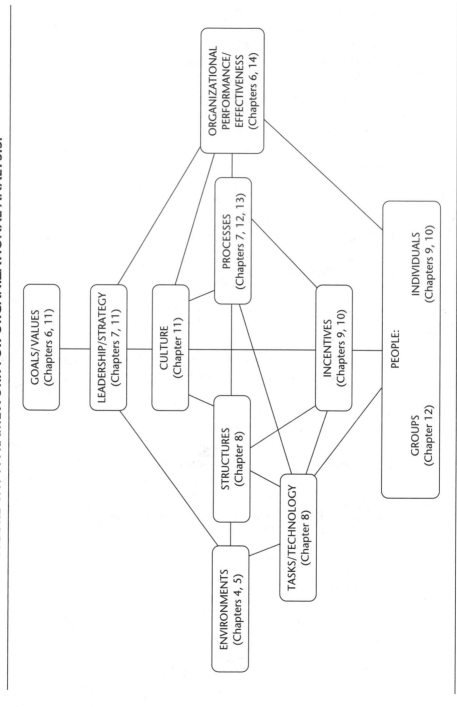

FIGURE 1.2. A FRAMEWORK FOR ORGANIZATIONAL ANALYSIS (ELABORATION OF FIGURE 1.1).

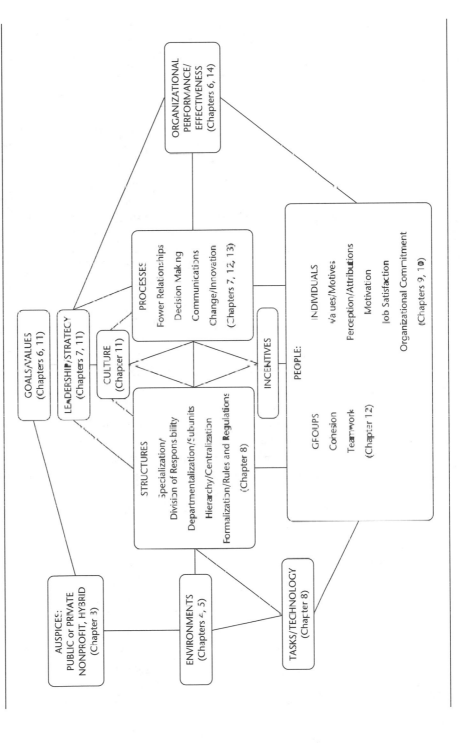

the organization, achieved through such means as hierarchies of authority, rules and regulations, and specialization of individuals, groups, and subunits. The division of responsibility determined by the organizational structure divides the organization's goals into components that the different groups and individuals can concentrate on—hence the term *organ*ization, referring to the set of organs that make up the whole. This division of responsibility requires that the individual activities and units be coordinated. Structures such as rules and regulations and hierarchies of authority can aid coordination. *Processes* are less physically observable, more dynamic activities that also play a major role in the response to this imperative for coordination. They include such processes as determining power relationships, decision making, evaluation, communication, conflict resolution, and change and innovation. Within these structures and processes, *groups* and *individuals* respond to *incentives* presented to them, making the contributions and producing the products and services that ultimately result in effective performance.

Implications of the Framework and Definition

This definition and this framework may seem very general and noncontroversial. They have some strong implications, however, that can be controversial among people who study organizations and management. Some of these implications are illustrated in the historical overview in Chapter Two, which will show why some of the parts of the framework are included and treated as they are.

Some of the characteristics of the framework and definition raise important issues about organizations that organization theorists have debated over the years. For example, some experts on organizations and management would point out that the definition is rather idealized, since it implies that leaders "guide" strategy development (implying both that strategies are developed and that this development is participative), that people work together to achieve common goals, and that organizational structures and processes support the strategy and provide incentives to the people. Actually, people in organizations may not always work together—they may work against each other in important ways. Furthermore, organizations' goals are often very hard to identify—as we will discuss in detail later—and the people in an organization may differ sharply about what they think the goals are or ought to be. The definition also implies that the efforts of an organization's members—its leaders and other participants—determine its performance, but some organization theorists have produced evidence that external forces, such as economic, political, and market conditions, may determine organizational performance. For example, experts have pointed out for years that elected officials will sometimes assign impossible tasks to public agencies, give them inadequate funding, and then blame them for failing to perform the required tasks.

On the other hand, some organization and management theorists would say that my definition and framework are not idealized enough. They might criticize them for being too "top-down" in their orientation, for exalting too highly the role of high-level leaders and placing too much emphasis on the control by structures and processes of people at lower levels. Some leaders develop poor strategies or none at all, and some actually damage their organization and its people, either intentionally or inadvertently. Later chapters will show that contemporary discussions of management often concern giving authority and freedom to organization members to prevent higher-level managers and organizational structures from stifling their creativity and productivity. So this criticism of my definition and conceptual framework raises some very important issues. If it concerns you, please turn Figures 1.1 and 1.2 upside down to put the people at the top of each figure.

This is not simply a flippant suggestion. In Chapter Thirteen we will encounter the example of the executive who had her agency's organizational chart inverted to put its clients at the top. The idea was to make a symbolic statement emphasizing the importance of the agency's clients, as a way of promoting that value among the people in and around the agency. But she could do the same for the individuals in the agency as well.

The point is that the placement of the components in Figure 1.1 is not meant to depict what is most important. For example, it does not mean to assert that leaders play a more grandiose role than the other people in the organization because they are placed at a higher level on the figure. Nor does the figure propose causal precedence among its components—for example, that environments determine structures, processes, organizational performance, and so on. For many of the boxes in the diagram, the lines connect them to indicate that the two parts interrelate with each other. Influence can run both ways. For example, an organization's environment can influence its executive-level leaders. In public agencies, they are often influenced by directives from the chief executive, the legislature, and other authorities, such as personnel and purchasing agencies. Yet, as later chapters describe, leaders in public agencies also act on their environments, by working with legislators, developing and employing the support of interest groups, seeking to influence public opinion, and in many other ways. Similarly, structures and processes influence people, but people also influence structures and processes. The same is true of all the components of Figures 1.1 and 1.2. They virtually all interrelate.

Is the framework in these figures simpleminded and obvious? In a way it is, but it has important implications and a lot of value. In Peters and Waterman's

In Search of Excellence (1982), a best-selling management book that had a tremendous following among managers in industry and government during the 1980s, the authors present a schematic called the McKinsey 7-S framework in the introductory part of the book. It consists of seven circles, with one of the following terms in each circle: strategy, structure, systems, shared values, skills, style (referring to management style), and staff. Each circle has a line connecting it to each of the other circles. Peters and Waterman said that they had found the figure very useful as a guide for analyzing excellent corporations in the United States. They described other, very prominent management consultants, professors, and researchers who also used the framework.

The success of the McKinsey framework underscores several points in relation to Figures 1.1 and 1.2. First, part of the challenge of organizing and managing involves deciding how to *think about* organizing and managing. What do you look at? What is important? What do you analyze? What decisions do you need to make? The next chapter shows that the way scholars and practicing managers think about managing plays a major role in determining how organizations look and operate and how managers manage. We will see that the evolution in thinking about organizations and management across this century has had such effects. The next chapter will show that earlier in this century, management experts and organization theorists would have produced a different diagram from that in Figure 1.1 and 1.2 or the McKinsey framework. The McKinsey framework proved valuable because it offered a guide to important topics, issues, and components in deciding how to organize and manage. Later chapters will show how the framework in Figures 1.1 and 1.2 can be useful in approaching the question of how to manage privatization and volunteer programs and how to approach the topic of organizational performance, effectiveness, and assessment.

This evolution in management thought raises another point. One of the major challenges in organizing and managing is the challenge of achieving comprehensive, coordinated thought and action. The McKinsey framework has lines running back and forth between all the circles to emphasize the need to coordinate all those components. Figures 1.1 and 1.2 have lines between components to show their interrelatedness and to emphasize this point about comprehensive thinking. The challenge in developing comprehensive thinking and coordinating the different aspects of organizing is one of the primary challenges of management. Unfortunately, we have no scientific, systematic procedure for achieving this integration. Organizational leaders have to try to manage the elements in Figures 1.1 and 1.2 and coordinate them using their judgment and experience. This book seeks to help with that process by providing a review of what organization theorists and researchers have learned about the topics in the framework and the figures. We start with a review of developments in the field across this century to show how the parts of the figure got there to begin with, and then later chapters will go into more depth about them.

Summing Up Some Key Points

This chapter has advanced the following points and assumptions for the book.

An antigovernment trend is evident in the public's attitudes and actions in the United States and many other nations. Many people assume that government organizations cannot perform as effectively or efficiently as private ones. Yet this assumption is not grounded in sound evidence, and it runs against some important themes in organization theory and management.

In the United States this antigovernment trend involves a measure of ambivalence. Citizens support a strong role for government in many ways and make many demands of government and government agencies. They support the delegation of large amounts of authority and funding to government agencies and officials. These pressures indicate the continuing need to improve the performance of government agencies.

We can improve public management and the performance of public agencies by learning about the literature on organization theory, organizational behavior, and general management and applying it to government agencies and activities.

The literature on organizations and management has not paid enough attention to public sector organizations and managers. This book integrates research and thought on the public sector context with the more general organizational and management theories and research.

This integration has important implications for the debates over whether public management is basically ineffective or often excellent and over how to reform and improve public management and education for people who pursue it. A sustained, careful analysis, drawing on available concepts, theories, and research and organized around the general framework presented above, can contribute usefully to advancing our knowledge of these topics.

CHAPTER TWO

UNDERSTANDING THE STUDY OF ORGANIZATIONS

A Historical Review

Large, complex organizations have existed for many centuries, but they have proliferated tremendously within the last two centuries. Writing about organizations and their administration—and training for managing them—has gone on for many centuries. Yet most of the large body of research and writing available today, like large organizations themselves, has proliferated only fairly recently. This chapter reviews major developments in the research, theory, and thinking about organizations and management over the last century. Table 2.1 provides a summary of developments reviewed in this chapter.

My analysis of public organizations begins with this review for a number of reasons. It illustrates the generic theme mentioned in the previous chapter. It shows that the major contributors to this field have usually treated organizations and management as being generally similar in all contexts, not drawing much of a distinction between the public and private sectors. The generic emphasis has much value, and this book will draw upon it. But it also sets the stage for the controversy over whether public organizations can be treated as a reasonably distinct category. Later chapters will show evidence supporting this claim.

Managers need to be aware of the historical developments summarized in this chapter. The review covers terms, ideas, and names that serve as part of the vocabulary of management, and well-prepared managers need to develop a sound understanding of them. For example, managers regularly refer to "Theory X" and "Theory Y." Warwick (1975) describes how the U.S. secretary of state once

TABLE 2.1. MAJOR DEVELOPMENTS IN ORGANIZATION AND MANAGEMENT THEORY IN THE TWENTIETH CENTURY.

I. *Classic Theories.* Implied a "one best way" to organize and a "closed-system" view of organizations and the people in them.
   A. *Max Weber (Rational-Legal)*
   - Provided one of the early influential analyses of bureaucracy. Defined its basic characteristics, such as hierarchies of authority, career service, selection and promotion on merit, and rules and regulations that define procedures and responsibilities of offices.
   - Argued that these characteristics grounded bureaucracy in a rational-legal form of authority and made it superior to organizational forms based on traditional authority (such as aristocracy) or charismatic authority. Of these alternatives, bureaucracy provides superior efficiency, effectiveness, and protection of clients' rights.
   - Also argued that bureaucracies are subject to problems in external accountability since they are very specialized and expert in their areas of responsibility and may be subject to self-serving and secretive behaviors.
   B. *Frederick Taylor (Scientific Management)*
   - Most prominent figure in the Scientific Management movement.
   - Advocated the use of systematic analyses, such as "time-motion" studies, to design the most efficient procedures for work tasks (usually consisting of high levels of specialization and task simplification).
   - Argued that management must reward workers with fair pay for efficient production so that workers can increase their well-being through productivity. This implies that simplified, specialized tasks and monetary rewards are primary motivators.
   C. *Administrative Management School*
   Sought to develop "principles of administration" that would provide guidelines for effective organization in all types of organizations. The principles tended to emphasize specialization and hierarchical control:
   - Division of Work. Work must be divided among units based on task requirements, geographic location, or interdependency in the work process.
   - Coordination of Work. Work units must be coordinated back together, through other principles:
       Span of Control. A supervisor's "span of control" should be limited to five to ten subordinates.
       One Master. Each subordinate (and subunit) should report directly to only one superior.
       Technical Efficiency. Units should be grouped together for maximum technical efficiency based on work requirements, technological interdependence, or purpose.
   - The Scalar Principle. Authority must be distributed in an organization like locations on a scale; as you move higher in the hierarchy, each position must have successively more authority, with ultimate authority at the top.

II. *Redirections, New Directions, and New Insights.* Toward the middle of the century, new authors challenged the previous perspectives and moved the field in new directions.
   A. *Human Relations and Psychological Theories.*
       1. *Hawthorne Studies: Motivating Factors*
       While studying physical conditions in the workplace, researchers found that weaker lighting in the workplace did not reduce productivity as predicted. They concluded that the attention they paid to the workers during the study increased the workers' sense of importance, the attention they paid to their duties, and their

BLE 2.1. MAJOR DEVELOPMENTS IN ORGANIZATION
NAGEMENT THEORY IN THE TWENTIETH CENTURY, cont'd.

communication, and this raised their productivity. Other phases of the research indicated that the work group played an important role in influencing workers to attend to their job and be productive. The studies have come to be regarded as a classic illustration of the importance of social and psychological factors in motivating workers.

2. *Maslow: The Needs Hierarchy*

Maslow held that human needs and motives fall into a hierarchy, ranging from lower-order to higher-order needs—from physiological needs (food, freedom from extremes of temperature) to needs for safety and security, love and belonging, self-esteem, and finally self-actualization. The needs at each level dominate an individual's motivation and behavior until they are adequately fulfilled, and then the next level of needs will dominate. The highest level, self-actualization, refers to the need to fulfill one's own potential. The theory influenced many other theories, largely due to its emphasis on the motivating potential of higher-order needs.

3. *McGregor: Theories X and Y*

Drawing on Maslow's theory, McGregor argued that management in industry was guided by "Theory X," which saw workers as passive and without motivation and dictated that management must therefore direct and motivate them. Rejecting the emphasis on specialization, task simplification, and hierarchical authority in the scientific and administrative management movements, McGregor argued that management in industry must adopt new structures and procedures based on "Theory Y," which would take advantage of higher-order motives and workers' capacity for self-motivation and self-direction. These new approaches would include such structures and procedures as job enrichment, management by objectives, participative decision making, and improved performance evaluations.

4. *Lewin: Social Psychology and Group Dynamics*

Driven out of Europe by Naziism, Kurt Lewin came to the United States and led a group of researchers in studies of group processes. They conducted pathbreaking experiments on the influence of different types of leaders in groups and the influence of groups on groups members' attitudes and behaviors (for example, they documented that a group member is more likely to maintain a commitment if it is made in front of the group).

This work influenced the development of the field of social psychology and of the group dynamics movement. The group dynamics movement actually developed in two directions. One involved a wave of experimental research on groups in laboratories and organizational settings. For example, a classic study by Coch and French (1948) found that work groups in factories carried out changes more readily if they had participated in the decision to make the change; this study contributed to the growing interest in participative decision making in management. The second direction involved the widespread use of group processes for personal and organizational development, using such methods as encounter groups, "T-groups," and "sensitivity groups."

Lewin developed ideas about attitude and behavior change, based on "force field analysis" and the concept of "unfreezing, moving, and refreezing" group and individual attitudes and behaviors. These ideas are still used widely in the writing about and practice of organizational development.

TABLE 2.1. MAJOR DEVELOPMENTS IN ORGANIZATION AND MANAGEMENT THEORY IN THE TWENTIETH CENTURY, cont'd.

B. *Chester Barnard and Herbert Simon*

   1. *Chester Barnard*

Barnard's sole book, *The Functions of the Executive* (1938), became one of the most influential management books ever written. Departing from the emphases of the administrative management school, he argued the importance of "informal" organizational structures. An organization is an economy of incentives, in which the executive must obtain resources to use in providing incentives for members to participate and cooperate. The executive must stimulate cooperation and communication and must draw on a complex array of incentives, including not just financial incentives but such rewards as fulfilling mutual values, conferring prestige, affirming the desirability of the group, and others (see Table 9.3).

   2. *Herbert Simon*

In his 1946 *Public Administration Review* article "Proverbs of Administration," Simon drew on Barnard's insights to attack the administrative management school. He criticized their "principles" as being more like vague proverbs, in some cases too vague to apply and in some cases contradictory. He called for greater analysis of administrative conditions and behaviors to determine when different principles actually apply.

His book *Administrative Behavior* (1948) pursued these points and called for the scientific study of administrative behavior, with decision making as the central focus. He observed that actual administrative decision making is less rational than many economic theorists had assumed, in that decision makers are less likely to pursue clearly identified and precisely valued goals—with an exhaustive review of alternatives and consistent selection of the path that will maximize goal attainment with minimal expenditure of resources—than such theorists had believed. Instead, administrators' ability to act rationally is often limited by incomplete knowledge and information, limited skills and mental abilities, the inability to predict or anticipate events, and other factors. Instead, they select the best available alternatives after a limited search, using available rules of thumb. Simon later referred to this as "satisficing."

Cyert and March, in a study of business firms reported in *A Behavioral Theory of the Firm* (1963), provided evidence supporting Simon's observations. With others, March's later work along these lines would lead to development of the "garbage can model" of decision making, one of the most prominent current perspectives (see Chapter Seven).

March and Simon's *Organizations* (1958) provided elaborate conceptual frameworks and hypotheses about behavior in organizations, especially about individuals' decisions to join an organization and actively participate in it. Their work influenced the development of empirical research on organizational behavior. Pursuing his interest in decision making, Simon became a leader in research on artificial intelligence, the use of computers to make complex decisions.

Simon's insights about bounded rationality and satisficing, based on his analysis of administrators' challenges in making decisions under conditions of complexity and uncertainty, influenced the development of open-systems and contingency theory (described below). In part because his ideas challenged basic assumptions in much of economic theory, he won the Nobel Prize for economics in 1978.

TABLE 2.1. MAJOR DEVELOPMENTS IN ORGANIZATION AND MANAGEMENT THEORY IN THE TWENTIETH CENTURY, cont'd.

C. *Organizational Sociology and Bureaucratic Dysfunction*
Following in the tradition of Weber, sociologists began studying the characteristics of organizations and bureaucracies.
   1. *Merton (1940): Bureaucratic Structures and Member Personalities*
Some of these authors began to observe that the bureaucratic characteristics Weber had regarded as good could actually lead to bad, or dysfunctional, conditions when they interacted with human characteristics, such as personalities. Merton, for example, observed that specialization, elaborate rules, and an emphasis on adhering to the rules can lead to "trained incapacity," in which people had trouble with problems that did not fit within the rules or their specialization. Also, "displacement of goals" can occur, in which people worry so much about adhering to the rules that their behavior conflicts with the goals of the organization. In addition, people in different departments may pursue the goals of their department more than those of the overall organization.
   2. *Victor Thompson: Bureaupathology*
Victor Thompson, a public administration scholar, argued that bureaucratic organizations can cause "bureaupathology" in their members, who may become overly concerned with protecting the authority of their office and too impersonal in their relations with clients and other members of the organization.
   3. *Selznick: Leadership and Institutionalization*
Many other scholars studied other organizational processes. Selznick, in *TVA and the Grass Roots* (1966), analyzed the ways in which organizations and their leaders develop relationships with external environments, through such processes as "co-optation," or drawing external groups into the decision-making processes of the organization to gain their support. In *Leadership and Administration* (1957), he analyzed the ways in which leaders develop their organizations as "institutions," by influencing the organizational environment, setting major directions for the organization, and supporting these efforts through recruiting, training, and other enhancements of the organization's capacity.
   4. *Kaufman: Socialization*
In his study *The Forest Ranger* (1960), Kaufman analyzed the ways in which the U.S. Forest Service developed the commitment of forest rangers and coordinated the activities of its widely dispersed employees through socialization processes that developed shared values and through accepted rules and procedures.
III. *Relatively Recent Developments*
  A. *Organizational Behavior and Organizational Psychology*
The analysis of humans in organizations described above has led to the development of an elaborate body of theory and research on topics such as the psychology of individuals in organizations, work motivation, and work-related attitudes such as job satisfaction (Chapter Ten), leadership (Chapter Eleven), and group processes in organizations (Chapter Twelve). The group dynamics movement described above has contributed to develop a body of knowledge about organizational development (Chapter Thirteen). These bodies of research, theory, and practice provide an understanding of human behavior and psychology in organizations that far exceeds what the "classic" theories can offer.
  B. *Organization Theory and Design*
The stream of sociological research on organizations described above contributed to a burgeoning field of theory and research on large organizations that has taken many directions and covered many topics in recent years.

TABLE 2.1. MAJOR DEVELOPMENTS IN ORGANIZATION AND MANAGEMENT THEORY IN THE TWENTIETH CENTURY, cont'd.

1. *Adaptive Systems and Contingency Theory*
   One major development—the adaptive-systems perspective—has supplanted the classic view of organizations as machinelike, closed systems with one proper way of organizing. This perspective regards organizations as being varied in their characteristics because of their needs to adapt to the conditions they face. Contingency theories developed the idea that organizations vary between more bureaucratized, highly structured entities and more flexible, loosely structured entities, depending on such contingencies as the nature of their operating environment, their tasks and technologies, their size, and the strategic decisions made by their leadership. The following are examples of influential adaptive systems and contingency-theory studies and analyses:
   - Burns and Stalker (1961), in their research on firms in Great Britain, found that the managerial and structural characteristics of the most successful firms were different in different industries. In industries where the operating environments (competitors, prices, products, technologies) of the firms were stable and predictable, "mechanistic" organizations with classic bureaucratic structures performed well. In industries where these environments were rapidly changing and complex, more flexible, loosely structured, "organic" organizations performed best.
   - Joan Woodward (1965), in studying firms in Great Britain, found that the most effective firms in particular industries did not have the same structural characteristics as the most effective firms in other industries. Rather than there being one best pattern of organization for all industries, the study indicated that the most effective pattern depended on the requirements raised by technological aspects of the work in each industry.
   - Lawrence and Lorsch (1967), in a study of businesses in the United States, found that the best-performing firms have structures that are as complex as their environment. Firms in environments with low levels of uncertainty (more predictable, less complex) operate well with less complex internal structures. Firms in more uncertain, less predictable, more complex environments have higher levels of differentiation (variation among units) and integration (arrangements for coordinating units, such as task forces or liaison roles).
   - Peter Blau and his colleagues (1971) conducted a series of studies that showed that organizational size has an important relationship to organizational structure.
   - Katz and Kahn (1966) published an influential book analyzing organizations as systems.
   - James Thompson (1967) published a highly influential analysis of organizations that integrated the closed- and open-systems perspectives. Drawing on Simon's observations about the challenges of decision making under conditions of bounded rationality, Thompson observed that "dominant coalitions" in organizations strive to set up closed-system conditions and rational decision-making processes, but that as tasks, technologies, environmental conditions, and strategic decisions produce more complexities and uncertainties, organizations must adapt by adopting more flexible, decentralized structures and procedures.
2. *Extensions to Organization Theory*
   Later discussions describe many extensions to the adaptive-systems perspective, such as new theories about the effects of organizational environments (Chapter Four) and more dynamic or adaptive management processes such as organizational culture and market-type arrangements (Chapter Eleven).

opposed an executive's efforts to reorganize a division of the State Department because the secretary thought the reorganization would make the "span of control" too wide. Managers need to know the meaning of such terms and understand their historical context and implications.

We should look at the developments covered in this review for the same reason we study history in general: to gain wisdom, perspective, a knowledge of the alternatives that have been developed, and a sense of the successes and failures of the past. Still another reason is to appreciate a central theme in the study and practice of management—the important role of theory and expert opinion. The review provided here will show that the different bodies of theory about how to organize and manage have strongly influenced, and been influenced by, the way managers and organizations behave. Some of the general trends involve profoundly important beliefs about the nature of human motivation and successful organizations. The review shows, for example, that management theory and practice have evolved over this century. Theories about the motives, values, and capacities of people in organizations have evolved, and this evolution has in turn prompted additional theories concerning how organizations must respond to these new perspectives and how organizations must look and behave in response to the increasing complexity and rapid change in the contexts in which they operate. The review shows that theories are not impractical abstractions but frameworks of ideas that often play a major role in management practice. In fact, as we go through the review, it will illustrate why the framework in Figures 1.1 and 1.2 looks as it does. It will show that the framework actually reflects many of the major developments in the field over the century.

The Systems Metaphor

Figures 1.1 and 1.2 and the accompanying definition of organization in Chapter One implicitly reflect one major organizing theme for these developments. The theme concerns how the field has moved from early (now classical) approaches that emphasized a single appropriate form of organization and management to more recent approaches that reject this "one best way" concept. Recent perspectives emphasize the variety of organizational forms that can be effective under the different "contingencies," or conditions, organizations face.

This trend in organization theory borrows from the literature on general systems theory. This body of theory has developed the idea that there are various types of systems in nature that have much in common. Analyzing them, according to systems theorists, provides insights about diverse entities and a common language for specialists in different fields (Daft, 1995, pp. 11–15; Kast and Rosenzweig, 1973, pp. 37–56; Katz and Kahn, 1966, pp. 19–29).

A system is an ongoing process that transforms certain specified *inputs* into *outputs;* these in turn influence subsequent inputs into the system in a way that supports the continuing operation of the process. One can think of an organization as a system that takes in various resources and transforms them in ways that lead to attaining additional supplies of resources (the definition in Chapter One includes this idea). Systems have subsystems, such as communications systems or production systems within organizations, and *throughput processes,* sets of internal linkages and processes that make up the transformation process. The outputs of the system lead to *feedback,* the influences that the outputs have on subsequent inputs. The systems theorists, then, deserve credit (or blame) for making terms such as *input* and *feedback* part of our everyday jargon. Management analysts have used systems concepts—usually elaborated far beyond the simple description given here—to examine management systems and problems.

A major trend in this century among organizational theorists has been to distinguish between *closed* systems and *open* or *adaptive* systems. Some systems are closed to their environment; the internal processes remain the same regardless of environmental changes. A thermostat is part of a closed system that transforms inputs, in the form of room temperature, into outputs, in the form of responses from heating or air conditioning units. These outputs feed back into the system by changing the room temperature. The system's processes are stable and machinelike. It consistently responds in a programmed pattern.

One can think of a human being as an open or adaptive system. Humans transform their behaviors to adapt to their environment when there are environmental changes for which the "system" is not programmed. Thus, its internal processes are more open to the environment and better able to adapt to shifts in it.

Some organization theorists have expressed skepticism about the usefulness of the systems approach (Meyer, 1979), but others have found it helpful as a metaphor for describing how organization theory has evolved during this century. They say that the earliest, "classical" theories treated organizations and employees as if they were closed systems.

Classical Approaches to Understanding Organizations

These early theories, and the advice they gave to managers, emphasized stable, clearly defined structures and processes, as if organizational goals were always clear and managers' main challenge was to design the most efficient, repetitive, machinelike procedures to maximize attainment of the organization's goals. Some organization theorists also characterize this view as the "one best way" approach to organization.

Frederick Taylor and Scientific Management

Frederick Taylor (1919) is usually cited as one of the pioneers of managerial analysis. He was the major figure in the scientific management school, which in Taylor's own words involved the systematic analysis of "every little act" in tasks to be performed by workers. Taylor asserted that scientific management involved a division of labor that was relatively new in historical terms. Whereas for centuries work processes had been left to the discretion of skilled craftspeople and artisans, scientific management recognized a division of responsibility between a managerial group and a group that performed the work. The role of management was to gather detailed information on work processes, analyze it, and derive rules and guidelines for the most efficient way to perform the required tasks. Workers were then to be selected and trained in these procedures so that they could maximize their output, the quality of their work, and their own earnings.

Taylor and others developed procedures for analyzing and designing tasks which are still in use today. They conducted time-motion studies, which involved the detailed measurement and analysis of physical characteristics of the workplace, such as the placement of tools and machinery in relation to the worker and the movements and time that the worker had to devote to using them. The objective was to achieve the most efficient physical layout for the performance of a specified task. Analytical procedures of this sort are still widely used in government and industry.

Taylor's emphasis on the efficient programming of tasks and workers provoked controversy even in its heyday. In later years critics attacked his work for its apparent inhumanity and its underestimation of psychological and social influences on worker morale and productivity. Some of this criticism is overdrawn and fails to give Taylor credit for the positive aspects of his pioneering work. Taylor actually felt that his methods would benefit workers by allowing them to increase their earnings and the quality of their work. In his own accounts of his work he said that he originally became interested in ways of encouraging workers without supervisors' having to place pressure on them. As a manager, he had been involved in a very unpleasant dispute with workers, which he attributed to the obligation to put them under pressure (Burrell and Morgan, 1980, p. 126). He wanted to find alternatives to such situations.

Yet Taylor did emphasize pay as the primary reward for work. He stressed minute specialization of worker activities, as if the worker were a rather mindless component of a mechanistic process. He did not improve his image with later organizational analysts when he used as an illustration of his techniques a description of his efforts to train a Scandinavian worker, whom he said was as dumb as an ox, in the most efficient procedures for shoveling pig iron. Though the value of his contribution is undeniable, as a guiding conception of organizational analysis, scientific management severely oversimplified the complexity of the needs of humans in the workplace.

Max Weber: Bureaucracy as an Ideal Construct

Also in the early decades of the century, Max Weber's writings became influential, in a related but distinct way. Organization theorists often treat Weber as the founder of organizational sociology—the analysis of complex organizations. His investigations of bureaucracy as a social phenomenon provided the most in fluential early analysis of the topic (Gerth and Mills, 1946).

The proliferation of organizations with authority formally distributed among bureaus or subunits is actually a fairly recent development in human history. Weber undertook to specify the defining characteristics of the bureaucratic form of or ganization, which he saw as a relatively new and desirable form in society. He saw the spread of bureaucratic organizations in society as part of a movement toward more legal and rational forms of authority and away from authority based on tradition (such as monarchical power) or charisma (such as that possessed by a ruler like Napoleon). The bureaucratic form was distinct even from the administrative systems of the ancient Orient (such as in Mandarin China) and others regarded as similar to modern systems. In traditional feudal or aristocratic systems, he said, people's functions were assigned by personal trustees or appointees of the ruler. Further, their offices were more like avocations than modern-day jobs; authority was discharged as a matter of privilege and the bestowing of a favor.

The bureaucratic form was distinct in its legalistic specification of the authorities and obligations of office. Weber wrote that the fully developed version of bureaucracy had the following characteristics:

1. Fixed, official jurisdictional areas are established by means of rules. The rules distribute the regular activities required by the organization among these fixed positions or offices, prescribing official duties for each. The rules distribute and fix the authority to discharge the duties, and they also establish specified qualifications required for each office.
2. There is a hierarchy of authority, involving supervision of lower offices by higher ones.
3. Administrative positions in the bureaucracy usually require expert training and the full working capacity of the official.
4. Management of subunits follows relatively stable and exhaustive rules, and knowledge of these rules and procedures is the special expertise of the official.
5. The management position serves as a full-time vocation, or career, for the official.

Weber regarded this bureaucratic form of organization as having technical advantages compared to administrative systems in which the officials regarded their service as an avocation, often gained by birthright or through the favor of a ruler, to be discharged at the official's personal discretion. In Weber's view, the existence of qualified career officials, a structured hierarchy, and clear, rule-based specifications of duties and procedures made for precision, speed, clarity, consistency, and reduction of costs. In addition, the strict delimiting of the duties and authority of career officials and the specification of organizational procedures in rules supported the principle of the objective performance of duties. Duties were performed consistently, and clients were treated without favoritism; the organization was freed from the effect of purely personal motives. With officials placed in positions on the basis of merit rather than birthright or political favoritism, constrained by rules defining their duties, and serving as career experts, bureaucracies represented the most efficient organizational form yet developed, from Weber's perspective.

Weber did express concern that bureaucratic routines could oppress individual freedom (Fry, 1989) and that problems could arise from placing bureaucratic experts in control of major societal functions. Nevertheless, he described bureaucracy as a desirable form of organization, especially for efficiency and the fair and equitable treatment of clients and employees. He thus emphasized one model of organization, involving clear and consistent rules, a hierarchy of authority, and role descriptions. For this reason, Weber is often grouped with the other classic figures as a proponent of what would later be characterized as the closed-system view of organizations.

The Administrative Management School: Principles of Administration

Also in the first half of the century, a number of writers began to develop the first management theories that encompassed a broad range of administrative functions that we now include under the topic of management and the proper means of discharging them. They sought to develop principles of administration to guide managers in such functions as planning, organizing, supervising, controlling, and delegating authority. This group became known as the administrative management school (March and Simon, 1958).

The members of the administrative management school emphatically espoused one proper mode of organizing. They either implied or directly stated that their principles would provide effective organization. The flavor of their work and their principles are illustrated in prominent papers by two of the leading figures in this group, Luther Gulick and James Mooney. In "Notes on the Theory of Organization," Gulick (1937) discussed two fundamental functions of management, the division of work and the coordination of work. Concerning the division of work, he discussed the need to create clearly defined specializations. Specialization, he said, allows the matching of skills to tasks and the clear, consistent delineation of tasks. He noted certain limits on specialization. No job should be so narrowly specialized that it does not take up a full work day, leaving the worker idle. Certain technological conditions, or traditions or customs, may constrain the assignment of tasks; and there are certain tasks, such as licking an envelope, that involve steps so organically interrelated that they cannot be divided.

Once a task has been properly divided, coordinating the work then becomes imperative. On this matter, Gulick proposed principles that were much clearer than his general points about specialization. Work can be coordinated through organization or through a dominant idea or purpose that unites efforts. Coordination through organization should be guided by several principles. First is the *span of control*—the number of subordinates reporting to one supervisor. The span of control should be kept narrow, limited to between six and ten subordinates per supervisor. Effective supervision requires that the supervisor's attention not be divided between too many subordinates. Gulick also proposed the principle of *one master*—each subordinate should have only one superior. There should be no confusion as to who the supervisor is. A third principle is *technical efficiency through the principle of homogeneity*—tasks must be grouped into units on the basis of their homogeneity. Dissimilar tasks should not be grouped together. In addition, a specialized unit must be supervised by a homogeneous specialist. Gulick gave examples of problems resulting from violation of this principle in government agencies: in an agricultural agency, for instance, the supervisor of the pest control division must not be given supervisory responsibility over the agricultural development division.

In the same paper, Gulick sought to define the job of management and administration through what became one of the most widely cited and influential acronyms in general management and public administration: POSDCORB. The letters stand for planning, organizing, staffing, directing, coordinating, reporting, and budgeting. These are the functions, he said, for which principles needed to be developed in subsequent work.

In "The Scalar Principle," Mooney (1930) presented a generally similar picture of the effort to develop principles. He said that an organization must be like a scale, a graded series of steps, in terms of levels of authority and corresponding responsibilities. The principle involved several component principles. The first of these was leadership. Under this principle, Mooney said that a "supreme coordinating authority" at the top must project itself through the entire "scalar chain" to coordinate the entire structure. This was to be accomplished through the principle of delegation, under which higher levels assign authority and responsibility to lower levels. These processes accomplished the third principle of functional definition, under which each person is assigned a specific task.

These two papers reflect the characteristics of the administrative management school. If certain of the "principles" seem vague, that was typical, as critics would later point out. In addition, these two authors clearly emphasize formal structure in the organization and the hierarchical authority of administrators. While some of the principles were vaguely discussed, some of them were quite clear. Tasks should be highly specialized. Lines of hierarchical authority must be very clear, with clear delegation down from the top and clear accountability and supervisory relations. Span of control should be narrow. There should be unity of command; a subordinate should be directly accountable to one superior. Like Weber and Taylor, these authors tend to emphasize consistency, rationality, and machinelike efficiency. They wrote about organizations as if they could operate most effectively as closed systems, designed according to the "one proper form" of organization.

The historical contribution of this group is undeniable; the tables of contents of many contemporary management texts reflect the influence of their early efforts to conceive the role of management and administration. Even recently in some highly successful corporations top executives have made this literature required reading for subordinates (Perrow, 1970b).

Gulick identified very strongly with public administration. He and other members of the administrative management school played important roles in the work of various committees and commissions on reorganizing the federal government, such as the Brownlow Committee in 1937 and the Hoover Commission in 1947. The reforms these groups proposed reflected the views of the administrative management school; they were aimed at such objectives as grouping federal agencies according to similar functions, strengthening the hierarchical authority of the chief executive, and narrowing the executive's span of control.

The immediate influence of these proposals on the structure of the federal government was complicated by political conflicts between the president and Congress (Arnold, 1995). They had a strong influence, however, especially on the development of an orthodox view of how administrative management should be designed in government. Many observers argue that the influence has continued across the years. They contend that structural developments in public agencies and the attitudes of government officials about such issues still reflect an orthodox administrative management school perspective (Golembiewski, 1962; Knott and Miller, 1987; Warwick, 1975, pp. 69–71). The influence of the administrative management school on these reform efforts can be considered the most significant direct influence on practical events in government that organization theorists, especially those oriented toward public administration, have ever had. Nevertheless, critics later attacked the views of the administrative management theorists as too limited for organizational analysis. And as described below, researchers began to find that many successful contemporary organizations violate the school's principles drastically and enthusiastically.

Before turning to the reaction against the administrative management perspective, however, we should note the context in which the administrative management theorists as well as the preceding early theorists worked. The administrative management theorists' work was related to the broad progressive reform movement earlier in the century (Knott and Miller, 1987). Those reformers sought to eradicate corruption in government, especially on the part of urban political machines and their leaders. They sought to institute more professional forms of administration through such means as establishing the role of the city manager. In addition, the growth of government over the earlier part of the century had led to a great deal of sprawling disorganization among the agencies and programs of government; there was a need for better organization. In this context, the administrative management theorists' emphasis on basic organizational principles appears not only well justified but absolutely necessary.

It is also important to acknowledge that these early theorists did not advance their ideas as simplemindedly as some later critics depict it. For example, Henri Fayol, one of the earliest of the writers who might be grouped into this school, noted the importance of esprit de corps in organizations. Mary Parker Follett, who wrote very approvingly of the effort to develop administrative principles, also wrote a classic essay on "the giving of orders" (Follett, [1926] 1989). In the essay she proposed a cooperative, participative process for giving orders, in which superiors and subordinates develop a shared understanding of the particular situation and what it requires. They would then follow the "law" of the situation rather than having a superior impose an order on a subordinate. Follett's perspective both foreshadowed later movements and influenced them in the direction of the kind of participatory and egalitarian management described below. It also foreshadowed very contemporary developments in feminist organization theory (Guy, 1995; Hult, 1995).

Still, the several contributions covered so far concentrated on a relatively limited portion of the framework for organizational analysis given in Figures 1.1 and 1.2 and the definition of organization in Chapter One. They emphasized the middle and lower parts of the framework, particularly organizational structure. They paid some attention to tasks and to incentives and motivation, but it was quite limited in comparison to the work of later authors. Additional developments would rapidly begin to expand the analysis of organizations, with increasing attention paid to the other components in Figures 1.1 and 1.2.

Reactions, Critiques, and New Developments

Developments in the emerging field of industrial psychology led to a sharp reaction against Taylor's ideas about scientific management and the principles of the administrative management school. These developments also led to a dramatic change in the way organizational and managerial analysts viewed the people in organizations. Researchers studying behavior and psychology in industry began to develop more insight into psychological factors in work settings. They analyzed the relationships between such factors as fatigue, monotony, and worker productivity. They studied working conditions, analyzing variables such as rest periods, hours of work, methods of payment, routineness of work, and the influence of social groups in the workplace (Burrell and Morgan, 1980, p. 129).

The Hawthorne Studies: The Discovery of Human Beings in the Workplace

A series of experiments beginning in the mid 1920s at the Hawthorne plant of the Western Electric Company provided a more subtle view of the psychology of the workplace than previous theorists had produced. The Hawthorne studies involved a complex series of experiments and academic and popular reports of their results over a number of years. Controversy continues over the interpretation and value of the studies (Burrell and Morgan, 1980, pp. 120–143); however, most organization theorists describe them as pathbreaking illustrations of the influence of social and psychological factors on work behavior, conditions that often have stronger effects than factors such as pay or physical conditions of the workplace. An employee's work-group experiences, a sense of the importance of one's work, and attention and concern on the part of supervisors are among a number of important social and psychological influences on workers.

The leaders of the project identified several major experiments and observations as the most significant in the study (Roethlisberger and Dickson, 1939). In one, the researchers lowered the level of illumination in the workplace and found that productivity nevertheless increased, because the workers responded to the attention of the researchers. In another, they improved the working conditions in a small unit through numerous alterations in rest periods and working hours. Increases in output were at first taken as evidence that the changes were influencing productivity. When the researchers tested that conclusion by withdrawing the improved conditions, however, they found that, rather than falling off, output remained high. In the course of the experiment, the researchers had consulted the workers about their opinions and reactions, questioned them sympathetically, and displayed concern for their physical well-being. Their experiment on the physical conditions of the workplace had actually altered the social situation in the workplace, and that appeared to account for the continued high output.

In observing another work group, the researchers found that it enforced strict norms regarding group members' productivity. To be a socially accepted member of the group, a worker had to avoid being a "rate buster," who turns out too much work; a "chiseler," who turns out too little; or a "squealer," who says something to a supervisor that could be detrimental to another worker. This suggested to the researchers a distinction between the formal organization, as it is officially presented in organization charts and rules, and the informal organization. The informal organization develops through unofficial social processes within the organization, but it can involve norms and standards that are just as forceful influences on the worker as formal requirements.

The Hawthorne studies were widely regarded as the most significant demonstration of the importance of social and psychological factors in the workplace up to that time, and they contributed to a major shift in research on management and organizations. The emphasis on social influences, informal processes, and the motivating power of attention from others and a sense of significance for one's work constituted a major counterpoint against the principles of administrative management and scientific management.

Chester Barnard and Herbert Simon:
The Inducements-Contributions Equilibrium and the Limits of Rationality

A successful business executive turned organization theorist and an academic who would become a Nobel laureate provided additional major contributions that weighed against the administrative management school and moved research in new directions. These contributions added substantially to attention organization theorists paid to organizational processes (especially decision making), people, environments, leadership, and goals and values.

Encouraged by the members of the Harvard group who were responsible for the Hawthorne studies and related work (Burrell and Morgan, 1980, p. 148), Chester Barnard wrote *The Functions of the Executive* (1938). It became one of the most influential books in the history of the field.

Barnard's definition of an organization—"a system of consciously coordinated activities or forces of two or more persons" (1938, p. 73)—illustrates the sharp difference between his perspective and that of the classical theorists. Barnard focused on how leaders induce and coordinate the cooperative activities fundamental to an organization. He characterized an organization as an "economy of incentives," in which individuals contribute their participation and effort in exchange for incentives that the organization provides. The executive cadre in an organization must ensure the smooth operation of this economy. The executive must keep it in equilibrium by ensuring the availability of the incentives to induce the contributions from members that earn the resources for continuing incentives, and so on. (Notice that the definition of organization in Chapter One speaks of leaders' and organizations' seeking to gain resources from the environment to translate into incentives. This reflects the influence of Barnard's perspective.)

Barnard offered a rich typology of incentives, including not just money and physical and social factors but also power, prestige, fulfillment of ideals and altruistic motives, participation in effective or useful organizations, and many others. (Chapter Nine provides a complete listing of the possible incentives he named.)

Barnard also saw the economy of incentives as being interrelated with other key functions of the executive—specifically, communication and persuasion. The executive must use communication and persuasion to influence workers' subjective valuations of various incentives. The executive can, for example, raise the salience of major organizational values. The persuasion process requires a communication process, and Barnard discussed both at length. He also distinguished between formal and informal organizations, but he saw them as interrelated and necessary to each other's success. He thought of the informal organization as the embodiment of the communication, persuasion, and inducement processes that were essential to the cooperative activity he saw as the essence of organization. Some authors now cite Barnard's ideas on these topics as an early recognition of the importance of organizational culture, a topic that has received a lot of attention in management in recent years (for example, see Peters and Waterman, 1982).

Barnard's divergence from the classical approaches is obvious. Rather than stating prescriptive principles, Barnard sought to describe the empirical reality of organizations. He treated the role of the executive as central, but he deemphasized formal authority and formal organizational structures, suggesting that those factors are not particularly important to understanding how organizations really operate. Compared to other authors up to that time, Barnard offered a more comprehensive analysis of the organization as an operating system, to be analyzed as such rather than bound by a set of artificial principles. His approach was apparently exhilarating to many researchers, including one of the preeminent social scientists of the century, Herbert Simon.

Simon attacked the administrative management school much more directly than Barnard had. In an article entitled "The Proverbs of Administration" in *Public Administration Review* (1946), he criticized the administrative management school's principles of administration as vague and contradictory. He compared them to proverbs because he saw them as prescriptive platitudes, such as "Look before you leap," that are useless because they are unclear. Often, too, they are countered by a contradictory proverb: "He who hesitates is lost." The principle of specialization, for example, never specified whether one should specialize by function, clientele, or place. Specialization also contradicts the principle of unity of command, which requires that a subordinate report to a superior within his or her specialization. But if a school has an accountant, who is obviously a specialist, that accountant must report to an educator. The two principles conflict.

Similarly, the principle of span of control also conflicts with unity of command. In a large organization, narrow spans of control require many hierarchical levels. There must be many small work units, with a supervisor for each. Then there must be many supervisors above those supervisors to keep the span of control narrow at that level, and so on up. This makes communication up, down, and across the organization very cumbersome, and it makes it difficult to maintain clear, direct hierarchical lines of authority.

Simon called for a more systematic examination of administrative processes to develop concepts and study their relationships. Researchers, he said, should determine when individuals in administrative settings should choose one or the other of the alternatives represented by the principles. As indicated by his critique, such choices are seldom clear. Such limits on the ability of organizational members to perform well and to be completely rational are major determinants of organizational processes and their effects. Simon argued that these limits on rationality and ability must be more carefully analyzed. In sum, he argued for a more empirical and analytical approach to organizational analysis, with decision making as the primary focus.

Hammond (1990) contends that Simon's critique of Gulick and others in the administrative management school overlooked major strengths of that approach. As mentioned above, the administrative management school did seek to analyze challenges that managers constantly face, challenges that later researchers have not really found answers for and that have a continuing influence on organizational structures in government. Still, most organization theorists agree that Simon's rejection of the school's principles had the stronger influence on subsequent work in the field and changed its direction.

Simon pursued his ideas further in *Administrative Behavior* (1948). As the title indicates, he emphasized analysis of actual behavior rather than stating formal prescriptions or principles. He drew on Barnard's idea of an equilibrium of inducements and contributions and extended it into a more elaborate discussion of an organization's need to provide sufficient inducements to members, external constituencies, and supporters for it to survive. (The definition and framework in Chapter One also reflect the influence of Simon's perspective.)

Like Barnard, Simon was concerned with the complex process of inducement and persuasion and with abstract incentives such as prestige, power, and altruistic service in addition to material incentives. He emphasized the uncertainties and contradictions posed by the classical principles purporting to guide administrative decisions. He displayed a continuing interest in a fundamental question: Amid such uncertainty and complexity, how are administrative choices and decisions made? The classical principles of administration were based on the assumption that administrators could and would be rational in their choice of the most efficient mode of organization. Much of economic theory assumed the existence of "economic man"—an assumption that firms and individuals are strictly rational in maximizing profits and personal gain. Simon observed that in administrative settings, there are usually uncertainties. "Administrative man" is subject to cognitive limits on rationality. Strictly rational decisions and choices are impossible in complex situations, because information and time for making decisions are limited, and human cognitive capacity is too limited to process all the information and consider all the alternatives. Whereas most economic theory assumed maximizing behavior in decision making, Simon coined a new concept. Rather than maximize, administrative man "satisfices." Satisficing involves choosing the best of a limited set of alternatives so as to optimize the decision within the constraints of limited information and time. Thus, an administrator does not make maximally rational decisions, because that is essentially impossible. The administrator makes the best possible decision within the constraints imposed by the available time, resources, and cognitive capacity.

This conception of the decision-making process challenged a fundamental tenet of economic theory. It influenced subsequent research on decision making in business firms, as amplified by *A Behavioral Theory of the Firm* by Richard Cyert and James March (1963; see Table 2.1). It provided a major step toward more recent approaches to organizational decision making, as we will see later. With James March, Simon later published another influential book, *Organizations* (March and Simon, 1958), in which they further elaborated the theory of an equilibrium between inducements and worker contributions. They presented an extensive set of propositions about factors influencing the decision by an employee to join and stay with an organization and, once in it, to produce. Simon's conception of decision making in administrative settings appears to be the foremost reason that he was later awarded the Nobel Prize in economics, however.

Social Psychology, Group Dynamics, and Human Relationships

Another important development began in the 1930s when Kurt Lewin, a psychological theorist, arrived in the United States as a refugee from Naziism. An immensely energetic intellectual, Lewin become one of the most influential social scientists of the century. Lewin developed "field theory" and "topological psychology," which sought to explain human actions as a function of both the characteristics of the individual and the conditions impinging on the individual at a given time. This may not sound original now, but it differed from other prominent approaches, such as Freudian psychology, which emphasized unconscious motives and past experiences.

Lewin's emphasis on the field of forces influencing an individual's actions drew on his interest in group behaviors and change processes in groups and individuals (Back, 1972, p. 98). He studied power, communication, influence, and "cohesion" within groups, and he developed a conception of change that has been valuable to analysts of groups and organizational change for years.

Lewin argued that groups and individuals maintain a "quasi-stationary equilibrium" in their attitudes and behaviors. This equilibrium results from a balance between forces pressing for change and those pressing against change. To change people, you must change these forces. Groups exert pressures and influences on the individuals within them. If a person is removed from a group and persuaded to change an attitude but is then returned to the same field of group pressures, the change is unlikely to last. One must alter the total field of group pressures, through a three-phase process. The first is "unfreezing," or weakening, the forces against change and strengthening the forces for change. Next, the "changing" phase moves the group to a new equilibrium point. Finally, the "refreezing" phase firmly sets the new equilibrium through such processes as expressions of group consensus.

One of Lewin's better-known experiments in group dynamics illustrates his meaning. Lewin conducted "action research," which involved analysis and sometimes manipulation of ongoing social processes of practical importance, such as race relations and group leadership. During World War II, Lewin sought to aid the war effort by conducting research on methods of encouraging consumption of underutilized foods as a way of conserving resources. He conducted an experiment in which he attempted to convince housewives that they should use more beef hearts in preparing meals. He assembled the housewives in groups and presented them with information favoring the change. They then discussed the matter, aired and resolved their concerns about the change ("unfreezing"), and came to a consensus that they should use more beef hearts. In groups in which the housewives made a public commitment to do so, more of them adopted the new behavior than in groups where the members made no such public commitment. The group commitment is an example of "refreezing," or setting group forces at a new equilibrium point.

As the intellectual leader of a group of social scientists interested in research on group processes, Lewin was instrumental in establishing the Research Center for Group Dynamics at MIT and the first National Training Laboratory, which served for years as a leading center for training in group processes. These activities produced an interesting set of diverse, sometimes opposing influences on later work in the field.

Lewin's efforts were among the first to apply experimental methods (such as using control groups) to the analysis of human behavior. The work of Lewin and his colleagues set in motion the development of experimental social psychology, which led to elaborate experimentation on group processes. Some of the important experiments on groups were relevant to organizational behavior. In another classic experiment conducted by members of this group, Lester Coch and John R. P. French (1948) compared different factory work groups faced with a change in their work procedures. One group participated fully in the decision to make the change, another group had limited participation, and a third group was simply instructed to make the change. The participative groups made the change more readily and more effectively, with the most participative group doing the best. These sorts of projects were instrumental in making "participative decision making," or PDM, a widely discussed and utilized technique in management theory and practice. Numerous experiments of this sort contributed to the growing literature on industrial psychology and organizational behavior.

Interestingly, Lewin's influence also led to an opposing trend in applied group dynamics. The National Training Laboratory conducted training in group processes for governmental and industrial organizations. After Lewin's death, the group dynamics movement split into two movements. In addition to the researchers who emphasized rigorous experimental research on group concepts, a large group continued to emphasize industrial applications and training in group processes. They tended to reject experimental procedures in favor of learning through experience in group sessions. Their work contributed to the development of the field of organization development (described in Chapter Thirteen). It also led to the widespread use of T-groups, sensitivity sessions, and encounter-group techniques during the 1960s and 1970s (Back, 1972, p. 99). The work of Lewin and his colleagues substantially influenced analysts' conception of the components of Figures 1.1 and 1.2, especially those concerned with processes of change and decision making and those concerned with people, especially groups.

The Human Relations School

The Hawthorne experiments and related work and the research on group dynamics were producing insights about the importance of social and psychological factors in the workplace. They emphasized the potential value of participative management, enhancing employee self-esteem, and improving human relations in organizations. Numerous authors began to emphasize such factors.

The psychologist Abraham Maslow developed a theory of human needs that became one of the most influential theories ever developed by a social scientist. Maslow argued that human needs fall into a set of major categories, arranged in a "hierarchy of prepotency." The needs in the lowest category dominate a person's motives until they are sufficiently fulfilled, and then those in the next-highest category dominate, and so on. The categories, in order of prepotency, were physiological needs, safety needs, love needs, self-esteem needs, and self-actualization needs. The self-actualization category referred to the need for self-fulfillment, for reaching one's potential and becoming all that one is capable of becoming. Thus, once a person fulfills his or her basic physiological needs, such as the need for food, and then fulfills the needs at the higher levels on the hierarchy, he or she ultimately becomes concerned with self-actualization. This idea of making a distinction between lower- and higher-order needs was particularly attractive to writers emphasizing human relations in organizations (for more detail on Maslow's formulation, see Chapter Nine).

Douglas McGregor, for example, published a book whose title foretells its message: *The Human Side of Enterprise* (1960). McGregor had been instrumental in bringing Kurt Lewin to MIT, and the influence of both Lewin and Maslow was apparent in his conceptions of "Theory X" and "Theory Y." He argued that management practices in American industry were dominated by a view of human behavior that he labeled Theory X. This theory held that employees were basically lazy, passive, resistant to change and responsibility, and indifferent to organizational needs. Hence management must take complete responsibility for directing and controlling the organization. Managers must closely direct, control, and motivate employees. McGregor felt that Theory X guided organizational practices in most industrial organizations and was at the heart of classic approaches to management such as scientific management.

Theory Y involved a diametrically different view of employees. Drawing on Maslow's conception of higher-level needs for self-esteem and self-actualization, McGregor defined Theory Y as the view that employees are fully capable of self-direction and self-motivation. Underutilized though it was, management based on this approach would be more effective, because individual self-discipline is a more effective form of control than authoritarian direction and supervision. McGregor advocated management approaches that would allow more worker participation and self-control, such as decentralization of authority, management by objectives, and job enlargement.

Theory Y clearly rejected the classical approach to organization; that rejection was emphatic in other major works of the time that placed a similar value on releasing human potential in the workplace. Argyris (1957), for example, argued that there were inherent conflicts between the needs of the mature human personality and the needs of organizations. When management applies the classical principles of administration, healthy individuals will experience frustration, failure, and conflict. Healthy individuals desire relative independence, activeness, and use of their abilities. These motives clash with the classical principles, such as those that call for narrow spans of control, a clear chain of command, unity of direction, and narrow specialization. These principles foster dependence on superiors and organizational rules, promote passiveness due to reduced individual discretion, and limit workers' opportunities to use their abilities. Argyris, too, called for further development of such techniques as participative leadership and job enlargement to counter this problem.

Like the classical theorists before them, the proponents of human relations theories in turn became the targets of scathing criticism. Critics complained that they concentrated too narrowly on one dimension of organizations—the human dimension—and were relatively inattentive to other major dimensions, such as organizational structure, labor union objectives, and environmental pressures. They argued that the human relations types were repeating the mistake of proposing one best way of approaching organizational and managerial analysis, that they always treated interpersonal and psychological factors as the central, crucial issues. Some critics also grumbled about the tendency of these theories to always serve the ends of management, as if the real objective were to get workers to acquiesce in the roles management imposed on them. Even where the motives were pure, some critics asserted, the approach was often naive.

Probably the most damaging critique of the human relations approach concerned its lack of empirical support, that is, the lack of evidence that improved human relations would lead to improved organizational performance (Perrow, 1970b). The upsurge in empirical research that occurred in the 1950s and 1960s produced evidence of considerable conflict in some very successful organizations. Research also produced little evidence of a strong relationship between individual job satisfaction and productivity.

Like the criticisms of the classical approaches, these criticisms tend to be overblown and a bit unfair. They often overlook the historical perspective of the writers, underestimating the significance of what they were trying to do at the time. The insights that these organizational analysts provided remain valuable—and dangerous to ignore. Examples still abound of management practices that cause damage because of inattention to the factors emphasized by the human relations theorists. When improperly implemented, scientific management techniques have created ludicrous situations in which workers slow down or disguise their normal behaviors when management analysts try to observe them.

For example, a consulting firm once tried to implement a management improvement system in a large state agency in Florida. The system involved a detailed analysis of work procedures through a process similar to time-motion methods. The process involved having observers spot-check employees at random intervals to note their activities. If an employee was idle, the observer would record that fact. A university professor went to the office of a midlevel administrator in the agency to discuss a research project. Finding the administrator on the phone, the professor began to back out of his office, in case the administrator wanted privacy for the phone call. The administrator beckoned her back in, explaining that he was not on the phone; he was sitting there trying to think. He was holding the phone to his ear to be sure that the observer would not happen by and record him as being idle. Another administrator was not so careful. After working late into the night on a project and coming in early to complete it, he finally finished and sat back to take a break, without thinking. Too late! The observer happened by and checked his record sheet. Idle!

Another example involved a management trainee in a large manufacturing firm who was assigned to work with the firm's systems engineers on the design of the assembly line. One step in the production process involved having an employee sit and watch two glass water tanks, through which refrigerator compressors would be dragged by a wire. If there was a leak in the compressor, an air bubble would be released, and the employee would remove it as defective. The management trainee expressed disgust at the incompetence of the employees, who were constantly failing at this simple task, where all they had to do was sit and watch two tanks of water for eight hours. As a solution, the systems designers changed the procedure so that an employee would sit directly facing a tank and would have to watch only one tank. The management trainee expressed even more disgust to find that the employees were so stupid that they could not even handle this simple task! Later, representatives from this company contacted a university, looking for consultants to help them deal with the problems of absenteeism and vandalism on the assembly line. As these examples illustrate, even several decades after the human relations material began to appear, there are still plenty of instances of unenlightened management attitudes that could be improved by some reading in the human relations literature.

Open-Systems Approaches and Contingency Theory

Criticism of the human relations approach, increasing attention to general-systems theory, and new research findings forced a more elaborate view of organizations. Researchers found that organizations successfully adopt different forms under different circumstances or contingencies. Organizational analysts became convinced that different forms of organization can be effective under certain contingencies of tasks and technology, organizational size, environment, and other factors. The effort to specify these contingencies and the organizational forms matched to them made "contingency theory" the dominant approach in organizational analysis in the 1960s and 1970s. The contingency perspective still provides a guiding framework, although researchers have either moved beyond the earlier versions of it or moved in different directions (Daft, 1995, pp. 23–25).

Around the middle of the century, researchers associated with the Tavistock Institute in Great Britain began conducting research on "sociotechnical systems," emphasizing the interrelationships between technical factors and social dimensions in the workplace (Burrell and Morgan, 1980, pp. 146–147). For example, Trist and Bamforth (1951) published an analysis of a change in work processes in a coal-mining operation that is now regarded as a classic study. They found that the technical changes in the work process changed the social relationships within the work group. They depicted the organization as a system with interdependent social and technical subsystems that tend to maintain an equilibrium. In response to disturbances, the system moves to a new point of equilibrium, a new ongoing pattern of interrelated social and technical processes. Additional studies by the Tavistock researchers further developed this view that organizations are systems that respond to social, economic, and technological imperatives that have to be satisfied for effective operation of the system—that is, that there are group and individual characteristics, task requirements, and interrelations among them that must be properly accommodated in the design of the organization.

Consistently with their emphasis on organizations as ongoing systems seeking to maintain equilibrium in response to disturbances, Tavistock researchers also began to devote attention to the external environments of organizations. In a widely influential article entitled "The Causal Texture of Organizational Environments," Emery and Trist (1965) noted the increasing flux and uncertainty in political, social, economic, and technological settings in which organizations operate and discussed the influence on the internal operations of organizations of the degree of "turbulence" in their environment. Thus, the emphasis moved toward analysis of organizations as open systems facing the need to adapt to environmental variations.

In the United States, the most explicit systems approach to organizational analysis appeared in a very prominent text by Daniel Katz and Robert L. Kahn (1966), *The Social Psychology of Organizations.* They showed how the systems language of inputs, throughputs, outputs, and feedback could be usefully applied to organizations. In analyzing throughput processes, for example, they differentiated various major subsystems, including maintenance subsystems, adaptive subsystems, and managerial subsystems. Scholars regard Katz and Kahn's effort as a classic in the organizational literature (Burrell and Morgan, 1980, p. 158), but it also provides an example of the very general, heuristic nature of the systems approach. Because of its very general concepts, organizational researchers increasingly treated systems theory as a broad framework for organizing information, a "macroparadigm" (Kast and Rosenzweig, 1973, p. 16), but not as a clearly articulated theory. The metaphor of organizations as open, adaptive systems remained powerful, however, as an expression of the view of organizations as social entities that adapt to a variety of influences and imperatives.

Besides the efforts to apply systems concepts to organizations, research results supported the view that organizations adopt different forms in response to contingencies. (Chapter Eight provides further description of the studies cited in the following paragraphs.) In England, Joan Woodward conducted a pathbreaking study of British industrial firms. She found that the firms fell into three categories on the basis of the production process or "technology" they employed: small-batch or unit production systems were used by such organizations as shipbuilding and aircraft manufacturing firms, large-batch or mass-production systems were operated by typical mass-manufacturing firms, and continuous production systems were used by petroleum refiners and chemical producers. Most importantly, she concluded that the successful firms within each category showed similar management-structure profiles, but those profiles differed among the three categories. The successful firms within a category were similar on such dimensions as the number of managerial levels, spans of control, and the ratio of managerial personnel to other personnel, yet they differed on these measures from the successful firms in the other two categories. This indicated that the firms within a category had achieved a successful fit between their structure and the requirements of the particular production process or technology with which they had to deal. The successful firms appeared to be effectively adapting structure to technology.

Another very influential study, reported by Burns and Stalker (1961) in *The Management of Innovation,* further contributed to the view that effective organizations adapt their structures to contingencies. Burns and Stalker analyzed a set of firms in the electronics industry in Great Britain. The industry was undergoing rapid change, with new products being developed, markets for the products shifting, and new information and technology becoming available. The firms faced considerable flux and uncertainty in their operating environments. Burns and Stalker classified the firms into two categories on the basis of their managerial structures and practices: *organic* and *mechanistic* organizations. Their descriptions of the characteristics of these two groups depict mechanistic organizations as bureaucratic organizations designed along the lines of the classical approaches. The name of the category also has obvious implications: these were organizations designed to operate in machinelike fashion. Burns and Stalker argued that the organic type, so named to underscore the analogy with living, flexible organisms, performed more successfully in the rapidly changing electronics industry. In these organizations there was less emphasis on communicating up and down the chain of command, on the superior controlling subordinates' behavior, and on strict adherence to job descriptions and organizational charts. There was more emphasis on networking and lateral communication, on the supervisor as facilitator, and on flexible and changing work assignments. Such organizations adapted and innovated more effectively under changing and uncertain conditions because they had more flexible structures and emphasized flexibility in communication, supervision, and role definition. The mechanistic form can be more successful under stable environmental and technological conditions, however, where its emphasis on consistency and specificity makes it more efficient than a more loosely structured organization. Thus, Burns and Stalker also emphasized the need for a proper adaptation of the organization to contingencies.

Another important research project heavily emphasized organizations' environment as a determinant of effective structure. Paul Lawrence and Jay Lorsch (1967) studied U.S. firms in three separate industries that confronted varying degrees of uncertainty, complexity, and change. The researchers concluded that the firms successfully operating in more uncertain, complex, changing environments had more highly differentiated internal structures. By differentiated structures, they meant that the subunits differed a great deal among themselves, in their goals, time frames, and internal work climates. Yet these highly differentiated firms also had more elaborate structures and procedures for integrating the diverse units in the organization. The integrating structures included task forces, liaison officers and committees, and other ways to integrate the more diverse units. Successful firms in more stable, certain environments, on the other hand, showed less differentiation and integration. Lawrence and Lorsch concluded that successful firms must have internal structures as complex as the environments in which they operate.

Other researchers continued to develop the general contingency perspective and to analyze specific contingencies. Perrow (1973) published an important analysis of organizational technology. He proposed two basic dimensions for the concepts of technology: the predictability of the task (the number of exceptions and variations encountered) and the analyzability of the problems encountered (the degree to which, when one encounters a new problem or exception, one can follow a clear program for solving it). Routine tasks are more predictable (fewer exceptions or variations) and more analyzable (exceptions or variations can be resolved through an established program or procedures). Organizations with routine tasks have more formal, centralized structures. They use more rules, formal procedures, and plans. Organizations with nonroutine tasks, where tasks have more exceptions and are harder to predict and where exceptions are harder to analyze and resolve, must have more flexible structures. They use more formal and informal meetings than rules and plans. (Chapter Eight describes a study confirming these relationships in public organizations.)

At about the same time, James Thompson (1967) published *Organizations in Action*, a very influential book that further developed the contingency perspective. Drawing on Herbert Simon's ideas about bounded rationality and satisficing, Thompson depicted organizations as reflecting their members' striving for rationality and consistency in the face of pressures against it. He advanced numerous propositions about how organizations use hierarchy, structure, units designed to buffer the environment, and other arrangements to try to "isolate the technical core"—that is, to create stable conditions for the units doing the basic work of the organization. Thompson suggested that organizations will try to group subunits on the basis of their technological interdependence—their needs for information and exchanges with each other in the work process (see Chapter Eight). Organizations, he proposed, will also adapt their structures to their environment. Where environments are more shifting and unstable, organizations will adopt more decentralized structures, with fewer formal rules and procedures, in order to provide more flexibility for adapting to the environment (Chapter Four provides further description). One of Thompson's important achievements was to provide a driving logic for contingency and open-systems perspectives by drawing on Simon's ideas. Organizations respond to complexity and uncertainty in their technologies and their environments by adopting more complex and flexible structures. They do so because the greater demands for information processing strain the bounded rationality of managers and the information processing capacity of more formal bureaucratic structures. Clear chains of command and vertical communication up and down them and strict specialization of tasks and strict rules and procedures can be too slow and inflexible in processing complex information and adapting to it. In the 1990s, probably without realizing it, an executive of one of the major computer corporations in the world expressed this kind of logic. His corporation was suffering operating losses and was losing out in competition with smaller, more innovative firms. The corporation, the executive said, had been taking too long to make decisions and to respond to new conditions. It had too many levels, and innovations required too many reviews and approvals within the hierarchy. The corporation, he said, was trying to decentralize into many smaller, more independent units that could respond to markets and competitors more rapidly. The executive said that the corporation had to push authority down in its organizational structure so that decisions could be made rapidly by the people with the necessary information.

Through the 1960s and 1970s, an upsurge in empirical research on organizations extended and tested the open-systems and contingency-theory approaches and added new "contingencies" to the set. Many of these studies took place in public and nonprofit organizations. Peter Blau and his colleagues (Blau and Schoenherr, 1971) reported a series of studies—of government agencies, actually—showing relationships between organizational size and structure. These and other studies added size to the standard set of contingencies. Hage and Aiken (1969) reported on a series of studies of social welfare agencies that provided evidence that routineness of tasks, joint programs among organizations, and other factors were related to organizational structure and change. In England, a team of researchers (Pugh, Hickson, and Hinings, 1969) conducted what became known as the Aston studies, a major effort at empirical measurement of organizations, and developed an empirical taxonomy, grouping organizations into types based on the measured characteristics. They interpreted differences in their taxonomic categories as the results of differences in age, size, technology, and external auspices and control. (Chapter Eight discusses important implications of these studies for theories about public organizations.) Child (1972) pointed out that in addition to the other contingencies that contingency theorists emphasized, managers' strategic choices play an important role in adapting organizational structure. These and numerous other efforts had by the mid 1970s established the contingency approach—the argument that organizational structures and processes are shaped by contingencies of technology, size, environment, and strategic choice—as the central school or movement in organization theory. Authors began to translate the contingency observations into prescriptive statements for use in "organizational design" (Galbraith, 1977; Starbuck and Nystrom, 1981; Mintzberg, 1989).

Like the other theories covered in this review and in later chapters, contingency theory soon encountered criticisms and controversies. Researchers disputed how the key concepts should be defined and measured. Different studies produced conflicting findings. Some studies found a relation between technology and structure, some did not (Hall, 1996, pp. 91–96). The basic idea that organizations must adapt to conditions they face, through such responses as adopting more flexible structures as they contend with more environmental uncertainty, still serves as a central theme in organization theory (Daft, 1995) and management practice (Peters, 1987).

The developments in organizational research reviewed here have produced an elaborate field with numerous professional journals carrying articles reporting analyses of a wide array of organizational topics. These journals and a profusion of books cover organizational structure, environment, effectiveness, change, conflict, communication, strategy, technology, interorganizational relations, and related variables.

In the last two decades, the field has moved in new directions, many of which represent extensions of contingency and open-systems theories, with increased or redirected emphasis on organizational environments. Later chapters will describe how organization theorists have developed "natural selection" and "population ecology" models for analysis of how certain organizational forms survive and prosper in certain environmental settings while others do not (Aldrich, 1979; Hannan and Freeman, 1989). Other theorists have analyzed external controls on organizations, with emphasis on organizations' dependence on their environments for crucial resources (Pfeffer and Salancik, 1978).

The research and theory described earlier on people and groups in work settings have similarly led to an elaboration of closely related work, in organizational behavior and organizational psychology. This included a similar trend toward elaborate empirical studies and conceptual development during the 1960s and 1970s. Thousands of articles and books reported work on employee motivation and satisfaction, work involvement, role conflict and ambiguity, organizational identification and commitment, professionalism, leadership behavior and effectiveness, task design, and managerial procedures such as management by objectives and flextime.

As the different fields have progressed, relatively new topics have emerged. In the last decade a major trend toward adopting Total Quality Management programs in industry and government has swept the United States. This wave developed out of writings earlier in the century by some key American authors such as W. Edwards Deming and Joseph Juran that had been embraced by the Japanese but virtually ignored in the United States until recently (note that the historical overview above has said nothing about these authors). The topic of organizational culture has received a lot of attention and is featured in Figures 1.1 and 1.2. While some important earlier authors such as Barnard and Philip Selznick (see Table 2.1) had devoted attention to related themes, organizational culture surged to prominence in the management literature in the 1980s. Advances in technology, especially computer, information, and communications technology, have presented organizations and managers with dramatic new challenges and opportunities, and researchers have been pressing to develop the theoretical and research grounding needed to understand and manage these developments. The increasing presence in the work force of women and racial and ethnic groups that were severely underrepresented in the past has given rise to a body of literature focusing on diversity in organizations (Ospina, 1996) and feminist organization theory (Hult, 1995). Later chapters will give more attention to many of these recent topics.

The Dubious Distinctiveness of Public Organizations and Management in Organization Theory

The rich field of organization theory provides many valuable concepts and insights that this book will draw on. It also raises an important issue for those interested in public organizations and public management: Have the characteristics of public organizations and their members been adequately covered in this voluminous literature? Has it paid sufficient attention to the governmental and political environments of organizations, which seem so important for understanding public organizations? As mentioned in Chapter One and further described in later chapters, there has been a literature on public bureaucracies for many years. But the historical review above illustrates the inattention on the part of most of the organization theorists regarding this literature.

The analysts discussed in the preceding historical review have either concentrated on industrial organizations or have sought to develop generic concepts and theories that apply across all types of organizations. For example, Peter Blau (Blau and Schoenherr, 1971) examined government agencies for his studies of organizational size, but he drew his conclusions as if they applied to all organizations. So have replications of Blau's study (Beyer and Trice, 1979), even though Argyris (1972, p. 10) suggested that Blau may have found the particular relationship he discovered because he was studying organizations governed by civil service systems. Such organizations might respond to differences in size in different ways than do other organizations, such as business firms. When the contingency theorists analyzed environments, they typically concentrated on environmental uncertainty, especially as a characteristic of business firms' market environments, and showed very little interest in political or governmental dynamics in organizational environments.

Providing a more classical example of this tendency, Weber argued that his conception of bureaucracy applied to government agencies and private businesses alike (Meyer, 1979). Major figures such as James Thompson (1962) and Herbert Simon (Simon, Smithburg, and Thompson, 1950) have stressed the commonalities among organizations and have suggested that public agencies and private firms are more alike than different. The contributions to organization theory and behavior described in the review above were aimed at the worthy objective of developing theory that would apply generally to all organizations. The theorists repeatedly implied or aggressively asserted that distinctions such as public and private, market and nonmarket, governmental and nongovernmental offered little value for developing theory or understanding practice.

Interestingly, research and writing about public bureaucracies had been appearing for many decades when many of these studies were published, and they were related to organizational sociology and psychology in various ways. They developed separately from organizational sociology and psychology, however. Political scientists or economists did the writing on public bureaucracies. They usually emphasized the relationship between the bureaucracy and other elements of the political system. The economists concerned themselves with the effects of the absence of economic markets for the outputs of public bureaucracies (Downs, 1967; Niskanen, 1971). The organizational sociologists and psychologists described above, while interested in environments, paid relatively little attention to these political and economic market issues. As noted above, they worked much more intensively on internal and managerial dimensions—organizational structure, tasks and technology, motivation, and leadership.

Authors interested in the management of public organizations began to point to this gap between the two literatures (Rainey, 1983). As described in more detail in Chapter Three, various authors cited in this book mounted a critique of the literature on organization theory, saying that it offers an incomplete analysis of public organizations and the influences of their political and institutional environments (Wamsley and Zald, 1973; Warwick, 1975; Meyer, 1979; Hood and Dunsire, 1981; Pitt and Smith, 1981; Perry and Kraemer, 1983). Yet they also complained that the writings on public bureaucracy had been too anecdotal and too discursively descriptive, lacking the systematic empirical and conceptual analyses common in organization theory. Also, the literature on public bureaucracies showed too little concern with internal structures, behavior, and management, topics that had received extensive attention from researchers in organizational sociology and psychology and from general management analysts. Researchers began to provide more explicit organizational analyses of the public bureaucracy, of the sort described in this book. As Chapter One mentioned, recently a profusion of books and articles have provided many additional contributions. But all this activity has actually dramatized, rather than fully resolved, the question of whether we can clarify the meaning of public organizations and public management and show evidence that such categories have significance for theory and practice. Thus the next chapter turns to the challenge of formulating a definition and drawing distinctions.

CHAPTER THREE

WHAT MAKES PUBLIC ORGANIZATIONS DISTINCTIVE

The overview of organization theory in Chapter Two leads us to a fascinating and important controversy. Leading experts on management and organizations have spurned the distinction between public and private organizations as a crude oversimplification or a relatively unimportant issue. Other very knowledgeable people have called for the development of a field recognizing the distinctive nature of public organizations and public management. Meanwhile, policymakers around the world struggle with decisions, involving billions of dollars, concerning the privatization of state activities and the proper roles of the public and private sectors. Figure 1.2 depicts government organizations' status as public bodies as a major influence on their environment, goals, and values and hence on their other characteristics. This characterization sides with those who see public organizations and managers as sufficiently distinct to deserve special analysis.

This chapter discusses important theoretical and practical issues that fuel this controversy, and it begins to develop some answers. First, it examines in greater depth the problems with the distinction between public and private. It shows that research and leading figures in organization theory have downplayed this distinction. In addition, the chapter describes the overlapping of the public, private, and nonprofit sectors in the United States, which erodes simple distinctions drawn between them. The discussion then turns to the other side of the debate: the meaning and importance of the distinction. If they are not distinct from other organizations such as businesses in any important way, why do public organizations exist? Answers to this question point to the inevitable need for public organizations and to their distinctive attributes. Still, given all the complexities, how can we define public organizations and managers? This chapter discusses some of the confusion over the meaning of *public* and then describes some of the best-developed ways of conducting research to clarify it. After analyzing some of the problems that arise in conducting such research, the chapter concludes with a description of the most frequent observations about the nature of public organizations and managers. The remainder of the book examines the research and debate on the accuracy of these observations.

Public Versus Private: A Dangerous Distinction?

Many authors caution against making oversimplified distinctions between public and private management (Bozeman, 1987; Murray, 1975). Objections to such distinctions deserve careful attention, because they provide valuable counterpoints to invidious stereotypes. But they also point out realities of the contemporary political economy and raise challenges that we must face when clarifying the distinction.

The Generic Tradition in Organization Theory

A distinguished intellectual tradition bolsters the generic perspective on organizations—that is, the position that organization and management theorists should emphasize the commonalities among organizations in order to develop knowledge that will be applicable to all organizations, avoiding such popular distinctions as public versus private and profit versus nonprofit. As serious analysis of organizations and management burgeoned early in this century, leading figures argued that their insights applied across commonly differentiated types of organizations. Many of them pointedly referred to the distinction between public and private organizations as the sort of crude oversimplification that theorists must overcome. From their point of view, such distinctions pose intellectual dangers: they oversimplify, confuse, mislead, and impede sound theory and research.

The historical review of organization theory in the last chapter illustrates how virtually all of the major contributions to the field were conceived to apply broadly across all types of organizations, or in some cases to concentrate on industry. Throughout the evolution described in that review, the distinction between public and private organizations received short shrift.

In some cases, the authors either clearly implied or aggressively asserted that their ideas applied to public, private, and other types of organizations. Weber claimed that his analysis of bureaucratic organizations applied to both government agencies and business firms. Frederick Taylor applied his scientific management procedures in government arsenals and other public organizations, and such techniques are widely applied in both public and private organizations today. Similarly, members of the administrative management school sought to develop standard principles to govern the administrative structures of all organizations. The emphasis on social and psychological factors in the workplace in the Hawthorne studies, McGregor's Theory Y, and Kurt Lewin's research pervades the organizational development procedures that consultants apply in government agencies today (Golembiewski, 1985).

Herbert Simon (1946) implicitly framed much of his work as being applicable to all organizational settings, both public and private. Beginning as a political scientist, he coauthored one of the leading texts in public administration (Simon, Smithburg, and Thompson, 1950). It contains a sophisticated discussion of the political context of public organizations. It also argues, however, that there are more similarities than differences between public and private organizations. Accordingly, in his other work he concentrated on general analyses of organizations (Simon, 1948; March and Simon, 1958). He thus implied that his insights about satisficing and other organizational processes apply across all types of organizations. Even his recent work asserts that public, private, and nonprofit organizations are equivalent on key dimensions (Simon, 1995). Thus, the leading intellectual figure of organization theory clearly assigned relative unimportance to the distinctiveness of public organizations.

Chapter Two also showed that contingency theory regards the primary contingencies affecting organizational structure and design to be environmental uncertainty and complexity, the variability and complexity of organizational tasks and technologies (the work that the organization does and how it does it), organizational size, and the strategic decisions of managers. Thus, even though this perspective emphasizes variations among organizations, it downplays any particular distinctiveness of public organizations. James Thompson (1962), a leading figure among the contingency theorists, echoed the generic refrain—public and private organizations have more similarities than differences.

During the 1980s, the contingency perspective evolved in many different directions, some involving more attention to governmental and economic influences (Scott, 1987). Still, the titles and coverage in management and organization theory journals and in excellent overviews of the field (Daft, 1995; Hall, 1996) reflect the generic tradition. Public organizations as a distinctive category receive sporadic, speculative attention, with the clear implication that their distinctiveness plays a minor role compared to other influences.

Findings from Research

Objections to distinguishing between public and private organizations draw on more than theorists' claims. Studies of variables such as size, task, and technology in government agencies show that those variables may influence public organizations more than anything related to their status as a governmental entity. These findings agree with the commonsense observation that an organization becomes bureaucratic not because it is in government or business but because of its large size.

Major studies that analyzed many different organizations to develop taxonomies and typologies have produced little evidence of a strict division between public and private organizations. Some of the prominent efforts to develop a taxonomy of organizations based on empirical measures of organizational characteristics have failed to show any value in drawing a distinction between public and private (Haas, Hall, and Johnson, 1966). Others have produced inconclusive results (Pugh, Hickson, and Hinings, 1969). Haas, Hall, and Johnson (1966) measured characteristics of a large sample of organizations and used statistical techniques to categorize them according to which ones they shared. A number of the resulting categories included both public and private organizations.

This finding is not surprising, since organizations' tasks and functions can have much more influence on their characteristics than their status as public or private. A government-owned hospital obviously resembles a private hospital more than it does a government-owned utility. Consultants and researchers frequently find in both the public and the private sectors organizations with highly motivated employees, as well as severely troubled organizations. They often find that more proximal factors, such as leadership practices, influence employee motivation and job satisfaction more than whether the employing organization is public, private, or nonprofit.

Pugh, Hickson, and Hinings (1969) classified some fifty-eight organizations into categories based on their structural characteristics; they had predicted that the government organizations would show more bureaucratic features, such as more rules and procedures, but they found no such differences. They did find, however, that the government organizations showed higher degrees of control by external authorities, especially over personnel procedures. The study included only eight government organizations, all local government units with functions similar to those of business organizations (for example, a vehicle repair unit and a water utility). Consequently, the researchers interpreted their findings as inconclusive concerning whether government agencies differ from private organizations in terms of their structural characteristics. Studies such as these have consistently found the public-private distinction inadequate for a general typology or taxonomy of organizations (McKelvey, 1982).

The Blurring of the Sectors

Those who object to the claim that public organizations make up a distinct category also point out that the public and private sectors overlap and interrelate in a number of ways.

Mixed, Intermediate, and Hybrid Forms. A number of important government organizations are designed to resemble business firms. A diverse array of state-owned enterprises, government corporations, government-sponsored corporations, and public authorities perform crucial functions in the United States and other countries (Seidman, 1983; Musolf and Seidman, 1980; Walsh, 1978). Usually owned and operated by government, they typically perform business-type functions and generate their own revenues through sales of their products or other means. Such enterprises usually receive a special charter to operate more independently than government agencies. Examples include the U.S. Postal Service, the Resolution Trust Corporation, the National Parks Service, port authorities in many coastal cities, and a multitude of other organizations at all levels of government. Such organizations are sometimes the subjects of controversy concerning whether they operate in a sufficiently businesslike fashion, on the one hand, and whether they show sufficient public accountability, on the other. The magnitude of the resources involved in these hybrid arrangements is striking. In 1996, the U.S. comptroller general voiced concerns over the results of audits by the General Accounting Office (GAO) of federal loan and insurance programs. These programs provide student loans, farm loans, deposit insurance for banks, flood and crop insurance, and home mortgages. The programs are carried out by government-sponsored enterprises such as the Federal National Mortgage Association ("Fannie Mae"). The comptroller general said the GAO audits indicated that cutbacks in federal funding and personnel have left the government with insufficient financial accounting systems and personnel to properly monitor these liabilities. The federal liabilities for these programs total $7.3 trillion.

On the other side of the coin are the many nonprofit, or third-sector, organizations that perform functions similar to those of government organizations. Like government agencies, many nonprofits obviously have no profit indicators or incentives and often pursue social or public service missions. Finally, many private, for-profit organizations work with government in ways that blur the distinction between them. Some corporations, such as defense contractors, receive so much funding and direction from government that some analysts equate them with government bureaus (Weidenbaum, 1969; Bozeman, 1987).

Functional Analogies—Doing the Same Things. Obviously, many people and organizations in the public and private sectors perform virtually the same functions. General managers, secretaries, computer programmers, auditors, personnel officers, maintenance workers, and many other specialists perform similar tasks in public, private, and hybrid organizations. Organizations located in the different sectors—for example, hospitals, schools, and electric utilities—also perform the same general functions.

Complex Interrelations. Government, business, and nonprofit organizations interrelate in a number of ways (Kettl, 1993). Governments buy many products and services from nongovernmental organizations. Through contracts, grants, vouchers, subsidies, and franchises, governments arrange for the delivery of health care, sanitation services, research services, and numerous other services by private organizations. These entangled relations muddle the question of where government and the private sector begin and end. Banks process loans provided by the Veterans Administration and receive Social Security deposits by wire for Social Security recipients. Private corporations handle portions of the administration of Medicare by means of government contracts, and private physicians render most Medicare services. Private nonprofit corporations and religious organizations operate facilities for the elderly or for delinquent youths using funds provided through government contracts and operate under extensive government regulation. In thousands of examples of this sort, private businesses and nonprofit organizations become part of the service delivery process for government programs and further blur the public-private distinction. Chapters Four, Five, and Fourteen provide more detail on these situations and their implications for organizations and management (Moe, 1996; Provan and Milward, 1995).

Analogies from Social Roles and Contexts. Government uses laws, regulations, and fiscal policies to influence private organizations. Environmental protection regulations, tax laws, monetary policies, and equal employment opportunity regulations either impose direct requirements on private organizations or establish inducements and incentives to get them to act in certain ways. Here, again, nongovernmental organizations share in the implementation of public policies. They become part of government and an extension of it. Even working independently of government, business organizations affect the quality of life in the nation and the public interest. Members of the most profit-oriented firms argue that their organizations serve their communities and the well-being of the nation. Government agencies, on the other hand, sometimes behave too much like private organizations. One of the foremost contemporary criticisms of government concerns the influence that interest groups wield over public agencies and programs. According to the critics, these groups use the agencies to serve their own interests rather than the public interest.

The Importance of Avoiding Oversimplifications

Theory, research, and the realities of the contemporary political economy show the inadequacy of simple notions about differences between public and private organizations. For management theory and research, this poses the challenge of determining what role a distinction between public and private can play, and how. For practical management and public policy, it means that we must avoid oversimplifying the issue and jumping to conclusions about sharp distinctions between public and private.

That advice may sound obvious enough, but violations of it abound. Some public managers too quickly assume a sharp distinction between their context and the context of those in private organizations. Experienced consultants find that their management ideas are as applicable in many public organizations as in business firms, yet public administrators often resist those ideas, claiming that one simply cannot do such things in government. Robert Golembiewski (1984), a prolific researcher with extensive consulting experience in government and industry, calls this tendency the "Dr. No" syndrome; he says he runs into it in many public agencies. Surveys show that public managers often hold stereotypes about business managers and business organizations, and vice versa (Stevens, Wartick, and Bagby, 1988; Weiss, 1983).

In matters of public policy, some calls for privatization oversimplify the distinction between public and private (Donahue, 1990; Wise, 1990). They often call for government contracts with private or nonprofit service providers that may impose elaborate constraints, eliminate competition, and otherwise restrain free-market conditions. Similarly, proposals for voucher systems and other quasi-market arrangements often assume that making things a little more like a market and a little less like government produces great improvements.

For all the reasons discussed above, clear demarcations between the public and private sectors are impossible, and oversimplified distinctions between public and private organizations are misleading. We still face a paradox, however, because scholars and officials make the distinction repeatedly in relation to important issues, and public and private organizations do differ in some obvious ways.

Public Organizations: An Essential Distinction

If there is no real difference between public and private organizations, can we nationalize all industrial firms—or privatize all government agencies? Private executives earn significantly higher pay than their government counterparts; the financial press regularly lambastes corporate executive compensation practices as absurd. Can we simply put these executives on the federal executive compensation schedule? Such questions make it clear that there are some important differences between public and private administration. Scholars have provided useful insights into the distinction in recent years, and researchers and managers have reported more evidence of distinctive features of public organizations.

The Purpose of Public Organizations

Why do public organizations exist? The answers to this question lie in both political and economic theory. Even some economists who strongly favor free markets regard government agencies as inevitable components of freemarket economies (Downs, 1967).

Politics and Markets. Decades ago, Robert Dahl and Charles Lindblom (1953) provided a useful analysis of the raison d'être for public organizations. They analyzed the alternatives available to nations for controlling their political economies. Two of the fundamental alternatives are political hierarchies and economic markets. In advanced industrial democracies, the political process involves a complex array of contending groups and institutions that produces a complex, hydra-headed hierarchy, which Dahl and Lindblom call a *polyarchy.* Such a politically established hierarchy can direct economic activities. Alternatively, the price system in free economic markets can control economic production and allocation decisions. Most nations use some mixture of markets and polyarchies.

Political hierarchy, or polyarchy, draws on political authority, which can serve as a very useful, inexpensive means of social control. It is cheaper to have people relatively willingly stop at red lights than to work out a system of compensating them for doing so. However, political authority can be "all thumbs" (Lindblom, 1977). Central plans and directives often prove confining, clumsy, ineffective, poorly adapted to many local circumstances, and cumbersome to change.

Markets have the advantage of operating through voluntary exchanges. Producers must induce consumers to willingly engage in exchanges with them. They have the incentive to produce what consumers want, as efficiently as possible. This allows much freedom and flexibility, provides incentives for efficient use of resources, steers production in the direction of consumer demands, and avoids the problems of central planning and rule making inherent in a polyarchy. Markets, however, have a limited capacity to handle certain types of problems, for which government action is required (Lindblom, 1977; Downs, 1967). Such problems include the following:

- *Public goods and free riders.* Certain services, once provided, benefit everyone. Individuals have the incentive to act as free riders and let others pay, so government imposes taxes to pay for such services. National defense is the most frequently cited example; education and police protection are others. Even though private organizations could provide these services, government provides most of them because they entail general benefits for the entire society.
- *Individual incompetence.* People often lack sufficient education or information to make wise individual choices in some areas, so government regulation is required. For example, most people would not be able to determine the safety of particular medicines, so the Food and Drug Administration regulates the distribution of pharmaceuticals.
- *Externalities or spillovers.* Some costs may spill over onto people who are not parties to a market exchange. A manufacturer polluting the air imposes costs on others that the price of the product does not cover. The Environmental Protection Agency regulates environmental externalities of this sort.

Government acts to correct problems that markets themselves create or are unable to address—monopolies, the need for income redistribution, and instability due to market fluctuations—and to provide crucial services that are too risky or expensive for private competitors to provide. Critics also complain that market systems produce too many frivolous and trivial products, foster crassness and greed, confer too much power on corporations and their executives, and allow extensive bungling and corruption. Public concern over such matters bolsters support for a strong and active government (Lipset and Schneider, 1987).

Conservative economists argue that markets eventually resolve many of these problems and that government interventions simply make matters worse. Advocates of privatization claim that government does not have to perform many of the functions it does and that government provides many services that private organizations can provide more efficiently. Nevertheless, American citizens broadly support government action in relation to many of these problems.

Political Rationales for Government. A purely economic rationale for government ignores the many political and social justifications for government. In theory, government in the United States exists to maintain systems of law, justice, and social organization; to maintain individual rights and freedoms; to provide national security and stability; to promote general prosperity; and to provide direction for the nation and its communities. In reality, government often simply does what influential political groups demand. In spite of the blurring of the distinction between the public and private sectors, government organizations in the United States remain restricted to certain functions. For the most part, they provide services that are not exchanged on economic markets but are justified on the basis of general social values, the public interest, and the politically imposed demands of groups.

The Meaning and Nature of Public Organizations and Public Management

While the idea of a public domain within society is an ancient one, beliefs about what is appropriately public and what is private, in both personal affairs and social organization, have varied among societies and over time. The word *public* comes from the Latin for "people," and dictionaries define it as a reference to matters pertaining to the people of a community, nation, or state (Guralnick, 1980). The word *private* comes from the Latin word that means to be deprived of public office or set apart from government as a personal matter. In contemporary definitions, the distinction between public and private involves three major factors (Benn and Gaus, 1983): *interests* affected (whether benefits or losses are communal or restricted to individuals); *access* to facilities, resources, or information; and *agency* (whether a person or organization acts as an individual or for the community as a whole). These dimensions can be independent of one another and even contradictory. For example, a military base may operate in the public interest, acting as an agent for the nation, but deny public access to it.

Approaches to Defining Public Organizations and Public Managers. The multiple dimensions along which the concepts of public and private vary make for many ways to define public organizations, most of which prove inadequate. For example, one time-honored approach defines public organizations as those that have a great impact on the public interest (Dewey, 1927). Decisions about whether government should regulate have turned on judgments about the public interest (Mitnick, 1980). In their prominent typology of organizations, Blau and Scott (1962) distinguish between *commonweal* organizations, which benefit the public in general, and *business* organizations, which benefit their owners. The public interest, however, has proved notoriously hard to define and measure (Mitnick, 1980). Some definitions directly conflict with others; for example, defining the public interest as what a philosopher king or benevolent dictator decides versus defining it as what the majority of people prefer. Most organizations affect the public interest in some sense, especially large business firms. Manufacturers of computers, pharmaceuticals, automobiles, and many other products clearly have tremendous influence on the well-being of the nation.

Alternatively, researchers and managers often refer to auspices or ownership, an implicit use of the agency factor mentioned above. Public organizations are governmental organizations, and private organizations are nongovernmental, usually business firms. Researchers using this simple dichotomy have kept the debate going by producing impressive research results (Mascarenhas, 1989). The blurring of the boundaries between the sectors, however, shows that we need further analysis of what this dichotomy means.

Agencies and Enterprises as Points on a Continuum. In their analysis of markets and polyarchies, Dahl and Lindblom (1953) described a complex continuum of types of organizations, ranging from *enterprises* (organizations controlled primarily by markets) to *agencies* (public or government-owned organizations). For enterprises, they argued, the pricing system automatically links revenues to products and services sold. This creates stronger incentives for cost reduction in enterprises than in agencies. Agencies have more trouble integrating cost reduction into their goals and coordinating spending and revenue-raising decisions, since legislatures assign their tasks and funds separately. Their funding allocations usually depend on past levels, and if they achieve improvements in efficiency, their appropriations are likely to be cut. Agencies also pursue more intangible, diverse objectives, making their efficiency harder to measure. The difficulty in specifying and measuring objectives causes officials to try to control agencies through enforcement of rigid procedures rather than evaluations of products and services. Agencies also have more problems related to hierarchical control, such as red tape, buck passing, rigidity, and timidity, than do enterprises.

More important than Dahl and Lindblom's oversimplified comparison of agencies and enterprises is their conception of a continuum of organizations. They depict various forms of agencies and enterprises occupying this continuum, ranging from the most public of organizations to the most private (see Figure 3.1). Dahl and Lindblom did not explain how their assertions about the different characteristics of agencies and enterprises apply to organizations on different points of the continuum. Implicitly, however, they suggested that agency characteristics apply less and less as one moves away from that extreme, and the characteristics of enterprises become more and more applicable.

Ownership and Funding. Wamsley and Zald (1973) pointed out that an organization's place along the public-private continuum depends on at least two major

FIGURE 3.1. AGENCIES, ENTERPRISES, AND HYBRID ORGANIZATIONS.

The continuum between government ownership and private enterprise. Below the line are arrangements colloquially referred to as public, government-owned, or nationalized. Above the line are organizational forms usually referred to as private enterprise or free enterprise. On the line are arrangements popularly considered neither public nor private.

Above the line:

- Private nonprofit organizations totally reliant on government contracts and grants (Atomic Energy Commission, Manpower Development Research Corporation).

- Private corporations reliant on government contracts for most revenues (some defense contractors, such as General Dynamics, Grumman).

- Heavily regulated private firms (heavily regulated privately owned utilities).

- Private corporations with significant funding from government contracts but majority of revenues from private sources.

- Private corporations subject to general government regulations such as affirmative action, Occupational Safety and Health Administration regulations.

- Private Enterprise

On the line:

- Government ownership of part of a private corporation

Below the line:

- Government Agency

- State-owned enterprise or public corporation (Postal Service, TVA, Port Authority of NY).

- Government-sponsored enterprise, established by government but with shares traded on stock market (Federal National Mortgage Association).

- Government program or agency operated largely through purchases from private vendors or producers (Medicare, public housing).

Source: Adapted and revised from Dahl and Lindblom (1953).

elements, ownership and funding. Organizations can be owned by the government or privately owned. They can receive most of their funding from government sources, such as budget allocations from legislative bodies, or they can receive most of it from private sources, such as donations or sales within economic markets. Putting these two dichotomies together results in the four categories illustrated in Figure 3.2: publicly owned and funded organizations, such as most government agencies; publicly owned but privately funded organizations, such as the U.S. Postal Service and government-owned utilities; privately owned but governmentally funded organizations, such as certain defense firms funded primarily through government contracts; and privately owned and funded organizations, such as supermarket chains and IBM.

This scheme does have limitations; it makes no mention of regulation, for example. And many corporations, such as IBM, receive funding from government contracts but operate so autonomously that they clearly belong in the private category. Nevertheless, the approach provides a fairly clear way of identifying core categories of public and private organizations.

Economic Authority, Public Authority, and "Publicness." Bozeman (1987) draws on a number of the preceding points to try to conceive the complex variations across the public-private continuum. All organizations have some degree of political influence and are subject to some level of external governmental control.

FIGURE 3.2. PUBLIC AND PRIVATE OWNERSHIP AND FUNDING.

	Public Ownership	Private Ownership
Public Funding (taxes, government contracts)	Department of Defense Social Security Administration Police departments	Defense contractors Rand Corporation Manpower Development Research Corporation Oak Ridge National Laboratories
Private Funding (sales, private donations)	U.S. Postal Service Government-owned utilities Federal Home Loan Bank Board	General Motors[a] IBM General Electric Grocery store chains YMCA

[a]These large corporations have large government contracts and sales, but attain most of their revenues from private sales and have relative autonomy to withdraw from dealing with government.

Source: Adapted and revised from Wamsley and Zald (1973).

Hence, they all have some level of "publicness," although that level varies widely. Like Wamsley and Zald, Bozeman uses two subdimensions—political authority and economic authority—but treats them as continua rather than dichotomies. Economic authority increases as owners and managers gain more control over the use of their organization's revenues and assets and decreases as external government authorities gain more control over their finances.

Political authority is granted by other elements of the political system, such as the citizenry or governmental institutions. It enables the organization to act on behalf of those elements and to make binding decisions for them. Private firms have relatively little of this authority. They operate on their own behalf and for only as long as they support themselves through voluntary exchanges with citizens. Government agencies have high levels of authority to act for the community or country, and citizens are compelled to support their activities through taxes and other requirements.

The "publicness" of an organization depends on the combination of these two dimensions. Figure 3.3 illustrates Bozeman's depiction of possible combinations. As in previous approaches, the owner-managed private firm occupies one extreme (high on economic authority, low on political authority), and the traditional government bureau occupies the other (low on economic authority, high on political authority). A more complex array of organizations represents various combinations of the two dimensions. Bozeman and his colleagues have used this approach to design research on public, private, and intermediate forms of research and development (R&D) laboratories, and other organizations. Later chapters describe how they found important differences between the public and private categories, with the intermediate forms falling in between (Bozeman and Loveless, 1987; Crow and Bozeman, 1987; Emmett and Crow, 1988; Coursey and Rainey, 1990).

All these efforts to clarify the public-private dimension cannot capture its full complexity. Government and political processes influence organizations in many ways, through laws, regulations, grants, contracts, charters, franchises, direct ownership (with many variations in oversight), and numerous other ways (McGregor, 1981; Hood, 1983; Salamon, 1989). Private market influences also involve many variations. Perry and Rainey (1988) suggest that future research can compare organizations in different categories, such as those in Table 3.1. Analyses of the external controls on organizations could determine whether they are influenced primarily by polyarchies or by markets. Waste (1987) has developed measures of polyarchy for classifying cities, and such measures could be developed for organizations. One could also classify organizations by ownership and funding to develop a set of types that could be compared in research.

FIGURE 3.3. "PUBLICNESS": POLITICAL AND ECONOMIC AUTHORITY.

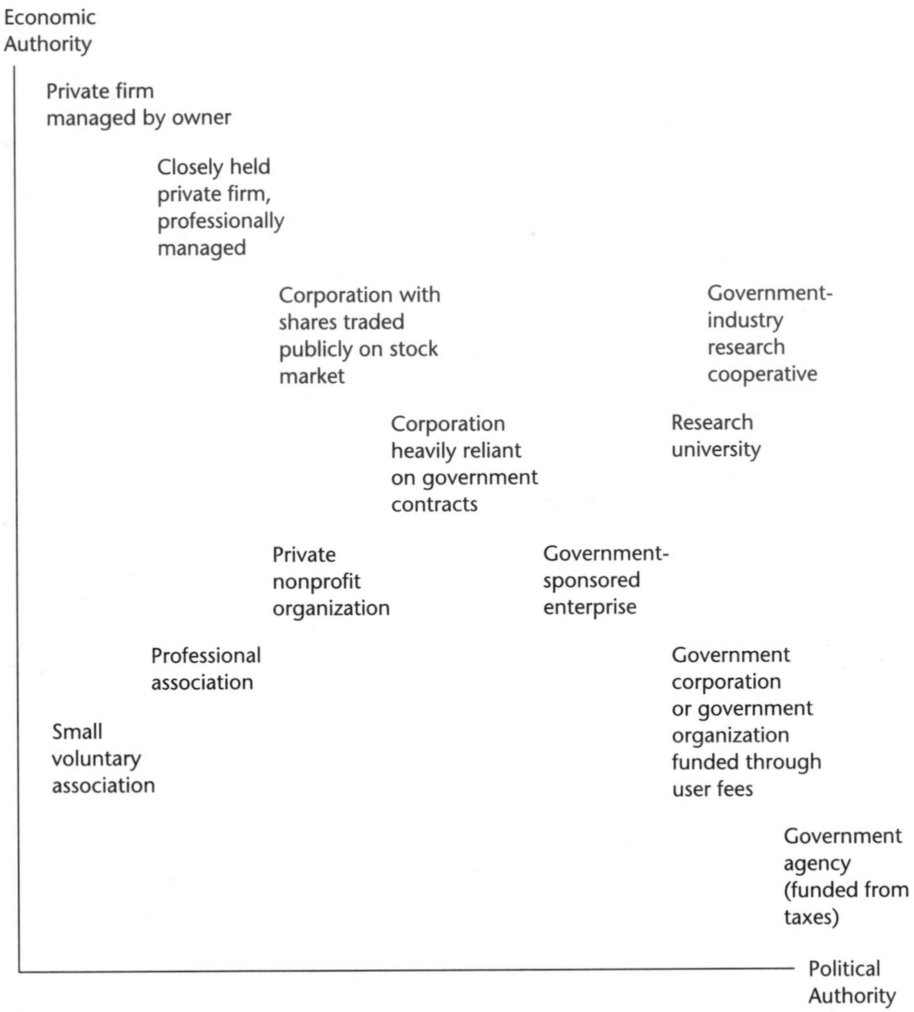

Economic
Authority

Private firm
managed by owner

    Closely held
    private firm,
    professionally
    managed

        Corporation with   Government-
        shares traded   industry
        publicly on stock   research
        market   cooperative

            Corporation   Research
            heavily reliant   university
            on government
            contracts

      Private   Government-
      nonprofit   sponsored
      organization   enterprise

    Professional   Government
    association   corporation
Small   or government
voluntary   organization
association   funded through
                     user fees

                          Government
                          agency
                          (funded from
                          taxes)

                                     Political
                                     Authority

Source: Adapted from Bozeman (1987).

No standard nomenclature exists for the hybrid organizations listed in Table 3.1. Such terms for hybrids as *government corporation* and *state-owned enterprise* are often used interchangeably (Seidman, 1983). Yet one could more carefully designate such categories and, within various industries and policy areas, compare organizations representing these different categories along the public-private continuum. Later chapters describe many useful studies comparing more limited sets of categories, such as state-owned enterprises versus private enterprises. Further refining such comparisons should help to clarify the effects of governmental and market influences on organizations.

While this topic needs further refinement, these analyses of the public-private dimension of organizations clarify important points. Simply stating that the public and private sectors are not distinct does little good. The challenge involves conceiving and analyzing the possible differences, variations, and similarities. In starting to do so, we can think with reasonable clarity about a distinction between public and private organizations, although we must always realize the complications. We can think of assertions about public organizations that apply primarily to organizations owned and funded by government, such as typical government agencies. At least by definition, they differ from privately owned firms, which get most of their resources from private sources and are not subject to extensive government regulations. We can then seek evidence comparing these two groups, and in fact such research often shows differences—although we need much more. The population of hybrid and third-sector organizations raises complications about whether differences between these core public and private categories apply to them. Yet we have increasing evidence that organizations in this intermediate group—even within the same function or industry—differ in important ways on the basis of how public or private they are. Designing and evaluating this evidence, however, involve some further complications.

Problems and Approaches in Public-Private Comparisons

Defining a distinction between public and private organizations does not prove that important differences between them actually exist. We need to consider those supposed differences and the evidence for or against them. First, however, some intriguing challenges in research on public management and public-private comparisons need consideration, because they figure importantly in sizing up the evidence.

The discussion of the generic approach to organizational analysis and contingency theory introduced some of these challenges. Many factors, such as size, task or function, and industry characteristics, can influence an organization more than its status as a governmental entity. Research needs to show that these alternative factors do not confuse analysis of differences between public organizations

TABLE 3.1. TYPOLOGY OF ORGANIZATIONS CREATED BY CROSS-CLASSIFYING OWNERSHIP, FUNDING, AND MODE OF SOCIAL CONTROL.

	Ownership	Funding	Mode of Social Control	Representative Study	Example
Bureau	Public	Public	Polyarchy	Meier (1993)	Bureau of Labor Statistics
Government corporation	Public	Private	Polyarchy	Walsh (1978)	Pension Benefit Guaranty Corporation
Government-sponsored enterprise	Private	Public	Polyarchy	Musolf and Seidman (1980)	Corporation for Public Broadcasting
Regulated enterprise	Private	Private	Polyarchy	Mitnick (1980)	Private electric utilities
Governmental enterprise	Public	Public	Market	Barzelay (1992)	Government printing office that must sell services to government agencies
State-owned enterprise	Public	Private	Market	Aharoni (1986)	Airbus
Government contractor	Private	Public	Market	Bozeman (1987)	Grumann
Private enterprise	Private	Private	Market	Williamson (1975)	IBM

Source: Adapted and revised from Perry and Rainey (1988).

and other types. Obviously, for example, if you compare large public agencies to small private firms and find the agencies more bureaucratic, size may be the real explanation. Also, one would not compare a set of public hospitals to private utilities as a way of assessing the nature of public organizations. Ideally, an analysis of the public-private dimension requires a convincing sample, with a good model that accounts for other variables besides the public-private dimension. Ideally, also, studies would have huge, well-designed samples of organizations and employees, representing many functions and controlling for many variables. No one has had the resources or inclination to conduct such studies. Instead, researchers and practitioners have adopted a variety of less comprehensive approaches.

Some theorize on the basis of assumptions, past literature, and their own experiences (Dahl and Lindblom, 1953; Downs, 1967). Similarly, but less systematically, some books about public bureaucracies simply provide a list of the differences between public and private, based on the authors' knowledge and experience (Gawthorp, 1969; Mainzer, 1973). Other researchers conduct research projects measuring or observing public bureaucracies and draw conclusions about their differences from private organizations. Some concentrate on one agency (Warwick, 1975), some on many agencies (Meyer, 1979). Although valuable, these studies leave doubts because they examine no private organizations directly.

Many executives and managers who have served in both public agencies and private business firms make emphatic statements about the sharp differences between the two settings (Blumenthal, 1983; Rumsfeld, 1983; Weiss, 1983). Quite convincing as testimonials, they apply primarily to the executive and managerial levels. Differences might fade at lower levels. Other researchers compare sets of public and private organizations or managers. Some compare the managers in small sets of government and business organizations (Buchanan, 1974, 1975; Rainey, 1979, 1983; Porter and Lawler, 1968). Questions remain about how well the small samples represent the full populations and how well they account for important factors such as tasks. More recent studies with larger samples of organizations still leave questions about representing the full populations. They add more convincing evidence of distinctive aspects of public management, however (Coursey and Bozeman, 1990; Coursey and Rainey, 1990; Hickson and others, 1986).

To analyze public versus private delivery of a particular service, many researchers compare public and private organizations within functional categories. They compare hospitals (Savas, 1987, p. 190), utilities (Atkinson and Halversen, 1986), schools (Chubb and Moe, 1988), and others. Somewhat similarly, other studies compare a function, such as management of computers, in government and business organizations (Bretschneider, 1990). Still others compare state-owned enterprises to private firms (Hickson and others, 1986; Mascarenhas, 1989; MacAvoy and McIssac, 1989). They find differences and show that the public-private distinction appears meaningful even when the same general types of organization operate under both auspices. Studies of one functional type, however, may not apply to other functional types. The public-private distinction apparently has some different implications in one industry or market environment (hospitals, for example) as compared to another (refuse collection). Still another complication is that public and private organizations within a functional category may not actually do the same thing or operate in the same way (Kelman, 1985). For example, private and public hospitals may serve different patients, and public and private electric utilities may have different funding patterns.

In some cases, organizational researchers studying other topics have used a public-private distinction in the process and have found that it makes a difference (Hickson and others, 1986; Chubb and Moe, 1988; Tolbert, 1985; Mintzberg, 1972; Kurke and Aldrich, 1983). These researchers have no particular concern with the success or failure of the distinction per se; they simply find it meaningful.

A few studies compare public and private samples from census data, large-scale social surveys, or national studies (Smith and Nock, 1980; U.S. Office of Personnel Management, 1979; U.S. General Accounting Office, 1990). These have great value, but often such aggregated findings prove difficult to relate to the characteristics of specific organizations and the people in them. In the absence of huge, conclusive studies, we have to piece together evidence from more limited analyses such as these. Many issues remain debatable, but we can learn a great deal from doing so.

Common Assertions About Public Organizations and Public Management

In spite of the difficulties, the stream of assertions and research findings continues. During the 1970s and 1980s, various reviews compiled the most frequent arguments and evidence about the distinction between public and private (Fottler, 1981; Meyer, 1982; Rainey, Backoff, and Levine, 1976). There has been a good deal of progress in research, but the basic points of contention have not substantially changed. Table 3.2 shows a recent summary and introduces many of the issues that later chapters examine. The table and the following discussion of it pull together theoretical statements, expert observations, and research findings. Except for those mentioned, it omits many controversies about the accuracy of the statements (these are considered in later chapters). Still, it presents a reasonable depiction of prevailing views and issues about the nature of public organizations and management, which amounts to something of a theory.

Unlike private organizations, most public organizations do not sell their outputs in economic markets. Hence, the information and incentives provided by

TABLE 3.2. DISTINCTIVE CHARACTERISTICS OF PUBLIC MANAGEMENT AND PUBLIC ORGANIZATIONS: A SUMMARY OF COMMON ASSERTIONS AND RESEARCH FINDINGS.

I. Environmental Factors

I.1. Absence of economic markets for outputs; reliance on governmental appropriations for financial resources.

    I.1.a. Less incentive to achieve cost reduction, operating efficiency, and effective performance.

    I.1.b. Lower efficiency in allocating resources (weaker reflection of consumer preferences, less proportioning of supply to demand).

    I.1.c. Less availability of relatively clear market indicators and information (prices, profits, market share) for use in managerial decisions.

I.2. Presence of particularly elaborate and intensive formal legal constraints as a result of oversight by legislative branch, executive branch hierarchy and oversight agencies, and courts.

    I.2.a. More constraints on domains of operation and on procedures (less autonomy for managers in making such choices).

    I.2.b. Greater tendency for proliferation of formal administrative controls.

    I.2.c. Larger number of external sources of formal authority and influence, with greater fragmentation among them.

I.3. Presence of more intensive external political influences.

    I.3.a. Greater diversity and intensity of external informal political influences on decisions (political bargaining and lobbying; public opinion; interest-group, client, and constituent pressures).

    I.3.b. Greater need for political support from client groups, constituencies, and formal authorities in order to obtain appropriations and authorization for actions.

II. Organization-Environment Transactions

II.1. Public organizations and managers are often involved in production of public goods or handling of significant externalities. Outputs are not readily transferable to economic markets at a market price.

II.2. Government activities are often coercive, monopolistic, or unavoidable. Government has unique sanctioning and coercion power and is often the sole provider. Participation in consumption and financing of activities is often mandatory.

II.3. Government activities often have a broader impact and greater symbolic significance. There is a broader scope of concern, such as for general public interest criteria.

II.4. There is greater public scrutiny of public managers.

II.5. There are unique expectations for fairness, responsiveness, honesty, openness, and accountability.

III. Organizational Roles, Structures, and Processes

The following distinctive characteristics of organizational roles, structures, and processes have been frequently asserted to result from the distinctions cited under I and II. More recently, distinctions of this nature have been analyzed in research with varying results.

III.1. Greater goal ambiguity, multiplicity, and conflict.

    III.1.a. Greater vagueness, intangibility, or difficulty in measuring goals and performance criteria; the goals are more debatable and value-laden (for example, defense readiness, public safety, a clean environment, better living standards for the poor and unemployed).

    III.1.b. Greater multiplicity of goals and criteria (efficiency, public accountability and openness, political responsiveness, fairness and due process, social equity and distributional criteria, moral correctness of behavior).

    III.1.c. Greater tendency of the goals to be conflicting, to involve more trade-offs (efficiency versus openness to public scrutiny, efficiency versus due process and social equity, conflicting demands of diverse constituencies and political authorities).

III.2. Distinctive features of general managerial roles

    III.2.a. Recent studies have found that public managers' general roles involve many of the same functions and role categories as those of managers in other settings but with some distinctive features: a more political, expository role, involving more meetings with and interventions by external interest groups and political authorities; more crisis management and "fire drills"; greater challenge to balance external political relations with internal management functions.

TABLE 3.2. DISTINCTIVE CHARACTERISTICS OF PUBLIC MANAGEMENT AND PUBLIC ORGANIZATIONS: A SUMMARY OF COMMON ASSERTIONS AND RESEARCH FINDINGS, cont'd.

III.3. Administrative authority and leadership practices.

    III.3.a. Public managers have less decision-making autonomy and flexibility because of elaborate institutional constraints and external political influences. There are more external interventions, interruptions, constraints.

    III.3.b. Public managers have weaker authority over subordinates and lower levels as a result of institutional constraints (for example, civil service personnel systems, purchasing and procurement systems) and external political alliances of subunits and subordinates (with interest groups, legislators).

    III.3.c. Higher-level public managers show greater reluctance to delegate authority and a tendency to establish more levels of review and approval and to make greater use of formal regulations to control lower levels.

    III.3.d. More frequent turnover of top leaders due to elections and political appointments causes more difficulty in implementing plans and innovations.

    III.3.e. Recent counterpoint studies describe entrepreneurial behaviors and managerial excellence by public managers.

III.4. Organizational structure.

    III.4.a. Numerous assertions that public organizations are subject to more red tape, more elaborate bureaucratic structures.

    III.4.b. Empirical studies report mixed results, some supporting the assertions about red tape, some not supporting them. Numerous studies find some structural distinctions for public forms of organizations, although not necessarily more bureaucratic structuring.

III.5. Strategic decision-making processes.

    III.5.a. Recent studies show that strategic decision-making processes in public organizations can be generally similar to those in other settings but are more likely to be subject to interventions, interruptions, and greater involvement of external authorities and interest groups.

III.6. Incentives and incentive structures.

    III.6.a. Numerous studies show that public managers and employees perceive greater administrative constraints on the administration of extrinsic incentives such as pay, promotion, and disciplinary action than do their counterparts in private organizations.

    III.6.b. Recent studies indicate that public managers and employees perceive weaker relations between performance and extrinsic rewards such as pay, promotion, and job security. The studies indicate that there may be some compensating effect of service and other intrinsic incentives for public employees and show no clear relationship between employee performance and perceived differences in the relationship between rewards and performance.

III.7. Individual characteristics, work-related attitudes and behaviors.

    III.7.a. A number of studies have found different work-related values on the part of public managers and employees, such as lower valuation of monetary incentives and higher levels of public service motivation.

    III.7.b. Numerous highly diverse studies have found lower levels of work satisfaction and organizational commitment among public than among private managers and employees. The level of satisfaction among public sector samples is generally high but tends consistently to be somewhat lower than that among private comparison groups.

III.8. Organizational and individual performance.

    III.8.a. There are numerous assertions that public organizations and employees are cautious and not innovative. The evidence for this is mixed.

    III.8.b. Numerous studies indicate that public forms of various types of organizations tend to be less efficient in providing services than their private counterparts, although results tend to be mixed for hospitals and utilities. (Public utilities have been found to be efficient somewhat more often.) Yet other authors strongly defend the efficiency and general performance of public organizations, citing various forms of evidence.

Source: Adapted from Rainey, Backoff, and Levine (1976) and Rainey (1989).

economic markets are weaker or absent in them. Some scholars theorize (as many citizens believe) that this reduces incentives for cost reduction, operating efficiency, and effective performance. In the absence of markets, other governmental institutions (courts, legislatures, the executive branch) use legal and formal constraints to impose greater external governmental control of procedures, spheres of operations, and strategic objectives. Interest groups, the media, public opinion, and informal bargaining and pressure by governmental authorities exert an array of less formal, more political influences. These differences arise from the distinct nature of transactions with the external environment. Government is more monopolistic, coercive, and unavoidable than the private sector, with a greater breadth of impact, and it requires more constraint. Therefore government organizations operate under greater public scrutiny and are subject to unique public expectations for fairness, openness, accountability, and honesty.

Internal structures and processes in government organizations reflect these influences, according to the typical analysis. Also, characteristics unique to the public sector—the absence of the market; the production of goods and services not readily valued at a market price; value-laden expectations for accountability, fairness, openness, and honesty as well as performance—complicate the goals and evaluation criteria of public organizations. Goals and performance criteria are more diverse, they conflict more often (and entail more difficult trade-offs), and they are more intangible and harder to measure. The external controls of government, combined with the vague and multiple objectives of public organizations, generate more elaborate internal rules and reporting requirements. They cause more rigid hierarchical arrangements, including highly structured and centralized rules for personnel procedures, budgeting, and procurement.

Greater constraints and diffuse objectives allow managers less decision-making autonomy and flexibility than their private counterparts have. Subordinates and subunits may have external political alliances and merit-system protections that give them relative autonomy from higher levels. Striving for control because of the political pressures on them but lacking clear performance measures, executives in public organizations avoid delegation of authority and impose more levels of review and more formal regulations.

Critics complain that these conditions, aggravated by rapid turnover of political executives, push top executives toward a more external, political role, with less attention to internal management. Middle managers and rank-and-file employees respond to the constraints and pressures with caution and rigidity. Critics and managers alike complain about weak incentive structures in government, lament the absence of flexibility in bestowing financial rewards, and point to other problems with governmental personnel systems. Complaints about difficulty in firing, disciplining, and financially rewarding employees generated major civil service reforms in the late 1970s at the federal level and in states around the country.

In turn, expert observers assert, and some research indicates, that public employees' personality traits, values, needs, and work-related attitudes differ from those of private sector employees. Some research finds that public employees place lower value on financial incentives, show somewhat lower levels of satisfaction with certain aspects of their work, and differ in some other work attitudes from their private sector counterparts.

Intriguingly, the comparative performance of public and nonpublic organizations and employees figures as the most significant issue of all and the most difficult one to resolve. It also generates the most controversy. As noted earlier, the general view has been that government organizations operate less efficiently and effectively than private organizations. Many studies have compared public and private delivery of the same services, mostly finding the private form more efficient. Efficiency studies beg many questions, however, and a number of authors defend government performance strongly. They cite client satisfaction surveys, evidence of poor performance by private organizations, and many other forms of evidence to argue that government performs much better than is generally supposed.

This is a fair characterization of the prevailing view of public organizations that one would attain from an overview of the literature and research. The picture is fairly unfavorable. Yet, for all the reasons given earlier, it is best to regard this as an oversimplified and unconfirmed set of assertions. The challenge now is to bring together the evidence from the literature and research to work toward a better assessment of these assertions and a better understanding of their real meaning.

CHAPTER FOUR

ANALYZING THE ENVIRONMENT OF PUBLIC ORGANIZATIONS

B efore encountering organization theory, a person might find peculiar the references to organizational "environments" in Figure 1.1 and the definition of organization in Chapter One. Why should there be a balloon in the figure with that word in it, and a reference to it in the definition? It is a bit like having a reference to "everything else" or "the rest of the world." Hearing the term *environment*, a lot of people outside this field probably think of the ecological environment, which we want to protect from pollution.

The historical overview should have made clear, however, why organizational environment has become one of the most important concepts in the study of management and organizations. The early contributors described in the historical review in Chapter Two concentrated on the middle parts of the framework in Figure 1.1— on structures, mainly, with limited attention to certain aspects of tasks, processes, incentives, and people. They placed little emphasis on an organization's environments or its managers' responses to them. The review in Chapter Two and the sections below show how dramatically this perspective has changed, to the point where researchers and experts now regard organizational environments, and the challenges of dealing with them, as absolutely crucial to analyzing organizations and leading them. This is certainly true for public organizations, since they are often more open than other organizations to certain types of environmental pressures and constraints. Public organizations tend to be subject to more directions and interventions from political actors and authorities who seek to direct and control them.

Management experts now exhort managers to analyze their environments, and consultants regularly lead executives and task forces through such analyses as part of strategic planning sessions (described in detail in Chapter Seven). In spite of all the attention to organizational environments, however, the management field provides no exact science for analyzing them, in part because the concept is complex and difficult in various ways. For example, the relevant environments usually involve many different dimensions, and they can differ for different issues and at different organizational levels (Starbuck, 1983).

Public organizations are often embedded in larger governmental structures (Meyer, 1979). The Food and Drug Administration, for example, operates as a subunit of the U.S. Department of Health and Human Services, which in turn is a component of the U.S. federal government. The larger units of government impose systemwide rules (Warwick, 1975) on all agencies. In many agencies, different subunits operate in very different policy areas and often have stronger alliances with legislators and interest groups than with the agency director (Seidman and Gilmour, 1986; Kaufman, 1979). All this can make it hard to say where an agency's environment begins and ends.

In addition, members of an organization often *enact* its environment (Weick, 1979). They choose which matters to pay attention to and to try to change. They make choices about the organization's *domain*, or field of operations, including the geographic areas, markets, clients, products, and services on which the organization will focus. Decisions about an organization's domain determine the nature of its environment. For example, leaders of the Ohio Bureau of Mental Retardation adopted a "deinstitutionalization" policy, moving patients out of the large treatment facilities operated by the agency and into smaller, private sector facilities. This changed the boundaries of the agency, its relations with its clients, and the set of organizations with which the agency worked. Organizations create or shape their environments as much as they simply react to them. This complicates the analysis of environments, but it makes it all the more important.

General Dimensions of Organizational Environments

One typical approach to working through some of the complexity of environmental analysis is to simply lay out the general dimensions or conditions, such as those in Table 4.1, that an organization encounters. These dimensions seem so general, however, that one might question their value. Consultants and experts often use such frameworks to lead groups in organizations through an *environmental scan* (described in Chapter Seven) as part of a strategic planning project, or in a general assessment of the organization (for example, see Morgan, 1988, pp. 18–19).

TABLE 4.1. GENERAL ENVIRONMENTAL CONDITIONS.

- *Technological conditions:* the general level of knowledge and capability in science, engineering, medicine, and other substantive areas; general capacities for communication, transportation, information processing, medical services, military weaponry, environmental analysis, production and manufacturing processes, and agricultural production.
- *Legal conditions:* laws, regulations, legal procedures, court decisions; characteristics of legal institutions and values, such as provisions for individual rights and jury trials as well as the general institutionalization and stability of legal processes.
- *Political conditions:* characteristics of the political processes and institutions in a society, such as the general form of government (socialism, communism, capitalism, and so on; degree of centralization, fragmentation, or federalism) and the degree of political stability (Carroll, Delacroix, and Goodstein, 1988). More direct and specific conditions include electoral outcomes, political party alignments and success, and policy initiatives within regimes.
- *Economic conditions:* levels of prosperity, inflation, interest rates, and tax rates; characteristics of labor, capital, and economic markets within and between nations.
- *Demographic conditions:* characteristics of the population such as age, gender, race, religion, and ethnic categories.
- *Ecological conditions:* characteristics of the physical environment, including climate, geographical characteristics, pollution, natural resources, and the nature and density of organizational populations.
- *Cultural conditions:* predominant values, attitudes, beliefs, social customs, and socialization processes concerning such things as sex roles, family structure, work orientation, and religious and political practices.

Anyone can provide examples of ways in which such conditions influence organizations. Technological and scientific developments gave birth to many government agencies, such as the Environmental Protection Agency and the Nuclear Regulatory Commission. Technological developments continually influence the operation of government agencies; they must struggle to keep up with advances in computer technology, communications, and other areas. Demographic trends currently receive much attention, as analysts project increasing percentages of women and minorities in government employment. This raises the challenge of managing diversity in the workplace (Ospina, 1996). Mainly due to the increasing size of the population of retired Americans, the Social Security Administration projected that its workload would increase 19 percent between 1993 and 1999 (U.S. Social Security Administration, 1995, p. 26). Public administrators attend carefully to legal developments, such as changes in public officials' legal liability for their decisions (Koenig and O'Leary, 1996). As for the political dimensions of organizational environments, much of the rest of this book pertains to such influences, especially this and the next chapter.

Another common approach to analyzing environments is to list specific elements of an organization's environment, such as important organizations and groups. A typical depiction of such elements of the environment might include competitors, customers, suppliers, regulators, unions, and associates. Similarly, Porter (1985) analyzes the major influences on competition within an industry: industry competitors, buyers, suppliers, new entrants, and substitutes. Consultants working with organizations on strategy formulation sometimes use such frameworks in a *stakeholder analysis,* to identify key stakeholders of the organization and their particular claims and roles (Bryson, 1995).

Research on Environmental Variations

Organizational researchers have also produced more specific evidence about the effects of environments. As Chapter Two described, early theorists paid little attention to external environments, but research has increasingly demonstrated their importance. Selznick (1966; Hall, 1996) helped lead this trend with a study of a government corporation, the Tennessee Valley Authority (TVA). He found that environmental influences play a crucial role in *institutionalization* processes in organizations. Values, goals, and procedures become strongly established, not necessarily because managers choose them as the most efficient means of production, but in large part as a result of environmental influences and exchanges. The TVA, for example, engaged in *co-optation,* absorbing new elements into its leadership to avert threats to its viability. The U.S. government established the TVA during the New Deal years to develop electric power and foster economic development along the Tennessee River. TVA officials involved local organizations and groups in decisions. This gained support for the TVA, but it also brought in these groups as strong influences on the organization's values and priorities. In some cases, these groups shut out rival groups, putting the TVA in conflict with other New Deal programs with which it should have been allied. Thus, an organization's needs for external support and its consequent exchanges with outside entities can heavily influence its primary values and goals.

Later research made the importance of the external environment increasingly clear. Prominent studies that led to the emergence of contingency theory found more and more evidence of the impact of environmental uncertainty and complexity. Burns and Stalker (1961), for example, studied a set of English firms and classified them into two categories. *Mechanistic* firms emphasized a clear hierarchy of authority, with direction and communication dependent on the chain of command, and specialized, formally defined individual tasks. Other firms were more *organic,* with less emphasis on hierarchy and more lateral communication and networking. Tasks were less clearly defined and changed more frequently. Managers in these firms sometimes spurned organizational charts as too confining or even dangerous. The mechanistic firms succeeded in stable environments—those with relative stability in terms of products, technology, competitors, and demand for their products. In such a setting, they could take advantage of the efficiencies of their more traditional structures. Other firms, such as electronics manufacturers, faced less stable environmental conditions, with rapid fluctuations in technology, products, competitors, and demand. The more organic firms, which were more flexible and adaptive, succeeded in this setting.

Lawrence and Lorsch (1967) studied firms in three industries whose environments exhibited different degrees of uncertainty as a result of more or less rapid changes and greater or lesser complexity. The most successful firms had structures with a degree of complexity matching that of the environment. Firms in more stable environments could manage with relatively traditional, hierarchical structures. Firms in more unstable, uncertain environments could not.

In addition, different subunits of these firms faced different environments. As these different environments imposed more uncertainty on the subunits' managers, the successful firms became more differentiated. The subunits differed more and more from one another in their goals, the time frames for their work, and the formality of their structure. This increased the potential for conflict and disorganization, however. Successful firms in more uncertain environments responded with higher levels of integration. They had more methods for coordinating the highly differentiated units, such as liaison positions, coordinating teams, and conflict-resolution processes. This combination of differentiation and integration made the successful firms in more complex, uncertain environments more internally complex. The authors' general conclusion advanced one of the prominent components of the contingency idea: organizations must adopt structures that are as complex as the environments they confront.

As many studies of this sort accumulated, James Thompson (1967) synthesized the growing body of research in a way that provided additional insights. Organizations must contend with the demands of their tasks and their environments. Organizations try to isolate the technical core, their primary work processes, so that their work can proceed smoothly. They use buffering methods to try to provide stable conditions for the technical core. For example, they use boundary-spanning units—such as inventory, personnel recruitment, and R&D units—to try to create smooth flows of information and resources. Yet environmental conditions can strain this process. In more complex environments, with more geographical areas, product markets, competitors, and other factors, organizations must become more internally complex. They establish different subunits to attend to the different environmental segments. More unstable environments create a need for greater decentralization of authority to these subunits and a less formal structure. The shifting environment requires rapid decisions and changes, and it takes too long for information and decisions to travel up and down a strict hierarchy.

Researchers have debated the adequacy of contingency theory, and many have moved off in other directions. Yet recent texts commonly deliver a standard message about the importance and implications of contingency theory perspectives on organizational environments (Daft, 1995, p. 92): an organization's structure must be adapted to environmental contingencies as well as other contingencies. In more simple, homogeneous, stable environments, organizations can successfully adopt more mechanistic and centralized structures. In more complex and unstable environments, successful organizations must be more organic and decentralized, partitioned into many departments with correspondingly elaborate integrating processes.

Scholars have also further developed contingency-theory concepts into more carefully conceived environmental dimensions. Table 4.2 illustrates prominent examples. Clearly these dimensions apply to public organizations. Tax revolts and pressures to cut government spending in recent years show the importance of environmental *capacity* (munificence or resource scarcity) for public organizations. The federal government has a regionalized structure, reflecting the influence of environmental heterogeneity and dispersion. The Florida Department of Health and Rehabilitative Services, one of the largest state agencies in the country, adopted a regionalized structure in the 1970s, partially in response to the heterogeneity and dispersion of its environment. The state created regional districts, in part to make the department more responsive to the different service needs in various parts of the state. In the southern part of the state there were greater demands for services for the elderly because of the populations of retirees in those areas. In other parts of the state such services were in less demand, but there was a greater need for services related to rural poverty. The regionalized structure allowed the organization to establish subunits targeted more directly to such local needs.

Even organization theorists who attach little significance to the public-private distinction agree that public organizations face particular complications in *domain consensus and choice* (Miles, 1980; Hall, 1996; Van de Ven and Ferry, 1980; Meyer, 1979). Jurisdictional boundaries and numerous authorities, laws, and political interests complicate decisions about where, when, and how a public organization operates. Research strongly supports the observation that public status influences strategic domain choices (Mascarenhas, 1989), although later chapters show how public managers often gain considerable leeway to maneuver.

Turbulence and *interconnectedness* characterize the environments of most public organizations. Studies of public policy implementation provide numerous accounts of policy initiatives that had many unanticipated consequences and implications for other groups. Public managers commonly encounter situations where a decision

TABLE 4.2. DESCRIPTIVE AND ANALYTICAL DIMENSIONS OF ORGANIZATIONAL ENVIRONMENTS.

Aldrich (1979)

Capacity: the extent to which the environment affords a rich or lean supply of necessary resources

Homogeneity-heterogeneity: the degree to which important components of the environment are similar or dissimilar

Stability-instability: the degree and rapidity of change in the important components or processes in the environment

Concentration-dispersion: the degree to which important components of the environment are separated or close together, geographically or in terms of communication or logistics

Domain consensus-dissensus: the degree to which the organization's domain (its operating locations, major functions and activities, and clients and customers served) is generally accepted or disputed and contested

Turbulence: the degree to which changes in one part or aspect of the environment in turn create changes in another; the tendency of changes to reverberate and spread

Dess and Beard (1984)

Munificence: the availability of needed resources

Complexity: the homogeneity and concentration of the environment

Dynamism: the stability and turbulence of the environment

Miles (1980)

Static dimensions

Complexity: the number of different external components and characteristics an organization must deal with

Routineness: the degree to which relations with the environment are routine and standardized

Interconnectedness: the degree to which environmental components and processes are intertwined such that changes at one point reverberate and spread

Remoteness: the immediacy and directness of an organization's relations with particular environmental components

Dynamic dimensions

Change rate: the rate of change in important elements and conditions

Unpredictability of change: the degree to which changes are patterned or predictable, as opposed to being sudden and difficult to anticipate

Receptivity dimensions

Resource scarcity: availability of needed resources

Output receptivity: demand for products and by-products and external constraints and opposition to outputs

Domain-choice flexibility: the extent to which an organization is free or constrained in choices of domain (that is, populations to be served, geographical areas in which to operate, technologies or procedures to apply, and goods, services, and functions to provide—what the organization does, where it does it, how it does it, and for whom it does it) touches off a furor, arousing opposition from groups that they would never have anticipated reacting (Chase and Reveal, 1983; Cohen and Eimicke, 1995). Similarly, environmental *stability, dynamism,* and *change rates* have major implications for public organizations. Rapid turnover of political appointees at the top of agencies and rapid external shifts in political priorities have major influences on public organizations and the people in them. For example, researchers find evidence that turbulence and instability in the environments of public agencies damage the morale of their managers and impede their acceptance of reforms (Ban, 1987; Rubin, 1985).

These environmental concepts are useful for enhancing our understanding of public organizations. As this discussion shows, however, no conclusive, coherent theory of organizations explains how these dimensions are related to one another and to organizations. In addition, organization theorists have defined these concepts at a very general level. Certainly they apply to public organizations, but to really understand public organizations we need to add more specific content to the environmental dimensions. There is a body of useful research and writing on public bureaucracies that can help in this task, to which this discussion will turn after a review of very recent work on organizational environments.

Current Research on Organizational Environments

Some of the most prominent current research in organization theory concentrates on organizational environments and moves beyond contingency theory. *Population ecology* theorists, for example, analyze the origin, development, and decline of populations of organizations, using biological concepts (Hannan and Freeman, 1989). Just as biologists analyze how certain populations of organisms develop to take advantage of a particular ecological niche, population ecologists analyze the development of populations of organizations within certain niches (characterized by their unique combinations of available resources and constraints).

Some population ecology theorists reject the contingency-theory depiction of organizations as rational, speedy adapters to environmental change. Indeed, they see environments as selecting organizational populations in a Darwinian fashion (Hannan and Freeman, 1989). This brings some criticism from other scholars, who complain that this view overlooks the importance of management strategies (Van de Ven, 1979). It also raises a profound question about management, one that is relevant to the public-versus-private debate. Belief in environmental selection of organizations implies that what managers do ultimately matters very little because environmental conditions determine outcomes. Consider this in relation to the claim that public managers face more constraints than do private ones. The environmental selection view in effect argues that all managers operate under sharp constraints; public managers do not appear to be unique. In addition, it looks at political influences on populations of organizations, such as laws and regulations that influence entry and exit in specific industries, and concludes that many organizations are influenced by governmental constraints; this again reduces the distinctiveness of public organizations.

On the other hand, this view raises some fascinating questions about public organizations that more research may enlighten. For example, why do some populations of organizations, such as schools, mostly inhabit the public sector? (About 00 percent of the schools in the United States are public schools.) This puts us back on the hunt for the meaning of a public organization.

Resource-dependence theories analyze how organizational managers try to obtain crucial resources from their environment—resources such as materials, money, people, support services, and technological knowledge. Organizations can adapt their structures in response to their environment, or they can change niches. They can try to change the environment by creating demand or seeking government actions that can help them. They can try to manipulate the way the environment is perceived by the people in the organization and those outside it. In these and other ways, they can pursue essential resources. These theorists stress the importance of internal and external political processes in the quest for resources. Chapter Six discusses how their analysis of resources in connection with internal power relationships applies to public organizations. They express their theories very generally, however, applying resource-dependency concepts to most or all organizations. Thus they, too, imply that public organizations do not represent a particularly distinct group (Pfeffer and Salancik, 1978, pp. 277–278).

Transaction-costs theories analyze managerial decisions to purchase a needed good or service from outside, as opposed to producing it within the organization (Williamson, 1975, 1981). Transactions with other organizations and people become more costly as contracts become harder to write and supervise. The organization may need a service very particular to itself, or it may have problems supervising contractors. Managers may try to hold down such costs under certain conditions by merging with another organization or permanently hiring a person with whom they had been contracting. These theories, which are much more elaborate than summarized here, have received much attention in business management research and have implications for government contracting and other governmental issues (Bryson, 1995). Yet they usually assume that managers in firms strive to hold down costs to maximize profits. Governmental contracting involves more political criteria and accountability and different or nonexistent profit motives, so leading theorists in this group express uncertainty about applications to government (Williamson, 1981).

Recent studies of *institutionalization* processes hark back to the work of Selznick. They analyze how certain values, structures, and procedures become institutionalized—widely accepted as the proper way of doing things—in and among organizations. Tolbert and Zucker (1983) show that many local governments reformed their civil service systems by adopting merit systems, because merit systems had become widely accepted as the proper form of personnel system for such governments. In addition, the federal government applied pressures for the adoption of merit systems. Meyer and Rowan (1983) argue that organizations such as schools often adopt structures on the basis of "myth and ceremony." They do things according to prevailing beliefs and not because the practices are clearly the means to efficiency or effectiveness. DiMaggio and Powell (1983) show that organizations in the same field come to look like one another as a result of shared ideas about how that type of organization should look. Dobbin and his colleagues (1988) found that public organizations have more provisions for due process, such as affirmative action programs, than do more private ones. These studies have obvious relevance for public organizations. Pfeffer (1982) suggests that this approach is particularly applicable to the public sector, where performance criteria are often less clear. There, beliefs about proper procedures may substitute more readily for firmly validated procedures. Public and nonprofit managers encounter many instances where new procedures or schemes, such as a new budgeting technique, become widely implemented as the latest, best approach—whether or not anyone can prove that it is. In addition, some of the research mentioned above shows how external institutions such as government impose structures and procedures on organizations. Some of these theorists disagree among themselves over these different views of institutionalization—whether it results from the spread of beliefs and myths or from the influence of external institutions such as government (Scott, 1987).

These developments show how elaborate and diverse the work on organizational environments has become, and each one provides insights. In fact, scholars are currently arguing more and more frequently that there is a need to bring these models together rather than argue about which is the best one (Hall, 1996, p. 314; Tolbert, 1985). Obviously they deal with processes that influence organizations in some combination, and all are true to some degree.

The Political and Institutional Environments of Public Organizations

The work on organizational environments provides a number of insights, many of them applicable to public organizations. The preceding review of the literature on organizational environments also shows, however, why people interested in public organizations call for more complete attention to public sector environments. The contingency-theory researchers express environmental dimensions very generally. They pay little attention to whether government ownership makes a difference or whether it matters if an organization sells its outputs in economic markets. They depict organizations, usually business firms, as autonomously adapting to environmental contingencies. Political scientists, however, see it as obvious that external political authorities often directly mandate the structures of public agencies, regardless of something called "environmental uncertainty" (Warwick, 1975; Pitt and Smith, 1981). The more current perspectives on organizational environments bring government into the picture, but they also express their concepts very generally, subsuming governmental influences under broader concepts. Sometimes they concentrate on business firms.

Major Components and Dimensions

Public executives commenting on public management and political scientists and economists writing about public organizations typically depict organizational environments as they are illustrated in Table 4.3. (Downs, 1967; Meier, 1993; Hood and Dunsire, 1981; Pitt and Smith, 1981; Stillman, 1996; Wamsley and Zald, 1973; Warwick, 1975; Wilson, 1989). The rest of this chapter will discuss the top part of the table, concerning general values and institutions. The next chapter will cover the bottom portion, covering institutions, entities, and actors.

General Institutions and Values of the Political Economy

Chapter Two defined public agencies as organizations owned and funded by government. They operate under political authority and without economic markets for their outputs. The political system of the nation and its traditions, institutions, and values heavily influence the exercise of this political authority. The U.S. Constitution formally states some of these values and establishes some of the nation's primary public institutions and rules of governance. Legislation and court cases have further defined and applied them. Rosenbloom (1983) has observed that the personnel systems in government are "law-bound." That observation applies to many other aspects of management and organization in government agencies as well.

Other values and rules receive less formal codification but still have great influence. For example, Americans have traditionally demanded that government agencies operate with businesslike standards of efficiency, although the Constitution nowhere explicitly expresses this criterion (Waldo, [1947] 1984). Relatedly, the nation maintains a free-enterprise system that affords considerable autonomy to

TABLE 4.3. MAJOR ENVIRONMENTAL COMPONENTS FOR PUBLIC ORGANIZATIONS.

General Values and Institutions of the Political Economy

Political and economic traditions
Constitutional provisions and their legislative and judicial development
    Due process
    Equal protection of the laws
    Democratic elections and representation (republican form)
    Federal system
    Separation of powers
Free-enterprise system (economic markets relatively free of government controls)

Values and performance criteria for government organizations

    Competence
        Efficiency
        Effectiveness
        Timeliness
        Reliability
        Reasonableness
    Responsiveness
        Accountability, legality, responsiveness to rule of law and governmental authorities, responsiveness to public demands
        Adherence to ethical standards
        Fairness, equal treatment, impartiality
        Openness to external scrutiny and criticism

Institutions, Entities, and Actors with Political Authority and Influence

Chief executives
    Executive staff and staff offices
Legislatures
    Legislative committees
    Individual legislators
    Legislative staff
Courts
Other government agencies
    Oversight and management agencies (GAO, OMB, OPM, GSA)
    Competitors
    Allies
    Agencies or governmental units with joint programs
Other levels of government
    "Higher" and "lower" levels
    Intergovernmental agreements and districts
Interest groups
    Client groups
    Constituency groups
    Professional associations
Policy subsystems
    Issue networks
    Interorganizational policy networks
    Implementation structure
News media
General public opinion
Individual citizens with requests for services, complaints, and other contacts

businesses and considerable respect for business values (Waldo, [1947] 1984; Lindblom, 1977). These values are not clearly and specifically codified in the Constitution. According to MacDonald (1987), the Constitution actually lacks some of the provisions necessary for a free-enterprise system, in part because some of the framers considered certain economic activities, such as trading debt instruments, to be immoral. Full development of the necessary governmental basis for a free-enterprise system required the actions of Alexander Hamilton, the first secretary of the treasury. Among other steps, he established provisions for the use of government debt as a source of capital for corporations. MacDonald, a conservative, would almost certainly disavow the conclusion that the private enterprise system in the United States was largely created through the efforts of a government bureaucrat, using government funding. More generally, however, these examples illustrate the existence, through formally codified instruments and less formally codified conditions, of general values and institutional arrangements that shape the operation of public authority.

These general values and institutional arrangements in turn influence the values, constraints, and performance criteria of public organizations. They sound abstract, but they link directly to practical challenges and responsibilities for public organizations and managers.

Constitutional Provisions

The Constitution places limits on the government and guarantees certain rights to citizens. These include provisions for freedom of expression and the press, equal protection of the laws, and protections against the denial of life, liberty, or property without due process of law. The provisions for freedom of association and expression and freedom of the press empower media representatives, political parties, and interest groups to assess, criticize, and seek to influence the performance of government agencies, in ways discussed in the next chapter.

Such provisions as those for equal protection and due process also have major implications for the operations of public organizations. The equal protection provisions, for example, provided some of the underlying principles and precedents for affirmative action requirements. The requirement for legal due process requires administrative due process as well and acts as one major form of control over public bureaucracies and bureaucrats (West, 1995, chap. 2). Agencies are often required to give notice of certain actions and to adhere to disclosure rules, to hold open hearings about their decisions, and to establish procedures for appealing agency decisions. For example, the Administrative Procedures Act requires federal agencies to adhere to certain procedures in rule making (and other legislation has established similar requirements at other levels of government). When the Department of Education makes rules about student loans or the Social Security Administration (SSA) makes rules about claims for coverage under its disability programs, the agencies have to adhere to such requirements. If the SSA denies or revokes an applicant's disability coverage, the applicant has the right to adjudication procedures, which may involve a hearing conducted by an administrative law judge. During a typical year in the 1970s, SSA had about 625 administrative law judges hearing such appeals (Mashaw, 1983, p. 18). More recently, the agency projected that its periodic reviews of disability cases—periodic checks on whether people are still disabled and still deserve coverage—would expand from its 1993 level of one hundred thousand to five hundred thousand by 1999 (U.S. Social Security Administration, 1995). This will expand the number of appeals and hearings, of course. These requirements strongly influence the agency's management of disability cases and the work of individual caseworkers. Generally, the requirement for all the appeals and hearings conflicts with the agency's goal of minimizing costs and maximizing efficiency of operations. More subtly, it raises complex issues about how efficiency relates to "bureaucratic justice" and the fair and proper handling of individual cases by individual caseworkers (Mashaw, 1983). (Chapters Eight and Ten show evidence that rules and procedures for disciplining and firing employees in the public service, based in part on due process principles, create one of the sharpest differences between public and private organizations confirmed by research.) These examples illustrate how general constitutional principles translate into a set of immediate challenges and issues in organizational behavior and management.

Democratic elections are another feature of the political system in the United States and other countries that has direct implications for organization and management. The electoral process produces regular, or at least frequent, changes in chief executives, legislative officials, and the political appointees that come and go with them. These changes in leadership often mean frequent changes in the top-level leadership of public agencies—every two years for many agencies. These changes often bring with them shifts in priorities that mean changes in agencies' focus and sometimes their power, their influence, and the resources available for their people and subunits.

The Constitution also established a federal system that allocates authority to different levels of government in ways that influence the organization and management of public agencies. State governments require that local governments establish certain offices and officers, such as sheriffs and judges, thereby specifying major features of the organizational structure of those governments. State legislation may mandate a formula to be used in setting the salaries of those officials. Many federal programs operate by granting or channeling funds to states and localities, often with various specifications about the structure and operations of the programs at those levels. When the human services agency in Florida undertook its reorganization into districts described earlier in the chapter, officials for vocational rehabilitation programs funded by the federal government instructed them that those programs could not be part of the reorganization. The legislation authorizing those programs included specifications for the program's structure that the agency was not allowed to change.

A particularly dramatic example of the implications for public organizations of societal values and institutions is the provision in the Constitution for separation of powers. As indicated in Table 4.3 and discussed below, government agencies face various pressures for efficient, effective operations. Separation of powers, however, represents a system that is explicitly designed with less emphasis on efficiency than on constraining the power of government authorities (Wilson, 1989). In the *Federalist Papers*, James Madison discussed the constitutional provision for dividing power among the branches of government as a way of constraining power. He pointed out that a strong central executive authority might be the most efficient organizational arrangement. But instead, he wrote, the government of the United States was being purposefully designed to constrain authority by dividing it among institutions. In one of the great exercises of applied psychology in history, he pointed out that if humans were angels, no such arrangements would be necessary. But since they are not, and since power can corrupt and overbear individuals, the new government would set ambition against ambition, dividing authority among the branches of government so that they would keep one another in check. Lower levels of government in the United States are designed with similar patterns of divided authority. For the organization and management of agencies, these arrangements have dramatic implications, since they subject the organizations and their managers to multiple authorities and sources of direction that are in part designed to conflict with one another. From its inception, the American political system has thus embodied a dynamic tension among conflicting values, principles, and authorities.

The controversy over whether this system works as intended never ends. Nevertheless, the political authorities and actors representing these broader values and principles impose on public organizations numerous performance criteria, such as those listed in Table 4.3. Authors use various terms to express the diversity of these criteria. Fried (1976), for example, refers to democracy, efficiency, and legality as the major performance criteria for the public bureaucracy in the United States. Rosenbloom (1989) considers law, management, and politics as the three dominant sources of administrative criteria. Table 4.3 uses Meier's distinction (1993) between *competence* and *responsiveness* criteria.

Competence Values

Public organizations operate under pressure to perform competently. Demands for efficiency come from all corners. Newspapers and television news departments doggedly pursue indications of wasteful uses of public funds at all levels of government. Political candidates and elected officials attack examples of waste, such as apparently excessive costs for components of military weaponry. The U.S. General Accounting Office (GAO), auditors general at the state and local levels, and other oversight agencies conduct audits of government programs, with an emphasis on efficiency. In 1979, the GAO set up a nationwide telephone hot line to receive reports of waste and fraud in federal programs. Legislative committees and city councils conduct hearings and reviews of agencies, with a similar concern. Special commissions, such as the Grace Commission (organized under the Reagan administration), investigate wasteful or inefficient practices in government. Similar commissions have been appointed in many states to examine state government operations and attack inefficiency. The Clinton administration's National Performance Review (mentioned in Chapter One and described more fully in Chapter Fourteen) emphasized streamlining federal operations and sharply reduced federal employment. Inefficiency in federal operations served as one of the justifications for its formation.

Public managers remain sensitive to these pressures because they know that evidence of inefficiency can damage public agencies and programs. They know of examples such as the severe pressures on the Department of Defense in 1987 that arose from allegations of excessive costs in defense contracts. At one point, a defense official temporarily suspended all contracts with the corporations involved. Surely this involved troublesome steps that defense officials did not want to take.

But efficiency was not necessarily the highest priority in the design of the U.S. government, as described above. External authorities, the media, interest groups, and citizens also demand effectiveness, timeliness, reliability, and reasonableness, even though these criteria may conflict with efficiency. Efficiency means producing a good or service at the lowest cost possible while maintaining a constant level of quality. These additional criteria concern whether a function is performed well, on time, dependably, and in a logical, sensible way. Government often performs services crucial to individuals or to an entire jurisdiction. People want the job done; efficiency is often a secondary concern. Also, in government the connection between a service and the cost of providing it is often difficult to see and analyze. Evidence that police, firefighters, emergency medical personnel, and the military lack effectiveness or reliability draws sharp responses that may relegate efficiency to a lesser status. Caspar Weinberger said in a television interview that the rapid military buildup he led as secretary of defense cost more than it would have if it had been conducted more slowly. He argued that the imperative to upgrade the military made faster, more expensive changes necessary. More recently, the Gulf War provided a striking example of an emphasis on effectiveness overriding concerns for costs and efficiency. At a time when surveys and voting patterns reflected widespread lack of confidence in government and resistance to public spending and taxation, an overwhelming majority of Americans voiced strong support for a very large, expensive, complex, risky military initiative. For supporters of the war, the priority of stopping Saddam Hussein's forces overwhelmingly outweighed considerations of cost and efficiency.

Sometimes one element of the political system stresses some of these criteria more vigorously than others (Pitt and Smith, 1981). This can increase conflicts for public managers, since different authorities emphasize different criteria. For example, the judiciary often appears to emphasize effectiveness over administrative efficiency because of its responsibility to uphold legal standards and constitutional rights. Judges rule that certain criteria must be met in a timely, effective way, virtually regardless of cost and efficiency. The courts have ordered that prisons and jails and affirmative action programs must meet certain standards by certain dates. They protect the right of clients of public programs to due process in decisions about whether they can be denied benefits. This increases the burden on public agencies, forcing them to conduct costly hearings and reviews and to maintain extensive documentation. The courts in effect leave efficiency and cost considerations for the agencies to worry about. The press and legislators, meanwhile, criticize agencies for slow procedures and expensive operations.

Casework by members of Congress, state legislators, and city council members can also exert pressure for results other than efficiency. (In this context, casework means action by an elected official to plead the case of an individual citizen or group who makes a demand of an agency.) A congressional representative or staff member may call about a constituent's late Social Security check. A city council member may call a city agency about a complaint from a citizen about garbage collection services. While these requests can promote effective, reasonable responses by an agency, responding to sporadic, unpredictable demands of this sort can tax both its efficiency and its effectiveness. Some of the worst abuses in the savings and loan scandal allegedly occurred when senators and representatives intervened with regulatory officials on behalf of major savings and loan executives.

Responsiveness Values

The responsiveness criteria in Table 4.3 often conflict sharply with competence criteria and also with each other. Public managers and organizations remain accountable to various authorities and interests and to the rule of law in general (Rosen, 1989; West, 1995). They must comply with laws, rules, and directives issued by government authorities and provide accounts of their compliance as required. (Chapter Four further discusses the means by which external authorities hold them accountable.)

Public organizations and their managers are often expected to remain open and responsive in various ways. Saltzstein (1992) points out that bureaucratic responsiveness can be defined in at least two ways, as responsiveness to the public's wishes or as responsiveness to the interests of the government, and that much of the discourse on the topic takes one or the other of these perspectives. These conflicting pressures sometimes coincide with accountability, in the sense of responding to directives and requests for information from government authorities. Yet public agencies also receive requests for helpful, reasonable, and flexible responses to the needs of clients, interest groups, and the general public. As they are public organizations, their activities are public business, and citizens and the media demand relative openness to scrutiny (Wamsley and Zald, 1973). For some programs, the enabling legislation requires citizen advisory panels or commissions to represent community groups, interest groups, and citizens. Administrative procedures at different levels of government require public notice of proposed changes in government agencies' rules and policies, often with provisions for public hearings at which citizens can attempt to influence the changes. The courts, legislatures, and legal precedent also require that agencies treat citizens fairly and impartially by adhering to principles of due process through appeals and hearings. The Freedom of Information Act and similar legislation at all levels of government require public agencies to make records and information available upon request under certain circumstances. Other legislation mandates the privacy of client records under certain circumstances.

Recently, the criterion of providing direct services to clients has received a lot of emphasis. The book *Reinventing Government* (Osborne and Gaebler, 1992), which has had such a broad impact in the 1990s, devotes a chapter to examples of "customer-driven government," proclaiming the value of staying in close touch with the customers of government programs and being responsive to their needs. As part of the National Performance Review, President Clinton directed federal agencies to issue and adhere to customer service standards and to in various ways be more responsive to clients and customers (Clinton and Gore, 1995). Chapter Fourteen describes these steps in more detail.

A related criterion, *representativeness*, pertains to various ways in which officials should represent the people. Representativeness is a classic issue in government and public administration, with discourse about the topic dating back for centuries. Important recent representativeness issues include equal employment opportunity, affirmative action, and more recently (as mentioned earlier), diversity. One view of representativeness holds that identifiable ethnic and demographic groups should be represented in government roughly in proportion to their presence in the population. The advisory groups mentioned above also reflect representativeness criteria in another sense. These criteria add to the complex set of objectives and values that public managers and organizations must pursue and seek to balance.

Later chapters describe examples and evidence of how conflicting values and criteria influence public organizations and pose very practical challenges for public managers. External authorities and political actors intervene in management decisions in pursuit of responsiveness and accountability and impose structures and constraints in pursuit of equity, efficiency, and accountability. Sharp conflicts over which values should predominate—professional effectiveness or political accountability, for example—lead to major transformations of organizational operations and culture (Maynard-Moody, Stull, and Mitchell, 1986; Romzek and Dubnick, 1987). Before examining these effects on major dimensions of organization and management, however, Chapter Five considers in more depth the elements in the lower portion of Table 4.3, the institutions, entities, and actors that seek to impose these values and criteria, and their exchanges of influence with public organizations.

CHAPTER FIVE

THE IMPACT OF POLITICAL POWER AND PUBLIC POLICY

Chapter Two defined public organizations as those that the government owns and funds and therefore directs and controls. The last chapter reviewed organization theorists' ideas about the crucial relationship between organizations, including public organizations, and their environment. It also argued that public organizations' environments impose a relatively distinctive set of values and criteria on them, through direction and influence by government institutions and entities (see Table 4.3, bottom). This chapter describes the sources of authority and influence—the power—of these entities over public organizations.

This chapter covers these topics in summary fashion. A complex literature analyzes these topics, but it is impossible to cover it fully in a brief chapter. One alternative would be simply to advise readers to go and study political science. Many will have already done that, and this discussion will mainly provide a review. Yet previous chapters have shown that the political institutions and entities discussed here play a central role in theories about the distinctiveness of public organizations. The analysis of public organizations and management requires that the insights gained from studies of public bureaucracy be integrated with the topics in general management and organization theory covered in later chapters. In addition, public managers need to understand and deal with the political entities discussed here. So, it is important to highlight some of the key points and issues.

Power and influence relationships are seldom simple, unidirectional, or entirely clear. Analyses of public organizations (or "public bureaucracies," as authors in the literature on bureaucratic power typically call them) certainly illustrate these complexities. For years, scholars analyzing public bureaucracies tended to characterize them as being out of the control of their political masters (Wood and Waterman, 1994, pp. 18–22). Some scholars depict regulatory agencies as having been "captured" by the interests they were supposed to regulate. Others have concluded that "iron triangles," or tight alliances of agencies, interest groups, and congressional committees, dominate agency policies and activities and close out other authorities and actors. These accounts describe bureaucracies as operating relatively independently of presidents, courts, and legislative bodies (except for special committees with which they might be allied).

A peculiar popular myth about public bureaucracies sees them as existing either for no reason and against everyone's better judgment or only for the selfish interests of the bureaucrats. In fact, a public agency that no one wants or that only the bureaucrats want is the easiest target for elimination in all the organizational world. Still, such popular views persist, and they correspond to very important political developments. Recent U.S. presidents, governors, and mayors have launched efforts to control bureaucracies, seeking to wrest from them their allegedly excessive power or to streamline and reduce them (Durant, 1992; Arnold, 1995).

Writers on public management often emphasize an opposing view, however. As mentioned in Chapter One, one source of concern about public management has been alleged constraints on public managers that deprive them of authority to carry out their jobs and frustrate them professionally. Thus the discussion on bureaucratic power has fallen into two conflicting camps, one in which bureaus and bureaucrats are seen as independent and influential and one in which they are regarded as impotent (Kingdon, 1984).

Recently, evidence has mounted that both these views have some merit, that bureaucratic power can more accurately be described as a dynamic mixture of both of these conditions. Researchers report numerous cases in which federal agencies have shown marked responsiveness to the authority of the president, the Congress, and the courts (Wood and Waterman, 1994; Rubin, 1985); on the other hand, Wood and Waterman (1994) also show evidence of "bottom-up" processes in which federal agencies initiate policy relatively independently. Similarly, recent studies of public management and leadership provide accounts of proactive behaviors by leaders of public agencies (Behn, 1991; Doig and Hargrove, 1987; Hargrove and Glidewell, 1990). The relative power of public organizations, their leaders, and the governmental institutions to which they are formally accountable is dynamic and depends on various conditions such as the salience of a particular issue, agency structure, agency expertise, public attitudes and support, and other factors. This chapter will review many of the formal powers of the external actors that influence public organizations, and as many of these dynamic factors as possible, because of their essential role in the fundamental organizational process of gaining resources from the environment—financial resources, grants of authority, and other resources. (Table 5.1 summarizes many of these formal powers and other bases of influence.) As Norton Long (1949, p. 257) declared in a classic essay, "the lifeblood of administration is power."

Public Organizations and the Public

Public organizations need support from what political scientists call *mass publics*, or broad, diffuse populations, and (especially) from *attentive publics*—more organized groups that are more interested in specific agencies.

Public Opinion and Mass Publics

General public opinion influences the management of public organizations more than much of the management literature acknowledges. Two types of mass opinion figure importantly: attitudes toward government in general and attitudes toward particular policies and agencies. Chapter One described the antigovernment trend of the last two decades and how elected officials responded with efforts to reform government bureaucracies. As noted in Chapter One, when President Carter reformed the civil service system, changing pay and disciplinary procedures and provisions for appointing senior executives, he promoted the reform as a means of motivating federal workers and making it easier to fire lazy ones. President Reagan more aggressively attacked the federal bureaucracy, cutting agency budgets and staffing, and sought to diminish the authority of career federal administrators (Rubin, 1985). Morale in the federal service plummeted. Surveys revealed that many career civil servants intended to leave the service and would discourage their children from pursuing a career in federal service (Volcker Commission, 1989). The general climate of unfavorable public opinion about the public bureaucracy thus had very significant effects on the morale and work behaviors of government employees, the structure of the federal government, and the functioning of major federal agencies.

The sharp public outcry in 1989 against a proposed pay raise for members of Congress, federal judges, and federal executives provides another good example of the effects of general public opinion on government employees and organizations. In opinion polls, more than 80 percent of the public opposed the increase. Ralph Nader and the National Taxpayers' Union fought the raise aggressively, exhorting voters to write and call their representatives to object to it. Congress overwhelmingly voted the raise down. After the defeat of the raise, stories in the *New York Times* and elsewhere reported bitter reactions by federal managers, including many who would

TABLE 5.1. SOURCES OF POLITICAL AUTHORITY AND INFLUENCE OF INSTITUTIONS, ENTITIES, AND ACTORS IN THE POLITICAL SYSTEM.

Chief Executives
Appointment of agency heads and other officials
Executive staff and staff offices (for example, budget office)
Initiating legislation and policy directions
Vetoing legislation
Executive orders and directives

Legislative Bodies
Power of the purse: final approval of the budget
Authorizing legislation for agency formation and operations
Approval of executive appointments of officials
Oversight activities: hearings, investigations
Authority of legislative committees
Initiating legislation

Courts
Review of agency decisions
Authority to render decisions that strongly influence agency operations
Direct orders to agencies

Government Agencies
Oversight and management authority (GAO, OMB, OPM, GSA)
Competitors
Allies
Agencies or government units with joint programs

Other Levels of Government
"Higher" and "lower" levels
Intergovernmental agreements and districts

Interest Groups
Client groups
Constituency groups
Professional associations

Policy Subsystems and Policy Communities
Issue networks
Interorganizational policy networks

News Media
Constitutional protections of freedom of the press
Open meetings laws, Sunshine laws

General Public Opinion
Providing (or refusing to provide) popular support

Individual Citizens
Requests for services, complaints, other contacts

not even have been in positions to receive the raise. They expressed sharp disappointment over the symbolic rejection of their value to the society.

During this period, the Federal Executive Institute Alumni Association (1991) reported survey responses from 1,140 members of the federal Senior Executive Service. The responses indicated that many of the senior executives felt that morale in their agency was low and declining and that the quality of its employees was also worsening. (About six hundred of the respondents felt that commitment to public service and writing ability among employees was worse than it had been ten years before). Forty-two percent of the executives said they would not encourage young people to consider a career in the federal government; only 29 percent said they would. These results suggest that the executives felt that the unfavorable climate surrounding the federal service affected morale, recruitment, and their own sentiments about the federal service. The responses illustrate the influence that the political environment and general public opinion can have on organizational behavior in government.

In state and local governments across this country and in other nations, unfavorable public attitudes about government have led to various reforms (Peters and Savoie, 1994). Some reforms have targeted government pay systems, seeking changes that would tie a government employee's pay more closely to his or her performance. The reforms are justified as a way to remedy allegedly weak motivation and performance on the part of public employees. Such efforts have apparently caused a lot of confusion and discouragement (Ingraham, 1993; Kellough and Lu, 1993; Gabris, 1987). In the state of Georgia, for example, the governor proposed in 1995 that merit system protections for state employees be abolished, in part so that it would be easier to fire them. The governor also aggressively pursued privatization initiatives, seeking, among other things, to authorize the operation of three large private prisons in the state. These sorts of reforms have been particularly prevalent in English-speaking countries, according to Peters and Savoie (1994). They reflect the decline in general public support for government spending and programs. As noted in Chapter One, this climate of opinion has strengthened in recent years and is reflected in the budget-balancing efforts in the U.S. Congress in 1995 and 1996, the Clinton administration's National Performance Review, and other developments.

Ambivalence and Paradoxes in Public Opinion

Chapter One also argued that public attitudes about government exhibit marked ambivalence and that this ambivalence also influences public managers and their agencies (Lipset and Schneider, 1987; Whorton and Worthley, 1981). Surveys consistently find that respondents say they would like lower taxes but do not want public spending reduced for most types of services (Ladd, 1983; Beck, Rainey, and

Traut, 1990). Surveys have also found that when respondents are asked how they feel about federal agencies in general, they give unfavorable responses. When asked for a specific evaluation of how they were treated by a particular agency in a specific instance, they give much more favorable responses (Katz, Gutek, Kahn, and Barton, 1975).

Ambivalent public attitudes contribute to the challenges of public management. In the absence of economic markets as mechanisms for measuring need and performance, public officials and public organizations often struggle with difficult questions about what the public wants. In recent decades, elected officials have often responded with reforms and decisions that directly influence structures, behavior, and management in public organizations. Nations cycle in and out of periods of antigovernment sentiment (Hirschman, 1982), and the climate in the United States may change. Nevertheless, these examples illustrate the influence on public management of general public sentiment.

Public Opinion and Agencies, Policies, and Officials

The general level of public support for a particular agency's programs affects its ability to maintain a base of political support. Certain agencies hold a more central place in the country's values (Wamsley and Zald, 1973) than do others, and the public regards their work as more crucial. The Department of Defense, police departments, and fire departments typically retain strong general public support because of the importance people attach to national defense and personal security. Some social programs, such as those perceived to involve "welfare" payments to the poor, receive weaker support in public opinion polls.

Hargrove and Glidewell (1990) propose a classification of public agencies and managerial jobs that places a heavy emphasis on public opinion. They classify public management jobs on the basis of how the public perceives the agency's clientele (for example, public sentiment toward prisoners and "welfare dependents" is usually negative), the level of respect it has for the professional authority of the agency and its head (for example, a scientific or medical professional basis usually gets more respect), and its general level of support for the mission and purpose of the agency. This discussion will return to such factors below in connection with the sources of authority for public agencies and managers.

Media Power: Obvious and Mysterious

The importance of public opinion bolsters the power of the news media. Congressional committees or state legislative committees summon agency executives before them to explain the events surrounding an embarrassing news story about an agency. Whistle blowers who go public with news about agency misconduct or incompetence have often received such harsh treatment that the federal government has made special provisions to protect them (Rosen, 1989). Bad press can sledgehammer an agency or an official, damaging budgets, programs, and careers. Chapter Thirteen describes a case in which bad press caused the removal of the head of a mental health services bureau and major changes in the bureau's operations.

Close media scrutiny of government plays an indispensable role in governance. The news media also report aggressively on scandals in private business (Dominick, 1981), yet they appear to emphasize scrutiny of government even more. Government is often more accessible, and it is more appropriate to watch it carefully, since government spends the taxpayers' money. In Columbus, Ohio, local newspaper photographers regularly checked the parking lots of bars and restaurants during normal working hours to try to take pictures of the license tags of any government vehicles parked there. An Atlanta, Georgia, television station carried a series of stories about the high costs of the furniture in the office of one of the county commissioners.

News reporters usually take a strong adversarial stance. They want to avoid seeming naive or co-opted. They need to focus on serious problems and generate an audience by reporting on controversial issues. The Volcker Commission (1989) report describes how Carter administration officials had trouble attracting interest in their proposals for civil service reforms until they developed a twenty-six-foot chart illustrating the tortuous steps it took to fire a bad federal employee. The news media immediately focused on this and provided more coverage. This apparently led the president to emphasize the negative, punitive aspects of the reforms in trying to build support for them. This emphasis almost certainly contributed to the disgruntlement of federal managers. Thus, media coverage influenced the tenor of reforms that shaped the personnel practices of the federal government and influenced the morale of employees throughout the public sector.

If anything, news coverage of government appears to be increasingly negative. Patterson (1994, pp. 20, 82) carefully documents that since 1960 news coverage has become much less descriptive, where reporters report facts about developments, and much more interpretive, where they interpret the developments. During the same period, coverage of candidates during presidential elections has become much more negative. Careful studies show that this negative coverage extends to government and the administrative branch. A study of news coverage of federal agencies during 1993 found that 72 percent of the coverage was negative (Patterson, 1996).

Instances where unfavorable press coverage damages a person, program, or agency make concern about media coverage part of the lore of government (Linsky, 1986). Officials and experts from Washington speak of managing in a "goldfish bowl" (Allison, 1983; Cohen and Eimicke, 1995), with media attention playing a stronger role than it does in business management (Blumenthal, 1983). Some federal executives apparently devote more time to creating a splash in the media than to performing well as managers (Lynn, 1981). Many public employees appear to feel that they will not get into much trouble for poor performance but will get into a *lot* of trouble for creating bad publicity (Lynn, 1981; Warwick, 1975; Downs, 1967). City and county officials will pack an auditorium to listen to consultants speak on how to handle media relations, and they regularly complain about unfair media coverage.

This apparent power of the media has mysterious qualities. The potential damage from bad coverage is often unclear. Ronald Reagan earned a reputation as the "Teflon president" by maintaining popularity in spite of sharp criticism in the media. As an additional irony, much of the worry over press coverage amounts to worrying over an entity in which the general public expresses little confidence. Public opinion polls find that public confidence in journalists and the news media is lower than public confidence in many other institutions and has been declining in recent decades (Patterson, 1996, p. 295). For a long time, many experts argued that the media exercise little influence over public voting patterns and attitudes about specific issues. Some experts on the news media now argue that the media exert a powerful influence on public attitudes, but in a diffuse way. Media coverage develops a climate that pervades the informational environment, and this in turn influences public opinion (Lichter, Rothman, and Lichter, 1986). In addition, some experts conclude that journalists come to develop a shared view of what constitutes the news, and this leads to a version of the news that is generally shared by the different news organizations (Patterson, 1996, p. 296).

Media attention also varies. Some agencies regularly get more media attention than others. Hood and Dunsire (1981) found that the foreign affairs office and the treasury get particularly high levels of press coverage in Britain, while other central government departments get relatively little. As the example of the Carter civil service reforms shows, the media often seriously neglect administrative issues. For years before the savings and loan scandal erupted as a major crisis, the media scarcely noticed the growing problem. Yet public officials also know that media attention can shift unpredictably. In one large state, where the department of administration ordinarily received little public attention, the director decided to change the set of private health insurance plans from which the state's employees chose their coverage. Many employees disliked the new set of plans. An outburst of complaints from state employees caused a sudden wave of coverage in the newspapers and television news around the state. A legislative committee soon called the director before special hearings about the changes.

Officials at higher levels and in political centers (capitals, large cities) often pay a great deal of attention to media strategies. Many city governments issue newsletters, televise city council meetings, and use other methods of public communication. Some federal and state agencies invest heavily in issuing public information. Even so, many public managers resist suggestions that they should devote time to media relations, regarding themselves as professionals rather than "politicians." More active approaches usually prove the most effective, however (Linsky, 1986). Various experts have offered advice on how to deal with the media; these are summarized in Table 5.2.

TABLE 5.2. GUIDELINES FOR MANAGING RELATIONS WITH THE NEWS MEDIA.

Experts on managing relations between government agencies and the news media propose such guidelines as the following:

- Understand the perspective of the media—their skepticism, their need for information and interesting stories, their time pressures.
- Organize media relations carefully—spend time and resources on them and link them with agency operations.
- Get out readable press releases providing good news about the agency; be patient if the media respond slowly.
- Respond to bad news and embarrassing incidents rapidly, with clear statements of the agency's side of the story.
- Seek corrections of inaccurate reporting.
- Use the media to help boost the agency's image, to implement programs, and to communicate with employees.
- To carry all this off effectively, make sure that the agency performs well, and be honest.

The Community Relations Office of the City of Claremont, California, published the following guidelines for managing relations with reporters:

- Prepare an agenda on each subject the media may be interested in. Include a list of three to five points you want to "sell" the reporter.
- Write or verbally deliver "quotable quotes" of ten words or less.
- Listen carefully to the question. The reporter may have made incorrect assumptions, and you will need to give clearer background information before answering the question.
- Avoid an argument with the reporter.
- If interrupted in midthought, proceed with your original answer before answering the new question.
- Challenge any effort to put words into your mouth.
- Don't just answer the question; use the question as a springboard to "sell" your agenda.
- If you do not know the answer, say so. Do not speculate.
- If you cannot divulge information, state why in a matter-of-fact way.
- Be positive, not defensive.
- Always tell the truth.

Sources: First half adapted from Cohen and Eimicke, 1995; Chase and Reveal, 1983; Garnett, 1992; second half adapted from Larkin, 1992.

Interest Groups, Clients, and Constituencies

The support of organized groups also determines the political well-being of public agencies. The role of organized interests in American politics generates continuing controversy. Special-interest politics poses the danger that the system will become (or has already become) too fragmented into self-interested groups, making it resistant to central coordination and hence unmanageable (Lowi, 1979). Critics say that the system favors richer, more powerful groups over the disadvantaged and allows private interests to control major domains of public policy. Influence peddling abounds in this system and creates ethical dilemmas for many public managers. Some face temptations, for example, to go easy on industries that they regulate in order to enhance their chance of acquiring a lucrative job in them.

Yet public managers also recognize that interest-group activities are not all bad. They play an important role in the current system and provide government with important information. As pointed out in Chapter Two, legislation requires that public managers consult with interested groups and their representatives. Often these groups voice reasonable demands—help our industry so we do not have to lay people off, help us with the economic development of your jurisdiction, help defend the country with this new weapons system, support education, aid the disadvantaged. Sometimes demands from different groups are reasonable but sharply conflicting.

Given the importance of these groups, many public managers have to cultivate their support and that of their constituencies (Hargrove and Glidewell, 1990; Doig and Hargrove, 1987; Meier, 1993; Rourke, 1984; Wildavsky, 1988; Chase and Reveal, 1983). Strong support from constituencies helps an agency defend itself against budget cuts or even secure budget increases from legislative bodies. It can also help agencies defend themselves against unwanted directives from legislators and chief executives. Constituent groups can promote an agency in ways that it cannot properly pursue itself. Interest groups can block an agency's actions, sometimes popping up unexpectedly as a manager tries to act.

What kind of group support bolsters an agency? Apparently, the most effective support comes from well-organized, cohesive groups that are strongly committed to the agency and its programs. On the other hand, *capture* of an agency by a constituency can damage the agency and bias it toward the self-interested priorities of that group (Rourke, 1984; Wilson, 1989). Critics have accused some regulatory agencies of being captives of the industries or professions that they supposedly regulate and complain that other agencies are captured by the clientele who receive their services (allegedly, the Forest Service has been captured by timber interests and the Bureau of Mines by mining interests). Agencies appear to have the most flexibility when they have the support of multiple groups; they can then satisfy some groups, if not all, and even have them confront one another about their conflicting demands (Chase and Reveal, 1983; Meier, 1993; Rourke, 1984).

Viteritti (1990) points out that an important distinction sometimes exists between an agency's *clients,* who should receive certain services, and its *constituents,* who demand them. He notes that research shows that bureaucratic rules in urban agencies actually defend equitable distribution of services. In some cases, however, broader constituencies may pressure public managers *not* to apply rules on behalf of certain clients. For example, community groups may press against having minority or handicapped clients put in school classes with their children or against the location of homes for the mentally retarded in their neighborhoods. The public manager faces challenges in sorting out the demands of clients and constituencies.

Several studies report that managers in state and local government agencies often see interest-group involvement with their agency as beneficial and appropriate. State and local agency managers regard interest groups as having less influence on the operations of their agency than the chief executive (the governor or mayor) or the legislature. When groups do exert influence, they often provide useful information about policy issues and group positions (Abney and Lauth, 1986; Brudney and Hebert, 1987; Elling, 1983). Abney and Lauth (1986) found additional evidence that agency managers at the urban level see interest-group involvement as appropriate when it focuses directly on the agency and inappropriate when it is channeled through the city council or the mayor. The managers may be too forgiving of interest-group influences, but the findings also suggest a more positive or at least necessary side of interest groups. Experienced public managers see maintaining relations with these groups as a necessary part of their work, often frustrating but also challenging and sometimes helpful. Public managers have to be accessible to such groups, seriously attentive to what they have to say, patient and self-controlled when they are harshly critical, and honest (Chase and Reveal, 1983; Cohen and Eimicke, 1995).

Legislative Bodies

Congress, state legislatures, city councils, and county commissions exercise as much formal, legal authority over public organizations as does any other entity. Formal authority always operates in a political context, which may weaken it or bolster it in practical terms.

Formal Authority

Legislative bodies have substantial formal powers. These powers include authority to control agency budgets, to pass legislation that authorizes and directs agency actions, and to oversee agency activities through hearings, investigations, and other means.

Power of the Purse. Legislative bodies provide the money needed to operate public agencies. They exercise the final power of approval over budget allocations to agencies. They can fund new initiatives or cut and curtail agency activities aggressively.

Legislation. Government agencies are usually born through legislation, especially at the federal and state levels. (At local levels, the agencies of a city government are often required under state guidelines.) Such legislation states the basic missions and duties of the agencies and authorizes their activities. Additional legislation can give an agency new duties. Its policies and programs can be extended, given to some other agency, reformed, or abolished.

Much of this legislation transmits vague, idealized directives to agencies. For example, legislation directs various regulatory agencies to promote "just" and "reasonable" practices in the public interest and for the common welfare (Woll, 1977). These broad grants of authority give the agencies considerable discretion (Lowi, 1979). Yet legislatures sometimes do the opposite, delving into the precise details of agency management and procedures and engaging in micromanagement. They sometimes reform the general structure of the executive branch, combining certain departments and splitting others apart. They sometimes dictate the organizational structure of major agencies, including what subunits they establish. They produce legislation governing the details of personnel procedures for the agencies within their jurisdiction or dictate other administrative procedures very precisely. For example, state legislatures sometimes include in legislation detailed specifications about the types of computer records a state regulatory agency must maintain.

Oversight. Legislative bodies regularly conduct hearings, audits, and investigations into agency activities (Rosen, 1989). Hearings are a normal part of the appropriations process and of the process of developing legislation. Investigatory and oversight agencies are established under the authority of the legislative branch to carry out inquiries into agency activities and performance. The General Accounting Office at the federal level and auditors general or similar offices in the states conduct audits to support legislative oversight.

Congressional oversight at the federal level has intensified in recent decades and has increasingly focused on administrative processes, apparently in response to presidents' efforts to control the bureaucracy (West, 1995). Wood and Waterman (1994) report evidence that congressional oversight can significantly influence the outputs and actions of federal agencies. They show, for example, that it led to a sharp increase in enforcement actions by the Environmental Protection Agency's hazardous waste compliance division during one period in the 1980s.

Committees. Particular legislative committees oversee particular agencies, conducting hearings about them, examining their operations, and developing legislation pertaining to them. Names of some committees correspond almost exactly to the names of major federal and state agencies. City councils often have a committee structure as well, with committees corresponding to the major departments and functions of the city government. Harold Seidman, one of the leading experts on federal administrative reforms, argues that if one wants to reform the federal bureaucracy, one must first reform Congress. Congressional committees jealously guard their authority over agencies (Seidman and Gilmour, 1986). An appropriations committee chair once objected to extending the president's power to veto legislation, saying, "We don't want the agencies taking orders from the president. We want them to take orders from us" (Miller, 1990).

Informal Influence

Legislative influences can be relatively informal as well, rather than codified into law. For example, legislators call administrators on the phone to press them for information or to ask for certain actions. State and federal administrators trying to relocate their agencies' offices or facilities to save money or to reorganize their operations frequently hear from outraged legislators whose districts will lose the facilities and jobs. During the 1960s, the U.S. Department of Labor sought to better organize diverse work-training programs run by various bureaus by bringing them under the authority of a newly created Manpower Administration. In committee hearings, powerful members of Congress told the head of this new agency that he should leave the Bureau of Apprenticeship and Trades (BAT) alone, that it should not be brought into the new structure (Ruttenberg and Gutchess, 1970). Labor unions wanted to maintain a strong influence on BAT and had lobbied members of Congress to oppose moving BAT under the new structure. Similarly, legislators press for the hiring or against the firing of political friends and allies in agencies (Warwick, 1975). None of these actions is necessarily formally authorized, and some are quite improper. They illustrate an additional dimension of legislative influence on the bureaucracy and show why legislators strive to defend their alliances and influences with the bureaucracy.

Limits on Legislative Power

Some experts insist that, even armed with all these powers, legislative bodies exert little real control over administrative agencies (Woll, 1977). The agencies are specialized and staffed with experts who know much more about their functions than do legislators and their staffs. Legislators often have little incentive to be aggressive in supervising agency performance (Meier, 1993; Ripley and Franklin, 1984). Such "good-government" activities offer little political advantage, since constituents often cannot see the results. In addition, tough oversight of agencies could jeopardize relationships with them, removing them as potential sources of favors for constituents. Agencies also have independent sources of support from interest groups and from parts of the legislative bodies and executive branches that they can play off against other parts. As mentioned previously, however, recent evidence suggests that although legislative influence is a complicated subject, legislative bodies clearly influence agencies very significantly in many instances (Wood and Waterman, 1994).

Legislative authority also varies across jurisdictions. Certain states, such as Florida, have relatively powerful legislatures, based on the state's legal and institutional arrangements (Abney and Lauth, 1986). The authority and power of city councils and county commissions vary from place to place, depending, for example, on whether there is a "strong-mayor" or "weak-mayor" government in a city.

The Chief Executive

Presidents, governors, and mayors rival the legislative branch for the status of strongest political influence on agencies. Presumably, chief executives have the greatest formal power over the public bureaucracies in their jurisdiction. Yet, as with legislative bodies, the influence patterns are complex and dynamic, and chief executives face similar challenges in taming the unwieldy bureaucracy.

Appointments

Chief executives appoint heads of executive agencies and usually an additional array of patronage positions within those agencies. Wood and Waterman (1994) found that the appointment of a new agency head was often strongly related to a change in agency actions and outputs in the direction of the president's preferences. The chief executive's ability to influence agencies through these appointments varies by agency, jurisdiction, and political climate, however. President

Reagan mounted an aggressive effort to influence federal agencies through appointments. He filled the top positions of some major agencies with executives committed to reducing the regulatory role, size, and influence of the federal bureaucracy. As a result, certain agencies sharply curtailed their staff and activities (Rubin, 1985). Administration officials also added new levels of political appointees at the tops of agencies. This added layers between the top executives and the highest-level career civil servants, effectively demoting career service managers. These steps had so much impact that the Volcker Commission (1989) called for reductions in the number of appointments the president can make. This example illustrates the potential power that the authority to make appointments gives a chief executive. In certain states and localities, many major or cabinet-level agency executives are independently elected and thus not beholden to the chief executive. Jurisdictions also vary in the degree to which they have patronage appointments within agencies.

Executive Staff Offices

The executive offices of the U.S. president and of governors and mayors around the country give chief executives various resources that can bolster their influence. Units within an executive office can represent special constituencies and functions. A governor might have an office of minority affairs or veterans' affairs as a way of demonstrating concern for that constituency. Other subunits might concentrate on press relations or relations with the legislature. Some governors and local executives have inspector generals in their executive offices to conduct investigations into allegations of improprieties in agencies.

Budgeting Authority

The most significant of the staff offices are those that wrestle with budgets—the Office of Management and Budget (OMB) in the Executive Office of the President and similar offices on the staffs of mayors and governors. The legislative branch ultimately approves the budget, but the chief executive assembles agency budget requests and submits them to the legislature for approval. The chief executive tries to hammer his or her priorities into the budget by proposing extensions or cuts in funding for programs. The executive's influence over the budget depends on many factors—anticipated tax revenues, programs needing attention, developments in the political climate (such as strong midterm election results for the chief executive's party or strong popularity ratings). The legislative body may fight back, of course, putting money back into programs that the chief executive tries to cut, and vice versa. Agency officials engage in various ploys to maintain their funding and avoid cuts (Wildavsky, 1988). Their ability to do so depends on factors already described, such as group support. Yet through this process the chief executives have significant potential influence on public policy and public agencies.

Policy Initiatives and Executive Orders

Chief executives have certain formal powers to tell agencies what to do through directives and executive orders (Cooper, 1996). For example, some of the original equal employment opportunity (EEO) initiatives were implemented through executive orders from President Eisenhower and later presidents. They directed federal agencies and private companies holding federal contracts to establish EEO programs. Chief executives can also prompt agencies to develop programs and policies that the executive will support through the budgeting process.

Many of the proposals developed by the Clinton administration's National Performance Review were implemented through presidential executive orders. The president ordered agencies to reduce rules and red tape, to develop customer service standards, to establish "reinvention laboratories" to develop innovative new processes, among other actions. Cooper (1996) argues that executive orders can be very useful to presidents, and some of these actions illustrate their effects. Agencies responded rapidly in carrying out some of the actions the president directed as part of the National Performance Review. Cooper also notes, however, that executive orders can complicate the roles of agency executives, because they sometimes conflict with other legal mandates for the agency. They become part of the complex, often conflicting influences on agencies and their leaders.

The Courts

As with the other institutions surrounding public organizations, some experts say that the courts exert powerful controls over the public bureaucracy, while others see them as ineffectual. Various experts point to the courts as the strongest ultimate check on the power of the public bureaucracy, while others see bureaucratic power overwhelming the courts.

The federal and state courts operate under fairly conservative principles (Woll, 1977). Courts overrule the actions of agencies for two main reasons. They can stop an agency from going beyond the intent of the legislation that created it. They can also prevent an agency from violating correct procedures, such as those required under the due process of law provisions of the Constitution and related legal precedents. These standards actually focus the courts on preventing agency actions rather than on proactively directing policies and programs. In addition, a number of relatively conservative legal principles strengthen the position of public agencies in disputes with citizens or groups. Examples of these include provisions that make public officials immune to many types of liability or require citizens with complaints against agencies to exhaust all possible remedies that they can seek through the agency before a court will hear their complaint. Also, for the courts to settle a dispute, someone has to initiate a lawsuit; this is expensive and can take a long time. Agencies win a lot of suits because they have highly specialized personnel and legal expertise at their disposal (Meier, 1993).

In a sweeping critique of contemporary governmental processes in the United States, Lowi (1979) cites vague legislation as a major problem in weakening judicial oversight of the bureaucracy. To achieve compromise among diverse interests in the legislative process, Congress and other legislative units give diffuse grants of authority to agencies, passing legislation that communicates only very general objectives and standards. Courts then have difficulty enforcing adherence to congressional intent. The sheer size and complexity of the administrative branch of government, the wide range of specializations it encompasses, and the technical complexity of many of the policy issues that come before the courts make it extremely difficult for the courts to exercise strong control over bureaucratic actions (Stewart, 1975).

Yet under the right circumstances, the courts wield immense authority and can be very aggressive in the oversight of administrative agencies (O'Leary and Straussman, 1993; Rosenbloom, 1983). Through injunctions they can force or block an agency's actions. They can make an agency pay damages, thus making administrators very careful about assessing the legal implications of their rules and procedures. Limitations on judicial interventions concerning, for example, citizens' ability to sue government officials and exhaustion of administrative remedies have relaxed over time (Meier, 1993). A ruling making it easier for citizens to sue social workers when children under their supervision suffer child abuse has changed the procedures and expenses of agencies across the country. In surveys, administrators report that court decisions influence the allocation of funds at state and local levels for education, prisons, hospitals, and other services (Meier, 1993).

Congress has moved toward including more specific standards in some legislation (Wilson, 1989), and court rulings sometimes focus powerfully on one particular aspect of an agency's operations. Courts sometimes intervene in particular agency activities, often due to some constitutional principle such as due process of law or equal protection of the law. On occasion, courts have in effect taken over schools and prisons in certain jurisdictions. Lawsuits to force agencies to comply with legislation requiring environmental impact statements prior to any major building projects have delayed many projects in many agencies. The courts wait in the background, in a sense, directly intervening in day-to-day operations of public organizations only on occasion. Yet they pose an ominous background presence. Administrators frequently take actions and establish procedures expressly because of what a court has done or *might* do.

Recent research has strengthened the position that courts have a significant influence on agency operations (O'Leary, 1994; Wood and Waterman, 1994). O'Leary (1994) cites numerous examples of a "new partnership" between judges and public managers that entails significant judicial influence over agencies and their operations as well as extensive interaction with agencies' managers and staff. She has reviewed research on these developments in relation to personnel administration in agencies and found evidence of such interaction. Her research provides evidence that the courts sometimes dictate which issues an agency must attend to. Courts can diminish the authority of administrators, in part by dictating where they must devote agency resources. This can decrease the budgetary discretion of administrators (and can involve a judge's refusal to defer to an administrator's expertise). Court orders can also influence staff morale, sometimes demoralizing people in the agency and sometimes boosting their enthusiasm about their work. These examples and findings provide the beginnings of a body of research that needs much more development. The material from organization theory and organizational development reviewed in other parts of this book show that the legal and judicial environment have not received much attention from organizational researchers (O'Leary and Straussman, 1993). These examples, however, show how the governmental and legal institutions surrounding public organizations can directly influence organizational design and effectiveness and the behavior of the people within organizations. They show that most public managers and employees need a sound knowledge of the judicial environment (Rosenbloom, 1983; Cooper, 1996) and raise a number of important research questions for scholars.

Other Agencies and Levels of Government

Public organizations both work together and fight with one another. The participants in this contest represent all the different levels of government, the various agencies, and certain oversight bodies concerned with personnel administration, budgeting, and central purchasing. Later chapters describe many examples of ways in which this affects management within public organizations.

In the U.S. federal system of government, higher levels of government direct and regulate the lower levels in various ways. Some federal programs, such as Social Security, are actually carried out by state personnel following federal guidelines. Behind this generally cooperative structure, however, patterns of mutual influence operate.

Grants from higher levels of government exert some of this influence. Merit systems have disseminated throughout the personnel departments of state and local governments in the United States in part because federal grants were made available to set up such systems. Federal laws can mandate that federal money for programs be matched in certain ways by states and localities. Under federal law, for example, states must contribute to Medicare payments for individuals, adding to the amounts paid by the federal government. With these funding arrangements come influences on state and local governments' structures and procedures. In Florida, the Department of Health and Rehabilitative Services adopted a new structure that brought together many services (for indigent medical care, family and youth counseling, and others) in the same government offices and established a regionalized, district structure. Yet federal vocational rehabilitation officials forced the department to exclude vocational rehabilitation activities from this arrangement and organize those services separately because the rules for these programs require that they be administered by a separate, independent organization.

Laws and regulations, whether or not they are attached to grants or other funding instruments, also exert such influences. State and federal environmental protection regulations and growth and economic development mandates dictate how programs must be managed by lower levels of government. Federal legislation sometimes directs a federal agency to do certain things in every state unless the states do them in a way that meets certain minimum standards established by the federal government. An example of this is the federal government's policy regarding mine safety regulations, under which the federal government must oversee mine safety within a state unless the state can finance and manage the program itself at least at the level required by federal standards.

The relationships between the different levels of government may be very smooth in many instances, but the lower levels do not necessarily accept higher-level influences and requirements lying down. During the Reagan administration, some state governments refused to carry out directives from the Social Security Administration requiring them to review the cases of many disability payment recipients and deny payments to some of them under more stringent rules. Early in the Bush administration, many states were very slow to comply with federal laws requiring that they increase their share of Medicare payments (Tolchin, 1989). Localities also work hard to influence state and federal legislation that may bear significantly on their activities. Associations such as the League of Cities lobby at the state and federal levels for legislation that they feel they need.

Organizations at a given level of government also cooperate and compete in many ways. The delivery of many local services in the United States often involves a complex network of joint agreements and contracts among localities. State and federal agencies typically have overlapping responsibilities and engage in joint planning and activity. The Equal Employment Opportunity Coordinating Commission was established to coordinate the various agencies at the federal level that had responsibilities for carrying out affirmative action and equal employment opportunity policies. Early in the Bush administration, a coordinating council was proposed as a means of facilitating the relationships between the various units of government that had some responsibility for programs to address homelessness. Agencies also compete with each other for the time and attention of higher-level executives (Chase and Reveal, 1983) and over turf, seeking to block other agencies and authorities from gaining control over their programs (Wilson, 1989).

Public Managers' Perceptions of the Political Environment

Later chapters describe a variety of studies that pertain to how public managers respond to these components of their political environments and how those environments influence public organizations. Some studies mentioned above, however, provide evidence of how public managers perceive various aspects of the political context, such as the relative influence of chief executives, legislatures, and interest groups (Abney and Lauth, 1986; Brudney and Hebert, 1987; Elling, 1983). These studies indicate that state agency managers see their legislature as the most influential, with the governor coming second (although there are variations among the states in the relative power of the governor and the legislature). Local managers see the chief executive—the mayor—as the most influential actor. State and local agency managers rate interest groups as much less influential than legislatures and chief executives but often see them as valuable contributors to decision making.

Aberbach, Putnam, and Rockman (1981) provide a similar account of the strong influence of the legislative branch at the federal level. They analyzed contacts between administrative officials and other actors in the federal systems of the United States and five other industrial democracies. In the United States they found much higher levels of contact between civil service administrators in agencies and congressional committee members than either of these two groups had with the executive heads of the agencies. The civil service managers had even more contacts with constituent groups than with Congress, however. Aberbach, Putnam, and Rockman referred to this pattern as the "end run" model, because it involves civil servants and legislators going around executive agency heads, and discovered that it occurs more often in the United States than in any of the other countries they studied.

Studies identifying how public managers perceive the nature of their own political activities are rare, but Olshfski (1989, 1990) identifies three conceptions of politics that emerge in state agency executives' descriptions of their political activities: *political astuteness*, the understanding of the political system and the processes of government and their own departments; *issue politics*, the political activities, such as bargaining and coalition building, necessary to advance an issue or achieve an objective; and *electoral politics*, the knowledge and activity related to gaining general political support for themselves, an elected official, or their departments.

The Public Policy Process

As analyses of public policy have burgeoned over the last several decades, so has the recognition that public organizations play an essential role in its formation and implementation. The research on the policymaking and implementation process helps explain many of the characteristics of public organizations and their management. It adds insights about the dynamic interplay of the political institutions and groups discussed above.

Many Arenas and Programs

Government activity at all levels encompasses a diverse array of functions and policy domains. Without any standard nomenclature, scholars and government officials refer to policy categories such as defense, health, science and technology, social welfare and poverty, environmental protection, energy, economic and fiscal policy (including tax policy), agricultural policy, industrial development policy, educational policy, and regulatory policy. Government activities at state and local levels, sometimes referred to as service delivery rather than public policy, include a similarly diverse list: industrial development, zoning and land use, police and firefighting services, transportation (including streets and roads), garbage collection, prisons and jails, parks and recreation, and many others. As mentioned earlier, state and local governments are also part of the policymaking process for major federal policies. Within these policy areas and spanning them, many specific programs operate at various levels of scope, size, and complexity.

Many Actors and Levels

All the institutions, levels, authorities, and groups discussed above play a part in shaping policy and carrying it out. Adding to the complexities already described, governmental policies draw many private organizations into the policymaking process. Many government programs operate largely through purchases and contracts with nongovernmental organizations, such as weapons manufacturers or private nonprofit organizations that seek, for example, to help troubled youths. Many people know about the massive contracting in the federal construction and procurement process but not about the similar linkages between government and the so-called private sector in most other areas of public policy and service delivery.

Government actually creates private or quasi-governmental organizations in some cases (Ripley and Franklin, 1982). Under human resource training or "manpower" programs, for example, nonprofit organizations were established to conduct research on labor policies. Reliance on private contractors creates complications for public managers. They are responsible for the performance of contractors but often have trouble holding them accountable (Rosen, 1989). In addition, the arrangements become so complicated that even public officials have trouble keeping up with them. In 1986, a new governor took over in the state of Florida, having campaigned on the promise to cut waste in government through businesslike administration of public programs. The governor's aides conducted discussions with the director of the Department of Health and Rehabilitative Services (DHRS), a huge state agency that administers social welfare programs. The aides felt that more contracts with private organizations for the delivery of services would make the agency's operations cheaper and questioned the director about working harder on contracting out. The director had to explain politely that about half of the agency's budget of around three billion dollars was already administered through contracts with other organizations—a fact of which the governor's aides had been unaware.

Policy Subsystems

As discussed above, the policy process is fragmented into a number of policy areas. For a long time, political scientists described these domains as being dominated by "iron triangles," which are tight alliances of congressional committees, administrative agencies, and interest groups that control major policy areas such as defense and environmental policy. Key people in the committees, agencies, and interest groups in the triangle exchange political favors and support. Authorities outside the triangle, even the president, can wield little influence over it. This situation has long been lamented as one of the fundamental problems of government in the United Sates. Ronald Reagan complained about iron triangles in one of his last public statements as president.

Although it refers to a very significant problem, political scientists now point out that the iron triangle analogy oversimplifies the true complexity and dynamism of these coalitions. Competition and conflict among groups and agencies may flare within the so-called triangles, making them much less solid than the analogy implies. Lawyers may fight doctors over a change in legislation on malpractice suits. One group of large corporations may line up on the other side of an issue from another group of equally large corporations. In addition, as problems change, different groups, organizations, and individuals move in and out of the policy arena. The iron triangle analogy fails to depict the instability and flux in the process. It also suggests that grim power politics is the driving force behind patterns of influence in the public sector (Kingdon, 1984, p. 131).

Recently proposed terms better characterize the situation. Heclo (1978) refers to "issue networks" of experts, officials, and interests that form around particular issues and that can shift rapidly. Milward and Wamsley (1982) describe what they call policy networks, or complex and shifting aggregations of groups, experts, public and private organizations, governmental authorities, and others whose interplay shapes the formation and implementation of policy. Others refer to subgovernments' implementation structures (Hjern and Porter, 1981), public service industries, policy subsystems (Rainey and Milward, 1983), and policy communities (Kingdon, 1984).

The policymaking process in which public organizations and managers participate is balkanized into domains akin to those suggested by the iron triangle idea. These subsystems or networks prove unwieldy and resistant to external control or coordination with other networks. Yet the depiction of the problem as one of staunch control by self-serving bureaucrats, politicians, and private interests oversimplifies the problem. Often the difficulties in coordination and control result largely from the flux and complexity of the issues, interests, and participants involved in the process.

Privatization, Government by Proxy, and the Hollow State

As mentioned in Chapter Three, one of the most striking phenomena in government in recent decades has been the expansion of nongovernmental organizations into the delivery of government services. Government agencies at all levels have increasingly contracted out portions of their functions and delivered more programs and services through grants to other levels of government or to entities that are not formally owned or operated by government (Gill, 1996). These developments involve increased sharing of power with these nongovernmental organizations and a pattern of "government by proxy," in which government provides a proxy to private organizations to carry out its programs and policies (Kettl, 1988, 1993). Privatization has extended even further in many policy areas, such as human and social service programs (Smith and Lipsky, 1993), environmental and energy programs, and prisons. As of this writing, for example, the governor of Georgia has appointed a commission on privatization to undertake aggressive privatization initiatives. The legislature is currently considering a proposal from the governor to authorize the operation of three large private prisons in the state. Unions are opposing the initiative, and the major newspaper in Atlanta has editorialized against it.

The roles of public agencies and their managers, and the nature of government, are sharply affected by these developments. As suggested by the titles of Kettl's books (1988, 1993), they extend the lines of accountability and make public managers responsible for organizational activities that they can control only through contracts and grants—or they can actually blur the lines of accountability. In some cases private and nonprofit contractors and grant recipients, instead of providing a competitive private sector alternative, become part of the political lobby for the programs with which they are involved (Smith and Lipsky, 1993). In other cases, government officials use private contractors to justify the pursuit of certain political and social objectives that they might not be able to justify through the normal legislative process. Moe (1996) argues that in these ways, privatization may involve more of a governmentalization of the private sector than a privatization of government.

In some policy areas, privatization has extended so far that government becomes "hollow," with private contractors taking over most or all of its authority and activity (Milward, Provan, and Else, 1993). Mental health programs, for example, may be provided by networks of private or nonprofit organizations, with government funding but virtually no involvement by government employees and fairly high autonomy on the part of the providers in making decisions about services and programs. Kettl (1993, pp. 131–132) and Gill (1996) report that in 1992, the Department of Energy (DOE) employed twenty thousand civil servants and 141,000 contractors and consultants, and that at DOE and the Environmental Protection Agency, contractors took charge of significant decisions about management and policy. Moe (1996, p. 143) dramatizes this trend when he cites the example of a new secretary of the Department of Energy who expressed dismay to find that his congressional testimony had been prepared by a contractor and that the agency had contractors supervising contractors.

These conditions raise dramatic issues for public agencies and managers. As noted, they strain lines of accountability and responsibility. They raise complex issues about how much authority and control government should retain and how much internal capacity agencies should have, both for supervising their own operations and for taking back functions from contractors when they perform poorly. They raise complicated issues about the meaning and nature of public service. They raise some new issues about organizational design and effectiveness in policy and program networks such as those described above, a question the next chapter will examine (Provan and Milward, 1995). Obviously, they make contract management and the management of other network or third-party arrangements, such as volunteer programs, a more important management skill for many public managers. Accordingly, Chapter Fourteen will cover the management of privatization and volunteer programs in considering managerial excellence in the public sector.

The Agenda-Setting Process and the Agenda Garbage Can

Public policy researchers also help characterize the complex context of public management by analyzing how certain matters gain prominence on the public agenda while others languish outside of public notice. John Kingdon (1984) says that this process resembles the "garbage can model" of decision making developed by James March and his colleagues (Cohen, March, and Olsen, 1972). As described in more detail in Chapter Seven, the garbage can model depicts decision making in organizations as being much less systematic and rational than is commonly supposed. People are not very sure about their preferences or about how their organization works. Streams of problems, solutions, participants, and choice opportunities flow along through time, sometimes coming together in combinations that shape decisions. (An example of a choice opportunity is a salient problem that has to be addressed by a newly formed committee with sufficient authority to have a chance at getting something done.) The process is more topsy-turvy than the organizational chart might suggest. Sometimes solutions actually chase problems, as when someone has a pet idea that he or she wants to find a chance to apply. Sometimes administrators simply look for work to do. Choice opportunities are like garbage cans in which problems, solutions, and participants come together in a jumbled fashion.

Kingdon revises this view when he applies it to public policy, referring to streams of problems, policies, and politics flowing alongside one another and sometimes coming together at key points to shape the policy agenda. Problems come to the attention of policymakers in various ways: through indicators (unemployment figures, figures on budget deficits); through events, such as crises that focus their attention on them; and through feedback, such as citizen complaints and reports on the operation of programs. Policies develop within the "policy community" as various ideas and alternatives emerge from the "policy primeval soup." Like microorganisms in a biological primeval soup, they originate, compete, evolve, and prosper or perish. They are evaluated in think tanks, conferences, staff meetings in legislative bodies and government agencies, and interest-group activities. They may be partially tried out in programs or legislation, and a long period of "softening up" often follows the original proposal, in which the alternative becomes more and more acceptable. Some alternatives have a long history of implementation, shelving, alteration, and retrial. For example, various versions of public works and job-training camps have appeared at different levels of government since the days of the Civilian Conservation Corps during the New Deal and the Job Corps during the Johnson administration's War on Poverty. At times, events in these streams converge to open "windows of opportunity" in which political forces align in support of a policy alternative for a particular problem, moving this combination to a central place on the public agenda.

In Kingdon's portrayal, the agenda-setting process appears difficult to predict and understand clearly but not wildly out of control. The processes of gestation and evaluation focus considerable scrutiny on ideas and alternatives and their workability. Still, this analysis illustrates the dynamism of the policymaking environment in which public managers must operate. In later chapters, the idea of identifying "windows of opportunity" figures usefully in the discussion of managing change in public organizations. Many of the challenges facing a public manager turn on effective assessment of the political feasibility of particular actions and alternatives and of the array of political forces shaping or curtailing various opportunities.

Policy Implementation: The "Too Many Cooks" Problem

The study of implementation of public policy once it has been formulated has also grown tremendously in the last two decades. Such studies describe the complications of implementing public policies that affect many levels, authorities, and interests. Government has to use directives and inducements to try to influence far-flung individuals and organizations. The system thus involves many "veto points," which can hinder implementation.

Recently researchers have offered better conceptions of implementation to replace the older case studies. They analyze such factors as the tractability of the problem a policy addresses, the types of inducements for implementation used by higher levels of government, and the capacities for implementation of lower levels—including their organizational structures and personnel (Goggin, Bowman, Lester, and O'Toole, 1990; Mazmanian and Sabatier, 1981). These analyses have not yet addressed many of the managerial issues that the remaining chapters take up. Analyzing their relationship to the problems of implementation remains a challenge for the field (Lynn, 1987). Nevertheless, the work on policy implementation adds meaning to analysts' assertions about complex objectives and constraints in public management. It also supports some suggestions in later chapters about how this implementation process may affect such elements as structure and motivation in public organizations.

Public managers, especially at higher levels, have to skillfully manage their relationship with these external authorities and actors. They also have to operate effectively within the pattern of interventions and constraints that these actors impose. As this discussion now turns to key dimensions of organizing and managing, the importance of these relationships in handling those dimensions will come up again and again. It will also become clear that, while many rank-and-file managers and employees have little direct involvement with this external political and administrative milieu, it shapes the context of their work. Evidence and examples will show how it affects organizational characteristics and individual attitudes and behaviors throughout public organizations.

PART TWO

KEY DIMENSIONS OF ORGANIZING AND MANAGING

CHAPTER SIX

ORGANIZATIONAL GOALS AND EFFECTIVENESS

The definition of organizations in Chapter One emphasizes goals as a basic element of that definition. Organizations are goal-directed, purposive entities. The framework in Figure 1.1 suggests that the organizational environment influences organizational goals, and as Chapter Four pointed out, the goals of an organization and its members can actually determine major dimensions of its environment. Figure 1.2 further suggests, and Chapters Four and Five argue, that the environments of public organizations bear a distinctive relationship to the goals and values of those organizations. The figures also show that goals and values influence leadership and strategy and that, in turn, a major function of leadership and strategy is to develop goals and values. Similarly, goals interrelate with the other components of Figure 1.1—culture, structure, incentives, and the others—in ways too elaborate to illustrate in the figure.

The figure and the definition of organizations also emphasize the relationship between goals and organizational performance and effectiveness. Virtually all of management and organization theory concerns performance and effectiveness, at least implicitly. Virtually all of it in some way concerns the challenge of getting an organization and the people in it to perform well. As previous chapters have discussed, beliefs about the performance and effectiveness of public organizations, especially in comparison to private organizations, have played a major role in some of the most significant political changes and government reforms in recent history, in nations around the world.

This chapter first discusses major issues about organizational goals and the goals of public organizations, including observations other authors have made about how public organizations' goals influence their other characteristics. Then the chapter reviews the models of organizational effectiveness that researchers have developed and discusses their implications for organizing and managing public organizations.

Despite the importance of these topics, when one turns to the literature on organizational goals and effectiveness, one finds something of a muddle, although a very insightful one. Experts in the field emphasize the difficulty of defining and determining organizational goals and effectiveness. Those who set out to study effectiveness soon realize that assessing whether an organization does its job well involves numerous complex technical, economic, ethical, and ideological issues. Their use of the somewhat unusual-sounding concept of *organizational effectiveness* attests to this. (While Figure 1.1 refers to organizational performance and effectiveness, the commonly used term in organization theory is just effectiveness.) Referring simply to organizational success bears less of an implication that the activities of the organization brought about the success. Effectiveness suggests not only that the organization had good results but also that it brought about these results through its own management, design, and other features.

Many other terms for doing well also have limitations. In assessing business firms, most investors look carefully at their profitability. Yet sophisticated investors realize that short-term profitability may in some cases mask long-term problems. In addition, consumer advocates and environmental groups object to assessments of business performance that disregard concerns for the environment and ethical concern for the consumer. In addition, profitability does not apply to government and nonprofit organizations. As with the generic approach in general, researchers have to consider the need for a general body of knowledge on organizational effectiveness that is not restricted to certain sectors or industries.

General Organizational Goals

An organizational goal is a condition that an organization seeks to attain. The discussion below recites many problems with the concept of goals, but clearly goals are very important to organizations and their employees. The next chapter provides numerous examples of goal statements from government agencies that have tried to make these organizations' goals clear in order to concentrate their efforts and motivate their members. In the last ten or fifteen years, it has become fashionable for organizations in both the public and private sectors to issue "mission statements," or expressions of their major goals and values. These statements, described more fully in the following chapter, express idealized versions of an organization's goals.

As such, they represent what organization theorists would call *official goals* (Perrow, 1961). Official goals are formal expressions of general goals that express an organization's major values and purposes. For example, as many public agencies have done, the Social Security Administration (SSA) and the Internal Revenue Service (IRS) have issued statements expressing a general commitment to providing excellent service to their clients. One tends to encounter official goals in mission statements and annual reports, where they are meant to enhance the organization's legitimacy and motivate and guide its members. *Operative goals* are the relatively specific immediate ends an organization seeks, reflected in its actual operations and procedures. For example, to better serve their clients, SSA has developed computerized systems for handling claims and IRS has developed automated returns processing.

As noted, people in organizations often consider goals important as expressions of guiding organizational values that can stimulate and generally orient employees to their organization's mission. In addition, clarifying goals for individuals and work groups can improve efficiency and productivity. The discussion of motivation in Chapter Ten reviews the research that shows that providing workers with clear, challenging goals can enhance their productivity. Nevertheless, the concept of a goal has many complications, with important implications for organizing and managing and for the debate over whether public and private organizations differ.

These complications include the problem that goals are always multiple (Rainey, 1993a). A goal is always one of a set of goals that one is trying to achieve (Simon, 1973). Goals in the set of goals often conflict with one another—maximizing one takes away from another. Short-term and long-term goals can conflict with each other. For example, while business firms supposedly have clearer, more measurable goals than public and nonprofit organizations, firms have to try to manage conflicts among goals for short-term and long-term profits, community and public relations, employee and management development, and social responsibility (such as compliance with affirmative action and environmental protection laws). Goals are arranged by linkages and hierarchies, and this makes it hard to express a goal in an ultimate or conclusive way. One goal leads to another or is an operative goal for a higher or more general goal. Many of the concepts related to organizational purpose—such as goals, objectives, values, incentives, and motives—are synonymous or overlap in various ways, leaving us with no conclusive or definitive terminology. Distinctions among these concepts are relatively arbitrary.

These complications appear to be related to a divergence among organization theorists between those who take the concept of goals very seriously and those who reject it as relatively useless (Rainey, 1993a). They present a problem for both theorists and practicing managers. The discussion of models of effectiveness below points out that these sorts of complications impede the assessment of organizational effectiveness—it can be difficult to say what an organization's goals really are and to measure their achievement. It is important for leaders and managers to help their organization clarify its goals, but these complications make that a very challenging process. The next chapter discusses some of the procedures members of organizations can use to clarify their goal statements.

Goals of Public Organizations

The complications also contribute to an interesting anomaly in the debate over the distinctiveness of public organizations. The complications imply that *all* organizations, including business firms, have vague, multiple, and relatively intangible goals. Without doubt, however, the most often repeated observations about public organizations are that their goals are particularly vague and intangible compared to those of private business firms and that they more often have multiple, conflicting goals (see III.1.a in Table 3.2; Rainey, 1993a). Previous chapters provided illustrations of the meaning of this observation. Public organizations produce goods and services that are not exchanged in markets. Through government auspices and oversight, they have imposed on them such multiple, conflicting, and often intangible goals as the constitutional, competence, and responsiveness values discussed in Chapters Four and Five (see Table 4.3). In addition, authorizing legislation often assigns very vague missions to government agencies and provides vague guidance for public programs (Lowi, 1979; Seidman and Gilmour, 1986). With such mandates, coupled with concerns over public opinion and public demands, agency managers feel pressured to balance conflicting, idealized goals. Conservation agencies, for example, receive mandates and pressures both to conserve natural resources and to develop them (Wildavsky, 1979, p. 215). Prison commissioners face pressures both to punish offenders and to rehabilitate them (DiIulio, 1990). Police chiefs must try to find a balance between keeping the peace, enforcing the law, controlling crime, preventing crime, assuring fairness and respect for citizen rights, and operating efficiently and with minimal costs (Moore, 1990).

In addition, many observers go on to assert that these goal complexities have major implications for public organizations and their management. Some researchers emphasize their effect on work attitudes and performance. Buchanan (1974, 1975) found that federal agency managers reported lower organizational commitment, job involvement, and work satisfaction than did managers in private business. He also found that the federal managers reported a weaker sense of having an impact on their organization and a weaker sense of finding challenge in their job. He concluded that the vagueness and value conflicts inherent in public organizations' goals were among several reasons the federal managers reported lower commitment, involvement, and satisfaction. He argued that the diffuseness of agencies' objectives made it harder to design challenging jobs for the public sector managers and harder for them to perceive the impact of their work. In turn, this weakened federal managers' commitment and satisfaction.

Boyatzis (1982), in a study of the competencies of a broad sample of managers, found that public managers displayed weaker "goal and action" competencies— those concerned with formulating and emphasizing means and ends. He concluded that the difference must result from the absence in the public sector of clear goals and performance measures such as sales and profits.

Other observations concern effects on organizational structure (pervasiveness of rules, number of levels) and hierarchical delegation. Some scholars say that the goal ambiguity in public agencies, and the consequent difficulties in developing clear and readily measurable performance indicators, lead to performance evaluation on the basis of adherence to proper procedure and compliance with rules (Barton, 1980; Dahl and Lindblom, 1953; Lynn, 1981; Meyer, 1979; Warwick, 1975). Under accountability pressures and scrutiny by legislative bodies, the chief executive, oversight agencies, courts, and the media, higher-level executives in public agencies demand compliance with rules and procedures mandated by Congress or oversight agencies or contained in their chartering legislation. Also, executives and managers in public agencies tend to add even more rules and clearance requirements in addition to externally imposed rules and procedures; plus, they add more hierarchical levels of review and generally resist delegation in an effort to control the units and individuals below them. The absence of clear, measurable, well-accepted performance criteria thus induces a vicious cycle of "inevitable bureaucracy" (Lynn, 1981) in which the demand for increased accountability increases the emphasis on rule adherence and hierarchical control. Some authors add the observation that these conditions breed a paradox in which the proliferation of rules and clearance requirements fails to achieve control over lower levels (Warwick, 1975; Buchanan, 1975). Rules provide some protections for people at lower levels, through civil service protections and the safety of strict compliance with other administrative rules. Superiors' efforts to control lower-level employees through additional rules and reporting requirements add to bureaucratic complexity without achieving control.

In this way, goal ambiguity also supposedly contributes to a weakening of the authority of top leaders in public organizations. Since they cannot assess performance on the basis of relatively clear measures, their control over lower levels is weakened. The absence of clear performance measures also allegedly contributes to a weakening of their attentiveness to developing their agencies. Since they cannot simply refer to their performance against unambiguous targets to justify continued funding, they must play more political, expository roles to develop political support for their programs. Blumenthal (1983), reflecting on his experiences as a top federal and business executive, begins his account of the differences between them with the observation that there is no "bottom line" in government. Media relations, general appearance and reputation, and political relations external to the agency figure more importantly in how others assess an executive's performance than do concrete indicators of the performance of his or her agency. Allison (1983) provides an account of the similar observations of John Dunlop and Richard Neustadt about the absence of a bottom line and of accepted and readily measurable performance indicators in public agencies.

Later chapters examine some of the research findings that support or fail to support these observations. The main point, however, is that many observers claim that the goals of public organizations have a distinct character that influences their other characteristics and their management. To further complicate this discussion, surveys of public and private managers indicate that they do not perceive these supposed differences in their organizations' goals. Several surveys covering different levels of government, different parts of the United States, and different organizations have asked managers in government agencies and business firms to respond to questions about whether the goals of their organization are vague, hard to define, and hard to measure. The results showed no particular differences between the government managers and business managers in their responses to such questions. This does not necessarily prove that there are no such differences, but it certainly complicates the debate. It illustrates the importance for researchers and managers of clarifying just what we mean by these repeated references to the vague, conflicting, multiple goals of public agencies and of proving or disproving their alleged effect on organizations and management in government.

Regardless of these complications in the analysis of the goals of public agencies, it is still very important and useful for agency leaders and managers to try to clarify their organization's goals and assess its effectiveness in achieving them. The next chapter provides many examples of efforts at clarifying goals and missions, and an expanding literature on public management provides many more (Behn, 1991, pp. 50; Hargrove and Glidewell, 1990, p. 95; Denhardt, 1993). In seeking to clarify goals, however, managers need to be aware of the attendant complications and conflicts. They need to be aware, also, of the concepts and models for assessing organizational effectiveness that researchers have developed, as well as the controversies over the strengths and weaknesses of the models and the trade-offs among them.

Models for Assessing Organizational Effectiveness

The people who study organizational effectiveness agree on many of the preceding points, but they cannot agree on one conclusive model or framework for assessing effectiveness (Goodman, Pennings, and Associates, 1977; Cameron and Whetten, 1983). The complexities described above, as well as numerous others, have caused them to try many approaches.

The Goal Approach

At the outset, it appeared obvious that one should determine the goals of one's organization and assess whether it achieves them. As suggested already, however, organizations have many goals, which vary along many dimensions and often conflict with one another. Herbert Simon (1973) once pointed out that a goal is always embedded in a set of goals, which a person or group tries to maximize simultaneously—achieve excellence in delivery of services to clients but keep the maintenance schedule up, keep the members happy and motivated, maintain satisfactory relations with legislators and interest groups, and so on. Many different coalitions or stakeholders associated with an organization—managers, workers, client and constituency groups, oversight and regulatory agencies, legislators, courts, people in different subunits with different priorities for the organization, and so on—can have different goals for the organization.

One can also state goals at different levels of generality, in various terms, and in various time frames (short-term versus long-term). Goals always link together in chains of means and ends, in which an immediate objective can be expressed as a goal but it ultimately serves as a means to a more general or longer-term goal. In addition, researchers and consultants can have a hard time specifying an organization's goals because the people in the organization have difficulty stating or admitting the real goals. Organizations have not only formal, publicly espoused goals but also actual goals. In their annual reports, public agencies and business firms often make glowing statements of their commitment to the general welfare as well as to their customers and clients. An automobile company might express commitment to providing the American people with the safest, most enjoyable, most efficient automobiles in the world. A transportation agency might state its determination to serve all the people of its state with the safest, most efficient, most effective transportation facilities and processes possible. Yet their actual behavior may indicate more concern with the economic security of the organization than with its clients and the general public. The goal model, in simplified forms, implies a view of management as a very rational, orderly process. Earlier chapters have described how management scholars increasingly depict managerial decisions and contexts as more turbulent, intuitive, paradoxical, and emergent than a rational, goal-based approach implies.

All these complications cause organizational effectiveness researchers to search for alternatives to a simple goal model. The discussion of strategy in Chapter Four demonstrated, however, that experts still exhort managers to identify missions, core values, and strategies. This may depart from a strict goal-based approach, but when you tell people to decide what they want to accomplish and to design strategies to achieve those conditions, you are talking about goals, even if you devise some other names for them. Goal clarification also plays a key role in managerial procedures described in later chapters, such as management by objectives (MBO).

Experts continue to suggest various terminologies and procedures for identifying organizational goals, and the goal model has never really been banished from the search for effectiveness criteria. These prescriptive frameworks, however, illustrate many of the complexities of goals mentioned above. Morrisey (1976), for example, illustrates the multiple levels and means-ends relationships of goals. He suggests a framework for public managers to use in developing MBO programs, which he describes as a funnel in which the organization moves from greater generality to greater specificity by stating goals and missions, key results areas, indicators, objectives, and, finally, action plans. Gross (1976) suggests a framework involving seven different groups of goals—satisfying interests (such as those of clients and members), producing output, making efficient use of inputs, investing in the organization, acquiring resources, observing codes (such as laws and budgetary guidelines), and behaving rationally (through research and proper administration). Under each of these general goals he lists multiple subgoals. Obviously, managers and researchers have difficulty clearly and conclusively specifying an organization's goals.

For similar reasons, researchers have grappled with complications in measuring effectiveness. As usual, they encounter the problem of choosing between subjective measures and objective measures. Some have asked respondents to rate the effectiveness of organizations, sometimes asking members for the ratings, sometimes comparing members' ratings of their own units in the organization with the ratings provided by other members (such as top managers or members of other units). Sometimes they ask people outside the organization for ratings. Others develop more objective measures, such as profitability and productivity indicators, from records or other sources. Some researchers develop both types of evidence, but they find this expensive. They also sometimes find that the two types of measures may not correlate with each other. In one frequently used variant of the goals approach, researchers do not seek to determine the specific goals of a specific organization; rather, they measure ratings of effectiveness on certain criteria or goals that they assume all organizations must pursue, such as productivity, efficiency, flexibility, and adaptability. Mott (1972), for example, studied the effectiveness of government organizations (units of NASA, the State Department, the Department of Health, Education, and Welfare, and a state mental hospital) by asking managers in them to rate the quantity, quality, efficiency, adaptability, and flexibility of their divisions.

The Systems-Resource Approach

Partly because of difficulties with goal models, Yuchtman and Seashore (1967) developed a systems-resource model. They concentrated on whether an organization can attain valued resources from its environment to sustain itself. They placed effectiveness criteria in a hierarchy, with the organization's ability to exploit external resources and opportunities as the ultimate criterion. They regarded this criterion as being ultimately unmeasurable by itself: it has to be inferred by measuring the next-highest, or penultimate, criteria, which they identified in a study of insurance companies. These criteria included such factors as business volume, market penetration, youthfulness of organizational members, and production and maintenance costs. They developed these factors by using statistical techniques to group together measures of organizational activities and characteristics such as sales and number of policies in force. Drawing on a survey they conducted in the same companies, they also examined the relationships between lower-order, subsidiary variables, such as communication and managerial supportiveness, and the penultimate factors.

Not many researchers followed this lead with subsequent research efforts. Critics raised questions about whether the approach confuses the conception and ordering of important variables. Some of the penultimate factors could just as well be called goals, others seem to represent means for achieving goals, and some of the factors seem more important than others. Critics have complained that the analytical techniques bunched unlike factors together inappropriately. Others pointed out that the criteria represent the interests of those in charge of the organizations, even though other actors, such as customers and public interest groups, might have very different interests.

Still, insights from the study influenced later developments in thinking about effectiveness. The study found that some subsidiary variables were related to *later* readings on penultimate variables. This shows that effective procedures now can lead to effective outcomes later and emphasizes the importance of examining such relationships over time. Some subsidiary measures are linked strongly to certain penultimate factors but not to others. This shows that one can point to different dimensions of effectiveness, with different sets of variables linking with them.

Also, while few researchers have reported additional studies following this model, at least one such study applied it to public agencies. Molnar and Rogers (1976) analyzed county-level offices of 110 public agencies, including various agricultural, welfare, community development, conservation, employment, and planning and zoning agencies. They argued that the resource-dependence model, which is applied to business firms, needs modification for public agencies for reasons similar to those discussed earlier in this book—absence of profit and of sales in markets, which blurs the link between inputs and outputs; consequent evaluation by political officials and other political actors; and an emphasis on meeting community or social needs that rivals emphases on internal efficiency.

Rogers and Molnar had people in the agencies rate their own organizations' effectiveness and the effectiveness of other organizations in the study. To represent the systems-resource approach for public agencies, they examined how many resources (equipment, funds, personnel, meeting rooms) an agency provided to other agencies in the study ("resource outflow") and how many they received from other agencies ("resource inflow"). They also calculated a score for how much resources flowing in exceeded resources flowing out. They found that the higher the level of resources flowing into an agency, the higher the level of resources flowing out. The more effective agencies thus appeared better able to develop effective exchanges with other agencies, using their own resources to attract resources from other agencies. Of course, effectiveness of public agencies involves many additional dimensions, but this study offers an interesting analysis of one means of examining it.

Participant-Satisfaction Models

Another approach involves asking participants about their satisfaction with the organization. This approach focuses on whether the members of an organization feel that it fulfills their needs or that they share its goals and work to achieve them. This approach can figure very importantly in managing an organization, but it has serious limitations if participation is conceived too narrowly. Participants include not just employees but suppliers, customers, regulators and external controllers, and allies. Some of the more recent studies of effectiveness ask many different participants from such categories for ratings of an organization (Cameron, 1978). Others have tried to build in more ethical and social-justice considerations by examining how well an organization serves or harms the most disadvantaged participants (Keeley, 1984). The participant-satisfaction approach thus adds crucial insights to our thinking about effectiveness, but even these elaborated versions of the approach encounter problems in handling the general social significance of an organization's performance. Organizations also affect the interests of the general public or society and of individuals not even remotely associated with the organization as participants.

Human Resource and Internal Process Models

These approaches to organizational effectiveness assess it by referring to such factors as internal communications, leadership style, motivation, interpersonal trust, and other internal states assumed to be desirable. Rensis Likert (1967) developed a four-system typology that follows this pattern, assuming that as one enhances open and employee-centered leadership, communication, and control processes, one achieves organizational effectiveness. Blake and Mouton's managerial grid (1984) involves similar assumptions, as do many organization development approaches.

Some who take positions quite at odds with the human relations orientation nevertheless share this general view. Management systems experts who concentrate on whether an organization's accounting and control systems work well make similar assumptions. These orientations have played an important role in the debate over what public management involves. Some writers see inadequacies in public management primarily because of weak management systems and procedures of the sort that purportedly exist in superior form in industry (Crane and Jones, 1982). They call for better accounting and control systems, better inventory controls, better purchasing and procurement, and better contracting procedures.

These human resource and internal process approaches do not involve complete conceptions of organizational effectiveness, but public managers often employ them. In interviews, managers in state agencies in Florida, chosen because they had reputations as excellent managers, gave very high ratings of the effectiveness of their own organization (Sherwood and Rainey, 1983). When asked how they knew that their organization was effective, they often mentioned internal processes or characteristics. They would point out that their staff and the subordinate managers got along very well and that things seemed to run smoothly. When they referred to external factors, they noted that they received few complaints from legislators, clients, or the press, which they took as evidence that things were running smoothly. Some mentioned that members of their organization received invitations to speak at professional conferences, which they took as evidence that they have an expert staff in place. Few referred to output indicators, systematic program or policy assessments, or other more performance-oriented measures. They may have interpreted the questions as asking how the organization achieved such results rather than how they *knew* that it did, but they showed a striking tendency to concentrate on internal processes and characteristics.

Alimard (1987) replicated the study with state agency managers in Virginia and found very similar results, especially in the tendency of managers to give very subjective impressions of the effectiveness of their agency. Whether managers in private industry would refer more frequently to bottom-line criteria is an interesting question. A study by Gold (1982), described in Chapter Fourteen, found that both public and private managers mentioned the sorts of criteria described above but that the private managers more often mentioned profit as a basic goal.

Toward Diverse, Conflicting Criteria

Increasingly, researchers try to examine multiple measures of effectiveness. Campbell (1977) and his colleagues, for example, reviewed various approaches to effectiveness, including those described above, and developed a comprehensive list of criteria (see Table 6.1). Obviously, *many* dimensions figure into effectiveness. Even this elaborate list does not capture certain criteria, such as effectiveness in contributing to the general public interest or the general political economy.

As researchers try to incorporate more complex sets of criteria, it becomes evident that organizations pursue diverse goals and respond to diverse interests, which imposes trade-offs. Cameron (1978) reported a study of colleges and universities in which he gathered a variety of types of effectiveness measures. Reviewing the literature, he noted that effectiveness studies use many types of criteria,

TABLE 6.1. ORGANIZATIONAL EFFECTIVENESS DIMENSIONS AND MEASURES.

1. Overall effectiveness	16. Planning and goal setting
2. Productivity	17. Goal consensus
3. Efficiency	18. Internalization of organizational goals
4. Profit	19. Role and norm congruence
5. Quality	20. Managerial interpersonal skills
6. Accidents	21. Managerial task skills
7. Growth	22. Information management and communication
8. Absenteeism	23. Readiness
9. Turnover	24. Utilization of environment
10. Job satisfaction	25. Evaluations by external entities
11. Motivation	26. Stability
12. Morale	27. Value of human resources
13. Control	28. Participation and shared influence
14. Conflict/cohesion	29. Training and development emphasis
15. Flexibility/adaptation	30. Achievement emphasis

Source: Campbell, 1977, "Comprehensive List of Effectiveness Criteria." Reprinted with permission.

including organizational criteria such as goals, outputs, resource acquisition, and internal processes. They also vary in terms of their universality (whether they use the same criteria for all organizations or different ones for different organizations), whether they are normative or descriptive (describing what an organization should do or what it does do), and whether they are dynamic or static. He also noted different sources of criteria. One can refer to different constituencies, such as the dominant groups in an organization, many constituencies in and out of an organization, or mainly external constituents. The sources also vary by level, from the overall, external system to the organization as a unit, organizational subunits, and individuals. Finally, one can use organizational records or individuals' perceptions as sources of criteria.

In his own study of educational institutions, Cameron (1978) drew on a variety of criteria: objective and subjective criteria; measures reflecting the interests of students, faculty, and administrators; participant criteria; and organizational criteria (see Table 6.2). Cameron developed profiles of different educational institutions according to the nine general criteria and found them to be diverse. One institution scored high on student academic and personal development but quite low on student career development. Another had the opposite profile—low on the first two criteria, high on the third. One institution scored high on community involvement, the others relatively low. This shows that even organizations in the same industry or service sector often follow different patterns of effectiveness. They may choose different strategies, involving somewhat different clients, approaches, and products or services. In addition, it shows that effectiveness criteria can weigh against one another. By doing well on one, an organization may show a weaker performance on another. Cameron points out that a university aiming at distinction in faculty research may pay less attention to the personal development of undergraduates than a college more devoted to attracting and placing undergraduates.

The Competing Values Approach

Quinn and Rohrbaugh (1983) draw this point about conflicting criteria into their competing values framework. They had panels of organizational researchers review the criteria in Table 6.1 to distill the basic dimensions out of the set. The panels' responses indicated that the criteria grouped together along three value dimensions (see Figure 6.1). The first, the organizational focus dimension, ranges from an internal emphasis on the well-being of the organization's members to an external focus on the success of the entire organization. A second dimension concerns control as opposed to flexibility. The third involves relative concentration on means (such as good planning) or ends (such as achieving productivity goals).

TABLE 6.2. EFFECTIVENESS DIMENSIONS FOR EDUCATIONAL INSTITUTIONS.

Perceptual Measures	Objective Measures
1. *Student educational satisfaction*	
Student dissatisfaction	Number of terminations
Student complaints	Counseling center visits
2. *Student academic development*	
Extra work and study	Percentage going on to graduate school
Amount of academic development	
3. *Student career development*	
Number employed in major field	Number receiving career counseling
Number of career-oriented courses	
4. *Student personal development*	
Opportunities for personal development	Number of extracurricular activities
Emphasis on nonacademic development	Number in extramurals and intramurals
5. *Faculty and administrator employment satisfaction*	
Faculty and administrators' satisfaction with school and employment	Number of faculty members and administrators leaving
6. *Professional development and quality of the faculty*	
Faculty publications, awards, conference attendance	Percentage of faculty with doctorates
Teaching at the cutting edge	Number of new courses
7. *System openness and community interaction*	
Employee community service	Number of continuing education courses
Emphasis on community relations	
8. *Ability to acquire resources*	
National reputation of faculty	General funds raised
Drawing power for students	Previously tenured faculty hired
Drawing power for faculty	
9. *Organizational health*	
Student-faculty relations	
Typical communication type	
Levels of trust	
Cooperative environment	
Use of talents and expertise	

Source: Adapted from Cameron (1978). The original table contains numerous additional measures for each dimension. See Cameron (1978) for the complete listing.

Quinn and Rohrbaugh point out that these dimensions reflect fundamental dilemmas that social scientists have debated for a long time—means versus ends, flexibility versus control and stability, internal versus external orientation.

The dimensions combine to represent the four models of effectiveness mentioned in Figure 6.1. The human relations model emphasizes flexibility in internal processes and improving cohesion and morale as a means of developing the people in an organization. The internal process model also has an internal focus, but it emphasizes control, through maintaining sound information, auditing, and review systems, as a means to stability. At the external end, the open-systems model emphasizes responsiveness to the environment, with flexibility in structure and process as a means to achieving growth and acquiring resources. The rational goal model emphasizes careful planning to maximize efficiency.

Quinn and Rohrbaugh recognize the contradictions between the different models and values. They argue, however, that a comprehensive model must retain

FIGURE 6.1. THE COMPETING VALUES FRAMEWORK.

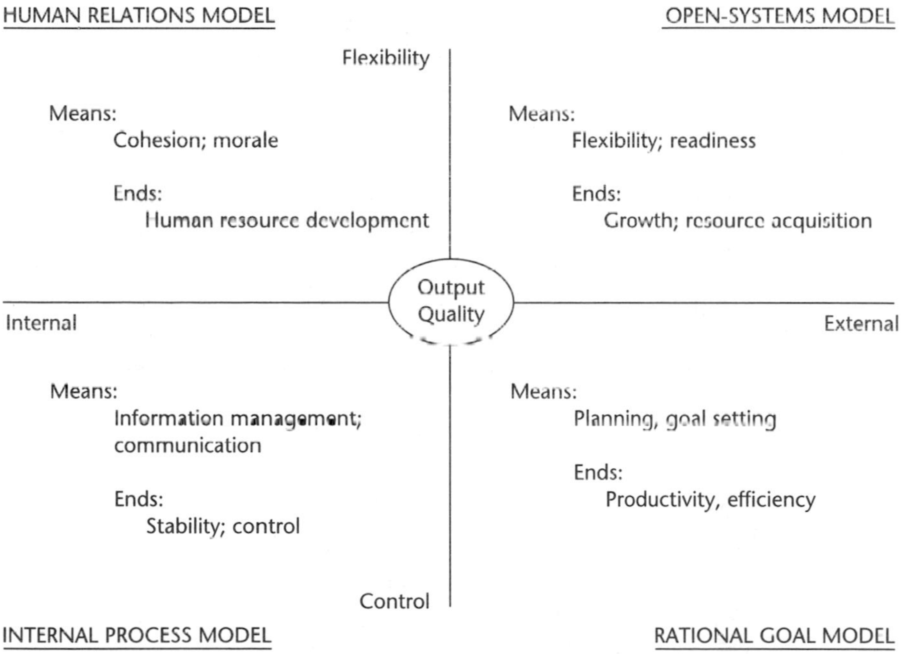

HUMAN RELATIONS MODEL   OPEN-SYSTEMS MODEL

Flexibility

Means: Means:
  Cohesion; morale   Flexibility; readiness

Ends: Ends:
  Human resource development   Growth; resource acquisition

Output Quality

Internal   External

Means: Means:
  Information management;   Planning, goal setting
  communication
                                        Ends:
Ends: Productivity, efficiency
  Stability; control

Control

INTERNAL PROCESS MODEL   RATIONAL GOAL MODEL

Source: Reprinted by permission of R. E. Quinn and J. Rohrbaugh, "A Spatial Model of Effectiveness Criteria: Towards a Competing Values Approach to Organizational Analysis," *Management Science,* 1983, *29.* Copyright © 1983, The Institute of Management Sciences.

them all, because organizations constantly face such competition among values. Organizations have to stay open to external opportunities yet have sound internal controls. They must be ready to change but maintain reasonable stability. Effective organizations and managers balance conflicting values. They do not always do so in the same way, of course. Quinn and Cameron (1983) drew amoebalike shapes on the diagram in Figure 6.1 to illustrate the different emphases that organizations place on the values. An organization that most heavily emphasizes control and formalization would have a profile illustrated by a roughly circular shape that expands much more widely on the lower part of the diagram than on the upper part. For an organization that emphasizes innovation and informal teamwork, the circle sweeps more widely around the upper part of the chart, showing higher emphasis on control and efficiency. This again underscores the point that different organizations may pursue different conceptions of effectiveness.

Quinn and Cameron also point out that effectiveness profiles apparently shift as an organization moves through different stages in its life cycle. In addition, major constituencies can impose such shifts. They describe how a unit of a state mental health agency moved from a teamwork and innovation profile to a control-oriented profile because of a series of newspaper articles criticizing the unit for lax rules, records, and rule adherence.

Still, the ultimate message is that organizations and managers must balance or concurrently manage competing values. Rohrbaugh (1981) illustrates the use of all the values with a measure of the effectiveness of an employment services agency. Quinn (1988) has developed scales for managers to conduct self-assessments of their own orientation within the set of values, for use in training them to manage these conflicts. The competing values framework expresses the values in a highly generalized form and does not address the more specific, substantive goals of particular agencies or the explicit political and institutional values imposed on public organizations. Nevertheless, it provides valuable insights into the effectiveness of public organizations, especially on the point that the criteria are multiple, shifting, and conflicting.

Effectiveness in Organizational Networks

Some very recent research provides particularly important new insights and directions for research and thought on effectiveness of government services, especially in relation to the increasing privatization and third-party governance discussed in Chapters Two and Five (O'Toole, forthcoming). Provan and Milward (1995) analyzed the mental health services of four urban areas in the United States. They found that these services were provided by networks of different organizations, each of which provided some type of service or part of the package of mental health services available in the area. Quite significantly, virtually none of the organizations was a government organization. The government—the federal government for the most part—provided most of the funding for the mental health services in these areas, but networks of private and nonprofit organizations provided the services.

The researchers pointed out that for such networks of organizations, a real measure of effectiveness should not be focused on any individual organization. Instead, one must think in terms of the effectiveness of the entire network. Provan and Milward focused on clients in measuring the network's effectiveness, using responses from clients, their families, and caseworkers concerning the clients' quality of life, their satisfaction with the services of the network, and their level of functioning. They then examined the characteristics of the network in relation to these measures of effectiveness. They found that the most effective of the four mental health service networks was centralized and concentrated around a primary organization. The government funds for the system went directly to that agency, which played a strong central role in coordinating the other organizations in delivering services. This finding runs counter to the organic-mechanistic distinction discussed in earlier chapters, which suggests that decentralized, highly flexible arrangements are most appropriate (Provan and Milward, 1995, pp. 25–26).

Managing Goals and Effectiveness

A reason to review this material on goals and effectiveness fairly early in the book, before the chapters to follow, is to raise basic issues concerning the goals of public organizations that allegedly influence their operations and characteristics. In addition, the concepts and models of effectiveness provide a context and basic theme for the topics to follow. The complications with these concepts and the absence of a conclusive model of effectiveness raise challenges for researchers and practicing managers alike. The next chapter and later chapters show how important these challenges are, however, and provide examples of how leaders have addressed them. Later chapters provide examples of mission statements and expressions of goals and values that members of public organizations have developed. The next chapter discusses strategic management, decision making, and power relationships that are part of the process of developing and pursuing goals and effectiveness. Later chapters discuss topics such as organizational culture and leadership, communication, motivation, organizational change, and managing for excellence—all topics that relate to goals and effectiveness. As Figures 1.1 and 1.2 in Chapter One indicate, a central challenge for people in public organizations is the coordination of such issues and topics in pursuit of goals and effectiveness.

Effectiveness of Public Organizations

As noted at the outset of this book and this chapter, beliefs about the effectiveness of public organizations, and their performance in comparison to business firms, are important parts of the culture of the United States and other countries. These beliefs and perceptions have influenced some of the major political developments in recent decades, and one could argue that they have helped shape the history of the United States and other nations. The preceding sections show, however, that assessing the effectiveness of organizations involves many complexities. Assessing the performance of complex populations of organizations such as public and private ones becomes still more complicated.

Chapter Fourteen returns to the topics of the effectiveness of public organizations and their effectiveness compared to private organizations. It argues that public organizations often operate very well, much better than suggested by the widespread public beliefs about their inferior performance indicated in public opinion polls. Chapter Fourteen makes this argument before covering additional ideas about the effective leadership and management of public organizations, claiming that public managers and leaders quite often perform well in managing goals and effectiveness.

CHAPTER SEVEN

FORMULATING AND ACHIEVING PURPOSE

Power, Strategy, and Decision Making

The framework presented in the first chapter indicates that organizational leadership teams lead the development of strategies aimed at achieving goals. It also suggests, however, that the relationship between strategies and goals works both ways. Major goals and values influence strategies, and strategic processes develop and shape major goals and values. The strategy-building process links the organizational environment, goals and values, structure, processes, and people in the pursuit of performance and effectiveness. To develop and carry out strategies, the members of the organization must exert their influence within it. They have to manage and work with internal power relationships and decision-making processes. As earlier chapters have emphasized, all of the topics and parts of the framework and definition from Chapter One are related to each other and mutually influential. The three topics covered here, power, strategy, and decision making, are closely interconnected in relation to forming and pursuing organizational goals.

Power and Politics Inside Organizations

External power and politics influence internal power and politics. Political scientists have long recognized the role of external politics in determining the power of public organizations and that units within the government bureaucracy engage in power struggles and turf warfare (Wilson, 1989). Yet, aside from case descriptions, political scientists have paid little attention to power relationships within individual public organizations. Writers on management have started looking at power within organizations only recently, but they have done more to analyze it than have political scientists. As discussed in other chapters, early management theories depicted managers as basing their decisions on rational choices and optimal alternatives. Researchers increasingly realized, however, that politics and power relationships figure importantly in all organizations (Pfeffer, 1981). Some make a point of claiming that the politics in business firms and government agencies are very similar (Yates, 1985). Management writers now warn managers of the dangers of overlooking power and politics within their organization and exhort managers to assess these dimensions of their setting (Yates, 1985). They also discuss power in a positive sense, as necessary to performing effectively and, when shared, as a means of motivating people (Kanter, 1987; Block, 1987).

The many rules and controls imposed by external authorities and political actors on public organizations weaken the authority of public sector managers. Political alliances between people in an agency and interest groups and legislators further weaken the authority of higher-level executives. This suggests that, in spite of the claims of management writers that business firms resemble public agencies in such matters, issues of power and influence are more complex for government managers (Allison, 1983). At the same time, rather paradoxically, observers typically depict the bureaucracy as quite powerful. Although constrained in many ways, then, public managers clearly can attain considerable power and authority within their organizations.

They also vary in power, just as agencies do. Agency power can be enhanced by a number of factors: strong, well-organized constituencies, skillful leadership, organizational esprit de corps or cohesion (a relatively strong commitment to the agency and its role, as with the Forest Service or the Peace Corps), and expertise—specialized technical knowledge required for the delivery of a service that the public values highly (Rourke, 1984; Meier, 1993). By implication, these factors also determine the power of people and units within public organizations. This chapter considers how concepts from the management literature can help us further sort out some of the determinants of power. A recent example of a power play in the federal bureaucracy provides a useful beginning. Newspaper accounts dramatized it as a perfect example of how power works in Washington, yet it also makes important points about how power does not work and illustrates the importance of analyzing the dimensions of power.

Shortly after Ronald Reagan left office, major newspapers carried reports on a controversial aide to the secretary of the Department of Housing and Urban Development (HUD) who had gained considerable power in the department. The reports claimed that the aide had little background related to housing and had gained her appointment because she came from a prominent family. According to the reports, the secretary had inattentively allowed her to make heavy use of his autopen—an apparatus that automatically signs the secretary's name—to influence major decisions on funding and agency policies. She garnered support from members of Congress by channeling projects and grants to their constituencies. She also allegedly used the authority of the secretary to move trusted associates into key positions in the agency where they could give her early information about the unit heads' plans so that she could devise ways to overrule them and channel their projects toward her supporters. In spite of her maneuvering, however, when she was nominated for the position of assistant secretary of HUD, Congress would not confirm her appointment because of her lack of credentials and qualifications. Ultimately, her influence on spending decisions in a housing rehabilitation program received intense scrutiny from federal auditors and news reporters and brought a deluge of bad publicity and the threat of legal action (Maitland, 1989; Waldman, Cohn, and Thomas, 1989).

Bases of Power in Organizations

The HUD official's inability to attain sustained, successful power raises the question of how one does so. Social scientists usually refer to French and Raven's typology of the bases for power in groups (1968): *Reward* power is the power to confer or withhold rewards that others want, such as pay. *Coercive* power comes from the ability to take forceful action against another. A person has *referent* power over others if they see him or her as someone they wish to be like, as a standard for them to emulate. *Expert* power derives from the control of knowledge, information, and skills that others need. A person holds *legitimate* power if others accept his or her authority to tell them what to do.

These types of power have important implications for managers. One might think of coercive power as the ultimate mode of influence. The capacity to tax, arrest, imprison, and execute individuals is a fundamental attribute of government. These powers justify strong controls on public organizations, which often have a coercive character themselves. As for their own leadership behaviors, however, public managers need to recognize that management theorists have long emphasized the relative clumsiness and costliness of coercive power (Etzioni, 1975). Forcing and threatening people require costly vigilance and oversight and can make enemies.

Managers may have authority to coerce, but their real challenge lies in finding ways to reward (Barnard, 1938); as Chapter Ten describes, public managers face particular constraints on their power over certain rewards. Managers may have some legitimate authority because of their rank and position, but they also have to maintain the less formal legitimacy that exists in the eyes of their subordinates and external authorities. To do so, good managers invest heavily in setting a good example and performing well in order to obtain referent power and expert power. For all the politics that surrounds public managers, experienced officials and observers still report that the skill, integrity, experience, and expert knowledge of a public administrator can give him or her a positive form of power over members of the organization and external authorities.

The HUD official described above rewarded certain supporters, illustrating the importance of political alliances. Yet her relatively coercive treatment of some agency officials probably contributed to her ultimate troubles. Also, she allegedly abused legitimate power (the secretary's autopen), and she lacked sufficient legitimate, expert, and referent power to sustain her position. Later chapters provide examples of more effective approaches. They, too, involve development of constituencies, but they entail a more effective vision of a contribution to society sustained by a reputation for expertise and integrity (Cohen and Eimicke, 1995; Doig and Hargrove, 1987; Chase and Reveal, 1983).

Dependency and Strategic Contingencies

In analyzing power, organization theorists also draw on the concept of dependency—how much a person or group must rely on another person or group for resources. Groups and units that have the most to do with obtaining key resources for their organization gain power. Studies of business firms find that their members rate the sales and production divisions of their firms as the most powerful units (Kenny and others, 1987; Perrow, 1970a). Businesses depend on these units to produce and sell the products essential to bringing in money. Others can also depend on a person or unit for information, completed tasks, and services.

Similarly, power accrues to units that manage *strategic contingencies*, or the factors and events that figure crucially in the operations of the organization and its ability to achieve goals (Hickson and others, 1971). Units that handle the biggest problems facing the organization gain power. Earlier chapters discussed the central role of environmental uncertainty in recent analyses of organizations; strategic contingencies include circumstances that impose major uncertainties on an organization, and those who handle these uncertainties become important. During the 1970s, many city governments faced the prospect of affirmative action suits, and many mayors and city managers began spending more time with their city attorneys and personnel officers to determine what kind of affirmative action plan would be legally defensible. The requests for support and resources from these officers and their units—for more funding and new personnel—and their capacity to tell other units what to do increased noticeably in some cities.

The study by Kenny and his colleagues (1987) further suggests that these concepts apply to public organizations, but with important distinctions. They analyzed major decisions in thirty public and private organizations in Great Britain. The private organizations included manufacturing and service firms. The public group included local governments, health districts, and state-owned enterprises such as a chemical manufacturer and an airline (both nationalized in the United Kingdom). The researchers asked managers of both types of organizations which internal and external units were involved in major decision making and how much influence they had. The two groups had similar patterns of unit involvement. For example, accounting, auditing, and production units were most frequently involved. In the public organizations, however, external government agencies became involved much more often. Sales, marketing, and production units had a great deal of influence in both groups. In the public organizations, adjudication units   committees or commissions that decide on resources and policies, such as a health services district commission—had the strongest influence rating. Yet this type of unit approached having the lowest rating in the private organizations. Surprisingly, also, external government agencies were rated as having little influence in the public organizations, in spite of their frequent involvement, but as being very influential in the private organizations. The authors suggest that this might mean that public sector managers take for granted the influence of external agencies, while business managers react more sharply to government interventions.

Overall, the study indicates that units that produce and distribute primary goods and services wield strong influence in both types of organizations. Even in public organizations with a high market or client orientation, like those in the study—government manufacturers, a health district, and so on—the institutional authority of government affects internal influence patterns; external agencies often become involved. The strong role of adjudication units in public organizations reflects the authority conferred on them by the institutions of government. In the organizations studied, those units also handled key strategic dependencies by representing external constituencies and making policy decisions. Later we will see that the same researchers also found that the strategic decision-making processes of the public organizations also reflected the effects of their public sector status.

Power at Different Organizational Levels

Management experts also consider how people at different levels and in different units obtain power. Daft (1995) points out that top managers have a variety of sources of power. They have considerable authority by virtue of their formal position, such as authority to control key decisions. They can also influence allocation of resources. In government agencies, in spite of external constraints and politics, the agency heads usually exert considerable influence over funding for subunits and allocation of other key resources, such as personnel. Top managers can control *decision premises*—fundamental values or principles that guide decision making—and information (Simon, 1948). Robert Dempsey, director of the Florida Department of Law Enforcement, became interested in Peters and Waterman's *In Search of Excellence* (1982), which emphasizes approaches such as concern for employees and open communication. Dempsey made it clear to his managers that the agency would adopt these orientations through open-door policies, improved communications, and other steps. This position became a guide for decision making by the other managers. Now when an employee asks to speak to a manager, the director has clear guidelines on how to respond—"You listen!" The basic premise behind the agency's decision-making procedure guides subsequent, more specific decisions. (Chapters Eleven, Thirteen, and Fourteen provide further examples of managers' efforts to communicate major values and premises to others.)

Top managers can also take advantage of *network centrality*. They occupy the center of networks of information, personal loyalty, and resource flows. The HUD official placed loyal associates in key positions to develop an information network. This worked effectively until deficits in other dimensions of her power eroded her position (Maitland, 1989).

Lower-level members of an organization can have substantial power as well. They may serve as experts on key tasks. They can obtain influence through effort, interest, informal coalitions (such as those formed by groups of friends), or formal organizations (such as unions). They can use rules and other organizational norms to their advantage. In his analysis of "street-level" government service providers, Lipsky (1980) points out that they have considerable autonomy. Civil service rules, vague performance measures, and extensive rules governing service delivery constrain higher officials' authority over them.

Middle managers have some of the influence potential of both executives and lower-level employees. Management experts interested in "empowerment" as a means of making managers more effective have lately focused increased attention on these managers (Kanter, 1987; Block, 1987). These authors often focus on business firms, but empowerment also has intriguing implications for public agencies. Middle managers occupy positions below corporate vice-presidents or major division and department heads. In government, this would include those below assistant secretaries or major bureau heads, such as managers in GS 13–15 positions in the federal government.

Kanter (1987) argues that middle managers in business firms have so little power that they cannot perform effectively. Many rules and routines govern their work, and there are few rewards for innovation. They rarely participate in important conferences or task forces. They lack resources and support to do useful things, such as rewarding excellent subordinates or pursuing a promising initiative. Higher-level managers must bestow a positive form of power on these middle managers. They must relax rules, increase participation, assign important tasks, and reward innovation (Kanter, 1987). This sharing of power *expands* power, giving more people in the organization the capacity and incentive to do good work. Excellent corporations and effective leaders employ such policies (see Chapters Eleven and Fourteen).

Interestingly, Kanter's analysis of problems in industry sounds like the complaints about heavy constraints on managers in government. The proposed solution, however, contrasts sharply with common approaches in government. Elected officials and top agency executives often impose *more* rules to try to improve performance and maintain control (Wilson, 1989; Lynn, 1981; Warwick, 1975); President Reagan aggressively sought to *dis*empower career federal civil servants. The accountability pressures in government complicate empowerment approaches. Yet government officials face a serious challenge in finding ways to allow civil servants sufficient authority and participation to maintain a competent and motivated public service (Volcker Commission, 1989; National Academy of Public Administration, 1986).

Power Among Subunits

Pfeffer and Salancik (1978) apply similar thinking to the analysis of power distributions among subunits. A department or bureau has more power when there is greater dependency on it, when it has more control over financial resources and greater centrality to the important activities of the organization, when there is less *substitutability* of services (when others have few or no alternatives to dealing with the unit for important needs), and when it has a larger role in coping with important uncertainties facing the organization.

Getting and Using Power

When they draw practical suggestions from this literature, management writers offer advice such as this (Daft, 1995):

- Move into areas of great uncertainty or strategic contingencies facing the organization and play an important role in managing those areas.
- Increase other departments' dependence on your own by making them depend on you for key resources and information. Incur obligations by doing additional work for others.
- Provide resources for the organization by bringing in money and other resources from external sources.

- Build coalitions and networks with others by building trust and respect through helpfulness and high motivation. Involve many people, including those who disagree with you.
- Influence the premises behind decision-making processes by such means as influencing the flow of information about one's department and shaping the agendas of important meetings.
- Enhance the legitimacy and prestige of your position and department.
- Be reasonably aggressive and assertive, but be quiet and subtle about power issues—do not make loud claims or demands about power.

Suggestions as general as these certainly apply in most management settings. For public management, they need to be interpreted in light of the points made here about legitimate authority and external political authority.

Decision Making in Organizations

Decision-making issues are closely related to power issues, since power determines who gets to decide. The literature often suggests that, as with power issues, public organizations should have distinct decision-making processes because of factors different from those faced by private organizations, such as political interventions and constraints and more diverse, diffuse objectives. The most recent evidence supports such assertions. Although it shows that the general decision-making processes of public organizations often resemble those of private organizations, it also indicates that major decisions in public organizations involve more complexity, dynamism, intervention, and interruption than those in their private counterparts. These conditions help to explain why when demands for accountability and efficiency have led to schemes for rationalizing government decision-making processes, they have often failed. At the same time, however, public employees engage in much routine decision making that can be highly standardized. This raises another key challenge for public managers—deciding when to try to standardize and rationalize decision-making processes. Concepts from general organization theory help in the analysis of this issue.

Many contemporary management scholars (for example, Daft, 1995) analyze decision-making processes according to a contingency-theory perspective of the sort described in Chapters One and Two. In some situations, managers can successfully adopt highly rationalized decision-making processes. Others involve too much uncertainty for such structured approaches and require more complex, intuitive decision making.

Rational Decision-Making Models

Rationality has various meanings and dimensions, but in the social sciences, a *strictly* rational decision-making process would involve the following components:

1. Decision makers know all the relevant goals clearly.
2. Decision makers clearly know the values used in assessing those goals and targeting levels of attainment for them, so they also know their preferences among the goals and can rank order them.
3. They examine all alternative means for achieving the goals.
4. They choose the most efficient of the alternative means for maximizing the goals.

These strict conditions are seldom met except in the most simple of situations, but we know that simple situations that require decisions come up all the time. A bureau chief receives a careful committee report demonstrating that three alternative vendors can sell the bureau identical copying machines. The bureau chief chooses the least expensive machine. To do otherwise would invite others to question the chief's competence, ethics, or sanity.

Rational Decision-Making Techniques in Public Organizations. Public agencies apply techniques akin to those of scientific management when they have consultants or in-house experts analyze work processes to design more efficient, effective work procedures. In one case, a client services agency conducted such an analysis when purchasing new computer terminals for use in recording intake interviews with new clients. The original plan called for the client to sit to the right of the interviewer while the interviewer keyed the client's responses into the computer. However, a consultant hired to conduct a time-motion study discovered that the terminals should be placed where the interviewer could face the client. The interviewers wanted to face the clients to make the interview more personable. In addition, if the client sat to the side of the interviewer, the interviewer would keep turning to face the client, wasting time and energy. A rational technique not only aided efficiency but also supported the organization's human relations objectives.

Similarly, management science techniques have wide applications in government (Downs and Larkey, 1986). These techniques involve mathematical models or other highly structured procedures for decision making. Linear programming, for example, uses mathematical formulas to determine how many units of output can be produced with given levels of inputs and thus the best mix of inputs for a production process. Other mathematical techniques support design of work flows and queuing processes. Many discussions of such techniques emphasize the greater difficulty of achieving successful applications in government because of such factors as vague performance criteria and political interventions (Drake, 1972; Morse and Bacon, 1967). For many technical areas of government work, however, these techniques have applications that are just as useful as those in industry.

Many of the proposals for improving government operations over the past several decades advocated approaches that involve elements of rational decision making (Downs and Larkey, 1986; Lynn, 1981). Lyndon Johnson issued a presidential directive ordering that the planning and program budgeting system (PPBS) be implemented in the budgeting processes of federal agencies. PPBS involves a systematic process of organizing budget requests according to major programs, with the plans and objectives for those programs specified and justified. Advocates proposed PPBS as a reform of previous budgeting techniques that concentrated on the items or activities to be funded and paid little attention to program objectives. The Department of Defense had used the system with some success prior to President Johnson's order. Problems in implementing PPBS more widely led to the order's cancellation a few years later, however.

When Jimmy Carter campaigned for president, he proposed the use of zero-based budgeting (ZBB) techniques as a way of exerting greater control over federal spending. This technique involves looking at the requests for funding of various activities as if their funding levels were zero. The idea is to force a very systematic, rational review of major commitments and possible reallocations rather than simply taking existing programs for granted. The procedure never came into use in any significant way.

Others have proposed that the public sector can use management by objectives (MBO) techniques as well as the private sector does (Morrisey, 1976). These techniques involve careful negotiation and specification of primary objectives for individuals and units, with performance evaluations concentrating on whether those objectives have been achieved (Swiss, 1991). As with the techniques discussed previously, debate goes on over prospects for such a systematic and explicit technique in public organizations (Bowsher, 1990).

Some public organizations use elements of these techniques, but their general implementation has foundered. Apparently the public sector conditions of diffuse goals, political complications, and highly complex programs often overwhelm such highly rationalized procedures.

Rationality Assumptions and the Behaviors of Public Managers and Officials. Another role that the concept of rationality has played in analyzing public organizations revolves around its use to interpret the behavior of public managers and other government officials. "Public choice" economists have developed a body of theory using approaches typical in economics to analyze how citizens and officials make political decisions. They argue, for example, that in political just as in economic contexts, individuals rationally maximize utility. Voters vote in their own self-interest, and political officials in essence try to buy votes by providing the government programs and services voters want. Since no market process ensures that one has to pay directly for the goods and services one receives, groups of voters use the political system to benefit themselves at the expense of others. They demand that their elected officials give them services and subsidies that *they* need, sometimes shifting much of the burden of paying for them to other voters. When these theorists turn to the public bureaucracy, they suggest similar problems. In some of the most prominent, widely cited academic works on public bureaucracies, they suggest that government organizations strive for ever greater budgets (Niskanen, 1971) and tend toward rigidity (Downs, 1967) and information distortion (Tullock, 1965).

Evidence about these assertions has accumulated, and some of it supports them. Clearly, they refer to serious challenges for public managers and potential shortcomings of public agencies. The evidence and careful assessment of the assertions, however, also indicate that they are oversimplified and, as depictions of many "bureaucrats" and public bureaucracies, simply inaccurate (Blais and Dion, 1991; Bendor and Moe, 1985). Chapters Thirteen and Fourteen will return to questions about the performance of government agencies and their managers. While acknowledging the severe performance problems that public agencies and managers sometimes exhibit, those chapters will also present evidence and assertions that public agencies and their managers often perform very well.

The Limits of Rationality. Chapter Two described how Herbert Simon (1948) advanced his observations about constraints on managers' ability to follow highly rational procedures, especially in complex decision-making settings. Simon argued that for large-scale decisions, the deluge of relevant information and uncertainties overloads the cognitive capacity of managers to process it. Managers strive for rationality — they are *intendedly rational*. But cognitive limits, uncertainties, and time limits cause them to decide under conditions of *bounded rationality*. They do not maximize in accordance with rationality assumptions; they "satisfice." They undertake a limited search among alternatives and choose the most satisfactory of them after as much consideration as they can manage within the constraints imposed by their situation. Cyert and March (1963) studied business firms and found that they approached major decisions largely as Simon had suggested. Rather than making decisions in highly rational modes, managers in the firms followed satisficing approaches. They engaged in "problemistic searches"—that is, they started searching for alternatives and solutions in relation to problems that came up rather than in a systematic, explicitly goal-oriented way. They also engaged in "sequential attention to alternatives," turning from possibility to possibility, looking at one alternative until they saw some problem with it and then turning to another. They tended to use benchmarks and rules of thumb rather than a careful explication of goals and a strategy for maximizing them. For example, without conclusive evidence to justify doing so, they might set a target of a 5 percent profit increase per year for the next five years, simply because that is almost what they have achieved in the past.

Contingency Perspectives on Decision Making

Current views of management typically follow this pattern of regarding strictly rational approaches to decision making as applicable within relatively limited domains of managerial activity. Where tasks and the operating context afford relatively stable, clear, simple conditions, managers find such approaches feasible. As conditions become more complex and dynamic, however, the deluge of information and uncertain conditions overwhelms procedures that require highly explicit statements of goals and painstaking analysis of numerous alternatives. More intuitive and experience-based judgment comes into play, supplementing or supplanting highly rational procedures.

James Thompson (1967) suggested a contingency framework to express these variations. Decision-making contexts vary along two major dimensions: the degree to which the decision makers agree on goals, and the degree to which they understand means-ends or cause-effect relationships—that is, the degree to which they have well-developed technical knowledge about how to solve the problems and accomplish the tasks. Where both goal agreement and technical knowledge are high, very rational procedures apply. The example above concerning the client services agency's intake interview system illustrates a situation where everyone agreed on the goals. Everyone wanted more efficient, effective interview procedures. In addition, the consultants had well-developed ways of analyzing the efficiency and effectiveness of the interviews in the trial runs. A rational procedure served very well.

The Internal Revenue Service deals each year with the problem of receiving a flood of tax returns and extracting and sorting them correctly. State departments of motor vehicles and the U.S. Social Security Administration process many routine applications and claims every day. In decisions about activities such as these, management science techniques and other forms of highly rationalized analysis have valuable applications (as long as they are properly implemented, in a humane and communicative fashion). For example, the U.S. Navy once effectively implemented a planned maintenance system with elaborate scheduling charts that directed when the various pieces of machinery and equipment on a ship should receive maintenance. Instruction cards detailed the maintenance tasks to be performed and included a system for recording the completion of tasks. In effect, the ships followed a strict recipe for maintenance.

At the other end of the scale, where decision makers have no clear consensus on goals and little clarity as to the technical means of achieving them, one can hardly follow a simple blueprint. Measurement, mathematical models and analysis, and strict guidelines for decisions become more tenuous. Under these conditions, managers engage in more bargaining and political maneuvering and more intuitive, judgmental decision making.

Incremental Decision-Making Processes

Much more in political science than in management, scholars have debated whether government decision-making processes follow an *incremental* pattern. This perspective on public sector decisions has features similar to those of the bounded rationality perspective and has similar intellectual origins. Incrementalism in decision making means concentrating on increments to existing circumstances, or relatively limited changes from existing conditions. Those who regard the policymaking process as having this characteristic argue that major, wrenching changes to federal budget categories seldom receive much consideration. Instead, the officials formulating the budget concentrate on the limited increments, up and down, proposed in any given year. Policymakers restrict the size of the changes that they propose. The bigger the change, the more opposition they stir up and the more complex the task of analyzing the change.

Political scientists have debated intensively over whether incrementalism accurately characterizes the policymaking and budgeting processes. In addition, they debate its desirability. Some argue that incremental processes stimulate useful bargaining among active political groups and officials and guard against ill-considered radical changes. Others complain that they make the policymaking and budgeting processes too conservative and shortsighted and too supportive of existing coalitions and policies.

The debate became mired in difficulties about what is meant by an increment—how large a change has to be to be large. It has led to the conclusion, however, that policy and budgetary changes tend to be incremental but are not always. Fairly drastic cuts in some portions of the federal budget during the Reagan administration, along with fairly sharp increases in military spending, illustrate that however one identifies an increment, cuts or increases can greatly affect public managers and their agencies (Rubin, 1985). More generally, however, the decision-making processes of public organizations play out within these larger incremental policymaking processes. Policy changes that agencies initiate or that influence them involve a complex interplay of political actors tugging and hauling over any significant change.

In fact, these aspects of the governmental context lead to prescriptions for using incremental approaches as the most feasible alternative. Charles Lindblom's article "The Science of Muddling Through" (1959) is a classic statement of this perspective. He notes that the requirement for political consensus and compromise results in vague goals for public policies and programs. In addition, public administrators carrying out these policies must maintain political support through public participation and consensus building. They have to remain accountable to elected officials, who usually have less experience than they do. As a result, stated goals and ends for policies provide little clarity, and means become inseparable from ends. Administrators find it difficult or politically unacceptable to state a precise societal impact for which a program aims. They must identify a package of means and ends that can achieve political consensus and support. Far-reaching, original procedures and goals evoke particularly strong opposition and usually must be modified if support is to be maintained. In addition, the need for political support often outweighs such criteria as efficiency and substantive impact. Thus, in formulating their packages of means and ends, administrators must strive for satisfactory decisions—that is, they must satisfice—after examining a relatively limited set of alternatives. Often they rely heavily on past practice. A good deal of intelligence may enter the decision-making process through the involvement of many groups, experts, and officials. Generally, however, the approach involves avoiding major departures and concentrating on relatively limited, politically feasible steps.

One can see why critics worry about the implications of such an approach (Rosenbloom, 1989). It can lead to unduly conservative decisions. It can favor politically influential groups over disadvantaged and less organized groups. Some critics end up calling for some version of greater central control by Congress or the president. The feasibility of these proposals, in turn, comes into question (Lindblom, 1977; Lowi, 1979).

Mixed Scanning. Etzioni (1967, 1986) proposes an approach aimed at reaching a compromise between the extreme versions of rational decision making and incrementalism. He argues that administrators and other officials make both decisions that have large-scale, long-term implications and decisions of more limited scope. The latter often follow major directions already selected by the former. Etzioni suggests that decision makers strive, through "mixed scanning," to recognize the points at which they concentrate on broader, longer-range alternatives and those at which they focus on more specific, incremental decisions that are a part of larger directions. Decision makers need to mix both perspectives, taking the time to conduct broad considerations of many major issues and alternatives to prevent the shortsightedness of incrementalism. Yet such broad scans cannot involve all the comprehensive analysis required by highly rational models; thus more intensive analysis must follow on decisions within areas of pressing need.

Logical Incrementalism. Quinn (1990) suggests a pattern of logical incrementalism in which long-range strategic decisions set a framework for incremental steps aimed at carrying out the broader objectives. Focused mainly on business organizations, the approach involves careful consideration of long-range, general priorities. Implementing these priorities, however, involves limited, experimental steps. Decision makers must recognize that the priorities need adaptation and that compromise remains important. These suggestions are consistent with some prescriptions for successful large-scale change in organizations discussed in Chapter Thirteen.

An Incremental Model of Decision-Making Processes Within Organizations.
Political scientists usually apply the concept of incrementalism to the process of creating broad public policy. Mintzberg, Raisinghani, and Theoret (1976) studied twenty-five major decisions in organizations and formulated an incremental model of decision-making processes within organizations. The model depicts decisions, even major ones, as involving numerous small, incremental steps, moving through certain general phases. During this process, "decision interrupts" can occur at any of the stages, causing the process to cycle back to an earlier point. The identification phase involves recognizing the problem and diagnosing it through information gathering. Then, in the development phase, a search process that identifies alternatives is followed by design of a particular solution. Finally, in the selection phase, the solution is evaluated, and through an authorization step the organization makes a formal commitment to the decision.

This process seldom flows smoothly. "Decision interrupts" at any of the steps make the decision-making process choppy and cyclical rather than smooth and carefully directed. An internal interruption may block diagnosis of a problem. Even when a solution has been designed, a new option may pop up and throw the process back. For example, a new executive may come in and refuse to authorize a decision that is otherwise ready for implementation, or an external interruption such as a government mandate may cause higher executives to push a proposal back for further development.

This incremental decision-making model has been used in research comparing private managers with managers from public and nonprofit organizations. Schwenk (1990) used it to analyze the managers' perceptions about decision processes in their organizations. He found that compared to the private business managers, public and nonprofit managers reported more interruptions, recycling to earlier phases, and conflicts in the decision processes in their organizations. This evidence of differences in decision processes in public and private organizations is consistent with the results of other research, such as the study by Hickson and others (1986) discussed later in this chapter.

The Garbage Can Model

The tendency to regard major organizational decisions as complex and dynamic rather than smoothly rational now dominates the management literature. It reaches its apex in the garbage can model. The garbage can metaphor comes from the observation that decisions in organizations are made when particular decision-making opportunities or requirements arise. Like garbage cans, these instances have a diverse array of material cast into them in a disorderly fashion. As noted above, James March participated in research validating Simon's observations about constrained rationality in organizational decisions (Cyert and March, 1963). In addition, March and his colleagues also observed that organizational decisions involve much more internal political activity than is generally supposed, with extensive bargaining and conflict among coalitions (March, 1962; Pfeffer, 1982).

These observations evolved into the garbage can model. It holds that in organizational decision-making processes, participation, preferences, and technology (know-how, techniques, equipment) are ambiguous, uncertain, and rapidly changing. Organizations tend to be "loosely coupled" (Weick, 1979; March and Olsen, 1986). The members and units have loose control and communication with one another. It is often unclear who has the authority to decide what and for whom. In addition, people may loosely engage even with very important issues, because other matters preoccupy them. People come and go in the organization and in decision-making settings such as committees. Problems and potential solutions come and go as well, as conditions change. Choice opportunities also come up—a committee may look for decisions to make, or a manager may look for work to do. A solution may go looking for a problem: a promising alternative may become available that virtually begs for some type of application, or a person or group may have a pet technique that they want to find a way to use. Thus, problems, decision-making participants, solutions, and choice opportunities flow along in time relatively independent of one another.

Decision making occurs when these elements come together in a way that is conducive to making a decision—the right problem arises when the right decision-making participants are receptive to an available solution, all coming together in a choice opportunity. The model emphasizes that the linkages between these elements are more temporal than consequential; that is, they result as much from coincidence as from rational calculation (March and Olsen, 1986).

The model has considerable intuitive appeal, since anyone who has worked in a complex organization knows of chaotic or accidental decisions. In addition, a number of studies have found that the model accurately depicts decision-making processes in a variety of organizations. March and Olsen (1986) stress that they intend the model not as a replacement for other perspectives on decision making but as a supplement to them, thus implying that they do not claim that it perfectly accounts for all decision-making processes and contexts. They do not rule out relatively rational approaches in certain instances. In addition, they point out that the model does not imply that all decisions involve unavoidable bedlam and chaos. Dominant values and norms, historical contexts, leaders with a firm sense of mission, and other factors can guide or bias decisions in systematic ways.

The proponents of the model do not state very clearly just where and when it applies. Early on in their theoretical work, they suggested (without explaining) that the model applies mainly to public and educational organizations (March and Olsen, 1976; Cohen, March, and Olsen, 1972). Most of the applications apparently have concentrated on educational and military organizations and courts. Yet at times they also suggest that it applies to business firms and generally to all organizations (March and Olsen, 1986, p. 12). Still, the model has important implications for public management. As discussed below, Hickson and his colleagues (1986) found that this type of decision making process occurs more frequently in public organizations than in private firms.

Strategic Management

Although most experts on managerial decision making emphasize the rather chaotic nature of the process, by no means do they deny that managers do and should engage in purposeful, goal-oriented actions. In fact, the topic of strategic management has advanced prominently in recent decades. Strategy *is* purposeful behavior. The term comes from the idea of military strategy, of using the resources and strengths of a military force to achieve goals—military victory, usually—by forming plans and objectives and executing them. The concept is more attractive than similar rubrics, such as planning and business policy, because of this emphasis on assessing one's own general goals, one's strengths and weaknesses, and the external threats and opportunities that one faces in deploying one's forces to best advantage in pursuit of those goals.

Prescriptive Frameworks for Strategic Management

Management consultants and experts propose a variety of approaches for developing strategy. Bryson and Roering (1996) provide an excellent summary of eight major approaches to strategic planning that provides more depth and detail on the models mentioned in this discussion. Bryson (1995) concludes that managers can apply virtually all of them in the public sector (although with several provisos, discussed below). Some of the models, such as that of the Boston Consulting Group, focus on high-level corporate decisions about the relative priority of the corporation's business activities. The Boston Consulting Group's "portfolio model" exhorts executives to treat the mix of business units in a large corporation as if they represented stocks in an individual's portfolio of assets. Executives assess the business units in the corporation on two dimensions—market growth and size of market share. The units high on both of these dimensions are "stars"; they should receive priority attention and reinvestment of profits. Units with small shares in slow-growing markets—low on both key dimensions—are "dogs" and candidates for divestiture. Mixed situations provide opportunities for strategic shifting of resources. A unit with a high market share in a slowly growing market brings in a lot of money but does not have strong growth prospects. These activities should be treated as "cash cows" and used to provide resources for units that provide growth opportunities. Units that are in a rapidly growing market but are not yet in command of a large share of it should be considered for infusions of resources from other units, especially the cash cows. The approach sounds cutthroat, but it actually emphasizes *synergy*—the effective meshing of all the activities in an organization to produce overall gains beyond what the activities would gain as the sum of their independent operations.

Ring (1988) applies a modified portfolio model to public sector strategy making. He uses "tractability of the problem" and "public support" as the key dimensions. Where problems are manageable and public support is high, public managers can seek to gain resources that they can then use to deal with more difficult policy problems in settings where public support is high but the problem is very difficult to solve. Where public support and tractability are both low, public managers simply seek to shift the priority away from those problems. Similarly, Rubin (1988) suggests that strategic patterns will differ according to whether the time horizon for the policy issue is long or short and whether the policy plays out within a disruptive or an anticipated environment.

Other approaches emphasize different levels and issues (Bryson, 1995). *Strategic planning systems* propose methods for formulating and implementing strategic decisions and allocating resources to back them up across units and levels of an organization. *Stakeholder management* approaches analyze how key stakeholders evaluate an organization and form strategies to deal with each stakeholder. (Stakeholders include individuals or groups who have a major interest in an organization, such as unions, customers, suppliers, and regulators.) *Competitive analysis* approaches analyze major forces acting on an industry, such as the power of buyers and suppliers, the prospects for substitute products, and competition in its markets. The aim is to gain competitive advantage through such strategies as differentiating oneself from competitors and selecting the segments of an industry in which one should compete (Porter, 1985). *Strategic issues management* focuses on identifying major issues that appear crucial to an organization's ability to achieve its objectives and deciding how a working group in the organization will respond to these issues and resolve them. *Process strategies* and *strategic negotiation* approaches treat strategic decision making as a highly political process and prescribe ways of managing the constant bargaining required. Similarly, *logical incrementalism,* as described earlier, emphasizes the incremental nature of strategic decisions and ways to guide bargaining along a consistent path. (For more detail, see Bryson, 1995, and Bryson and Roering, 1996.)

Applications of Strategic Management in the Public Sector

Numerous frameworks for strategic management in the public sector are now available (Bryson, 1995; Bryson and Roering, 1996; Nutt and Backoff, 1992). They focus on such procedures as strategic issue management, stakeholder analysis, environmental scanning, and SWOT analysis (described below). The procedures prescribed by scholars and consultants usually begin with a planning and organizing phase. A "strategic management group" (SMG) typically manages the process and must agree on who will be involved, how the strategic analysis will proceed, and what they expect to achieve. Usually the procedure requires a structured group process and a facilitator—a consultant skilled in helping groups make decisions. The facilitator often asks members of the group to list their views about important points, such as stakeholders, opportunities, and threats. Then the group follows a procedure for synthesizing their views, such as the nominal group technique described in Chapter Twelve.

The SMG usually begins with a preliminary assessment of the history and current status of the organization to produce a general statement of the organization's mission, such as those provided in Table 7.1. Bryson (1995) suggests that for public organizations, this step requires a careful review of the organization's mandates—the requirements imposed by external authorities through legislation and regulations. This review can clarify what external authorities dictate and can also provide insights about new approaches. For example, representatives of a public hospital who interpret their mandate as forbidding competition with private health services may find upon review that they have the authority to do so.

TABLE 7.1. MISSION AND VALUE STATEMENTS OF PUBLIC AGENCIES.

Social Security Administration

Mission. The mission of the Social Security Administration is to administer equitably, effectively, and efficiently a national program of social insurance, as prescribed by legislation.

Operating Priorities. The mission translates into six operating priorities:

- Maintain the fiscal integrity of the Social Security trust funds.
- Improve public confidence in Social Security and how its programs are operated.
- Provide the best possible service to SSA's customers.
- Improve management to facilitate greater effectiveness, efficiency, and accountability.
- Use the best and most appropriate technology available to administer SSA programs.
- Continue to insure that SSA can count on a properly skilled and highly motivated work force.

Two underlying principles guided the formulation of the strategic plan:

- Commitment to current beneficiaries of Social Security programs.
- Commitment to those who work for the Social Security Administration.

Strategic Recommendations. The plan presents twenty-nine strategic recommendations for improvements in program simplification, service delivery, technology, and organization and human resources.

Internal Revenue Service

Mission. The purpose of the IRS is to collect the proper amount of tax revenues at the least cost to the public, and in a manner that warrants the highest degree of public confidence in our integrity, efficiency, and fairness. To achieve that purpose, we will:

- Encourage and achieve the highest possible degree of voluntary compliance in accordance with the tax law and regulations.
- Advise the public of their rights and responsibilities.
- Determine the extent of compliance and the causes of noncompliance.
- Do all things needed for the proper administration and enforcement of the tax laws.
- Continually search for and implement new, more efficient and effective ways of accomplishing our mission.

Strategic Initiatives. The plan describes fifty-five strategic initiatives in the following areas:

- Balancing Efficiency and Effectiveness (Examples: Expand contracting of office automation and data processing services. Monitor public opinion. Identify and measure effectiveness goals.)
- Strengthening Voluntary Compliance (Examples: Establish a research project on withholding noncompliance. Conduct a survey of nonresponsive taxpayers. Strengthen training for IRS examiners.)
- Enhancing Recruitment and Retention of Employees. (Examples include initiatives in employee counseling, physical fitness, child care, rules of conduct, pride, involvement, and productivity, recruiting, and training.)
- Developing an Information Management Strategy. (Examples: Establish an information resources management function. Establish an information systems planning process.)

TABLE 7.1. MISSION AND VALUE STATEMENTS
OF PUBLIC AGENCIES, cont'd.

Alabama Division of Rehabilitation and Crippled Children Service
"Blueprint for the Future": Values and Goals

I. We value the worth, dignity, and rights of persons with disabilities.
Goals:
1. Provide quality services which lead to quality outcomes, giving priority to persons with severe disabilities.
2. Involve advocates and persons with disabilities in agency planning and policy development.
3. Advocate the rights of persons with disabilities.
II. We value the contribution of all staff in achieving our mission.
Goals:
1. Recruit, employ, and promote qualified staff.
2. Establish open and honest communication.
3. Provide staff opportunities for personal and professional growth.
4. Establish realistic performance and productivity standards.
5. Reward exemplary job performance.
6. Encourage staff creativity and innovation.
III. We value an agency management style that provides opportunities for staff participation.
Goals:
1. Develop an agency management philosophy that promotes creativity and innovation.
2. Provide management development opportunities for agency management staff.
3. Promote an agency management style that encourages teamwork among all staff.
4. Promote an agency management style that encourages greater staff participation in agency decision making.
IV. We value maximum acquisition and the efficient and effective management of resources.
Goals:
1. Acquire maximum financial and other resources.
2. Increase legislative support.
3. Develop a management information system to measure the effective and efficient use of our resources.
4. Develop and use appropriate technological resources.
V. We value public support.
Goals:
1. Inform the public of our mission and our goals.
2. Develop partnerships with business and industry.
3. Encourage greater staff commitment to and responsibility for development of community-based agency support.

Sources: U.S. Department of Health and Human Services (1988); U.S. Department of the Treasury (1984); Stephens (1988).

Working toward the mission statement, the SMG typically reviews trends in the operating environment, using a framework like those described in Chapter Four. It may also conduct a stakeholder analysis at this point and develop idealized visions of how it wants the organization to be in the future. Ultimately the mission statement expresses the general purpose of the organization and its major values and commitments.

Next, the SMG members assess the strengths and weaknesses of the organization and look outward to the environment and forward to the future to identify opportunities and threats facing the organization. This assessment of strengths, weaknesses, opportunities, and threats is called a SWOT analysis. The SMG can choose from an array of techniques for this analysis (Nutt and Backoff, 1992). A typical approach involves the nominal group technique mentioned above. From the SWOT analysis, the SMG develops a list of *strategic issues*—conflicts among opposing forces or values that can affect the organization's ability to achieve a desired future (Nutt and Backoff, 1992). Then the group develops plans for managing these issues (Nutt and Backoff, 1992; Ring, 1988; Eadie, 1996). A wide variety of public sector organizations now use this approach to strategic planning (Bryson, 1995; Boschken, 1988; Wechsler and Backoff, 1988).

Analytical Research on Managerial Strategies in the Public Sector

In addition to recommending procedures, researchers have studied the strategies that public organizations actually pursue and how their strategic decisions actually develop. Some of these studies show the effects of government ownership on strategy. In their study of strategic decisions in thirty British organizations, Hickson and his colleagues (1986) found that strategic decision-making processes in publicly owned service and manufacturing organizations differed from those in private service and manufacturing firms. The public organizations follow a "vortex-sporadic" decision-making process. This involves more turbulence, more shifting participation by a greater diversity of internal and external interests, more delays and interruptions, and more formal and informal interaction among participants. The type of decision made a great difference, as did the distinction between service and manufacturing organizations. The results, however, indicate that the public sector context does impose on internal strategic decision making the sorts of interventions and constraints described in earlier chapters.

Mascarenhas (1989) studied 187 public and private offshore drilling firms in thirty-four countries to analyze their strategic domains (markets served, product type, customer orientation, and technology applied). The government-owned firms operated mainly in domestic markets, with narrow product lines and stable customer bases. Publicly traded private firms (those whose stock is traded on exchanges) were larger, operated in many geographical markets, and offered a wider range of products. Privately held private firms were more like the state-owned firms but had less stable customer bases. The nationality and size of the firms also made a big difference, but the ownership distinctions persisted even with controls for those factors. The results support the point, mentioned in Chapter Three, that public organizations tend to have greater constraints on their strategic domains.

Other studies have analyzed important variations in strategy within the public sector. Wechsler and Backoff (1986) studied four state agencies in Ohio and found that they pursued four types of strategies. The Department of Natural Resources followed a *developmental* strategy. This agency had diverse tasks, constituencies, and independent funding sources. The managers had relative independence to pursue a strategy of enhancing the capabilities, resources, and general performance of the organization. Stronger external forces shaped the *transformational* strategy of the Department of Mental Retardation. Professional experts and legal rights groups advocated deinstitutionalization of the mentally retarded—getting them out of large hospitals and into normal living conditions. The agency also faced constant budgetary pressures. It responded by transforming itself from a manager of hospitals to a monitor and regulator of client services delivered through community-based programs and contracts. The Department of Public Welfare received intense criticism in the media and from legislators and faced increasing human service needs and potential cutbacks in funding, so its managers followed a *protective* strategy. They strengthened internal controls, lowered the agency's public profile ("getting the agency out of the newspapers"), mended relations with legislators, and worked to protect funding levels. The Public Utilities Commission, which regulates utility pricing decisions, adopted a *political* strategy. Nuclear energy issues and increasing fuel prices led to more political activity by consumer advocates. The agency's decisions became more favorable to consumers, reflecting a shift in response to changing configurations of stakeholders.

Boschken (1988) found that a private sector model of strategic variations applied well to government enterprises. Miles and Snow's prominent typology (1978) suggests that *defenders* react to stable environments by trying to protect their hold on their markets and their customers, emphasizing efficiency and centralization. *Analyzers,* operating in moderately changing contexts, take a similar approach but seek to innovate moderately, allowing looser control of innovative efforts. *Prospectors* are found in contexts of growth and dynamism; they seek opportunities and take risks, employing more decentralized and organic management. *Reactors* may appear in any context. They simply drift without clear purpose, responding to conditions as they arise. Boschken (1988) found this framework useful in analyzing the strategic behaviors of port authority organizations for various cities on the West Coast. Public authorities fall between public agencies and business firms. Nevertheless, the study suggests that the very general frameworks for the private sector can be useful in government.

These studies show that strategic orientation varies considerably among public organizations. Public managers, like private managers, engage in a variety of purposeful efforts to respond to their environment and achieve their objectives. This general perspective stands in sharp contrast to negative stereotypes of public managers as passive and inattentive to long-term purposes, which often get drawn into respectable academic theory. The research and writing also suggest that we can develop generalizations about power, decision making, and strategy formulation in the public sector.

Issues for Managers and Researchers

There are more observations about the general features of the public sector context than there is consensus about how to deal with the variations within it. The assertions in the literature about the general characteristics of public organizations that distinguish them from their private counterparts can be summarized as follows:

- There are more political intrusions into management in public organizations and a greater infusion of political criteria.
- A more elaborate overlay of formal, institutional constraints governs the management process, involving more formal laws, rules, and mandated procedures and policies.
- Goals and performance criteria are generally more vague, multiple, and conflicting for public organizations.
- Economic market indicators are usually absent, and the organizations pursue idealized, value-laden social objectives.
- The public sector must handle particularly difficult social tasks, often under relatively vague mandates from legislative bodies.
- Public organizations must jointly pursue all of the complex goals described earlier—accountability, responsiveness, representativeness, openness, efficiency, and accountability.

The literature on power in organizations reminds us that power is elusive and complex and that thinking too much in terms of power relationships can be deluding. Yet the best-intentioned of managers have to consider means of exerting influence for the good ends that they seek. We now have a considerable literature on the power of bureaucracies in general, with a growing set of case studies of effective public managers and how they gain and use influence within the political system (Olshfski, 1990; Doig and Hargrove, 1987; Allison, 1983; Lewis, 1980; Kotter and Lawrence, 1974). We do not, however, have many studies of large samples of public managers that analyze their power and influence within the system and what causes variations in it. Both managers and researchers, then, face the question of what to make of the current state of knowledge on this topic.

Pulling together the material from organization theory and political science suggests some answers. For one thing, public administrators apparently face relatively sharp constraints on their power and influence as a result of their particular context. High-level executives such as politically elected executives and appointed cabinet officers must share authority over their administrative units with legislators and other political authorities. Their authority over their subordinates and organizations is constrained by rules and procedures imposed by other units, such as those governing civil service procedures, purchasing, procurement and space-allocation decisions, and budgeting decisions. At lower managerial levels, managers' authority is further overshadowed by the stronger formal authority and resource control of the other institutional units. Kingdon (1984) reports a survey in which federal officials rated the president and Congress as having much more influence over the policy agenda than administrative officials.

Within this disadvantaged setting, however, administrative officials have varying degrees of influence. Given the assertions of the literature on organizational and bureaucratic power, one would expect that administrative officials, although always subject to the shifting tides of political, social, and technical developments, have greater influence under the following conditions:

- When they play important roles in relation to major policy problems and issues related to obtaining resources for their agency—when they are in key budgetary decision-making roles or in policymaking positions central to the agency's mandates and to the support of major constituencies.
- When they have effective political support from committees and actors in the legislative branch, in other components of the executive branch, and in interest and constituency groups.
- When they have strong professional capabilities and credentials. Some agencies are dominated by a particular professional group, such as attorneys, foreign service officers, police officers, or military officers. Managers without strong credentials and abilities in these specializations will need other strengths, such as excellent preparation or a reputation as a strong generalist manager.
- When they have excellent substantive knowledge of government and its operations and institutions (for example, the legislative and administrative lawmaking processes) and of the policies and programs of the agencies in which they work.

- When they achieve or have the capacity to achieve a reputation for general stature and competence, including high energy, intelligence, integrity, and commitment to serving the public.

Public managers have to consider these power and influence issues because they are directly related to the autonomy and authority they exercise in decision-making processes and to the nature of the decision-making process itself. The evidence and analysis discussed in this chapter and earlier suggest more political intrusions and institutional constraints on decision making in public organizations than in private organizations. Executives who have had experience in business and government echo these observations (Perry and Kraemer, 1983).

More explicitly, Ring and Perry (1985) synthesized literature and research on management strategy for public organizations and came to a similar conclusion. They found that existing research and observations indicate that public sector strategic decision making takes place under such conditions as the following:

- Policy ambiguity (policy directives that are more ill-defined than those in business firms)
- Greater openness to the participation and influence of the media and other political officials and bodies, and greater attentiveness from a more diverse array of them
- More artificial time constraints due to periodic turnover of elected and appointed officials and mandated time lines from courts and legislatures
- Shaky coalitions (relative instability in the political coalitions that can be forged around a particular policy or solution)

Besides the implications of the political science literature and these observations, recent research increasingly validates this general scenario. A number of studies show more constraints, interruptions, interventions, and external contacts in the public sector than in the private sector. Porter and Van Maanen (1983) compared city government administrators with industrial managers and found that city administrators feel they have less control over how they allocate their own time, feel more pressed for time, and regard demands from people outside their organization as a much stronger influence on how they manage their time. The study by Hickson and his colleagues (1986) described earlier emphasizes the more turbulent pattern of participation, delay, interruption, and participation in public sector decision making.

Ring and Perry (1985) also suggest some of the consequences of this context for strategic management. They say that because public managers must often shoot for more limited objectives, they are more likely to have to follow incremental decision-making patterns, and thus their strategies are more likely to be emergent than intended (that is, their strategic decisions and directions are more likely to emerge from the decision-making process than to follow some originally intended direction). Effective public managers must maintain greater flexibility in their orientation toward staff assignments and controls and avoid premature commitments to a given set of objectives. According to Ring and Perry, they must straddle competing demands for efficiency, equity, high moral standards, and political responsiveness to constituent groups by showing open-mindedness, shunning dogmatism, and skillfully integrating competing viewpoints. They must effectively "wield influence rather than authority" and minimize discontinuities in the process. These suggestions from Ring and Perry are noticeably similar to suggestions for garbage can management, but they give more explicit attention to the external political context surrounding major decisions in public organizations.

The question of political influences on decisions raises one final issue addressed in the organizational literature on decision making: Which contingencies determine that decisions must be less structured and systematically rational? As illustrated in earlier examples, many decisions in public organizations are not pervaded with politics and institutional constraints but take place much as they might in a business firm. A challenge facing practitioners and researchers alike is the clarification of where, when, and how deeply the political environment of public organizations affects their decision-making processes. Researchers on public management have not clarified when such contingencies occur. Public managers appear to have more encapsulated, internally manageable decision-making settings, where rational decision-making processes are often more appropriate, when tasks and policy problems are clear, routine, and tractable; at levels of the organization and in geographical locations that are remote from political scrutiny; when issues are minimally politically salient or enjoy consistent public support; when legislative and other mandates are clear as opposed to "fuzzy" (Lerner and Wanat, 1983); and when administrative decision makers gain stronger authority to manage a situation autonomously, without political intervention. Given the present state of research and knowledge, researchers and managers alike have to struggle to analyze such variations in decision-making contexts to determine the most appropriate approaches.

This theme of appropriately assessing and managing the political context in relation to other organizational contingencies comes up again in later chapters. In the next chapter we address additional issues about structure and technology in public organizations, issues related to decision-making processes and influence within the political environment, which in turn relate to later questions about human behavior and performance in public organizations.

CHAPTER EIGHT

ORGANIZATIONAL STRUCTURE, DESIGN, AND TECHNOLOGY

The historical overview in Chapter Two and the discussion of organizational environments in Chapter Four show why so many factors, such as environmental complexity, public sector status, goals, leadership, and others, affect organizational structures and their design. Management researchers use the term *structure* to refer to the configuration of the hierarchical levels and specialized units and positions within an organization, and the formal rules governing these arrangements. They use *technology* and *tasks* to refer to the work processes of an organization that often serve as major influences on the design of organizational structure.

As the historical review in Chapter Two showed, the concept of organizational structure has played a central role in organization and management theory from the beginning. Researchers have analyzed organizational technologies and tasks as important elements affecting the best structure. In spite of the constraints placed on them, public managers have considerable authority over their organizations' structure and make many decisions in relation to technology and tasks, so current thinking on these topics is important to effective public management.

This chapter first discusses the interesting division of opinion about whether public organizations have distinctive structural characteristics, such as more red tape than private organizations. It then discusses the importance of organizational structure and its relation to political power, strategy, and other topics. Next it describes major concepts and findings from the research on organizational structure, technology, and design. Organization theorists have generally addressed structure from a generic perspective, devoting little attention to the distinctive structural attributes of public organizations, even though some important studies have concentrated on public agencies. These general points apply to most organizations, however, and the discussion here gives examples specifically involving public organizations. The chapter concludes by turning more directly to the evidence about whether public organizations differ in structure and design from private organizations.

Novels, essays, and popular stereotypes have all bemoaned the absurdity and inhumanity of government bureaucracies. Often their observations focus on structural matters, such as rigid rules and hierarchies. More formal scholarship often follows suit. In a virtual tradition among some economists, government bureaucracies play the role of villain, sometimes threatening both prosperity and freedom. In probably the most widely cited book on bureaucracy ever published, Downs (1967) argues that government bureaucracies inevitably move toward rigidity and hierarchical constraints. He states a "law of hierarchy" that holds that large government organizations, with no economic markets for their outputs, have more elaborate and centralized hierarchies than do private business firms. Downs's "law" represents a broad consensus that government bureaucracies have exceedingly complex rules and hierarchies, even in comparison to large private sector organizations (Dahl and Lindblom, 1953; Lindblom, 1977; Barton, 1980; Sharkansky, 1989).

An opposite consensus also exists, however. Organization theorists' research on organizational structure offers the best-developed concepts and empirical findings on the topic. Yet as the first several chapters of this book pointed out, most organization theorists have not regarded public organizations as a particularly distinctive category. They have usually adopted a generic perspective that holds that their concepts of structure apply broadly across many types of organizations and that such distinctions as public and private are oversimplified and based on crude stereotypes. Many organization theorists regard other factors, such as organizational size, environmental complexity, and technology, as more important influences on structure than public or private status. Mainstream organization theory in effect sharply disputes the view among some economists and political scientists—described above—that public bureaucracies have excessive red tape and highly centralized and elaborate hierarchies.

Later in this chapter, we will examine the evidence about this controversy over whether public and private organizations differ in structural characteristics. First, however, we will review the concepts and insights about organizational structure developed by organization theorists and how they apply to public organizations—because they do. An important reason to review these concepts, however, is that most of the research comparing public and private organizations' structures uses concepts and methods from organization theory. After reviewing these concepts, we can turn to the evidence comparing public and private organizational structures. There we will see very interesting developments in this research, some of them quite recent. To some people, carefully examining research on the structures of public bureaucracies and business firms sounds about as inviting as reading the telephone book. But if you like to base your thinking on well-developed evidence instead of stereotypes and the half-baked assertions we hear in popular discourse, following and interpreting the research on this topic are intriguing challenges.

The Development of Research on Structure

We have already seen many examples of political actors' and government authorities' influence on the structures of public agencies: rules and clearances imposed on federal managers by oversight agencies; micromanagement by legislators who specify rules and organizational structure; legislators and interest groups jealously guarding the structural autonomy of an agency, preventing its reorganization under the authority of another; President Reagan's demoting federal career civil servants by creating new positions above them. Presidents have created new agencies and placed them outside existing agencies to keep them away from those agencies' powerful political and administrative coalitions (Seidman and Gilmour, 1986). John Kennedy placed the Peace Corps outside the State Department, and Lyndon Johnson kept the youth employment training programs of the Office of Economic Opportunity away from the Department of Labor.

Interestingly, however, early in this century, public administration experts leading the development of the field left political dynamics out of their analyses. Luther Gulick and others in the administrative management school advocated such administrative principles as highly specialized, clearly described task assignments (because, they said, when people specialize they become very well versed in what they have to do and therefore better at it); clear chains of command and authority (with "unity of command," where each person has "one master"—one supervisor—and therefore receives clear directions); a centralized authority structure, with authority residing mainly at the top of the organization; and narrow "spans of control" to help maintain clear lines of authority (a span of control is the number of subordinates reporting to a superior; a narrow span of control means relatively few people report to any given supervisor).

These principles were to guide decisions about structure that would maximize efficiency and performance. Although later criticized and abandoned, this drive toward developing efficient, effective structure drew strength from important issues in government at the time. A reform movement in the later part of the nineteenth century and the earlier decades of the twentieth attacked government corruption and mismanagement, particularly in urban areas. Reformers saw these principles guiding the efficient structuring of organizations as a means of purging political patronage and slovenly management (Knott and Miller, 1987).

Later, government growth during the New Deal and after World War II brought a vast proliferation of government agencies. Gulick and other proponents of the principles of the administrative management school influenced major proposals for reorganizing the sprawling federal bureaucracy and played an important role in major developments in the structure of the federal government in this century. For example, some of the reforms proposed grouping various federal agencies under larger "umbrella" agencies as a means of narrowing the chief executive's span of control. Some experts feel that many government officials still hold the general view of proper organization espoused by the administrative management school (Knott and Miller, 1987; Warwick, 1975; Seidman and Gilmour, 1986). The school's proponents argued that its principles of administration applied equally well in government and business organizations. After all, the object was to make government more efficient, more businesslike, and less "political."

As explained in Chapter Two, the classic approach to structure came under criticism as research on organizations burgeoned during the middle of the twentieth century. The contingency perspective on organizational structure held that an organization's structure must be adapted to key contingencies facing the organization, such as environmental variations and uncertainty, the demands of technology or the production process, the size of the organization, and strategic decisions by managers and coalitions within the organization.

A profusion of empirical studies in the 1960s and 1970s added to this perspective, seeking to define and measure structural concepts. By the 1970s, research journals were filled with empirical studies analyzing these concepts. The activity led to the fairly typical version of contingency frameworks that we will examine next and to the topic of *organizational design*, which we will take up after that.

During the 1980s and 1990s, the literature on organizations and the practice of management within them moved still further in the direction described in Chapter Two—away from more bureaucratized, mechanistic structures and toward more flexible, organic structures. Management mavens touted extremely loose and informal structure as the ideal (Peters, 1988). Many large corporations launched initiatives to decentralize their structure and make themselves more flexible, and business periodicals carried stories about "bureaucracy-busting" executives. These efforts often targeted middle management positions for elimination. By the 1990s, large-scale reductions in personnel through layoffs and "downsizing" had become so common that newsmagazines ran cover stories about the problem and it became an issue in political campaigns. These reductions were aimed in part at developing more flexible organizational structures, with less bureaucracy.

The public sector followed the lead of the private sector in these directions. The National Performance Review (described in Chapters One and Fourteen) sought sharp reductions in federal employment, particularly in oversight staff and middle management. In addition, the president ordered a 50 percent reduction in agency rules, eliminated the federal personnel manual as a symbolic gesture toward reducing personnel rules, and took other steps toward decentralizing and loosening up the bureaucratic structure of the federal government. The Winter Commission, which proposed ways of revitalizing state and local public service, also proposed reducing bureaucratic rules and decentralizing procedures. Among other proposals, the commission called for "flattening" the bureaucracy by eliminating middle layers in public agencies, and "deregulating" government by eliminating many personnel rules and decentralizing procedures (Thompson, 1993). Within a few years, state governments began efforts to eliminate layers of middle management (Walters, 1996). These trends show that the topic of organizational structure and its design and management remain key challenges for public managers.

Structural Dimensions and Influences

Researchers trying to work out clear definitions and measures of organizational structure have run into many complications. For example, you can measure structural features objectively (by counting the number of rules, for example) or subjectively (by asking people how strictly they must follow the rules). In addition, organizations can be very complex, with different units having markedly different structures, and this makes it hard to develop an overall measure of an organization's structure.

Dimensions of Structure

While the issue is a complex one, research has produced concepts that help clarify the topic of structure. Researchers typically use such dimensions as the following to define organizational structure.

Centralization. The degree of centralization in an organization is the degree to which power and authority concentrate at its higher levels. Some researchers measure this with questions about the location of decision-making authority (asking, for example, whether decisions have to be approved at higher levels).

Formalization. Formalization refers to the extent to which an organization's structures and procedures are formally established in written rules and regulations. Some researchers measure this by asking employees how much they have to follow established rules, whether they must go through "proper channels," and whether a rule manual exists (Hage and Aiken, 1969). Others determine whether the organization has organization charts, rule manuals, and other formal instructions (Pugh, Hickson, and Hinings, 1969).

Complexity. Organizational complexity is measured in terms of the number of subunits, levels, and specializations in an organization. Researchers break this dimension down further into subdimensions (Hall, 1996). Organizations vary in *horizontal differentiation,* or the specialized division of labor across subunits and individuals. To measure horizontal differentiation, some researchers simply count the number of subunits and individual specializations in an organization (Blau and Schoenherr, 1971; Meyer, 1979). *Vertical differentiation* refers to the number of hierarchical levels in an organization—its "tallness" or "flatness."

Influences on Structure

The research has also analyzed a number of factors that influence organizational structure, concentrating on the following:

Size. Various studies have shown that larger organizations tend to be more structurally complex than smaller ones, with more levels, departments, and job titles (for example, Pugh, Hickson, and Hinings, 1969). Blau and Schoenherr (1971) also concluded, however, that the rate at which complexity increases with size falls off at a certain point; organizations that reach this point grow larger without adding new departments and levels as rapidly. In addition, this research indicates that larger organizations tend to have less administrative overhead. So, contrary to stereotypes and popular books about bureaucracy (Parkinson, 1957), larger organizations often have smaller percentages of their personnel involved in administrative work.

Argyris (1972) criticized the findings on public organizations of some studies of organizational size. He noted that Blau studied government agencies controlled by civil service systems and applied the results to *all* organizations in drawing his conclusions. Civil service regulations may have caused these organizations to emphasize task specialization and narrow spans of control and thus grow in the patterns that Blau observed. Business organizations might not follow these patterns, however. In contrast to the findings of a study of state employment agencies by Blau and Schoenherr (1971), Beyer and Trice (1979), studying a set of federal agencies, found no direct relationship between size and vertical or horizontal differentiation. Ultimately, they concluded that increased size increases the division of labor, which in turn increases vertical and horizontal complexity. In addition, the relationships of size, division of labor, and vertical and horizontal differentiation were stronger in federal units doing routine work than in those doing nonroutine work. Thus, larger public organizations tend toward somewhat greater structural complexity (more levels and subunits, greater division of labor). Much larger organizations almost certainly show more complexity than much smaller ones, but the effects of size are not clear-cut.

Other researchers have reported further evidence that size has little clear influence on structure. Reviewing this research, Kimberly (1976) pointed out that size is actually a complex variable with different components, such as number of employees and net assets. Since different researchers use different measures of size, it is difficult to consolidate their findings and draw conclusions from them.

Environment. Chapter Four showed that the effects of organizational environment dominate many current analyses of organizational structures, including those based on the contingency perspective. One of the central arguments of this perspective is that a formalized, centralized structure performs well enough in a simple, stable environment, where it can take advantage of specialization and clear patterns of communication and authority, but as the environment presents more changes and more uncertainty, strict rules, job descriptions, and chains of command become more cumbersome and are unable to evolve and process information rapidly enough. Therefore, rules and assignments have to become more flexible. Communication needs to move laterally among people and units, not strictly up and down a hierarchy. People working at lower levels must be given more authority to decide without having to ask permission up the chain of command. As its environment becomes more fragmented, an organization must reflect this complexity in its own structure, giving the people in the units that confront these multiplying environmental segments the authority they need to respond to the conditions they encounter. Although somewhat outdated, this general perspective still exerts a great influence on current prescriptions for managers (Peters, 1988; Daft, 1995).

More recent approaches, such as institutional models, contend that organizations adopt rules and structural arrangements because of prevailing beliefs about their appropriateness or because of influences from external institutions such as government. As we have seen, a number of researchers have advanced claims and evidence about the effects on structure of governmental ownership and funding.

Technology and Tasks. A number of studies indicate that an organization's structure also depends on the nature of its work processes, or technologies and tasks. Researchers use a wide variety of definitions of technology and tasks, such as the interdependence required by the work and the routineness of the work. The effects on structure depend on which of these definitions one uses (Tehrani, Montanari, and Carson, 1990).

In a much-respected book, Thompson (1967) analyzes technology in terms of the type of *interdependence* among workers and units that the work requires. Organizations such as banks and insurance companies have *mediating* technologies. They deal with many individuals who need largely the same set of services, such as checking accounts or insurance policies. Their work involves *pooled* interdependence because it "pools" together such services and sets of clients. They establish branches that have little interdependence with one another and formulate standardized rules and procedures to govern them. *Long-linked technologies,* such as typical assembly line operations, have a *sequential* pattern of interdependence. One unit completes its work and passes the product along to the next unit, which completes another phase of the work, and so on. Plans and schedules become a more important coordination tool for these units. Units with *intensive* technologies have a *reciprocal* pattern of interdependence. The special units in a hospital or an R&D laboratory need to engage in a lot of back-and-forth communication and adjustment in the process of completing the work. These units must be closer together and coordinated through more mutual adjustments and informal meetings. Analyzing many studies of structure, Tehrani, Montanari, and Carson (1990) found some support for Thompson's observations. The studies tended to find that organizational units with high interdependence were much less likely to have a lot of standardized work procedures.

Public organizations often follow these patterns. The Social Security Administration operates regional service centers around the country to process benefits applications and claims—an example of mediating technology. For a long time, the agency also processed claims through a long-linked technology. (Thompson points out that in many organizations, different units have different technologies.) Social Security Administration service centers would forward claims to the main office in Baltimore, one large unit performing a single processing phase (adjudication), and the claims would then be passed to another office (for disbursement, for example), and so on. As Social Security eligibility rules became more complex, however, the people working on different parts of the claims processing procedure needed to communicate with one another more and more about individual cases. This created backlogs as they sent cases back and forth between units. As Chapter Thirteen describes, the agency reorganized to establish modular work units, which brought people from the different phases together in single units. They could communicate and adjust more rapidly—an example of a more intensive technology. Other factors besides work processes influenced the reorganization, but Thompson's ideas about interdependence clearly apply.

Perrow's (1973) analysis of technology, the most frequently cited, argues that work processes vary along two main dimensions: the frequency with which exceptions to normal procedures arise and the degree to which these exceptions are analyzable (that is, the degree to which they can be solved through a rational, systematic search). If a machine breaks down, often a clear set of steps can lead to fixing it. If a human being breaks down psychologically, usually few systematic procedures lead as directly to diagnosis and treatment.

Organizational technologies can rank high or low on either of these two main dimensions. *Routine* technologies involve few exceptions and provide clear steps in response to any that occur (high analyzability). In such cases, the work is usually programmed through plans and rules, since there is little need for intensive communication and individual discretion in performing the work. For examples of routine technology, researchers usually point to the work of many manufacturing personnel, auditors, and clerical personnel. At the opposite extreme, nonroutine technologies involve many exceptions, which are less analyzable when they occur. Units and organizations doing this type of work tend toward flexible, "polycentralized" structures, with power and discretion widely dispersed and with much interdependence and mutual adjustment among units and people. Units engaged in strategic planning, research and development, and psychiatric treatment apply such nonroutine technologies.

Between these extremes, Perrow suggests two intermediate categories, *craft* technology and *engineering* technology. Craft technology involves infrequent exceptions but offers no easily programmed solutions when they occur. Government budget analysts, for example, may work quite routinely but with few clear guidelines on how to deal with the unpredictable variations that may arise, such as unanticipated shortfalls. These organizations tend to be more decentralized than those with routine technologies. Engineering technology involves many exceptions but also offers analyzable responses to them. Engineers may encounter many variations, but often they can respond in systematic, programmed ways. Lawyers and auditors often deal with this type of work. When an Internal Revenue Service auditor examines a person's income tax return, many unanticipated questions come up about whether certain of the person's tax deductions can be allowed. The auditor can resolve many of the questions, however, by reference to written rules and guidelines. Organizations with engineering technologies tend to be more centralized than those with nonroutine technologies but more flexibly structured than those with routine technologies. Tehrani, Montanari, and Carson (1990) also found support for Perrow's observations. The studies they analyzed found that organizational units with routine technologies had more formal rules and procedures and fewer highly educated and professional employees.

Perrow's analysis clearly has applications to public organizations. In a study of state employment agencies, Van de Ven, Delbecq, and Koenig (1976) used questionnaire items about task variability and task difficulty based on Perrow's work. The questions asked about how much the work involves the same tasks and issues, how easy it is to know whether the work is being done correctly, and similar issues. The researchers found relationships between the structures and coordination processes in organizational units and the nature of their tasks. Some units, such as clerical claims-processing units, were characterized by tasks low in uncertainty (low in variability and difficulty), more plans and rules, fewer scheduled and unscheduled meetings, and relatively little horizontal communication among individuals and units. Units with high task uncertainty, however, such as employment counseling units, relied less on plans and rules and had more scheduled and unscheduled meetings and more horizontal communication. Units that were intermediate on the task dimensions fell in the middle ranges on the structural and coordination dimensions. So, in many government agencies, in spite of the external political controls, subunits tend toward more flexible structures when they have uncertain, nonroutine, variable tasks.

Yet Perrow himself pointed out that organizations doing the same work can define the nature of it differently. Job Corps training centers for disadvantaged youths in the 1960s were first operated by personnel from the U.S. Office of Economic Opportunity, who adopted a nurturant approach to running the centers. Serious disciplinary problems led to the transfer of some of the centers to the Department of the Interior, after which they increasingly emphasized strict rules and discipline and highly structured routines and procedures. The same organization in effect altered its definitions of its task. Similarly, many organizations have purposely tried to transform routine work into more interesting, flexible work to better motivate and utilize the skills of the people doing it. The Social Security Administration changed to modular work units partly for such reasons.

Also complicating the analysis of technology, various studies have found weak relationships between structure and technology, sometimes finding that size influences structure more than technology does. Recent studies also suggest that technology shows stronger effects on structure in smaller organizations than in larger ones (Tehrani, Montanari, and Carson, 1990). Similarly, the effects of task characteristics on structure are strongest within task subunits; that is, the task of a bureau within a larger organization has a stronger relationship to the structure of that bureau than to the structure of the larger organization. Size shows stronger effects on the structure of government agencies with routine technologies than on the structure of agencies with nonroutine technologies (Beyer and Trice, 1979). In sum, size, technology, structure, and other factors have complex interrelationships.

Strategic Choice. Managers' strategic choices also determine structure. Managers may divide up an organization into divisions and departments designed to handle particular markets or products that have been chosen for strategic emphasis. The product divisions described below are one example. As described in earlier chapters, Florida's Department of Health and Human Services adopted a district structure, with district directors in charge of the department's activities in different geographic areas of the state. The aim, in part, was to create divisions that would be more responsive to the particular needs of the different regions.

Organizational Design

Work on contingency theory led to the development of literature offering guidelines for managers and others engaged in designing organizations (Galbraith, 1977, 1995; Mintzberg, 1979, 1983; Daft, 1995). Although these authors usually do not consider the distinctiveness of public organizations, many of the concepts they discuss apply in public management.

Design Strategies

Jay Galbraith (1977) proposes a set of techniques for designing and coordinating activities in organizations that is based on an information processing approach. Organizations face varying degrees of uncertainty depending on how much more information they need than they actually have. As this uncertainty increases, the organizational structure must process more information. Organizations employ a mix of alternative modes for coordinating these activities. First they use the organizational *hierarchy of authority*, in which superiors direct subordinates, answering their questions and specifying rules and procedures for managing the information processing load. As uncertainty increases, it overwhelms these approaches. The next logical strategy, then, is to set *plans and goals* and allow subordinates to pursue them with less referral up and down the hierarchy and with fewer rules. They can also narrow *spans of control* so that superiors must deal with fewer subordinates and can process more information and decisions.

Many contemporary organizations operate under such great uncertainty that these basic modes become overloaded, so they must pursue additional alternatives. First, managers can try to reduce the need for information. They can engage in *environmental management* to create more certainty through more effective competition for scarce resources, public relations, and cooperation and contracting with other organizations. They can create *slack resources* (that is, create a situation in which they have extra resources) by reducing the level of performance that they seek to attain or create *self-contained* tasks, such as profit centers or groups working independently on individual components of the work. Alternatively, managers can increase information processing capacity by investing in *vertical information systems,* such as better computerized information management systems, or by creating *lateral relations,* such as task forces or liaison personnel. Thus, managers have to adopt coordination modes in response to greater uncertainty and information processing demands.

Mintzberg's Synthesis

Mintzberg (1979) presents one of the most comprehensive reviews of the literature on structure, summarizing the set of structural alternatives that managers can pursue. He begins by setting forth his own scheme for describing the major components of organizations. Organizations have an *operating core,* including members directly involved in the organization's basic work—police officers, machine operators, teachers, claims processors, and so on. The *strategic apex* consists of the top managerial positions—the board of directors, chief executive officer, president, and president's staff. The *middle line* includes the managers who link the apex to the core through supervision and implementation—the vice-presidents down through the supervisors. Finally, two types of staff units complete the set of components. The *technostructure* consists of analysts who work on standardizing work, outputs, and skills—the policy analysts and program evaluators, strategic planners, systems engineers, and personnel training staff. The *support staff* units support the organization outside the work flow of the operating core—for example, mail room, food service, and public relations personnel.

Design Parameters. Organizations establish structures to divide and then coordinate work within and among these units through the design of four different structural categories: positions, superstructures, lateral linkages, and decision-making systems.

Design of Positions. Individual positions can be established through *job specialization, behavior formalization* (written job descriptions, written work instructions, general rules), and *training and indoctrination* (in which individuals learn the skills that they will apply using their own judgment).

Design of Superstructures. Then the different positions must be coordinated through the design of the organization's superstructure. All organizations do this in part through *unit grouping,* based on any of a number of criteria: knowledge and skill (lawyers, engineers, social workers), function (police, fire, or parks and recreation employees; military personnel), time (night shift, day shift), output (the products produced by the different divisions of a corporation), clients (inpatients or outpatients; beneficiaries of insurance policies), or place (the regional offices of business firms, the federal government, and many state agencies; precincts in a city police department).

Managers choose among these bases or some combination of them. We have little conclusive scientific guidance for those choices, but Mintzberg offers suggestions about criteria for grouping. Choices about grouping can follow *work-flow interdependencies,* where natural phases in the work require certain people to communicate closely or to be located near one another. *Process interdependencies* make it useful to group together people who perform the same type of work (attorneys, claims eligibility experts) so that they can learn from one another and share tools and materials. Because of *scale interdependencies,* certain units may become large enough to need their own functional categories—their own set of attorneys, for example. Also, *social interdependencies* may make it useful to group individuals to facilitate social relations, morale, and cohesiveness. Military units that have trained together are often kept together for these reasons.

Design of Lateral Linkages. Mintzberg suggests that coordination also requires linking operations laterally. For this purpose, organizations can use *performance-control systems, action-planning systems,* or *liaison devices.* Performance-control systems specify general results to be attained, as indications that operations are effectively coordinated. For example, as described in Chapter Thirteen, in large "service centers" operated by the Social Security Administration, employees are organized into "modules." A module is a work unit that includes all the personnel required to handle a client's application for Social Security benefits (as well as other types of services)—people who authorize the benefits, people who calculate what the benefit payment will be, file clerks, typists, and other specialists. Administrators keep track of the average time that the modules take in handling clients' requests—how many days, on average, does each module take to complete the handling of a client's application? They can compare these times across modules and to national standards. A low average time (that is, fast processing of the requests) indicates effective coordination within the module. Good average times for all the modules suggest that the service center is effectively coordinated, in that all modules are performing well. When a module falls behind the others and has backlogs of applications and slower times, however, this indicates a possible coordination problem, not just in the module but among the modules. Sometimes a module may have an overload of particularly difficult cases or some personnel problems such as high absenteeism or a lot of newer employees who need training. The slower time for the module may thus indicate that the assignments of cases and personnel are not effectively coordinated among the modules, and administrators may shift some of the caseload to other modules or transfer some personnel among modules temporarily, so as better to coordinate the work of the modules. Thus, the performance-control information provides evidence about coordination within and among units. (We should be careful to note, of course, that simple reviews of limited performance information, such as time taken to complete the processing of an application, can have serious pitfalls as an evaluation system, and managers must be sensitive to these weaknesses.)

An action-planning system, by contrast, specifies not the general result or standard but the details about actions that people and groups are to take. In the modules mentioned above, the applications from clients are placed in file folders that move from point to point in the modules as different people do their part of the work on the case. The filing clerks are trained in a system for moving and keeping track of the files so that they will not be lost—there are many thousands of them for each module—and they can be located at any given time. As the clerks move the files around the module, they log them in when they arrive at certain points, using a bar-code scanner similar to those used in supermarkets. The careful specification of the actions of the file clerks in this file-tracking system is essential to coordinating the different specialists in the module and to assessing the coordination of the work among all the modules.

Liaison devices include such arrangements as a person in a special position to serve as "ambassador" to another unit who keeps track of developments there and who facilitates communication with the other unit. Task forces or standing liaison committees can also address problems of coordination. One of the service centers used a task force to respond to a major coordination problem. The first three digits of a person's Social Security number indicate the place where that person was born or the person's location when the number was issued. In the service centers, cases are usually assigned to modules on the basis of these three first digits. That alone can create coordination problems because certain regions of the country produce more cases that are difficult to handle than other regions. Modules assigned certain geographical areas on the basis of the first three digits of the Social Security numbers may get more difficult cases than other modules. One service center considered moving to "terminal digit case allocation" among the modules—allocating cases on the basis of the last four digits of the Social Security number to achieve a fairer allocation of cases. Yet moving to this new allocation system required extensive coordination among the modules because they had to transfer all the files among themselves to redistribute them according to the new system. The director of the center appointed a task force to consider and plan the new system. The task force was highly representative, with people from all levels and many different modules and units. Empowered by the director to plan and implement the new system as they saw fit, the task force effectively managed the transition to the new system.

Designing Decision Systems Through Decentralization. Organizations can also decentralize. *Vertical decentralization* involves pushing decision-making authority down to lower levels. *Horizontal decentralization* involves spreading authority out to staff analysts or experts or across individuals involved in the work of the organization.

Types of Organizational Structures. Mintzberg also proposes a typology of five types of organizational structures, based on the employment of these design alternatives and shifts in the roles of the components described earlier. *Simple structures* are usually adopted by new, small government agencies, small corporations run by an entrepreneur, and other new, small, aggressive organizations headed by strong leaders. They tend toward vertical and horizontal centralization and coordination by means of direct supervision from a strong strategic apex. *Machine bureaucracies* include the prototypical large bureaucracies in the public and private sectors. They evolve from simple structures as growth, age, or external control leads to greater emphasis on standardizing work processes. The technostructure becomes more important as experts and staff specialists assume roles in this process. Mintzberg suggests a subcategory—*public* machine bureaucracies—consisting of government agencies that assume this form because they are required to standardize for political oversight. Alternatively, simple structures with a strong professional component (law firms, research organizations) evolve toward *professional bureaucracies,* with a profession that dominates their operating cores, coordination primarily through standardization of skills (through professional training) rather than standardization of tasks, and general decentralization. Machine bureaucracies may further evolve into *divisionalized forms* as further growth leads to economies of scale for product-oriented subunits. It becomes more cost-effective to break the organization up into product divisions with their own versions of the various functional components—for example, their own manufacturing and marketing divisions. Mintzberg (1989) observes that public machine bureaucracies cannot do this. Without profit and sales measures by which their general performance can be monitored, and because they operate under more intensive, political oversight, public machine bureaucracies face more constraints than their private counterparts on their ability to decentralize to relatively autonomous divisions. Finally, an *adhocracy,* such as NASA or an innovation-oriented firm, has a very organic structure, with great emphasis on fluid communication and flexibility, largely through decentralization to project teams.

Major Design Alternatives:
Functional, Product, Hybrid, and Matrix Structures

Management writers also contrast the pros and cons of the major design alternatives from which organizations choose (Davis and Lawrence, 1977; Daft, 1995). *Functional* structures, the classical prototype, organize according to major functions—marketing and sales, manufacturing, finance, R&D. The advantages include economies of scale within the functional units (all the attorneys in the legal department can use the same law library; the manufacturing personnel share plants and machinery). Departments concentrate on their functions and enhance their specialized skills. Yet this may weaken coordination with other functions to ensure overall product quality or the implementation of needed changes.

As organizations grow, producing more diverse products and competing in more diverse, rapidly changing markets, the functional structure proves too slow in responding to changes and too hierarchical to allow rapid coordination across functional divisions. Large corporations, such as the major automobile manufacturers, thus adopt *product* structures, with separate divisions responsible for their own product line. Each division possesses its own units to perform major functions such as sales and manufacturing (for example, the Oldsmobile, Chevrolet, and Buick divisions of General Motors). This sacrifices some of the advantages of the functional form, but it provides for more rapid responses to environmental changes (in product technology, customer demands, competitors) and greater concentration on the quality of the products rather than on individual functions. In fact, many corporations actually employ *hybrid* structures, with major product divisions (for example, chemicals, fuels, lubricants; see Daft, 1995) but also some major functional units (finance, human resources).

Some firms have developed a *matrix* structure in response to demands for both high-quality products in highly technical areas (product emphasis) and rapid and reliable production (functional emphasis). Military weapons manufacturers, for example, face pressure to produce highly technical weapons systems according to demanding standards and to do so within sharp time constraints. Matrix structures purposely violate the classic prescriptions for "one master" and clear chains of authority. High-level managers share authority over the same activities, with some exercising functional authority (vice-presidents for product development, manufacturing, marketing, procurement) and others having responsibility for the particular products or projects that cross all those functions. Thus, one manager may have responsibility for pushing the completion of a particular aircraft project, while others share responsibility for the particular functions involved in getting the craft built. The authority of the product executives crosses all the functions, while the functional executives have authority over their functions across all the products. Diagrammed, this appears as a matrix of two sets of executives with crosshatched lines of authority. This offers the advantage of the ability to rapidly share or shift personnel or other resources across product lines and to coordinate the organization's response to dual pressures from the environment. It requires a heavy investment in coordination, liaison activities, and conflict resolution, however. Successful matrix designs often require a good deal of training and good interpersonal skills on the part of managers, because they typically produce high levels of stress and conflict that must be resolved.

Some structures in the public sector have been equated with matrix structures. Simon (1983) describes the use of a matrix management arrangement at the U.S. Consumer Product Safety Commission. The commission had been organized into functional bureaus, including as the Bureau of Engineering, Bureau of Economics, Bureau of Biomedical Science, and so on. Each bureau had partial responsibility for developing regulations issued by the commission, but none had overall responsibility. The matrix arrangement involved establishing six functional directorates and the Office of Program Management. The Office of Program Management had a program manager for each of a set of new product-oriented programs, including a chemical products program, an electrical products program, and a children's products program. These program managers chaired program teams made up of representatives from the various functional directorates. The teams managed the overall development of regulations for the products their programs were responsible for and coordinated the work of the functional directorates pertaining to those programs. The commission's executives felt that the matrix arrangement improved productivity, morale, effective use of resources, communication, and accountability. It also increased stress and turf battles and evoked some resistance, as matrix arrangements usually do.

The executive director of the commission observed that public managers face particular challenges in adopting matrix designs. He felt that private executives have more authority over rewards and have profit targets to use as incentives for cooperation. Public executives can impose fewer sanctions and have weaker authority to reassign those who resist a new design. Here again we see that a design developed in industry has potential value in government but requires skillful implementation within the constraints imposed by the public sector. Swiss (1991) provides further examples of the use of matrix organization in city governments.

Actually, structures in industrial organizations show a great deal of variation, and managers apply heavy doses of pragmatism in working them out (Webber, 1979). Some large corporations, for example, appoint staff vice-presidents to act as the eyes and ears of the presidents of their various divisions. Complexity and even conflict are built into many contemporary corporate structures. Management experts currently propose that many organizations should adopt highly adaptive, permeable, fluid, loosely arranged structures (Peters, 1988).

The function-versus-product distinction is not always clear in government. For example, do the military, police, firefighters, public works programs, youth services, elderly services, and family services provide functions or products? Generally, however, government agencies have tended to adhere to the functional form (Golembiewski, 1987). Before its reorganization, the Social Security Administration, for example, had a typical organization-by-function structure—claims intake, claims adjudication, claims disbursement. Demands for accountability, absence of profits and sales measures, and public officials' adherence to the old principles of administration (clear chains of command, unity of command, and so on) drive this functional emphasis (Warwick, 1975; Golembiewski, 1987, 1995; Mintzberg, 1989). Golembiewski calls for more efforts to organize around *purpose* in public organizations, through such designs as variants of the matrix form. For example, the Florida Department of Health and Rehabilitative Services established district directors who shared authority over programs in their districts with program officials in the central headquarters. In addition, functions can be organized around a purpose, such as service to clients as individuals. The Social Security Administration's reorganization brought the agency's functions together within individual modular units, so that each unit could process a client's claim from beginning to end. The Florida Department of Health and Rehabilitative Services set up service units with representatives of each of the agency's programs—youth services, family counseling, drug treatment programs—in the same location. Developing and assessing such alternatives remain challenges for public managers and researchers.

Organizational Structures in Public Organizations

The question of alternative designs for public organizations brings us back to whether public organizations have distinctive structures. As mentioned earlier, some academic theories and observations suggest that they are inherently different from private organizations, since governmental oversight and the absence of performance indicators such as sales and profits cause them to emphasize rules and hierarchy. If true, this suggests that public organizations cannot adopt some structural forms, such as decentralized and flexible designs, or that they can do so only with great difficulty. On the other hand, many organization theorists regard public sector status as unimportant (in part because their research has often found little evidence that public organizations have distinctive structures). Pugh, Hickson, and Hinings (1969), for example, predicted that government organizations in their sample would show higher levels of formalization (they used a measure called "structuring of activities") but found that they did not. Over the years, additional studies concurred. Buchanan (1975) also sought to test the proverbial red-tape differences by comparing federal managers to business managers on a "structure salience" scale. Unexpectedly, the public managers perceived a *lower* level of salience assigned to structure in their organizations. Bozeman and Loveless (1987) found that public sector R&D units differed only slightly from private sector R&D units in the amount of red tape with which they had to contend.

Yet other evidence suggests that public organizations do differ. Although Pugh, Hickson, and Hinings (1969) did not find greater "structuring of activities" in government organizations, those organizations had more concentration of authority at the top of or outside the organization, especially concerning personnel procedures. The researchers concluded that an organization's size and technological development act as the main determinants of how it structures its activities but that government ownership exerts an influence independent of size and technology, causing this concentration of authority in public organizations at the top or with external authorities. The study included only eight public organizations, all local government units with tasks similar to those of many business firms, including a local water department and a manufacturing unit of a government agency. This might explain why they did not show as much bureaucratic structuring as anticipated. It also indicates, however, the effects of government ownership even on organizations that are much like business firms. A public manager would probably comment that the researchers simply observed the effects of civil service systems.

Mintzberg (1979) cited this evidence from Pugh, Hickson, and Hinings when he designated public machine bureaucracies as a subtype within the machine bureaucracy category in his typology of structures. He argued that many public bureaucracies tend toward the machine bureaucracy form because of external governmental control. Other studies have come to similar conclusions. Warwick (1975) concluded from his case study of the U.S. State Department that public bureaucracies inherently incline toward elaborate hierarchies and rules. Meyer (1979) analyzed a national sample of state and local finance agencies and found their vertical hierarchies to be very stable over time. Political pressures forced frequent changes in their subunit composition, however, and pressures from the federal government led to formalization of their personnel systems. He concluded that public bureaucracies have no alternative to elaborate hierarchies. Their managers' political strength and skill, however, determine how well they can defend themselves from external forces that can strip away their subunits and assign them to some other organization.

Holdaway, Newberry, Hickson, and Heron (1975) found, in a study of Canadian universities, that higher degrees of government control are related to correspondingly higher levels of formalization, standardization of personnel procedures, and centralization. Chubb and Moe (1990) reported that public school employees in the United States perceive more externally imposed formal constraints on personnel procedures and school policies than do private school employees. Rainey's sample of middle managers in state agencies (1983) perceived more organizational formalization, particularly concerning going through channels and adhering to standard operating procedures, than did middle managers in business firms. This study and a number of others found that government managers report much stronger constraints on the administration of extrinsic rewards such as pay and promotion under the existing personnel rules for their organizations than do business managers. Chapters Nine and Ten cite various studies that have found this difference at all levels of government. Also indicating the effects of public sector status on personnel procedures, Tolbert and Zucker (1983) showed how federal pressures influenced the diffusion of civil service personnel systems across governments in the United States.

Studies by professional associations and government agencies, and the testimony of public managers, paint a similar picture. A National Academy of Public Administration (1986) report laments the complex web of controls and rules governing federal managers' decisions and the adverse effects of these constraints on their capacity and motivation to manage. The report complained that managers in charge of large federal programs often face irritating limits on their authority to make even minor decisions. The head of a program involving tens of millions of dollars might have to seek the approval of the General Services Administration before he or she can send an assistant to a short training program. Very large surveys of federal employees have found that a large percentage of federal managers and executives say they do not have enough authority to remove, hire, promote, and determine the pay of their employees. Large percentages also feel that federal personnel and budgeting rules create obstacles to productivity (U.S. Office of Personnel Management, 1979, 1980, 1983). Executives who have served in both business and government say similar things about the constraints on managers' authority in government positions imposed by overarching rules and oversight agencies (Allison, 1983; Blumenthal, 1983; Chase and Reveal, 1983).

These studies and reports provide increasing evidence that public sector status influences an organization's structure in a number of ways, particularly regarding rules and structural arrangements over which external oversight agencies have authority, such as personnel and purchasing procedures. Bozeman and Bretschneider (1994) provide explicit evidence of these patterns. They analyzed them in R&D laboratories based on the labs' public or private status and the amount of government funding they receive. The government labs had highly structured personnel rules. The private labs did not, even when they received high levels of government funding. They did, however, receive more contacts and communications from government officials when they received more public funding. This suggests that government funding brings with it a different pattern of governmental influence than does governmental ownership. Ownership brings with it the formal authority of oversight agencies to impose rules, usually governing personnel, purchasing, and accounting and budgeting procedures. Bretschneider (1990) provided more evidence in an analysis of decisions about computer systems in public and private organizations. Managers in the public organizations experienced longer delays in getting approval to purchase computer equipment and in the processing of those purchases. The delays apparently reflect the procurement rules imposed by central procurement agencies such as the General Services Administration. In sum, these studies provide evidence, consistent with the pattern that began to emerge with the Pugh, Hickson, and Hinings (1969) study, that government ownership often subjects organizations to central oversight rules over such matters as personnel, purchasing, and budgeting and accounting procedures.

Recent survey evidence supports this observation more strongly than ever. Rainey, Facer, and Bozeman (1995) reported results of surveys in several different states, involving all levels of government, many different organizations, and different points across a fifteen-year period, and compared the responses of public and private managers to numerous questions about constraints under personnel rules. The questions asked about whether the rules made it hard to fire a poor manager or reward a good manager with higher pay, and similar matters. The differences between the public and private managers were huge by the standards of survey research. Roughly 90 percent of the public managers agreed that their organization's personnel rules make it hard to fire poor managers and hard to reward good managers with higher pay, while 90 percent of the business managers disagreed. These differences shape the context of leadership and motivation in public organizations discussed in later chapters.

Another recent research initiative provides some of the most convincing evidence yet of distinctive structural characteristics of public organizations, because the findings are based on a large representative sample of work organizations in the United States (Kalleberg, Knoke, Marsden, and Spaeth, 1994). The researchers undertook the National Organizations Study (NOS) project in part because the samples in most studies of organizations are not large, representative ones since such samples are expensive and hard to attain. The Aston studies described in Chapters One and Two found some distinctive attributes of the public organizations in their sample. The researchers included only eight public organizations in their sample of nearly sixty organizations, however, and they expressed reservations about their findings for the public organizations. The NOS, by contrast, surveyed representatives of a carefully designed representative sample consisting of 725 work organizations. About ninety-four of these organizations were state, local, or federal government agencies. Status as a public agency turned out to be one of the strongest correlates of structural characteristics in the study.

The NOS researchers asked the respondents in the organizations they surveyed to reply to questions aimed at measuring the structural characteristics of their organizations, including decentralization and formalization (defined earlier in this chapter). Status as a public organization was among the variables most strongly related to these two structural characteristics. The public organizations tended to be less decentralized (more centralized) and more formalized (Marsden, Cook, and Kalleberg, 1994). In addition, the method of measuring formalization makes this finding consistent with the evidence mentioned above about the formalization of personnel rules and procedures in public organizations that appears to result from government civil service personnel systems. The researchers followed a procedure similar to that of the Aston studies in which they asked whether the organization had written documentation for various important organizational matters. In the NOS, almost all of the questions used to measure formalization asked about written documentation of personnel matters—documentation on fringe benefits, hiring and firing procedures, personnel evaluation, and the requirement for written job descriptions and written performance records (Marsden, Cook, and Knoke, 1994). Thus, this study of a nationally representative sample of organizations, while not intended as a study of public organizations, provides some of the most important evidence to date of the tendencies toward distinctive structural characteristics among the population of public organizations in the United States.

Researchers have also found distinctive structural characteristics of public organizations that are not tied to rules imposed by oversight agencies. Tolbert (1985) found differences in the subunit structures of public and private universities related to external influences from public and private institutions and the universities' dependence on them for resources. Crow and Bozeman (1987) and Emmert and Crow (1987, 1988) report that public R&D units differ from private units in the size and structure of the administrative component of the organization and the way the research teams were organized. The public labs actually had more team-based organization. This again emphasizes the fact that government organizations vary a great deal and by no means all follow a rigid bureaucratic pattern. In fact, these government labs appeared to respond more directly than the private labs to task contingencies of the sort discussed earlier.

The Macrostructure of Public Organizations

The evidence of the influence of government ownership on the structures of public organizations brings up another structural topic, one that needs much further attention from both researchers and managers. Structure *within* public organizations cannot easily be separated from structures *outside* the organization that are an inherent part of government. In other words, the internal structures of public agencies reflect, in part, the jurisdictional structures of the government body under which they operate. Legislatures, oversight agencies, and other governmental institutions impose systemwide rules and configurations on all the agencies within their jurisdiction (Warwick, 1975; Meyer, 1979; Hood and Dunsire, 1981).

The examples above show that external authorities often directly impose rules and structural configurations on public agencies. Managers in government point out, however, that external oversight also influences their own decisions about structure. For example, at one point in Florida, bureaus—relatively small units—proliferated rapidly within state agencies. Apparently, to escape the constraints of the state's rules regarding pay raises, managers got raises for their assistants by creating bureaus and appointing them as bureau chiefs. To curb this tendency, the Department of Administration, the agency in charge of personnel systems, adopted regulations governing when an agency could establish a new bureau. This example illustrates a constant tension in governments at all levels, between oversight and operating agencies. The former emphasize relatively uniform rules—often for good reasons, such as fairness and equal treatment (such as preventing unequal pay for the same work in different agencies). Yet this imposes on the operating agencies overarching structures that dominate their own and constrain their managers' ability to respond to their own problems.

In addition, different units of government differ in the structural arrangements of their major institutional attributes, such as their formal, constitutional powers (Abney and Lauth, 1986). In some states the governor has less formal power than in others, and the legislature has more formal authority. The governor of Florida, for example, appoints fewer of the cabinet officers of the state government than do governors in other states. Instead, some run for independent election, and consequently the agencies they head tend to have more independence from the governor than in other states. Meyer (1979) found that independently elected heads of finance agencies more effectively defend their agencies against the loss of subunits than do political appointees. At the local level, the structure of city governments determined the authority of mayors, city councils, and city managers. In strong-mayor forms, the mayor is elected by the citizens, appoints department heads, and has veto power over some of the actions of the city council. In weak-mayor forms, the mayor may appoint few department heads, have no veto power over the council, and share authority for city administration with the council. In the council-manager form, there may not even be a mayor. If there is, he or she is not elected by the people but is a member of the council, serving on a rotating basis with other council members; the city's administrative duties are largely under the authority of the city manager, who is accountable to the council.

Another important macrostructural dimension involves structural relationships between jurisdictions. Different units at the same level may engage in joint activities or agreements. For example, large federal agencies share responsibility for programs and have joint policymaking committees; the same is true of large state agencies. Local units of government now engage in elaborate partnerships with other local units through regional councils, areawide planning agencies that link a number of counties, and service agreements and contracts between local governments for provision of services such as police protection and water. In addition, special districts for services such as these, like traditional school districts, are proliferating rapidly around the country, operating within and between other jurisdictions, such as counties. The management field has no term for these structural arrangements, but we might call them *lateral interjurisdictional structures*. Similarly, the complex relationships among levels of government, well recognized under the topic *intergovernmental relations*, involve structural issues that need further development. For example, the federal government implements many programs through state and local governments. Federal rules, grants, or other funding patterns essentially pay states and localities to hire people and establish offices to run these programs under federal guidelines. Thus, the structure of many federal agencies meshes with other agencies at so-called lower levels of government. We might refer to these structural arrangements as *vertical interjurisdictional structures*.

Complications such as these have been recognized in the large body of work on intergovernmental relations, public policy implementation (for example, Lester, Bowman, Giggin, and O'Toole, 1987), and interorganizational relations (Whetten, 1987). Yet we need to know much more about how these macrostructural complexities are related to the structures of particular agencies and to many other topics in public management. Even pending that development, however, the obvious characteristics of this complex macrostructural terrain support the observation that public organizations operate within larger structures that heavily influence their own.

Summing Up the Literature on Structure

The researchers on organizational structure who reject a public-private distinction have shown us that structure is multidimensional and that both types of organization vary widely on different structural dimensions. Often these variations are related to the major contingencies of size, strategy, technology and tasks, and environmental uncertainty and complexity. Obviously, technological similarities cause government-owned electric utilities, hospitals, railroads, airlines, R&D

labs, and manufacturing units to show stronger structural similarities to private or nonprofit versions of the same types of organizations than to other types of government organizations. The same holds true for organizations or organizational units engaged in similar tasks, such as R&D labs and legal offices. Indeed, the general structure of subunits of public organizations often resembles the structure of their private sector counterparts more than they resemble that of other units in their parent organization. Also, relatively small, independent organizations usually have simpler structures (Mintzberg, 1979), so a smaller unit of government may exhibit quite a bit less red tape or hierarchical complexity than a large private firm. Obviously, government agencies respond to environmental complexities and uncertainties just as private organizations do, as is reflected in district structures. Thus we can see that it is incredibly simplistic to treat all public organizations as a uniform mass that is inherently subject to intensive red tape and bureaucracy. These researchers rightfully condemn such stereotypes.

Other research, including that on macrostructures and government environments, supports a balanced conclusion. This research suggests that public organizations generally tend toward higher levels of internal structural complexity, centralization, and formalization than do private organizations. Size, task, technology, and environmental contingencies make a difference, often figuring more importantly than public or private ownership. Within given task categories, however, public organizations tend toward more stable hierarchies and more centralized and formalized rules, especially rules pertaining to the functions governed by oversight agencies—personnel, purchasing and procurement, and budgeting and accounting. Very general measures of red tape and complexity may not reflect large differences between public and private organizations because of the multidimensionality of organizational structure. Government organizations may not have more formalized and elaborate rules than private organizations of similar size, but they often have more centralized, formalized rules for functions such as personnel and procurement. Comparisons of government and nongovernment organizations engaged in the same type of work tend to support such conclusions.

Still, wide variations are likely—R&D labs or other special units may have even more general structural flexibility under government ownership. In addition, government ownership and influence are multidimensional in that hybrid organizations such as public enterprises may be owned by government but privately funded and exempt from some central rules and controls. Privately owned organizations with extensive public funding often show heavy governmental influences on certain aspects of their structures; for example, defense contractors have small armies of government auditors on site, making sure their spending and record-keeping practices adhere to government regulations. Here again, government rules tend to follow from government ownership or funding.

Finally, researchers point out that typical government agencies that are fully owned and funded by government (as opposed to public enterprises or other hybrids), especially at the federal level, often engage primarily in administrative functions—making and enforcing regulations; administering grants, contracts, and transfer payments; and administering programs actually provided at other levels of government or in the private sector. Others point out that the absence of fairly concrete or quantifiable performance measures for many public and nonprofit activities makes government managers and officials rely more on rules as means of managing their organizations. Also, this inclines public and nonprofit organizations to adopt particular forms and structures because they represent the widely accepted way of doing the work or the way authorized by higher levels of government or professional associations. This inclination is even stronger when technologies and performance measures are vague.

All managers must deal with structural complexity and with external influences on their authority. Public managers usually face more elaborate structural arrangements and constraints, however, and must learn to work with them. Their understanding of the elaborate macrostructural patterns in government, of the structures of their own agencies, and of the origins and purposes of these arrangements can serve as a valuable component of their professional knowledge as public managers. Among other challenges, they must find ways to reward and encourage people working within these complex structures, even when the personnel rules they must follow do not readily provide much flexibility. The next chapter further considers that topic. Public managers need to understand the sources and nature of these constraints, not only so that they can adjust to them but also in consideration of the useful changes that they can hope to make. Later chapters discuss how public managers can and do make valuable changes, in part through effective knowledge of the structure of government and its agencies and in part through effective applications of the general body of knowledge on organizational structure that we have just covered.

CHAPTER NINE

UNDERSTANDING PEOPLE IN PUBLIC ORGANIZATIONS

Values and Motives

In 1990, Gary Larson's popular cartoon strip, *The Far Side,* expressed a long-standing stereotype about government employees. One Sunday morning's cartoon depicted a government employee who "made civil service history" by going to work for a couple of hours on a holiday. In an interview the next day, a manager with the U.S. Drug Enforcement Administration mentioned that the cartoon had really bothered him, since he felt that he and others in his office worked very hard. Surveys of government managers have found that the unfavorable public image of government weakens their motivation and increases their thoughts about leaving the public service (U.S. Merit Systems Protection Board, 1987; Volcker Commission, 1989; Perry and Miller, 1990). At the same time, however, some of these same managers, and other experts, have expressed concern about the challenges that public managers face in trying to motivate public employees, due to such factors as elaborate protections for employees faced with disciplinary actions. A prominent public management scholar argues that the problem of motivating employees is one of the most important issues in the field of public management (Behn, 1995).

This chapter and the next one concern the people in public organizations, emphasizing the motivation and work-related attitudes (such as job satisfaction) of public employees. This chapter defines motivation and discusses it in the context of public organizations. It then reviews concepts basic to the analysis of motivation and work attitudes, including the concepts about people's needs, values, and motives that serve as essential components of motivation theories niques. This discussion covers the values and motives that are particu portant in public organizations, such as the desire to perform a public service and values and attitudes about pay, security, work, and other matters that often distinguish public sector managers and employees from those in other settings.

The next chapter describes the major theories concerning work motivation. It also summarizes techniques that organizations use to enhance employee motivation. It then describes research on major work-related attitudes such as job satisfaction, organizational commitment, and professionalism. In covering all these topics, the discussion considers applications and examples in public organizations.

Motivation and Public Management

Human motivation is a fundamental topic in the social sciences, and people's motivation to work serves as a similarly basic topic in the field of organizational behavior (OB). The framework in Figures 1.1 and 1.2 indicates that the people in an organization, and their behaviors and attitudes, are interrelated with such factors as organizational tasks, organizational structures and processes, leadership processes, and organizational culture. These factors both influence and are influenced by the behavior and attitudes of organizational members. With all these factors impinging on people, motivating employees and stimulating effective attitudes in them become crucial and sensitive challenges for managers. This and the next chapter will show that, as with many topics in management and OB, the basic research and theory provide no conclusive "science of motivation." Leaders have to draw on the ideas and apply the available techniques pragmatically, blending their experience and judgment with the insights the literature provides.

These two chapters will show that OB researchers and management consultants often treat motivation and work attitudes as internal organizational matters, influenced by such factors as supervisory practices, pay, and the nature of the work. Such factors figure very importantly in public organizations; however, motivation in public organizations, like the other organizational attributes discussed in this book, is also greatly affected by the public sector environment. The effects of this environment require public managers to possess a distinctive knowledge of motivation that links OB with political science in ways essential to the analysis and practice of management.

The effects on people of the political and institutional environment of public organizations show up in numerous ways. As the *Far Side* cartoon suggests, beliefs and stereotypes about weak motivation on the part of government employees pervade our culture. Such opinions contributed to the budgetary impasse, described in Chapter One, that shut down large portions of the federal government, furloughed employees, and sharply complicated the work that the remaining employees had to do.

In recent decades, governments at all levels in the United States and in other nations have mounted efforts to reform civil service systems and government pay systems (Ingraham, 1993; Peters and Savoie, 1994). Typically, the reformers have sought to correct allegedly weak links between performance and pay, promotion, and discipline in government organizations, claiming that these weak links weaken motivation and hence performance and efficiency. These reforms came about not just because of public attitudes but also because government managers have for years complained about their weak authority concerning pay, promotion, and discipline (Macy, 1971; U.S. Office of Personnel Management, 1983). The reforms also reflect, then, the constraints on public managers that earlier chapters have described. The fact that such reforms have often foundered or backfired (Ingraham, 1993; Kellough and Lu, 1993; Perry, Petrakis, and Miller, 1989) raises the possibility that these constraints are inevitable in the public sector (Rainey, Facer, and Bozeman, 1995). Many analysts and experienced practitioners regard the constraining character of government personnel systems as *the* critical difference between managing in the public and private sectors (Thompson, 1989).

As with other topics in this book, however, another side argues that government differs little from business in matters of motivation. Businesses also have problems motivating managers and employees, because of union pressures, selfish and unethical behaviors, ineffective bonus and merit-pay systems, and other problems. Business managers worry over the paper work involved in firing an employee and about the potential for wrongful termination suits (Bryant, 1996). Ban (1995, p. 58) describes an amusing incident in which a government manager who had worked in a business firm shocked his peers by saying that he liked working for government because it is easier to fire incompetent employees than in a business firm. In a recent article, Herbert Simon (1995), characterized in earlier chapters as one of the most influential contributors to public administration theory and arguably the world's preeminent living behavioral scientist, proclaimed the equivalency of reward practices in public, private, and nonprofit firms: "Everything said here about economic rewards applies equally to privately owned, nonprofit, and government-owned organizations. The opportunity for, and limits on, the use of rewards to motivate activities towards organizational goals are precisely the same in all three kinds of organizations" (p. 283, note 3).

In addition, high motivation exists in many government organizations. Executives coming to government from business typically mention how impressed they are with how hard government employees work (Volcker Commission, 1989). In surveys, government managers have mentioned frustrations of the sort discussed above but have also reported high levels of work effort and satisfaction.

Specialists in public personnel administration have for a long time argued that the claim that you cannot fire a government employee is a myth and that one certainly can do so by following the proper procedures (Ban, 1995, p. 157). In sum, experts differ over the accuracy of the claim that government personnel systems constrain managers much more than those in business firms and that this leads to lower motivation among government employees.

This chapter takes the position that both sides are right, in a sense. Public managers often do face unique challenges in motivating employees, but they can also apply a great deal from the general motivation literature. (One of many examples of such an application is provided by the Federal Employee Attitude Survey, completed by about fourteen thousand federal employees in 1979 and repeated several times since. The survey had numerous questions drawn from research on the expectancy theory of work motivation, described in the next chapter, as well as many questions about other general work-related attitudes covered in the next chapter.) The challenge is to draw from the ideas and insights in the literature while taking into consideration the public sector context discussed in other chapters and basing one's conclusions on as much actual evidence as possible. The next section reviews the assertions about the public sector context discussed in earlier chapters before the discussion turns to the concept of motivation itself.

The Context of Motivation in Public Organizations

Previous chapters have presented observations and research findings that suggest a unique context for motivation in public organizations (Perry and Porter, 1982):

- The absence of economic markets for the outputs of public organizations and the consequent diffuseness of incentives and performance indicators in the public sector.
- The multiple, conflicting, and often abstract values that public organizations must pursue.
- The complex, dynamic political and public policy processes by which public organizations operate, which involve many actors, interests, and shifting agendas.
- The external oversight bodies and processes that impose structures, rules, and procedures on public organizations. These include civil service rules governing pay, promotion, and discipline and rules that affect training and personnel development.
- The external political climate, including public attitudes toward taxes, government, and government employees, which turned sharply negative during the 1970s and 1980s.

Earlier chapters have also related these conditions to various characteristics of public organizations that in turn influence motivation:

- Sharp constraints on public leaders and managers that limit their motivation and ability to develop their organization. Politically elected and appointed top executives and their appointees turn over rapidly. Institutional oversight and rules limit their authority. Lower-level public employees can develop external political alliances with interest groups and legislators, enhancing their independence.
- The relatively turbulent, sporadic decision-making processes in public organizations, which can influence managers' and employees' sense of purpose and their perception of their impact (Hickson and others, 1986).
- Relatively complex and constraining structures in many public organizations, including constraints on the administration of incentives (Rainey, Facer, and Bozeman, 1995; Thompson, 1989).
- Vague goals, both for individual jobs and for the organization; a weak sense on the part of employees of personal significance within the organization; more unstable expectations; and less cohesive collegial and work groups—all the result of the preceding factors (Buchanan, 1974, 1975; Perry and Porter, 1982). Many observers argue that people at the lower and middle levels of public organizations often become lost in the elaborate bureaucratic and public policy system. They work under elaborate rules and constraints that, paradoxically, fail to hold them highly accountable (Warwick, 1975; Barton, 1980; Lipsky, 1980; Michelson, 1980; Lynn, 1981).
- Differences in the type of people who choose to work in public management, in light of the constraints on pay and performance in public service. These differences often include higher levels of public service motivation (Crewson, 1995b; Perry and Wise, 1990).

Some of these observations are difficult to prove or disprove. For others we have increased evidence, which later sections and the next chapter will present. As we examine this evidence, it is important to examine how organizational researchers have treated the concept of motivation and its measurement.

The Concept of Work Motivation

A substantial body of theory, research, and experience provides a wealth of insight into motivation in organizations (Rainey, 1993b). Yet in scrutinizing the topic, scholars have shown its complexity more and more. Everyone has a sense of what we mean by *motivation*. The term derives from the Latin word for *move*, as do the words *motor* and *motif.* We know that forces move us, arouse us, direct us. Work motivation refers to a person's desire to work hard and work well—to the arousal, direction, and persistence of effort in work settings. Managers in public, private, and nonprofit organizations use motivational techniques all the time. Yet debates about motivation have raged for years, because the simple definition just given leaves many questions about what it means to work hard and well, how one measures such behavior, and what determines a person's desire to do so.

Measuring and Assessing Motivation

Motivation researchers have struggled with different ways of measuring motivation, none of which provides an adequately comprehensive measurement. For example, the typical definition of motivation such as the one above—the willingness and tendency to exert effort toward successful work performance—raises complications about what we actually mean by motivation. Is it an attitude or a behavior, or both? Must we observe a person exerting effort? Does it suffice to have the person tell us that she or he is working hard or trying as hard as possible?

As Table 9.1 shows, researchers have tried to measure motivation in different ways that imply different answers to these questions. Some researchers have asked about behavior and attitudes (Entries 1 through 4 in Table 9.1). At least one study (Guion and Landy, 1972) has tried to develop measures based on observations by a person's co-workers. As the set of examples in the table implies, OB researchers have attempted very few measures of general work motivation. One of the few available general measures—Entry 1 in Table 9.1—relies on questions about how hard one works and how often one does some extra work. Researchers have reported successful use of this scale (Cook, Hepworth, Wall, and Warr, 1981). One study using this measure, however, found that respondents gave very high ratings to their own work effort. Most reported that they work harder than others in their organization. They gave such high self-ratings that there was little difference among them (Rainey, 1983).

This example illustrates the problems of asking people about their motivation. It also reflects the cultural emphasis on hard work in the United States that leads people to report that they do work hard. Many people apparently want to think that they work hard and feel that they do. Yet what does it mean to work hard and exert effort? What standard applies? And if, as in the study cited earlier, most respondents report that they work harder than their colleagues, there must be organizations in which everyone works harder than everyone else! Obviously, motivation is hard to measure with simple questionnaires.

Partly due to such problems with general measures of motivation, researchers have used various alternative, more specific measures, such as job involvement and intrinsic or internal work motivation (Entries 2 and 3 in Table 9.1; see also Cook,

TABLE 9.1. QUESTIONNAIRE ITEMS USED TO MEASURE WORK MOTIVATION OR CLOSELY RELATED CONCEPTS.

1. *Job Motivation Scale* (Patchen, Pelz, and Allen, 1965)

   This questionnaire, one of the few direct measures of job motivation, poses the following questions:

   On most days on your job, how often does time seem to drag for you?

   Some people are completely involved in their job—they are absorbed in it night and day. For other people their job is simply one of several interests. How involved do you feel in your job?

   How often do you do some extra work for your job which isn't really required of you?

   Would you say that you work harder, less hard, or about the same as other people doing your type of work at (name of organization)?

2. *Job Involvement Scale* (Lodahl and Kejner, 1965)

   Job involvement concerns the extent to which an employee considers his or her work important and absorbing. Lodahl and Kejner's scale includes items such as the following:

   The major satisfaction in my life comes from my job.

   The most important things that happen to me involve my work.

   I'm really a perfectionist about my work.

   I live, eat, and breathe my job.

   I am very much involved personally in my work.

   Most things in life are more important than work.

3. *Intrinsic Motivation Scale* (Lawler and Hall, 1970)

   Intrinsic motivation refers to the motivating effects of the work itself. Researchers have measured it with items such as these:

   When I do my work well, it gives me a feeling of accomplishment.

   When I perform my job well, it contributes to my personal growth and development.

   I feel a great sense of personal satisfaction when I do my job well.

   Doing my job well increases my self-esteem.

4. *Reward Expectancies* (Rainey, 1983)

   Some surveys, such as the Federal Employee Attitude Survey, use questions about reward expectations, such as those following, to assess reward systems but also as indicators of motivation:

   Producing a high quality of work increases my chances for higher pay.

   Producing a high quality of work increases my chances for a promotion.

5. *Peer Evaluations of an Individual's Work Motivation*
   (Guion and Landy, 1972; Landy and Guion, 1970)

   For this method of measuring motivation, fellow employees evaluate an individual's work motivation on the following dimensions:

   Team attitude

   Task concentration

   Independence/self-starter

   Organizational identification

   Job curiosity

   Persistence

   Professional identification

Hepworth, Wall, and Warr, 1981). Researchers in organizational behavior define intrinsic work motives or rewards as those that are mediated within the worker—psychic rewards derived directly from the work itself. Extrinsic rewards are externally mediated and are exemplified by salary, promotion, and other rewards that come from the organization or work group. As the examples in Table 9.1 indicate, questions on intrinsic motivation ask about an increase in feelings of accomplishment, growth, and self-esteem through work well done. Measures such as these assess important work-related attitudes, but they do not ask directly about work effort or direction. They implicitly assume that if one feels this way at work, one must be motivated to exert effort.

Researchers and consultants sometimes use items derived from expectancy theory (to be described shortly) as proxy measures of work motivation. Such items (see Entry 4 in Table 9.1) have been widely used by consultants in assessing organizations and in huge surveys of federal employees used to assess the civil service system and efforts to reform it (U.S. Office of Personnel Management, 1979, 1980, 1983). Surveys have also found sharp differences between government and business managers on questions such as these (Rainey, 1983; Rainey, Facer, and Bozeman, 1995). This research has also shown, however, that worker expectations concerning rewards are not strongly related to self-reported motivation on general measures such as the Patchen, Pelz, and Allen scale. They are very useful questions, but they do not serve as good indicators of general motivation. The effort to use such scales as indicators of motivation implicitly acknowledges the limitations of asking people to report their level of motivation and effort.

If one cannot ask people directly about their motivation, one can ask those around them for their observations about their co workers' motivation (see Entry 5 in Table 9.1). Landy and Guion had peers rate individual managers on the dimensions listed in the table. Significantly, their research indicated that peer observers disagree a lot when rating the same person. This method obviously requires a lot of time and resources to administer, and few other researchers have used this very interesting approach. The method does provide a useful illustration of the many possible dimensions of motivation.

As an additional example of the different outcomes or directions that can motivate employees, one of the classic distinctions in the theory of management and organizations concerns the difference between motivation to join an organization and stay in it, on the one hand, and motivation to work hard and do well within it, on the other. These two motivations have related, but fairly distinct, determinants. Chester Barnard (1938), and later James March and Herbert Simon (1958), in books widely acknowledged as the most prominent contributions to the field, analyzed this distinction. You might get people to shuffle into work every day, rather than quitting, but they can display keen ingenuity at avoiding doing what you ask them to do if they do not want to do it. Currently, management experts widely acknowledge Barnard's prescience in seeking to analyze the ways in which organizational leaders must employ a variety of incentives, including the guiding values of the organization, to induce cooperation and effort (Williamson, 1990; Peters and Waterman, 1982; DiIulio, 1994).

Rival Influences on Performance

Motivation alone does not determine performance. Ability figures importantly in performance. One person may display high motivation but insufficient ability, while another may have such immense ability that he or she performs well with little apparent motivation. The person's training and preparation for a certain task, the behaviors of leaders or co-workers, and many other factors interact with motivation in determining performance. A person may gain motivation by feeling able to perform well or lose motivation through the frustrations brought on by lacking sufficient ability. Alternatively, a worker may lose motivation to perform a task he or she has completely mastered, as it fails to provide a challenge or a sense of growth. As we will see, the major theories of employee motivation try in various ways to capture some of these intricacies. The points may sound obvious enough, but major reforms of the civil service and of government pay systems have frequently oversimplified or underestimated these concepts (Ingraham, 1993; Perry, Petrakis, and Miller, 1989).

Motivation as an Umbrella Concept

The complexities of work motivation have given the topic the status of an umbrella concept that refers to a general area of study rather than a precisely defined research target (Campbell and Pritchard, 1983). Considerable research and theorizing about motivation continue, but they usually employ the term to refer to a general concept that incorporates many variables and issues (for example, see Klein, 1989; Klein, 1990; Kleinbeck, Quast, Thierry, and Harmut, 1990). Locke and Latham (1990a), for example, present a model of work motivation that does not include a concept specifically labeled "motivation." Motivation currently appears to serve as an overarching theme for research on a variety of related topics, including organization identification and commitment, leadership practices, job involvement, organizational climate and culture, and characteristics of work goals.

Needs, Values, Motives, and Incentives

An important dimension of motivation is the internal and external impetuses that arouse and direct effort—what needs, motives, and values push us and what incentives, goals, and objectives pull us. Every theory of work motivation discussed in Chapter Ten refers to these factors in some way. Classic debates have raged, however, over what to call them, what the proper set includes, and what roles they play.

These debates, like the problems involved in defining and measuring motivation, raise serious challenges for both managers and researchers. If anything, the concepts of values, motives, and incentives have become even more prominent in management in recent years. Studies of leadership, change, and organizational culture—topics covered in later chapters—have increasingly emphasized the importance of "shared values" in organizations (Huber and Glick, 1993). DiIulio (1994) shows how particularly important this can be in public organizations by describing how members of the Bureau of Prisons display a very strong commitment to the organization's values and mission in part because some of the bureau's long-term leaders have very effectively promoted those values. But since this topic is so important, it raises the question of how managers (and scholars) can deal with all the complications involved in defining and understanding motivation, values, motives, and related concepts. This chapter approaches the problem by reviewing many of the efforts to specify and define important needs, values, motives, and incentives. This review provides a complex array of approaches to the problem, but it gives a lot of examples and suggestions from which managers can draw.

Motivation theorists use the terms we have been using, such as *need, value, motive, incentive, objective,* and *goal,* in overlapping ways. We can, however, suggest definitions for them. A *need* is a resource or condition required for the well-being of an individual. A *motive* is a force acting within an individual that causes him or her to seek to obtain or avoid some external object or condition. An *incentive* is an external object or condition that evokes behaviors aimed at attaining or avoiding it. A *goal* is a future state that one strives to achieve, and an *objective* is a more specific, short-term goal, a step toward a more general, long-term goal. Rokeach (1973), an authority on human values, defines a *value* as "an enduring belief that a specific mode of conduct or end-state of existence is personally or socially preferable to an opposite or converse mode of conduct or end-state of existence" (p. 5).

Many people would disagree with these definitions and switch some of them around. The challenge for public managers, however, is to develop a sense of the range of values, motives, incentives, and goals that influence employees, even in view of all the quandaries that researchers raise. The research on motivation tells us to expect no simple list, since goals, needs, values, and motives always occur in complex sets and interrelationships. They are linked—one value takes on importance as a means to achieving another, more general or more important one. They are also grouped into sets, with workers pursuing all the members of a set simultaneously.

Attempts to Specify Needs, Values, and Incentives

Tables 9.2 and 9.3 present some of the prominent lists and typologies from the research on needs, motives, values, and incentives. These lists illustrate the diversity among theorists and provide some of the most useful enumerations of these topics ever developed.

Murray's typology of human needs, for example, provides one of the more elaborate inventories of needs ever attempted, but it still fails to exhaust all possible ways of expressing human needs and motives.

Maslow's needs hierarchy, one of the most prominent theories of human needs, has significantly influenced the field of management. As noted in Chapter Two, Maslow proposed five categories of needs, arranged in a "hierarchy of prepotency" from the most basic *physiological needs* up through *safety needs, social needs,* and *self-esteem needs* to the loftiest *self-actualization needs.*

Researchers trying to determine whether individuals rank their needs as the theory predicts have found that Maslow's five-level hierarchy does not hold. Instead, the evidence points to a two-step hierarchy: lower-level employees show more concern with material and security rewards, while higher-level employees place more emphasis on achievement and challenge (Pinder, 1984). Analyzing results of the 1979 Federal Employee Attitude Survey, Crewson (1995b) found this kind of difference between the employees at lower GS (salary grade) levels (GS 1–8) and the highest GS levels (GS 16 and above). He also found that executive-level employees gave a higher rating to the importance of public service and to having an impact on public affairs. This suggests that the self-actualizing motives among public sector executives focus on public service, a point the discussion returns to below.

Alderfer's typology of existence, relatedness, and growth (ERG) needs (1972) provides still another example of an effort to specify basic human needs. It comes closer to the smaller set of categories (that is, smaller than the five categories suggested by Maslow) supported by research in organizations.

As Crewson's analysis shows, this distinction between higher- and lower-order motives holds in public organizations. Surveys have shown that lower-level public employees attach more importance to job security and benefits, but public managers and executives say that they consider these factors less important than accomplishment and challenging work. Managers coming into government often say that they are attracted by the opportunity to provide a public service and to influence significant events. At the same time, as described below, prominent motivation theorists argue that employees at all levels can be motivated by higher-order motives and should be treated accordingly. Chapter Thirteen describes how that philosophy played a role in the reorganization of the Social Security Administration.

TABLE 9.2. THE COMPLEXITY OF HUMAN NEEDS AND VALUES.

Murray's List of Basic Needs (1938)	Maslow's Need Hierarchy (1954)	Alderfer's ERG Model (1972)	Rokeach's Value Survey (1973)	
			Terminal Values	Instrumental Values
Abasement	Self-actualization needs	Growth needs	A comfortable (prosperous) life	Ambitious (hard-working, aspiring)
Achievement	Esteem needs	Relatedness needs	An exciting (stimulating, active) life	Broad-minded (open-minded)
Affiliation	Belongingness/social needs	Existence needs	A sense of accomplishment (lasting contribution)	Capable (competent, effective)
Aggression	Safety needs		A world at peace (free of war and conflict)	Cheerful (lighthearted, joyful)
Autonomy	Physiological needs		A world of beauty (of nature and the arts)	Clean (neat, tidy)
Counteraction			Equality (brotherhood, equal opportunity for all)	Courageous (standing up for one's beliefs)
Defendance			Family security (taking care of loved ones)	Forgiving (willing to pardon others)
Deference			Freedom (independence, free choice)	Helpful (working for the welfare of others)
Dominance			Happiness (contentedness)	Honest (sincere, truthful)
Exhibition			Inner harmony (freedom from inner conflict)	Imaginative (daring, creative)
Harm avoidance			Mature love (sexual and spiritual intimacy)	Independent (self-reliant, self-sufficient)
Nurturance			National security (protection from attack)	Intellectual (intelligent, reflective)
Order			Pleasure (an enjoyable, leisurely life)	Logical (consistent, rational)
Play			Salvation (eternal life)	Loving (affectionate, tender)
Rejection			Self-respect (self-esteem)	Obedient (dutiful, respectful)
Sentience			Social recognition (respect, admiration)	Polite (courteous, well-mannered)
Sex			True friendship (close companionship)	Responsible (dependable, reliable)
Succorance			Wisdom (a mature understanding of life)	Self-controlled (restrained, self-disciplined)
Understanding				

TABLE 9.3. TYPES OF INCENTIVES.

Incentive Type	Definitions and Examples
Barnard (1938)	
Specific incentives	Incentives "specifically offered to an individual"
Material inducements	Money, things, physical conditions
Personal, nonmaterialistic inducements	Distinction, prestige, personal power, dominating position
Desirable physical conditions of work	
Ideal benefactions	"Satisfaction of ideals about nonmaterial, future or altruistic relations" (pride of workmanship, sense of adequacy, altruistic service for family or others, loyalty to organization, esthetic and religious feeling, satisfaction of hate and revenge)
General incentives	Incentives that "cannot be specifically offered to an individual"
Associational attractiveness	Social compatibility, freedom from hostility due to racial, religious differences
Customary working conditions	Conformity to habitual practices, avoidance of strange methods and conditions
Opportunity for feeling of enlarged participation in course of events	Association with large, useful, effective organization
Condition of communion	Personal comfort in social relations
Simon (1948)	
Incentives for employee participation	Salary or wage, status and prestige, relations with working group, promotion opportunities
Incentives for elites or controlling groups	Prestige and power
Clark and Wilson (1961) and Wilson (1973)	
Material incentives	Tangible rewards that can be easily priced (wages and salaries, fringe benefits, tax reductions, changes in tariff levels, improvement in property values, discounts, services, gifts)
Solidary incentives	Intangible incentives without monetary value and not easily translated into one, deriving primarily from the act of associating
Specific solidary incentives	Incentives that can be given to or withheld from a specific individual (offices, honors, deference)
Collective solidary incentives	Rewards created by act of associating and enjoyed by all members if enjoyed at all (fun, conviviality, sense of membership or exclusive-collective status or esteem)

TABLE 9.3. TYPES OF INCENTIVES, cont'd.

Incentive Type	Definitions and Examples
Purposive incentives	Intangible rewards that derive from satisfaction of contributing to worthwhile cause (enactment of a law, elimination of government corruption)
Downs (1967)	
General "motives or goals" of officials	Power (within or outside bureau), money income, prestige, convenience, security, personal loyalty to work group or organization, desire to serve public interest, commitment to a specific program of action
Niskanen (1971)	
Variables that may enter the bureaucrat's utility function	Salary, perquisites of the office, public reputation, power, patronage, output of the bureau, ease of making changes, ease of managing the bureau, increased budget
Lawler (1971)	
Extrinsic rewards	Rewards extrinsic to the individual, part of the job situation, given by others
Intrinsic rewards	Rewards intrinsic to the individual and stemming directly from job performance itself, which satisfy higher-order needs such as self-esteem and self-actualization (feelings of accomplishment and of using and developing one's skills and abilities)
Herzberg, Mausner, Peterson, and Capwell (1957)	
Job "factors" or aspects. Rated in importance by large sample of employees.	In order of average rated importance: security, interest, opportunity for advancement, company and management, intrinsic aspects of job, wages, supervision, social aspects, working conditions, communication, hours, ease, benefits
Locke (1969)	
External incentive	An event or object external to the individual which can incite action (money, knowledge of score, time limits, participation, competition, praise and reproof, verbal reinforcement, instructions)

Another application of Maslow's theory in public organizations is the use of measures of need satisfaction based on Maslow's hierarchy. As described in Chapter Ten, one study comparing public and private managers found that public managers were somewhat less satisfied in many of the need categories.

Human values are also basic components of motivation. Rokeach (1973) developed two corresponding lists of values—instrumental values and terminal values (see Table 9.2)—and designed questionnaires to assess people's commitment to them. Sikula (1973a) compared government and business executives using the Rokeach instrument, compiling responses from managers in twelve occupational groups. Six of the groups consisted of managers from industry, education, and government, including fifty-four executives in the U.S. Department of Health, Education and Welfare (HEW). The value profile of the HEW executives was similar to that of the other managerial groups; they all placed a higher priority on values related to competence (being wise, logical, and intellectual) and initiative (imagination, courage, sense of accomplishment) than did the other groups. Among all the groups, the government executives placed the highest priority on being responsible, honest, helpful, and capable. They rated higher than any other group on the terminal values of equality, mature love, and self-respect but lower than the other groups on the terminal values of happiness, pleasure, and a comfortable life. Sikula's limited sample leaves questions about whether the findings apply to all public managers. Yet, the emphasis on service (helpfulness) and integrity and the deemphasis on comfort and pleasure conform with other findings about public managers.

Incentives in Organizations

Other researchers have analyzed incentives in organizations. As described in Chapter Two, some very prominent theories about organizations have depicted them as economies of incentives. Organizational leaders must constantly maintain a flow of resources into their organization to cover the incentives that must be paid out to induce people to contribute to the organization (Barnard, 1938; Simon, 1948; March and Simon, 1958). In analyzing these processes, these theorists developed the typologies of incentives outlined in Table 9.3, which provides about as thorough an inventory as anyone has produced (although Barnard used some very awkward terms). The typologies reflect the development, earlier in the century, of an increasing emphasis in management theory on incentives besides material ones, such as personal growth and interest and pride in one's work and one's organization. Barnard, March, and Simon, of course, implied that all executives, in both public and private organizations, face these challenges of attaining resources and providing incentives.

Clark and Wilson (1961) and Wilson (1973) followed this lead in developing a typology of organizations based on the primary incentive offered to participants—material, solidary (defined as "involving community responsibilities or interests"), or purposive (see Table 9.3). Differences in primary incentives force differences in leadership behaviors and organizational processes. Leaders in solidary organizations, such as voluntary service associations, face more pressure to develop prestige and worthy service projects to induce volunteers to participate. Leaders in purposive organizations, such as reform and social protest organizations, must show accomplishments in relation to the organization's goals, such as passage of reform legislation. Subsequent research on this typology has concentrated on why people join political parties and groups; it has not specifically addressed public agencies. The concept of purposive incentives has great relevance for government, however.

For many public managers, a sense of valuable social purpose can serve as a source of motivation (although in many agencies, they appear to face impediments in fulfilling this motive). In the survey of the U.S. Merit Systems Protection Board (1987), only 20 to 40 percent of the respondents from most federal agencies agreed that "opportunity to have an impact on public affairs" provides a good reason to stay in government service. In the Environmental Protection Agency, however, more than 65 percent of the employees identified this as a reason to stay.

Extrinsic and Intrinsic Incentives. The distinction between extrinsic and intrinsic incentives described in Table 9.3 figures importantly in current research on motivation in organizations. Since the days of Frederick Taylor's pay-them-by-the-shovelful approach to rewarding workers (see Chapter Two), management experts have increasingly emphasized the importance of intrinsic incentives in work.

The "Most Important" Incentives. The variety of incentives in Table 9.3 shows why we can expect no conclusive rank-ordered list of the most important needs, values, and incentives of organizational members. There are too many ways of expressing the incentives, and employees' preferences vary according to many factors, such as age, occupation, and organizational level. Herzberg, Mausner, Peterson, and Capwell (1957) compiled the rankings shown in Table 9.3 from sixteen studies covering eleven thousand employees. Other studies have come to different conclusions, however. Lawler (1971), for example, disagrees with the Herzberg ranking, indicating that a wider review of research suggests that people rate pay much higher (averaging about third in importance in most studies). He argues that management scholars often underestimated the importance of pay because they objected to managerial approaches that rely excessively on pay as a motivator. He points out that pay often serves as a proxy for other incentives, because it can indicate successful achievement, recognition by one's organization, and other valued outcomes. Pay can serve as a very effective motivating incentive in organizations, if pay systems are designed strategically (Lawler, 1990).

Motives and Incentives in Public Organizations. In spite of these complications, there are some useful theories and research about the importance of certain motives and incentives in public organizations. Downs and Niskanen, two economists who developed theories about public bureaucracies, proposed the inventories of public managers' motives described in Table 9.3. They make the point that for public managers, political power, serving the public interest, and serving a particular government bureau or program become important potential motives. Downs (1967) developed a typology of public administrators on the basis of such motives. Some administrators, he argued, pursue their own self-interest. Some of these people are *climbers,* who seek to rise to higher, more influential positions. *Conservers* seek to defend their current positions and resources. Other administrative officials have mixed motives, combining a concern with their own self-interest with concerns for larger values, such as public policies and the public interest. They fall into three groups of managers who pursue increasingly broader conceptions of the public interest. *Zealots* seek to advance a specific policy or program. *Advocates* promote and defend an agency or a more comprehensive policy domain. *Statesmen* [*sic*] pursue a more general public interest. As public agencies grow larger and older, they fill up with conservers and become rigid (since the climbers and zealots leave for other opportunities or turn into conservers). Among the mixed-motive officials, few can maintain the role of statesmen, and most become advocates. In the absence of economic markets for outputs, the administrators must obtain resources through budget allocation, and they have to develop constituencies and political supports for their agency. This pushes them toward the advocate role and discourages statesmanship.

Downs's book (1967) is almost certainly the most widely cited work ever written on government bureaucracy, but researchers have never really tested his theory in empirical studies. Its accuracy remains uncertain, then, but it does make the important point that public managers' commitments to their agencies, programs, and the public interest become important motives for them. They also face difficult decisions about the relative importance of these motives and the relationships between them.

Niskanen (1971) was also interested in how bureaucrats "maximize utility," as economists put it. He theorized that, in the absence of economic markets, bureaucrats pursuing any of the incentives listed in Table 9.3 do so by trying to obtain larger budgets. Even those motivated primarily by public service and altruism have the incentive to ask for more staff and resources and hence larger budgets.

Government bureaucracies therefore tend to grow inefficiently. Although this theory, too, has received scant empirical testing, public managers clearly do defend their budgets and usually try to increase them. Yet many exceptions occur, in which agency budgets increase because of legislative adjustments to formulas and entitlements that agency administrators have not requested. Some agencies also initiate their own cuts in funding or personnel or accept such reductions fairly readily (Rubin, 1985). In 1986, the Social Security Administration launched a project to reduce its work force by seventeen thousand, about 21 percent of its staff (U.S. General Accounting Office, 1986). For reasons such as this, apparently, Niskanen's more recent work focuses on discretionary budgets—those parts of the organizational budget over which administrators have some discretion. An increasing body of research disputes many of Niskanen's basic assumptions about the motives and capacities of bureaucrats to engage in budget maximizing (Bendor and Moe, 1985; Blais and Dion, 1991).

Both of these theories reflect the tendency of some economists to argue that public bureaucracies incline toward dysfunctioning because of the absence of economic markets for their outputs. These theories may accurately depict problems to which public organizations are prone. Later chapters discuss the ongoing controversy over the performance of public organizations and point out that in fact they often perform very well.

Attitudes Toward Money, Security and Benefits, and Challenging Work. Government does not offer the large financial gains that some people make in business, although civil service systems have traditionally offered job security and well-developed benefit programs. One might expect these differences to be reflected in public employees' attitudes about such incentives. We have increasing evidence that they do, although with many complications. Numerous surveys have found that government employees place less value on money as an ultimate goal in work and in life than do employees in business (Khojasteh, 1993; Kilpatrick, Cummings, and Jennings, 1964; Lawler, 1971; Rawls, Ullrich, and Nelson, 1975; Rainey, 1983; Siegel, 1983; Wittmer, 1991). Yet such attitudes vary by time period, organizational level, geographical area, occupation, and type of agency. Below the highest levels of organizations, pay levels are often fairly comparable in the public and private sectors. A federal study in 1989 found that federal white-collar salaries were about 22 percent lower than private sector salaries for similar jobs (U.S. General Accounting Office, 1990). The federal government and many state and local governments conduct pay-comparability studies, however, and try to keep their pay levels competitive with those of the private sector.

Analyzing the comparability of pay between the two sectors can be complicated. Gold and Ritchie (1993), for example, point out that average salaries for state and local government employees tend to be higher than average salaries for private sector employees in the same state. Yet public sector workers with higher skill levels and those at higher levels make less than comparable private sector employees. These differences are due to a different skill mix in the two sectors. The private sector has a higher proportion of blue-collar workers, and the public sector has a higher proportion of technical and professional workers, who tend to get higher pay than blue-collar workers. So, the higher average in the public sector is apparently due to the employment of a larger proportion of higher-paid technical and professional employees, although these same employees may make less than comparable employees in the private sector (Gold and Ritchie, 1993).

As this suggests, at the highest executive levels and for professions such as law and medicine, the private sector offers vastly higher financial rewards, and the differences in these areas have been increasing (Volcker Commission, 1989; Gold and Ritchie, 1993; Kelman, 1989). Studies of high-level officials who entered public service have found that most of them took salary cuts to do so. Compensation did not influence their decision; challenge and the desire to perform public service were the main attractions (Hartman and Weber, 1980). In sum, many people who choose to work for government do not emphasize making a lot of money as a goal in life, even though at lower organizational levels many public employees do not work at markedly lower pay than people in similar private sector jobs. Since top executives and professionals in government work for much lower salaries than their private sector counterparts, they must be motivated by goals other than high earnings.

Nevertheless, pay issues can still have a very strong influence on the motivation of public sector employees. As pointed out above, pay can have a symbolic meaning, as a recognition of an employee's skill and performance (Lawler, 1990). Studies with limited samples have also found that some public managers attach higher importance to increases in their pay than do private sector managers. Apparently these midlevel public managers felt that they had little impact on their organizations and turned to pay rather than responsibility as a motive (Schuster, 1974).

Research also indicates that security and benefits serve as important incentives for many who join and stay with government. A major survey by Kilpatrick, Cummings, and Jennings (1964) found that vast majorities of all categories of public employees, including federal employees, cited job security and benefit security (retirement, other protective benefits) as their motive for becoming a civil servant. Sixty-two percent of their sample of federal executives (GS 12 and above) held this view. A survey of about seventeen thousand federal employees by the U.S. Merit Systems Protection Board (1987) found that 81 percent considered annual leave and sick leave benefits a reason to stay in government, and 70 percent saw job security as a good reason to stay. A rough version of the Maslow needs hierarchy tends to apply, however. Smaller percentages of the executives and managers surveyed attached this level of importance to benefits and job security (Crewson, 1995b).

Managers and executives report more attraction to opportunities for challenge and significant work (Hartman and Weber, 1980). The Federal Employee Attitude Survey asked newly hired employees to rate the importance of various factors in their decision to work for the federal government. Virtually all of the executive-level employees rated "challenging work" as the most important factor (97 percent of GS 16 and above). Employees at lower GS levels rated job security and fringe benefits more highly than did the executives, but about 60 percent of them also rated challenging work as the most important factor. Rawls, Ullrich, and Nelson (1975) found that students headed for the nonprofit sector—mainly government—showed higher "dominance," "flexibility," and "capacity for status" in psychological tests and a lower valuation of economic wealth than did students headed for the for-profit sector. The nonprofit-oriented students also played more active roles in the program. Guyot (1960) found that a sample of federal middle managers scored higher than their business counterparts on a need-for-achievement scale and about the same on a measure of their need for power. We have some evidence, then, that government managers express as much or more concern with achievement and challenge than do private managers. Khojasteh (1993) found that intrinsic rewards such as recognition had higher motivating potential for a sample of public managers than for a sample of private managers.

These studies suggest that challenging, significant work and the opportunity to provide a public service are often the main attractions for public managers. Perceptions of public service vary over time, however, with changes in the political climate. A recent survey of career preferences among top students at leading universities found that they placed a high priority on challenging work and personal growth and a low priority on salary. They saw government positions as less likely to provide challenging work and personal growth than positions in private industry, however (Sanders, 1989). They saw government employment as providing superior opportunities for service to society, but they rated that opportunity as intermediate in importance. Their attitudes may reflect the antigovernment climate of the 1980s and 1990s, and general perceptions about government may change. More recently, researchers have been finding that younger workers in the public sector are expressing higher levels of general job satisfaction than younger workers in the private sector (Steel and Warner, 1990) and that employees entering the public sector show higher levels on certain measures of skill and quality than do those entering the private sector. Yet if the public sector attracts increasingly high-quality employees, the challenge of providing them with challenging work becomes all the more important. The discussion of work-related attitudes such as organizational commitment in the next chapter returns to this issue, because scholars have debated whether it is particularly hard to provide challenging work in public organizations.

The Motive for Public Service: In Search of the Service Ethic

The topic of challenging work in the public service and motives for it brings us to the motive mentioned in discussions of why people want to work for government—the service ethic, the desire to serve the public. Interestingly, although this topic echoes again and again in research on public organizations, it has not been the subject of nearly as much systematic research as one might expect. Public executives and managers tend to express a higher motive to serve the public, as shown by Sikula's survey (1973a), described above. Similarly, Kilpatrick, Cummings, and Jennings (1964) found that federal executives, scientists, and engineers gave higher ratings than their counterparts in business to work-related values such as the importance of doing your best, even if you dislike your work; the importance of doing work that is worthwhile to society; and helping others as one's main source of occupational satisfaction. Rainey (1983) found that state agency managers rated the "opportunity to engage in meaningful public service" as more important than did managers in large business firms. As noted earlier, the Federal Employee Attitude Survey found that high percentages of managers and executives entering the federal government rated public service and having an impact on public affairs as the most important reasons for entering federal service, with very low percentages of these groups rating salary and job security as important attractions (Crewson, 1995b). Findings such as these suggest the common characteristics of persons motivated by public service: they place a high value on work that helps others and benefits society as a whole, involves self-sacrifice, and provides a sense of responsibility and integrity. Public managers often mention such motives (Hartman and Weber, 1980; Lasko, 1980; Kelman, 1989; Sandeep, 1989; Wittmer, 1991). Later, however, we will discuss evidence that people motivated by such ideals often experience frustration, which underscores the importance of public managers' understanding and nurturing of service motives.

The general references to public service motivation above and in some of the surveys cited in this chapter leave many questions about what we mean by service motivation and how we can assess it. Rainey (1982) asked middle managers in state agencies and business firms to rate the value of various rewards of their work, including "the opportunity to engage in a meaningful public service." The public managers rated this item much more highly than did business managers. These high ratings were strongly related to their job satisfaction but only weakly related to their job involvement (see Table 9.1 for a definition of job involvement).

This suggests that public service motivation apparently differs from job involvement and other generic concepts developed in organizational behavior research in ways that we need to understand more fully. As indicated in Tables 9.2 and 9.3, many analyses of values, motives, and incentives in organizational research and the social sciences do not focus directly on public service motivation. Many pay virtually no attention to such motives. Public service motives are by no means restricted to government employees, but the topic should play a major part in the development of theories of public management and behavior in public organizations.

Recently some researchers have begun to develop this topic with more detailed analysis and evidence about public service motives. Perry and Wise (1990) suggest that public service motives can fall into three categories: *instrumental motives,* including participation in policy formulation, commitment to a public program because of personal identification, and advocacy for a special or private interest; *norm-based motives,* including desire to serve the public interest, loyalty to duty and to government, and social equity; and *affective motives,* including commitment to a program based on convictions about its social importance and the "patriotism of benevolence." They draw the term *patriotism of benevolence* from Frederickson and Hart (1985), who define it as an affection for all the people in the nation and a devotion to defending the basic rights granted by enabling documents such as the Constitution.

Perry (1996a) provides more recent evidence of the dimensions of a general public service motive and ways of assessing it. He analyzed survey responses from about four hundred people, including managers and employees in various government and business organizations and graduate and undergraduate students. He analyzed the responses to questions such as those in Table 9.4 to see if the respondents answered them in ways that supported the conclusion that their public service motives fall into these dimensions (in technical terms, he analyzed the reliability of these subscales using a confirmatory factor analysis).

But public service motivation involves additional dimensions. It appears to vary over time, with changes in the public image of government service, and to take different forms in different agencies and service areas. It presents an elusive topic for analysis. Sociologists who have studied the altruistic motivations of civil rights workers found that these people have trouble putting into words the motives behind the sacrifices they make and the risks they take (Demerath, Marwell, and Aiken, 1971). Public managers' references to their own service motives often take a similarly diffuse form. Although complex, these motivations need more attention from managers and researchers. The constraints on extrinsic incentives in government jobs make intrinsic and public service incentives even more important, in part because managers have some influence over them (Cohen and Eimicke, 1995; Romzek, 1990).

TABLE 9.4. DIMENSIONS AND QUESTIONNAIRE MEASURES OF PUBLIC SERVICE MOTIVATION.

Dimension	Questionnaire Items
Attraction to Public	Politics is a dirty word. (Reversed)[a] The give and take of public policymaking doesn't appeal to me. (Reversed) I don't care much for politicians. (Reversed)
Commitment to the Public Interest	It is hard to get me genuinely interested in what is going on in my community. (Reversed) I unselfishly contribute to my community. Meaningful public service is very important to me. I would prefer seeing public officials do what is best for the community, even if it harmed my interests. I consider public service a civic duty.
Compassion	I am rarely moved by the plight of the underprivileged. (Reversed) Most social programs are too vital to do without. It is difficult for me to contain my feelings when I see people in distress. To me, patriotism includes seeing to the welfare of others. I seldom think about the welfare of people whom I don't know personally. (Reversed) I am often reminded by daily events about how dependent we are on one another. I have little compassion for people in need who are unwilling to take the first step to help themselves. There are few public programs I wholeheartedly support. (Reversed)
Self-Sacrifice	Making a difference in society means more to me than personal achievements. I believe in putting duty before self. Doing well financially is definitely more important to me than doing good deeds. (Reversed) Much of what I do is for a cause bigger than myself. Serving citizens would give me a good feeling even if no one paid me for it. I feel people should give back to society more than they get from it. I am one of those rare people who would risk personal loss to help someone else. I am prepared to make enormous sacrifices for the good of society.

[a]"Reversed" indicates items that express the *opposite* of the concept being measured, as a way of varying the pattern of questions and answers. The respondent should *disagree* with such statements if they are good measures of the concept. For example, a person high on the compassion dimension should *disagree* with the statement "I am rarely moved by the plight of the underprivileged."

Source: James L. Perry developed these questions. See Perry (1996a). Used with permission.

In spite of the complexities in analyzing all the possible motives, values, and incentives in organizations, the research has produced evidence about their patterns among public sector employees and the differences from private sector employees. The evidence in turn suggests challenges for leaders and managers in the public sector. Even though many public employees may value intrinsic rewards and a sense of public service—often more highly than private sector employees value them—the next chapter will describe some experts' concerns that the characteristics of the public sector context described in earlier chapters can impede leaders' effort to provide such rewards. Yet the next chapter and later ones will also present examples of how public organizations and their leaders can and do provide rewarding experiences for employees and enhance their motivation.

The next chapter will continue our analysis by covering theories that suggest how values and motives affect work motivation, techniques for increasing motivation, and other important work attitudes that are related to motivation.

CHAPTER TEN

UNDERSTANDING PEOPLE IN PUBLIC ORGANIZATIONS

Theories of Work Motivation and Work-Related Attitudes

Chapter Nine discussed motives, values, and incentives, which play essential roles in leadership, organizational culture, and employee motivation and performance. It also illustrated the complex array of values, motives, and incentives that researchers have identified. Both researchers and managers face the question of how these factors influence motivation. This chapter reviews the most prominent theories of motivation, which represent theorists' best efforts to explain motivation, to describe how it works. Some of the terms sound abstract, but the effort is quite practical—how do you explain the motivation of members of your organization and use this knowledge to enhance their motivation? No one has yet developed a conclusive theory of work motivation, but each theory provides important insights about motivation and can contribute to managers' ability to think comprehensively about it. Examples below will show that reforms in government have often revealed very simplistic thinking about work motivation on the part of the reformers—thinking that could be improved by more careful attention to the theories described in this chapter.

Chapter Nine also pointed out that OB scholars now treat motivation as an umbrella concept to refer to a set of attitudes and behaviors related to employee behavior, such as job satisfaction and organizational commitment. After reviewing the motivation theories, this chapter will describe those important work-related attitudes.

This and the preceding chapter emphasize the complexity of motivation and the array of concepts and factors related to it because this reflects the state of our knowledge about these topics and the challenges managers and scholars face in dealing with them. Managers and organizations invest very heavily in efforts and procedures designed to motivate employees; this chapter briefly summarizes many of these techniques.

Theories of Work Motivation

One way of classifying the theories of motivation that have achieved prominence is to distinguish between content theories and process theories. Content theories are concerned with analyzing the particular needs, motives, or rewards that affect motivation. Process theories concentrate more on the psychological and behavioral processes behind motivation, often with no designation of important rewards and motives. The two categories overlap, and the distinction need not be taken as confining. It serves largely as a way of introducing some of the major characteristics of the different theories.

Content Theories

Table 10.1 summarizes the needs, values, and incentives that play a part in prominent content theories of motivation. These theories go beyond the mere listing of factors that influence motivation (like the theories described in Chapter Nine) to specify how such factors influence motivation.

Maslow: Needs Hierarchy. Abraham Maslow's theory of human needs and motives (1954), described in Chapters Two and Nine and in Table 10.1, advanced some of the most widely influential ideas in social science. Contemporary work motivation scholars do not accept the needs hierarchy as an adequate theory of motivation, but it contributed concepts that are now regarded as classic and continues to influence important intellectual developments (for example, see Burns, 1978). Maslow's conception of self-actualization as the highest-order human need is his most influential idea. It has appealed widely to people searching for a way to express this ultimate human motive, to fulfill one's potential.

In later writings Maslow (1965) further developed his ideas about self-actualization, going beyond the summary in Table 10.1, and discussed the relationship of this motive to work, duty, and group or communal benefits. Maslow was

TABLE 10.1. CATEGORIES OF NEEDS AND VALUES EMPLOYED IN SELECTED CONTENT THEORIES.

Maslow's Needs Hierarchy (1954)

Physiological Needs: Needs for relief from hunger, thirst, and fatigue and for defense from the elements

Safety Needs: Needs to be free of the threat of bodily harm

Social Needs: Needs for love, affection, and belonging to social units and groups

Self-Esteem Needs: Needs for sense of achievement, confidence, recognition, and prestige

Self-Actualization Needs: The need to become everything one is capable of becoming, to achieve self-fulfillment, especially in some area of endeavor or purpose (such as motherhood, artistic creativity, or a profession)

Herzberg's Two-Factor Theory (1968)

Hygiene Factors	*Motivators*
Company policy and administration	Achievement
Supervision	Recognition
Relations with supervisor	The work itself
Working conditions	Responsibility
Salary	Growth
Relations with peers	Advancement
Personal life	
Relations with subordinates	
Status	
Security	

McClelland: Need for Achievement, Power, and Affiliation (1961)[a]

Need for Achievement: The need for a sense of mastery over one's environment and successful accomplishment through one's own abilities and efforts; a preference for challenges involving moderate risk, clear feedback about success, and ability to sense personal responsibility for success. Purportedly stimulates and facilitates entrepreneurial behavior.

Need for Power: A general need for autonomy and control over oneself and others, which can manifest itself in different ways. When blended with degrees of altruism and inhibition, and low need for affiliation, can facilitate effectiveness at management.

Need for Affiliation: The need to establish and maintain positive affective relations, or "friendship" with others.

Adams: The Need for Equity (1965)

The need to maintain an equitable or fair balance between one's contributions to an organization and one's returns and compensations from it (determined by comparing the balance maintained by others to one's own); the need to feel that one is not overcompensated or undercompensated for one's contributions to the organization.

[a]McClelland and other researchers do not provide concise or specific definitions of the need concepts.

Source: Adapted from Rainey (1993b).

concerned that during the 1960s some psychologists interpreted self-actualization as self-absorbed concern with one's personal emotional salvation or satisfaction, especially through the shedding of inhibitions and social controls; Maslow sharply rejected such ideas. Genuinely self-actualized persons achieve this ultimate state of fulfillment through hard work and dedication to a duty or mission that serves higher values than simple self-satisfaction, through work that benefits others or society. Genuine personal contentment and emotional salvation, he argued, are by-products of such dedication. In this later work, Maslow emphasizes that the levels of need are not separate steps from which one successively departs. Rather, they are cumulative phases of a growth toward self-actualization, a motive that grows out of the satisfaction of social and self-esteem needs and also builds on them.

Maslow's ideas have had a significant impact on many social scientists but have received little reverence from empirical researchers attempting to validate them. As described in Chapter Nine, researchers trying to measure Maslow's needs and test his theory have not confirmed a five-step hierarchy. Instead they have found a two-step hierarchy, in which lower-level employees show more concern with material and security rewards. Higher-level employees place more emphasis on achievement and challenge (Pinder, 1984).

Critics also point to theoretical weaknesses in Maslow's hierarchy. Locke and Henne (1986) point to the dubious behavioral implications of Maslow's emphasis on need deprivation—that is, Maslow's contention that unsatisfied needs dominate behavior. Being deprived of a need does not tell a person what to do about it, and the theory does not explain how people know how to respond. Locke and Henne also complain that Maslow's concept of self-actualization is so hazy that it is hard to evaluate it.

In spite of the criticisms, Maslow's theory has had a strong following among many other scholars and management experts. Maslow contributed to a growing recognition of the importance of motives for growth, development, and actualization among members of organizations. His ideas also influenced other developments in the social sciences and OB. For example, in a prominent book on leadership, James MacGregor Burns (1978) drew on Maslow's concepts of a hierarchy of needs and of higher-order needs such as self-actualization. Burns observed that *transformational* leaders—that is, leaders who bring about major transformations in society—do not engage in simple exchanges of benefits with their followers. Rather, they appeal to higher-order motives in the population, including motives for self-actualization that are tied to societal ends, involving visions of a society transformed in ways that fulfill such personal motives. As a political scientist, Burns concentrated on political and societal leaders, but writers on organizational leadership have acknowledged his influence on recent thought about transformational leadership in organizations (see Chapter Eleven). In addition, Maslow's work foreshadowed and helped to shape current discussions of organizational mission and culture, worker empowerment, and highly participative forms of management (for example, see Block, 1987; Golembiewski, 1985; Peters and Waterman, 1982).

McGregor: Theory X and Theory Y. Douglas McGregor's ideas about Theories X and Y (1960) also reflect the influence of Maslow's work and the penetration into management thought of an emphasis on higher-order needs. As described in Chapter Two, McGregor argued that industrial management in the United States has historically reflected the dominance of a theory of human behavior that he calls "Theory X." Theory X assumes that workers lack the capacity for self-motivation and self-direction and that managers must design organizations to control and direct them. McGregor called for wider acceptance of Theory Y, the idea that workers have needs like those Maslow described as higher-order needs—for growth, development, interesting work, and self-actualization. Theory Y should guide management practice, McGregor argued. Managers should use participative management techniques, decentralized decision making, performance evaluation procedures that emphasize self-evaluation and objectives set by the employee, and job enrichment programs to make jobs more interesting and responsible. McGregor's ideas offered only the rudiments of a theory, and researchers do not regard it as an adequately comprehensive theory of work motivation. Like Maslow's, however, McGregor's ideas have had profound effects on the theory and practice of management. Chapter Thirteen describes two examples of efforts to reform and change federal agencies that both drew on McGregor's ideas about Theory Y.

Herzberg: Two-Factor Theory. Frederick Herzberg's two-factor theory (1968) also emphasized the essential role of higher-order needs and intrinsic incentives in motivating workers. From studies involving thousands of people in many occupational categories, he and his colleagues concluded that two major factors influence individual motivation in work settings. They called these factors "motivators" and "hygiene factors" (see Table 10.1). Insufficient hygiene factors can cause dissatisfaction with one's job, but even when they are abundant they do not stimulate high levels of satisfaction. As indicated in Table 10.1, hygiene factors are extrinsic incentives—including organizational, group, or supervisory conditions—or externally mediated rewards such as salaries. While hygiene factors can only prevent dissatisfaction, motivators are essential to increasing motivation. They include intrinsic incentives such as interest in and enjoyment of the work itself and a sense of growth, achievement, and fulfillment of higher-order needs.

Herzberg concluded that since motivators provide the real sources of stimulation and motivation for employees, managers must avoid the negative techniques of controlling and directing employees and should instead design work to provide for the growth, achievement, recognition, and other elements people need, which are represented by the motivators. This requires well-developed job enrichment programs to make the work itself interesting and to give workers a sense of control, achievement, growth, and recognition, which produces high levels of motivation.

Herzberg's work sparked controversy among experts and researchers. He and his colleagues developed their evidence by asking people to describe events on the job that led to feelings of extreme satisfaction and events that led to extreme dissatisfaction. Most of the reports of great satisfaction mentioned intrinsic and growth factors. Herzberg labeled these "motivators" in part because the respondents often mentioned their connection to heightened motivation and better performance. Reports of dissatisfaction tended to concentrate on the hygiene factors.

Researchers using other methods of generating evidence did not obtain the same results, however (Pinder, 1984). Critics argued that when people are asked to describe an event that makes them feel highly motivated, they might hesitate to report such things as pay or an improvement in physical working conditions. Instead, in what social scientists call a *social desirability effect,* they might attempt to provide more socially acceptable answers. Critics also questioned Herzberg's conclusions about the effects of the two factors on individual behavior. Lawler (1971), for example, cited Herzberg as one of a number of researchers who understated the importance of pay in organizations. He pointed out that surveys show that workers rank pay fairly high in importance and that pay can serve as an indicator of achievement, recognition, and increased responsibility.

These concerns about the limitations of the theory have led to a decline in interest in it. Locke and Henne (1986), for example, find no recent attempts to test the theory and conclude that theorists no longer take it seriously. Nevertheless, the theory always receives attention in reviews of motivation theory because of its contribution to the stream of thought about restructuring work to make it interesting and to satisfy worker's needs for growth and fulfillment. While researchers have turned away from the theory because it does not provide a complete and well-validated explanation of motivation, its central theme contributes to the mainstream of current thinking about motivating people in organizations.

McClelland: Needs for Achievement, Power, and Affiliation.

In its day, David McClelland's theory about the motivations for seeking achievement, power, and affiliation (the desire for friendly relations with others)—especially his ideas about the need for achievement—was one of the most prominent theories in management and OB. It elicited thousands of studies (McClelland, 1961; Locke and

Henne, 1986). Need for achievement *(n Ach)*, the central concept in his theory, refers to a motivation—a "dynamic restlessness" (McClelland, 1961, p. 301) to achieve a sense of mastery over one's environment through success at achieving goals by using one's own cunning, abilities, and efforts. He originally argued that *n Ach* was a common characteristic of persons attracted to managerial and entrepreneurial roles, although he later narrowed its application to predicting success in entrepreneurial roles (Pinder, 1984).

McClelland measured *n Ach* through a variety of procedures, including the Thematic Apperception Test (TAT). The TAT involves showing a standard set of pictures to individuals, who then write brief stories about what is happening in each picture. One typical picture shows a boy sitting at a desk in a classroom reading a book. A respondent identified as low in *n Ach* might write a story about the boy daydreaming, while someone high in *n Ach* might write a story about the boy studying hard to do well on a test. Researchers have also measured *n Ach* through questionnaires that ask about such matters as work role preferences and the role of luck in outcomes.

McClelland (1961) argued that persons high in *n Ach* are motivated to achieve in a particular pattern. They choose fairly challenging goals with moderate risks, where outcomes are fairly clear and accomplishment reflects success through one's own abilities. Persons in roles such as research scientist, which requires waiting a long time for success and recognition, may have a motivation to achieve, but they do not conform to this pattern. As one example of the nature of *n Ach* motives, McClelland (1961) cited the performance of children and students in experiments where they chose how to behave in games of skill. Researchers had children and students participate in a ring-toss game. The participants chose how far from the target peg they would stand. The high–*n Ach* participants tended to stand at an intermediate distance from the peg, not too close but not too far away. McClelland interpreted this as a reflection of their desire to achieve through their own skills. Standing too close made success too easy and thus did not satisfy their desire for a sense of accomplishment and mastery. Standing too far away, on the other hand, made success a gamble, a matter of a lucky throw. The high–*n Ach* participants chose a distance that would likely result in success brought about by their own skills. McClelland also offered evidence of other characteristics of persons with high *n Ach*, such as physical restlessness, particular concern over the rapid passage of time, and an aversion to wasting time.

McClelland claimed that *n Ach* could determine the success of individuals in business activities and the success of nations in economic development (McClelland, 1961; McClelland and Winter, 1969). He analyzed the achievement orientation in the folktales and children's stories of various nations and produced some evidence that cultures high in *n Ach* themes also showed higher rates of economic development. He has also claimed successes in training managers in business firms in less-developed countries to increase their *n Ach* and enhance the performance of their firm (McClelland and Winter, 1969). He suggested more achievement-oriented fantasizing and thinking as a means to improving the economic performance of nations. Others have also reported the use of achievement motivation training with apparent success in enhancing motivation and increasing entrepreneurial behaviors (Miner, 1980, p. 67).

McClelland (1975) later concluded that *n Ach* encouraged entrepreneurial behaviors rather than success in managerial roles. He argued, however, that his conceptions of the needs for power and affiliation did apply in predicting success in management roles (although there is much less empirical research about these needs to support his claims). McClelland concluded that the most effective managers develop high motivation for power, but with an altruistic orientation and a concern for group goals. This stage also involves a low need for affiliation, however, since too strong a need for friendship with others can hinder a manager.

Reviewers vary in their assessments of the state of this theory. Some rather positive assessments (Miner, 1980) contrast with others who focus only brief attention on it (Pinder, 1984) or criticize it harshly (Locke and Henne, 1986). Locke and Henne condemn the body of research on the theory as chaotic. They say that the status of the theory has become confused since McClelland narrowed the focus of *n Ach* to entrepreneurial behaviors, but most of the huge set of empirical studies of the theory have not focused on entrepreneurs. One finds little very recent research on the theory in major management or organizational journals.

Regardless of its prestige among scholars, this theory adds another important element to a well-developed perspective on motivation. Individuals vary in the general level and pattern of internal motivation toward achievement and excellence that they bring to work settings. These differences suggest the importance of employee selection in determining the level of motivation in an organization.

Equity Theory. J. Stacy Adams (1965) argued that a sense of equity in contributions and rewards has a major influence on work behaviors. A sense of inequity brings discomfort, and people thus act to reduce or avoid it. People assess the balance between their inputs to an organization and the outcomes or rewards that they receive from it, and they perceive inequity if this balance differs from those of other employees. For example, if another person and I receive the same salary, recognition, and other rewards, yet I feel that I make a superior contribution (such as working harder, producing more, having more experience), I will perceive a state of inequity. Conversely, if the other person makes superior inputs but gets lower rewards than I get, I will perceive inequity in the opposite sense (I will feel overcompensated).

In either case, according to Adams, a person tries to eliminate such inequity. If people feel overcompensated, they may try to increase their inputs or reduce their outcomes to redress the inequity. If they feel undercompensated, they will do the opposite, slowing down or reducing their contributions. Adams advanced specific propositions about how workers react that depend on factors such as whether they receive hourly pay or are paid according to their rate of production. For example, he predicted that if workers are overpaid on an hourly basis, they will produce more per hour, to reduce the feeling that they are overcompensated. If they are overpaid on a piece-rate basis, however, they will slow down, to avoid making more money than other workers.

These sorts of predictions have received some confirmation in laboratory experiments. The theory proves difficult to apply in real work settings, however, because it is hard to measure and assess inequity, and some of the concepts in the theory are ambiguous (Miner, 1980). People vary in their sensitivity to inequity, and they may vary widely in how they react to the same conditions.

While this specific theory has not held up well, equity in contributions and rewards is very important in management. As described later, more recent models of motivation include perceptions about equity as important components. Equity issues also play a role in debates about civil service reforms and performance-based pay plans in the public sector. Governments at all levels in the United States and in other countries have tried to adopt performance-based pay plans (Ingraham, 1993). Supporters of such plans often cite equity principles akin to those stressed in this theory. They argue that people who perform better than others but receive no better pay perceive inequity and experience a loss of morale and motivation and that the highly structured pay and reward systems in government tend to create such situations (Schay, 1988).

For most managers, trying to ensure that people feel they are rewarded fairly in comparison to others is a major responsibility and challenge. A manager often finds it easier to rely heavily on the most energetic and competent people than to struggle with the problem of dealing with less capable or less enthusiastic ones. If a manager cannot or does not appropriately reward those on whom he or she places heavier burdens, these more capable people can become frustrated. Managers in government organizations commonly complain that the highly structured reward systems in government aggravate this problem. In work groups and team-based activities, too, the problem of a team member's not contributing as well as others can raise tensions. The OB literature does contain questionnaires for assessing fairness and equity to help in confronting such problems (Gordon, 1993, p. 135). Many of the motivational techniques described later in this chapter, and the leadership and cultural issues discussed in the next chapter, pertain to the challenge of maintaining equity in the work setting.

Process Theories

Process theories emphasize *how* the motivational process works. They describe how goals, values, needs, or rewards operate in conjunction with other factors to determine motivation. The content factors—the particular needs, rewards, and so on—are not specified in the theories themselves.

Expectancy Theory

Expectancy theory is the most promising theory of work motivation yet proposed, and it has produced the most important applications in public organizations. Expectancy theory holds that an individual considering an action sums up the values of all the outcomes that will result from the action, with each outcome weighted by the probability of its occurrence. The higher the probability of good outcomes and the lower the probability of bad ones, the stronger the motivation to perform the action. In other words, the theory draws on the classic utilitarian idea that people will do what they see as *most likely* to result in the *most good* and the *least bad*.

Although the theory draws on classic utilitarian ideas, it has assumed an important role in contemporary OB theory. Vroom (1964) stated the theory formally, with algebraic formulas (see Figure 10.1). The formula expresses the following idea: the force acting on an individual and causing him or her to work at a particular level of effort (or to choose to engage in a particular activity) is a function of the sum of the products of the perceived desirability of the outcomes associated with working at that level ("valences") and the "expectancies" for the outcomes. Expectancies are the person's estimates of the probability that the expected outcomes will follow from working at a particular level. In other words, multiply the value (positive or negative) of each outcome by the expectancy (perceived probability) that it will occur, and sum these products for all the outcomes. A higher sum reflects higher expectancies for more positively valued outcomes and should predict higher motivation.

Researchers originally hoped that this theory would provide a basis for the systematic research and diagnosis of motivation: ask people to rate the positive or negative value of important outcomes of their work and the probability that desirable work behaviors would lead to those outcomes or avoid them, and use the expectancy formula to combine these ratings. They hoped that this approach would improve researchers' ability to predict motivational levels and analyze good and bad influences on them, such as problems due to beliefs that certain outcomes were unattainable or that certain rewards offered little value. A spate of empirical tests soon followed, with mixed results. Some of the studies found that the

FIGURE 10.1. FORMULATIONS OF EXPECTANCY THEORY.

A Formulation Similar to Vroom's Early Version

$$F_i = \Sigma(E_{ij}V_j)$$

where F = the force acting on an individual to perform act i

   E = the expectancy, or perceived probability, that act i will lead to outcome j

   V = the valence of outcome j

and

$$V_j = \Sigma(V_k I_{jk})$$

where V = the valence of outcome j

   I = the instrumentality of outcome j for the attainment of outcome k

   V = the valence of outcome k

A Formulation Similar to Various Revised Formulations

Motivation = $f[EI \times EII(V)] = f[(E \rightarrow P) \times [(P \rightarrow O)(V)]]$

where $EI = (E \rightarrow P)$ = expectancy I, the perceived probability that a given level of work effort will result in a given level of performance

   $EII = (P \rightarrow O)$ = expectancy II, the perceived probability that the level of performance will lead to the attainment of outcome j

   V = the valence of outcome j

Source: Adapted from Rainey (1993b).

theory failed to predict effort and productivity. Critics soon began to point out weaknesses in the theory (Campbell and Pritchard, 1983). They complained that it does not accurately represent human mental processes, because it assumes that humans make exhaustive lists of outcomes and their likelihoods and sum them up systematically. Researchers found it difficult to list on a questionnaire all the possible outcomes important to people in an organization and to measure their valences.

Nevertheless, expectancy theory still stands as one of the most prominent work motivation theories, and researchers continue to propose various improvements on it (Evans, 1986). More recent versions relax the mathematical formula and simply state that motivation depends generally on the positive and negative values of outcomes and their probabilities, in ways we cannot precisely specify (see Figure 10.1). Some of these more recent forms of the theory have broken down the concept of expectancies into two types, as illustrated in the figure. Expectancy I (EI) perceptions reflect an individual's beliefs about the likelihood that effort will lead to a particular performance level. Expectancy II (EII) perceptions reflect the perceived probability that a particular performance level leads to a given level of reward. The distinction helps to clarify some of the components of motivational responses. For example, the Performance Management and Recognition System (PMRS), one of the many pay-for-performance plans adopted by governments during the 1980s, applied to middle managers in federal agencies (GS 13–15). Under PMRS, a manager's superior would rate the manager's performance on a five-point scale, and the manager's annual salary increase would be based on that rating. PMRS got off to a bad start in many federal agencies, however. In some agencies, the vast majority of the managers received very high performance ratings, and their EI perceptions strengthened—it became clear that they had a high likelihood of performing well enough to receive a high rating. Yet, about 90 percent of the managers in some agencies received pay raises of 3 percent or less, and fewer than 1 percent of them received pay raises of as much as 10 percent. EII perceptions, then, naturally weaken. One may expect to perform well enough to get a high rating (EI), but performance at that level may not lead to a high probability of getting a significant reward (EII). PMRS, like many other performance-based pay plans in government, applies expectancy theory implicitly but fails to do so adequately (Perry, 1986; Perry, Petrakis, and Miller, 1989). Soon after its introduction, PMRS was canceled.

Some recent versions of the theory also draw in other variables. They point out, for example, that a person's self-esteem can affect EI perceptions. Organizational characteristics and experiences, such as the characteristics of the pay plan or the perceived equity of the reward system, can influence EII perceptions—as in the PMRS case. Some of the most recent versions bring together expectancy concepts with ideas about goal setting, control theory, and social learning theory, discussed in the sections below (Klein, 1989). These examples show how recent formulations of the theory provide useful frameworks for analyzing motivational plans and pinpointing the sources of problems.

Expectancies as Dependent Variables. In spite of the controversies over the theory, researchers and management consultants regularly use expectancy-type questions as *dependent variables*. Individuals' beliefs about the relationship between performance and pay, job security, promotion, and other incentives often show significant relationships to other important attitudes, such as work satisfaction and self-reported work effort. Researchers use EI scales with items concerning beliefs about the relationship between effort and performance, asking whether effort will lead to high-quality and high-quantity output. For example, one item asks for agreement or disagreement with the statement "Trying as hard as I can leads to high-quality output." EII items ask about the link between performance and rewards: "Producing a high-quality output increases my chances for promotion." Other EII items ask about the relationship of quantity, quality, and timeliness of output to rewards such as promotion, higher pay, job security, and recognition.

Expectancy Theory and Public Organizations. The PMRS and pay-for-performance examples show why expectancy theory has had important applications in the public sector. It has served as the implicit theoretical underpinning for reforms of many civil service and other government pay systems. In addition, expectancy questions of the sort described above have been used in major surveys of government employees that were intended in part as a means of evaluating some of the reforms (U.S. Office of Personnel Management, 1979, 1980, 1983). As described below, these and other surveys using expectancy items have found some consistent distinctions between public sector and private sector incentive structures.

Operant Conditioning Theory and Behavior Modification

Another body of research that has influenced motivation theory and practice and that has implications similar to those of expectancy theory applies operant conditioning and behavior modification concepts to the management of employees. This approach draws on the theories of psychologists such as B. F. Skinner. Skinner argued that we can best analyze behavior by studying the relationships between observable behaviors and contingencies of reinforcement.

The term *operant conditioning* stems from a revision Skinner and others made to older versions of stimulus-response psychology. Skinner (1953, p. 65) pointed out that we animals do not develop behaviors simply in response to stimuli. We exhibit behaviors as well, and those behaviors operate on our environment, generating consequences. We repeat or drop behaviors depending on the consequences. We acquire behaviors or extinguish them in response to the conditions or contingencies of reinforcement.

A *reinforcement* is an event that follows a behavior and changes the probability that the behavior will recur. (We might call this a reward or punishment, but Skinner apparently felt that the term *reinforcement* was a more objective one, since it assumes less about what goes on inside the subject.) Learning and motivation depend on "schedules" of reinforcements, referring to how regularly they follow a particular behavior. For example, a manager can praise an employee every time he or she does good work, such as completing a task on time, or the manager can praise the behavior once out of every several times it occurs. According to the operant conditioning perspective, such variations make a lot of difference.

Operant theory derives from what psychologists have called the behaviorist school of psychology. Behaviorism gained its label because it emphasizes observations of the overt behaviors of animals and humans without hypothesizing about what goes on inside them. In a classic debate in psychology, some theorists (the precursors to the expectancy theorists) argued that motivation and learning theories should refer to what goes on inside the organism. Behaviorists, such as Skinner, rejected the use of such internal constructs, arguing that since one cannot observe them scientifically, they can only add confusing speculation to the analysis of motivation. Skinner argued that one can scientifically analyze only those behaviors that are overtly observable. As described below, in recent years psychologists have worked toward reconciling operant behaviorism with cognitive concepts (Kreitner and Luthans, 1987; Bandura, 1978).

Skinner and other behaviorists analyzed relationships between reinforcements and behaviors and developed principles concerning various types and schedules of reinforcement. For example, Skinner pointed out that a subject more rapidly acquires a behavior under a constant reinforcement schedule, but the behavior will extinguish (stop occurring) faster than one brought about using a variable-ratio schedule. For the example above, the behaviorists would suggest that constant praise by the manager might have more immediate effects on the employee, but the effects would fall off rapidly if the manager stopped the constant praise. More intermittent praise—every few times—might be slower to take effect, but it would have a more lasting effect. Behaviorists also point out that positive reinforcement works better than negative reinforcement or punishment. Table 10.2 summarizes the concepts and principles from this body of theory.

Behavior modification refers to techniques that apply principles of operant conditioning to modify human behavior. The term apparently comes from the way in which the behaviorists studied the principles of reinforcement, by modifying and shaping behaviors. They would, for example, develop a behavior by reinforcing portions of it, and then larger portions, and so on, until they developed the full behavior. (For example, inducing an anorexic patient to eat by first reinforcing related behaviors such as picking up a fork, and then eating a small amount, and so on). Behavior modification has come to refer broadly and somewhat vaguely to a wide variety of techniques for changing behaviors, such as programs for helping people to stop smoking. Some of these techniques adhere closely to behaviorist principles; others may have little to do with them. Behavior modification practitioners claim successes in psychological therapy, improving student behavior and performance in schools, supervision of mentally retarded patients, and rewarding the attendance of custodial workers (Bandura, 1969; Sherman, 1990). Many organizations, including public ones such as garbage collection services, have adopted variants of these techniques to improve performance and productivity.

As these examples show, managers and consultants have applied behavior modification techniques in organizations. The ideas about intermittent schedules

TABLE 10.2. CONCEPTS AND PRINCIPLES
OF OPERANT CONDITIONING.

Types of reinforcement

Positive reinforcement: Increasing a behavior by providing a beneficial stimulus, contingent on workers' exhibiting that behavior. Example: An agency director announces that she will reward her assistant directors in their performance appraisals for their efforts to help their subordinates with professional development. She praises and rewards those efforts in the appraisals. As a result, the assistant directors devote even more attention to their subordinates' professional development.

Negative reinforcement: Decreasing behavior by removing or withholding an aversive stimulus (withholding punishment). Example: A supervisor stops reprimanding an employee for arriving late when the employee arrives on time; the probability increases that the employee will thereafter arrive on time.

Operant extinction: The result of withholding or removing a positive reinforcement. Example: A new agency director replaces the one described above and ignores the assistant directors' efforts at promoting their subordinates' professional development. As a result, the assistant directors reduce their efforts.

Punishment: Application of an aversive stimulus to reduce occurrence of a behavior. Example: Docking the pay of a habitually late worker.

Schedules of reinforcement

Fixed schedule: Applies the reinforcement on a regular basis or after a fixed period of time or a fixed number of occurrences of the behavior.

Variable schedule: Varies the time period or number of repetitions.

Ratio schedule: Applies reinforcements according to a designated ratio of reinforcements to responses, such as once for every five occurrences.

Interval schedule: Applies reinforcement after a designated time interval.

These categories can be combined

A fixed-interval schedule—a weekly paycheck.
A variable-interval schedule—a bonus every so often.
A fixed-ratio schedule—piece-rate pay scales.
A variable-ratio schedule—intermittent praise for a behavior.

Selected principles of reinforcement

Positive reinforcement provides the most efficient means of influencing behavior. Punishment is less efficient and effective in shaping behavior (Skinner, 1953).

A low-ratio reinforcement schedule—reinforcement after each occurrence of a behavior, for example—produces rapid acquisition of the behavior but more rapid extinction when the reinforcement stops.

Intermittent reinforcement, especially in highly variable intervals or according to a variable-ratio schedule (reinforcement after long, varying periods or after varied numbers of occurrences), requires more time for behavior acquisition, but extinction occurs more slowly when the reinforcements cease.

mentioned above and in Table 10.2, for example, lead some behavior modification proponents (Kreitner and Luthans, 1987) to prescribe such managerial techniques as *not* praising a desired behavior constantly. They advise praise on a varying basis, after a variable number of repetitions of the behavior. They might also prescribe periodic bonuses to supplement a worker's weekly paycheck, arguing that the regular check will lose its reinforcing properties over time but the bonuses will act as variable-interval reinforcements, strengthening the probability of sustained long-term effort. They have also offered useful suggestions about incremental shaping of behaviors by reinforcing successively larger portions of a desired behavior.

These kinds of prescriptions provide examples of those offered by practitioners of organizational behavior modification (OB Mod). OB Mod often involves this approach:

1. Measure and record desirable and undesirable behaviors, to establish baselines
2. Determine the antecedents and consequences of these behaviors
3. Develop strategies for using reinforcements and punishments—such as praise and pay increases—to change the behaviors
4. Apply these strategies, following the reinforcement schedules mentioned above
5. Assess the resultant behavioral change

A number of field studies of such projects have reported successes in improving employee performance, attendance, and adherence to safety procedures (Pinder, 1984). A highly successful effort by Emery Air Freight, for example, received widespread publicity (Kreitner and Luthans, 1987). That project involved having employees monitor their own performance, setting performance goals, and using feedback and positive reinforcements such as praise and time off.

Yet controversy over explanations of the success of this project reflects more general controversies about OB Mod. Critics have argued that the success of the Emery example, as well as other applications of OB Mod, was not the result of their using operant conditioning principles. They succeeded, according to the critics, because they included such steps as setting clear performance goals and making rewards contingent upon them (Locke, 1977). Therefore, the critics contend, these efforts do not offer any original insights derived from OB Mod. One might draw similar conclusions from expectancy theory, for example. Other criticisms focus on the questionable ethics of the emphasis on manipulation and control of people. Also, behavior modification and OB Mod appear to be most successful in altering relatively simple behaviors amenable to clear measurement. Even then, the techniques often involve practical difficulties because of all the measuring and reinforcement scheduling required.

For their part, proponents of OB Mod, and behavior modification more generally, point to the successes of the techniques. They counter attacks on the ethics of their approach by arguing that they cut through a lot of obfuscating fluff about values and internal states and move right to the issue of correcting bad behaviors and augmenting good ones. ("Do you want smokers to be able to stop, anorexics to eat, and workers to follow safety precautions, or do you not?") Similarly, OB Mod advocates claim that their approach succeeds in developing a focus on desired behaviors (getting the filing clerk to come to work on time), as opposed to making attributions about attitudes ("The filing clerk has a bad attitude"), and an emphasis on strategies for positive reinforcement of desired behaviors (Kreitner and Luthans, 1987).

Social Learning Theory

Recent work on social learning theory reflects both the limitations and the value of operant conditioning theory and OB Mod. Developed by psychologist Albert Bandura (1978, 1989) and others, social learning theory (and, later, "social cognitive theory" [Bandura, 1986]) blends ideas from operant conditioning theory with greater recognition of internal cognitive processes such as goals and a sense of "self-efficacy," or personal effectiveness. It gives attention to forms of learning and behavior change that are not tied tightly to some external reinforcement.

For example, individuals obviously learn by modeling their behaviors on those of others and through vicarious experiences. If you see another person burned by a hot object, you do not need to touch the object yourself to know to avoid it. Humans also use anticipation of future rewards, mental rehearsal and imagery, and self-rewarding behaviors (such as praising oneself) to influence their behavior. Applications of such processes in organizational settings have included frameworks for developing leadership and self-improvement, and studies have suggested that the sorts of techniques mentioned above can improve performance. For example, Sims and Lorenzi (1992) propose models and methods for motivating oneself and others through self-management that make use of some of the techniques suggested above—setting goals for oneself and developing the capacity of others to set their own goals, developing self-efficacy in oneself and others, employing modeling and self-rewarding behaviors (such as self-praise). Sims and Lorenzi propose that this approach can support the development of more decentralized, participative, empowering leaders and teamwork processes in organizations. These extensions are unlikely to satisfy the critics of OB Mod (Locke and Henne, 1986)— they in fact acknowledge some of its limitations—and few motivation theorists consider these approaches to be adequate by themselves for a complete analysis of motivation in organizations (Pinder, 1984).

Goal-Setting Theory

The psychologist Edwin Locke and his colleagues have advanced a theory of goal setting that has been very successful in that it has been solidly confirmed by well-designed research (Pinder, 1984; Locke and Latham, 1990a). The theory simply states that difficult, specific goals lead to higher performance than easy goals, vague goals, or no goals (for example, "Do your best") do. Difficult goals enhance performance by directing attention and action, mobilizing effort, increasing persistence, and motivating the search for effective performance strategies. Commitment to the goals and feedback about progress toward achieving them are also necessary for higher performance. Commitment and feedback do not by themselves stimulate high performance without difficult, specific goals, however. Research findings also indicate that while participation in setting a goal does not enhance commitment to it, expecting success in attaining the goal does enhance commitment. As the value of the goal increases, commitment to the goal increases. If money is contingent on the goal, that may lead to the setting of higher goals and to higher goal commitment. Individual differences also show strong relationships to the effectiveness of goal setting.

Locke and Latham (1990b) contend that assigning difficult, specific goals enhances performance because of the goals' influence on an individual's personal goals and his or her self-efficacy. Self-efficacy refers to a person's sense of his or her capability or effectiveness in accomplishing outcomes (Bandura, 1989). Assigned goals influence personal goals through a person's acceptance of and commitment to them. They influence self-efficacy by providing a sense of purpose and standards for evaluating performance, and they create opportunities for accomplishing lesser and proximal goals that build a sense of self-efficacy (Earley and Lituchy, 1991).

Although many studies support this theory, another reason for its success may be its compactness and relatively narrow focus (Pinder, 1984). The theory and much of the research that supports it concentrate on task performance in clear and simple task settings, which is amenable to the setting of specific goals. Also, a few studies have examined complex task settings (Locke and Latham, 1990a). However, some of the prominent contributions to organization theory in recent decades, such as the contingency theory and garbage can models of decision making (described in previous chapters), have emphasized that in many situations clear, explicit goals are quite difficult to specify. This suggests that in many of the most important settings, such as high-level strategy development teams, clear, specific goals may be impossible or dysfunctional. Similarly, precise goals can raise potential problems for public organizations, given their complex goal sets. Nevertheless, this body of research emphasizes the value of clear goals for work groups.

Whether or not it applies precisely to higher-level goals for public agencies, developing reasonably clear goals remains one of the major responsibilities and challenges for public executives and managers. The literature on public management now offers numerous examples of leaders in public agencies who have developed effective goals (Behn, 1991; DiIulio, 1990; Moore, 1990; Allison, 1983).

Recent Directions in Motivation Theory

As mentioned above, no theory has provided a conclusive general explanation of work motivation, and reviewers tend to agree that motivation theory is in a disorderly state (Landy and Becker, 1987; Pinder, 1984; Katzell and Thompson, 1990). Some theorists are calling for the development of separate theories to apply to different settings or dependent variables. Pinder (1984) argues that the effort to develop and evaluate the existing motivation theories as general, universal theories is fruitless. He proposes the development of a typology of motivational settings (the motivational attributes of a work setting), combined with a typology of motivational types (the motivation-related attributes of individuals in a work group), and the development of middle-range theories to be applied within such categories. Landy and Becker (1987) reject the quest for a universal theory and contend that the existing theories should be treated as theories that apply to different combinations from a set of dependent variables (choice, effort, satisfaction, performance, and withdrawal).

Others try to integrate some of the theories described above (Katzell and Thompson, 1990). There has been a good deal of attention to the integration of goal-setting theory and expectancy theory (Evans, 1986; Klein, 1989; Landy and Becker, 1987; Locke and Latham, 1990b), sometimes including other theories, such as control theories. Klein (1990) proposes a feasibility theory of motivation—emphasizing the availability of resources for task performance—that brings in need theory and draws on expectancy theory. Because of the success of goal-setting theory, there has been a strong trend toward including goal-related concepts in theories and integrating them with other cognitive concepts, such as those from social learning theory (Bandura, 1989; Pervin, 1989; Locke and Latham, 1990a, 1990b). For the time being, however, motivation theory remains a body of interesting and useful, but partial, efforts to apprehend a set of phenomena too complex for any single theory to capture.

Motivation Practice and Techniques

The state of motivation theory just described confronts both managers and researchers with the problem of what to make of it. The theorists lament their inability to provide a universal, conclusive work motivation theory, but that is quite a demanding standard. As illustrated above by the use of expectancy theory to analyze the PMRS, the individual theories provide useful frameworks for thinking about motivation and trying to lead and manage it. Taken together, they make up a broader, looser, but still valuable framework for analyzing motivational issues in practical settings. The content theories remind us of the importance of intrinsic incentives and equity and provide concepts for expressing them. This may seem obvious enough, but civil service and pay reforms in government in the last several decades have concentrated heavily on extrinsic incentives, to the virtual exclusion of the intrinsic incentives the content theorists emphasize.

Expectancy and operant conditioning theories emphasize an analysis of what is rewarded and punished in organizations and work settings. Kerr (1989), in an article now considered a classic, pointed out that leaders in organizations very frequently fail to reward the behaviors they say they want and in fact reward those that they say they do not want. The theories discussed above provide concepts and suggestions for analyzing such reward practices.

In addition, as mentioned in the discussion of operant conditioning theory, these theories direct attention to rewards and disincentives rather than to dubious assumptions about a person's reasons for behaving as he or she does. Consider, for example, an actual case in which two supervisors disciplined file clerks in a claims-processing agency for coming to work late or missing work altogether. At least one of the supervisors felt that the file clerks were being irresponsible and showed weak commitment to showing up on time (or at all). Both supervisors felt bound by the rules of their organization to carry out disciplinary actions. The file clerks were young minority females, and the supervisors were white males. A minority administrator at a higher level in turn verbally reprimanded the supervisors for being insensitive to the problems of the young females, who were unwed mothers with low incomes and had difficulties with child care that kept them out of work.

One immediate solution to this mess would have been better communication among all the parties from the outset. The supervisors were not aware of the difficulties the file clerks faced, and the higher-level administrator did not fully realize the obligation the supervisors felt to bring the disciplinary action. The supervisors thought that they themselves would be punished for lost productivity, that they were legally bound to discipline absentee employees (which they were, actually). They were also concerned that the other employees would perceive inequity if they did not. (Although they had never heard of equity theory, they were applying an informal version of it.)

Applying the theories discussed in this chapter, one could suggest that the supervisors' first impulse should have been to consider the various incentives acting on the file clerks; they might then have communicated with them more carefully about why they were showing up late. They should have been thinking about positive incentives to get them to show up on time rather than, as one supervisor did, assuming that they have weak motivation or bad habits. The administrator should have considered the incentives acting on the supervisors rather than jumping to the conclusion that they are insensitive. The more elaborate formulations of expectancy theory would also emphasize the influences on EI (the perception that a level of effort will lead to performance) of such factors in the agency as work design and arrangements (such as support for parental responsibilities), among others. Those ideas would have led the supervisors to think about what external factors might make the clerks feel that they could not make it to work on time and to analyze these obstacles and complications rather than simply decide that they are weak in character or have a bad attitude. Ultimately, such analysis might have led to organizational efforts to provide child care support for employees. More careful analysis by the administrator might have led to leadership activities that would relax pressures on supervisors, address the problems of equity, and provide support for employees. This example could be elaborated even further to show how motivation theories can apply to analyzing and understanding motivational issues and how managers actually use implicit versions of them in practice.

Also, in spite of the travails of the theorists, organizations need motivated members, and they address this challenge in numerous ways. Table 10.3 provides a description of many of the general techniques used to motivate employees, several of which have a large literature devoted to them. Real-world practice often loosely reflects theory, stressing pragmatism instead. Far from making theory irrelevant, however, the practices of organizations often justify the apparently obvious advice of the theorists and experts, since organizations frequently have trouble achieving desirable motivational strategies on their own (Kerr, 1989). For example, surveys find that fewer than one-third of employees in organizations feel that their pay is based on performance (Katzell and Thompson, 1990). As illustrated in the example about PMRS above, often these techniques involve implicit motivational assumptions and theories that could be improved through more careful analysis.

Incentive Structures and Reward Expectancies in Public Organizations

The challenge of tying rewards, especially extrinsic rewards, to performance is even greater in many public organizations than it is in private ones. Chapter Eight described numerous studies that demonstrate that organizations under government ownership usually have more highly structured, externally imposed personnel

TABLE 10.3. METHODS COMMONLY USED TO ENHANCE WORK MOTIVATION IN ORGANIZATIONS.

- *Improved performance appraisal systems.* Reforms involving the use of group-based appraisals (ratings for a work group rather than an individual), appraisals by a member's peers, and other approaches mentioned below.
- *Merit pay and pay-for-performance systems.* A wide variety of procedures for linking a person's pay to his or her performance.
- *Bonus and award systems.* One-time awards for instances of excellent performance or other achievements.
- *Profit-sharing and gain-sharing plans.* Sharing profits with members of the organization (usually possible only in business organizations, for obvious reasons). Employee stock ownership plans are roughly similar, providing a means of rewarding employees when the organization does well.
- *Management by Objectives (MBO) and other performance-targeted procedures.* Organizations of all types have tried MBO programs, which involve evaluating people on the basis of stated work objectives. Superiors work with subordinates on developing objectives for their work, thus enhancing communication. Performance appraisals then concentrate on those objectives. This focuses employees' attention on the most important outcomes of work, gives them more say in what they do, and enhances decentralization and autonomy, since agreement on the objectives provides a basis for allowing employees to go ahead and work their own way rather than relying on constant directions from the boss. The most elaborate MBO programs involve mapping broad organizational objectives down through more specific objectives at the different levels of the organization. Organizations also use a wide variety of "performance targeting" procedures emphasizing productivity or performance targets for groups.
- *Participative management and decision making.* These involve a sustained commitment to engage in more communication and sharing of decisions, through teams, committees, task forces, general meetings, open-door policies, and one-to-one exchanges.
- *Work enhancement: job redesign, job enlargement, and rotation.* Usage varies, but job redesign usually means changing jobs to enhance control and interest for the people doing the work. Job enlargement, or "horizontal loading," involves giving employees more different tasks and responsibilities at the same skill level. Job restructuring, or "vertical loading," involves giving employees more influence over decisions normally made by superiors, such as work scheduling, or, more generally, to enlarge employees' sense of responsibility by giving them control of a complete unit of work output (for example, having work teams build an entire car or having caseworkers handle all the needs of a client). These approaches may involve job sharing and rotation among workers and various team-based approaches.
- *Quality of Work Life (QWL) programs and Quality Circles (QCs).* Organizations of all types have tried QWL programs, which typically involve efforts to enhance the general working environment of an organization through representative committees, surveys and studies, and other procedures designed to improve the work environment. Quality circles, used successfully in Japanese companies, are teams that focus directly on improving the quality of work processes and products.
- *Organizational Development (OD) interventions.* OD, employed widely in the public and private sectors, applies behavioral science techniques to improving communication, resolving conflicts, and building trust.

procedures than private organizations have. The civil service systems and centralized personnel systems in government jurisdictions apparently account for these effects.

Of course, public organizations also vary among themselves in how much such systems affect them. The U.S. General Accounting Office, for example, has a relatively independent personnel system and uses a pay-for-performance plan. Government enterprises often have greater autonomy in their personnel procedures than typical government agencies. In demonstration projects, some federal units have adopted pay-for-performance plans with apparent success (Schay, 1988). Debate continues over whether pay constraints are an inherent feature of government (Gabris, 1987; Ingraham, 1993). At present, public organizations more often have more formalized, externally imposed personnel systems than private organizations do.

This evidence of more formalized personnel rules does not in itself prove that people in public organizations perceive them as such. Chapter Eight also described surveys revealing that public managers, in comparison to their private sector counterparts, report more formalized personnel procedures and greater structural constraints on their authority to administer extrinsic rewards such as pay, promotion, and discipline and to base these on performance (Rainey, Facer, and Bozeman, 1995; U.S. Office of Personnel Management, 1979, 1980, 1983; Elling, 1986). Recently, Ban (1995) reported on extensive interviews with federal managers; again, they consistently described the federal personnel rules and procedures as constraining and cumbersome.

The feelings of the public managers in these studies may reflect shared stereotypes. Business managers may have personnel problems that are just as serious as those faced by public sector managers, despite the stereotype of a stronger relationship between rewards and performance in private business than in government. Even if that is the case, these findings indicate that the perception among public managers of having greater difficulty with such matters currently forms part of the culture at all levels of government in the United States.

The existence of formalized personnel systems and managers' perceptions of constraints under them do not prove that public employees see no connection between extrinsic rewards and their performance. For years, expert observers (Thompson, 1975) have pointed out that some public managers find ways around formal constraints on rewards by isolating poor performers, giving them undesirable assignments, or establishing linkages between rewards and performance in other ways. Ban (1995) describes how managers in different federal agencies respond differently to the federal personnel rules depending on the culture of the agency. In some agencies the managers resist the strictures of the rules more aggressively and try to manipulate them in constructive ways. In other agencies the managers abide more strictly by the rules.

Nevertheless, a number of surveys have indicated that public employees perceive weaker relationships between performance and pay, promotion, and disciplinary action than private employees do (Porter and Lawler, 1968; Rainey, 1979, 1983; Lachman, 1985; Rainey, Traut, and Blunt, 1986; Solomon, 1986; Coursey and Rainey, 1990). These studies used expectancy-theory questionnaire items about such relationships and found that public sector samples rated them as weaker. Similarly, the U.S. Office of Personnel Management (1979) surveys found that sizable percentages of federal employees feel that pay, promotion, and demotion do not depend on performance. Again, these results may reflect shared stereotypes. In fact, there are some conflicting findings. Analysts in the Office of Personnel Management compared results from their survey question about pay and performance to results from a similar item on a large survey of private sector workers; they found little difference in the percentages of employees who expect to get a pay raise for good performance.

Self-Reported Motivation Among Public Employees

The reforms of the civil service systems and numerous writers on public organizations assume that these differences in incentive structure diminish motivation among public employees. One can more readily make that claim than prove it. As noted earlier, organizational researchers have difficulty measuring motivation. A few studies have compared public and private managers and employees on scales of self-reported motivation, however, and have found no large differences. Rainey (1979, 1983), using the Patchen scales described earlier, found no differences in self-reported motivation between middle managers in public and private organizations. Virtually all of the public and private managers said that they work very hard. Baldwin (1990) also found no difference in self-reported motivation between groups of public and private managers. Rainey (1983) found no difference in responses to expectancy items about the connection between performing well and intrinsic incentives such as the feeling of accomplishing something worthwhile, although the public managers perceived stronger connections between performance and the sense of "engaging in a meaningful public service." Bozeman and Loveless (1987) report somewhat higher levels of positive work climate in public R&D labs than in less public, more private labs.

Similarly, in spite of the stereotype of the cautious government bureaucrat (Downs, 1967; Warwick, 1975), public managers have claimed in response to surveys that they feel open to change and to new ways of doing things (Rainey, 1983). Many federal employees express skepticism about prospects for changing their organization, but most federal managers and executives (65 to 75 percent) see change as possible (U.S. Office of Personnel Management, 1979). Bellante and Link (1981) report a study showing that more risk-averse people join the public sector. Their measures of risk aversion, however, included smoking and drinking less, using automobile seat belts, and having higher medical and automobile insurance coverage. These could just as well serve as indicators of the sort of dutiful, public service–oriented, somewhat ascetic individuals suggested in studies of work-related values (Kilpatrick, Cummings, and Jennings, 1964; Sikula, 1973a) and do not themselves indicate aversion to professional and managerial risks. Golembiewski (1985; Golembiewski, Proehl, and Sink, 1981) reviewed 270 organizational development efforts in public organizations and concluded that more than 80 percent of them were apparently successful. Roessner (1983) notes scant evidence concerning the comparative innovativeness of public and private organizations but found no indication of private sector superiority in rates of diffusion of technological innovations.

In addition, the very large surveys of public employees and managers mentioned earlier found that they report high levels on measures related to motivation. They report very high work effort, a strong sense of challenge in their job, a strong sense of their organization's being important to them, high ratings of their organization's effectiveness, and high general work satisfaction (National Center for Productivity and Quality of Working Life, 1978; U.S. Office of Personnel Management, 1979; U.S. Merit Systems Protection Board, 1987).

Self-reports about one's effort and about these other factors have obvious limitations. The research indicates, nevertheless, that although many public employees and managers perceive relatively weak connections between performance and extrinsic rewards such as pay and promotion, they report attitudes and behaviors consistent with high motivation.

Other Motivation-Related Work Attitudes

The use of these techniques is also part of the reason that public employees express favorable attitudes on an array of motivation-related variables: work satisfaction, the importance of their organization, and a sense of challenge in their job, for example. These concepts return us to the point that motivation as a general topic covers numerous dimensions. Motivational techniques often aim at enhancing these attitudes as well as work effort. Researchers have developed many of these, often distinguishing them from motivation in the sense of work effort. These distinctions have importance in their own right, but researchers have also used some of them to compare public and private managers.

Job Satisfaction. Thousands of studies and dozens of different questionnaire measures make job satisfaction the most intensively studied variable in organizational research. Job satisfaction is a measure of how an individual feels about his or her job and various aspects of it (Gruneberg, 1979), usually in the sense of how favorable—how positive or negative—those feelings are. Job satisfaction is often related to other important attitudes and behaviors such as absenteeism, the intention to quit, and actually quitting.

Years ago, Locke (1983) pointed out that researchers had published about 3,500 studies of job satisfaction without coming to any clear agreement on its meaning. Job satisfaction nevertheless continues to play an important role in recent research (Cranny, 1992). The different ways of measuring job satisfaction illustrate different ways of defining it. Some studies use only two or three summary items, such as the following:

- In general, I like working here.
- In the next year, I intend to look for another job outside this organization.

General or global measures ask questions about enjoyment, interest, and enthusiasm to tap general feelings in much more depth. They often employ multiple-item scales, with the responses to be summed up or averaged, such as the following from the Minnesota Satisfaction Questionnaire (Weiss, Dawis, England, and Lofquist, 1967):

- I definitely dislike my work [reversed scoring].
- My job is pretty uninteresting [reversed scoring].
- I feel happier in my work than most other people.
- I find real enjoyment in my work.
- Most days I am enthusiastic about my work.

Specific, or facet, satisfaction measures ask about particular facets of the job. The following examples are from Smith's Index of Organizational Reactions (1976):

> *Supervision:* "Do you have the feeling you would be better off working under different supervision?"
>
> *Company identification:* "From my experience, I feel this organization probably treats its employees _____" [five choice responses, from "poorly" to "extremely well"].

Smith also includes scales for kind of work, amount of work, co-workers, physical work conditions, financial rewards, and career future. Porter's Needs Satisfaction Questionnaire (1962) asks respondents to rate thirteen factors concerning fulfillment of a particular need, rating how much of each factor there is now and how much there should be. The degree to which the "should be" rating exceeds the "is now" rating measures need dissatisfaction, or the inverse of satisfaction. The following are examples of the items included:

Security needs: "The feeling of security in my management position."

Social needs: "The opportunity, in my management position, to give help to other people."

Self-actualization needs: "The opportunity for personal growth and development in my management position."

Porter's questionnaire, which is not used very frequently anymore, employs categories based on Maslow's need theory. Some of the research on public sector work satisfaction described below used this method.

Determinants of Job Satisfaction. Different measures of job satisfaction use different definitions of it, and this complicates the research on the topic. Different studies using different measures—and hence different definitions—often come to conflicting conclusions about how job satisfaction is related to other variables. Partly because of these variations, researchers do not agree on a coherent theory or framework of what determines job satisfaction. Research generally finds higher job satisfaction associated with better pay, sufficient opportunity for promotion, consideration from supervisors, recognition, good working conditions, and utilization of skills and abilities. Even so, some studies report contradictory findings for almost any possible determinant.

This situation actually makes sense, because it is obviously unrealistic to try to generalize about how much any single factor affects a worker's satisfaction. Any particular factor in a given setting contends with other factors in that setting. Various studies suggest the importance of *individual differences* between workers: level of aspiration, level of comparison to alternatives (whether the person looks for or sees better opportunities elsewhere), level of acclimation (what a person is accustomed to), educational level, level in the organization and occupation, professionalism, age, tenure, race, gender, national and cultural background, and personality (values, self-esteem, and so on). The influence of any one of these, however, depends on other factors. For example, tenure and organizational level usually correlate with satisfaction. Those who have been in an organization longer and are at a higher level report higher satisfaction. This makes sense. Unhappy people leave; happier people stay. People who get to higher levels should be happier. Yet some studies find the opposite. In some organizations, longer-term employees feel undercompensated for their long service. Some people at higher levels may feel the same way or may feel that they have hit a ceiling on their opportunities. Career civil servants sometimes face this problem (Rainey, 1983).

Researchers also look at *job characteristics* and *job design* as determinants of job satisfaction. The most prominent recent approach, by Hackman and Oldham (1980), also draws on Maslow's need-fulfillment theory. These researchers report higher job satisfaction for jobs higher on the dimensions measured by their Job Diagnostic Survey, which includes the following subscales: skill variety, task identity, task significance, autonomy, feedback from the job, feedback from agents, and dealing with others. Hackman and Oldham's findings conform to a typical position among management experts, that more interesting, self-controlled, significant work, with feedback from others, improves satisfaction.

Besides looking at the person and the job, researchers have analyzed factors extrinsic to the work itself: pay, promotion, job security, supervision, work-group characteristics, participation in plans and decisions, and organizational structure and climate. These factors often influence satisfaction, but they too depend on the other factors in a given setting

Consequences of Job Satisfaction. Controversy also persists regarding the consequences of job satisfaction. For years, authors regularly pointed out that job satisfaction showed no consistent relationship to individual performance (Pinder, 1984). They typically cite Porter and Lawler's interpretation of this disappointing evidence (1968), which pointed out that good performance can lead to higher satisfaction just as well as satisfaction might lead to performance. A good performer who gets better rewards feels greater satisfaction. Yet a good performer who gets no better rewards experiences dissatisfaction, thus dissolving any positive link between satisfaction and performance. The link between performance and rewards, they concluded, plays a key role in determining the performance-satisfaction relationship. Though many individual studies have reported weak relationships between satisfaction and performance, recent meta-analytical studies—analyses of many studies to look for general trends in their results—suggest that the relationship of job satisfaction to performance is generally stronger than this typical interpretation suggests (Petty, McGee, and Cavender, 1984).

Researchers have also pointed out that satisfaction shows fairly consistent relationships with absenteeism and turnover. These behaviors cost organizations a lot of money, so since satisfaction helps to explain them, they are important variables. Although fairly consistent, these relationships have not proved extremely strong either. Obviously, practical factors such as health and family problems influence these behaviors. Satisfaction shows a stronger relationship with the expressed *intention* of turnover, but this does not always predict turnover very well.

In spite of these complexities, job satisfaction figures very importantly in organizations. Distinct from motivation and performance, it can nevertheless influence them, as well as other important behaviors such as turnover and absenteeism. Some studies have found work satisfaction to be related to life satisfaction and physical health (Gruneberg, 1979). In addition, measures of satisfaction have proved valuable in assessing attitudes in public organizations (Volcker Commission, 1989). As described below, studies find public sector respondents to be somewhat lower on such measures than private business employees. We know a good deal about influencing satisfaction and motivation, and we need to put that knowledge to better use in public organizations.

Role Conflict and Ambiguity. In an influential book published some years ago, Kahn and his colleagues (1964) argue that characteristics of an individual's "role" in an organization determine the stress that the employee experiences in his or her work. A number of "role senders" impose expectations and requirements on the person through both formal and informal processes. If these expectations are ambiguous and conflicting, the stress level increases. Other researchers later developed questionnaire items to measure role conflict and role ambiguity (Rizzo, House, and Lirtzman, 1970; House and Rizzo, 1972). *Role ambiguity* refers to a lack of necessary information at a given organizational position. The role ambiguity questionnaire asks about clarity of objectives, responsibilities, amount of authority, and time allocation in the person's job.

Role conflict refers to the incompatibility of different role requirements. A person's role might conflict with his or her values and standards or with his or her time, resources, and capabilities. Conflict might exist between two or more roles that the same person is expected to play. There might be conflict among organizational demands or expectations or conflicting expectations from different "role senders." The survey items on role conflict ask whether there are adequate labor and other resources to carry out assignments, whether others impose incompatible expectations, and whether the respondent has to buck roles in order to carry out assignments.

The two role variables consistently show relationships to job satisfaction and some similar measures, such as "job-related tension" (Miles and Petty, 1975; Miles, 1976), but are not so consistently related to measures of job performance (Schuler, 1977, p. 164). They also show a relationship to a number of other organizational factors, such as participation in decision making, leader behaviors, and formalization. Individual characteristics such as need for clarity and perceived locus of control (whether the individual sees events as being under his or her control or as being controlled externally) also influence how much role conflict and ambiguity a person experiences. These concepts have importance by themselves, since managers increasingly concern themselves with stress management and time management. Managing one's role can play a central part in these processes. In addition, however, research on public managers has also employed role questionnaires.

Job Involvement. In observing increasingly technical, professional, and scientific forms of work, researchers find differences among individuals in their involvement in their work. For some people, especially advanced professionals, work plays a very central part in their lives. Researchers measure job involvement by asking people whether they receive major life satisfaction from their jobs, whether their work is the most important thing in their life, and similar questions. Job involvement is distinct from general motivation and satisfaction but resembles intrinsic work motivation (Cook, Hepworth, Wall, and Warr, 1981). It figures importantly in the work attitudes of highly professionalized people who serve in crucial roles in many organizations. The concept has also played an interesting role in the research on public managers, as described below.

Organizational Commitment. The concept of organizational commitment has also figured in research on public and private managers (discussed later in this chapter). Individuals vary in their loyalty and commitment to the organizations in which they work. Certain people may consider the organization itself to be of immense importance to them, as an institution worthy of service, as a location of friends, as a source of security and other benefits. Others may see the organization only as a place to earn money. Professionals such as doctors, lawyers, and scientists often have loyalties external to the organization—to the profession itself and their professional colleagues.

Scales for measuring organizational commitment ask whether the respondent sees the organization's problems as his or her own, whether he or she feels a sense of pride in working for the organization, and similar questions (Mowday, Porter, and Steers, 1982). Studies also show the complex, multidimensional nature of commitment. For example, Angle and Perry (1981) show the importance of the distinction between calculative commitment and normative commitment. One form of organizational loyalty can be calculative, based on the perceived material rewards that the organization offers. Another basis for organizational loyalty is normative: the individual is committed to the organization because he or she sees it as a mechanism for enacting personal ideals and values.

Balfour and Wechsler (1996) further elaborated the concept of organizational commitment in a model for the public sector based on a study of public employees. Their evidence suggested three forms of commitment. Identification commitment is based on the employee's degree of pride in working for the organization and the sense that the organization does something important and does it competently. Affiliation commitment derives from a sense of belonging to the organization and of the other members of the organizations as "family" who care about one another. Exchange commitment is based on the belief that the organization recognizes and appreciates the efforts and accomplishments of its members.

Balfour and Wechsler's is part of an interesting stream of research and thought on public organizations to which we will return below. In addition, we will return to the point that their study and others suggest ways that public sector leaders and managers can seek to enhance commitment and other work experiences in their organizations.

Professionalism. For years, sociological researchers have studied the way in which highly trained specialists control complex occupations. Technological advances have made certain valuable types of work increasingly complex and difficult to apprehend. Specialists in these areas must have advanced training and must maintain high standards. Only specialists, however, have the qualifications to establish and police the standards. From the point of view of society and of large organizations, these factors raise problems involving monopolies, excessive self-interest, and mixed loyalties. Government and business organizations also face challenges in managing the work and careers of highly trained professionals.

Researchers have offered many definitions of the term *profession,* typically including these elements:

- Application of a skill based on theoretical knowledge
- Requirement for advanced education and training
- Testing of competence through examinations or other methods
- Organization into a professional association
- Existence of a code of conduct and emphasis on adherence to it
- Espousal of altruistic service

Occupational specializations that rate relatively highly on most or all of these dimensions are highly "professionalized." Medical doctors, lawyers, and highly trained scientists are usually considered advanced professionals without much argument. Scholars usually place college professors, engineers, accountants, and sometimes social workers in the professional category. Often they define less developed specializations, such as librarians and computer programmers, as semi-professions, emerging professions, or less professionalized occupations.

In turn, management researchers analyze the characteristics of individual "professionals," because they play key roles in contemporary organizations. They point out that, as a result of their selection and training, professionals tend to have certain beliefs and values (Filley, House, and Kerr, 1976):

- Belief in the need to be expert in the body of abstract knowledge applicable to the profession
- Belief that they and fellow professionals should have autonomy in their work activities and decision making

- Identification with the profession and with fellow professionals
- Commitment to the work of the profession as a calling, or life's work
- A feeling of ethical obligation to render service to clients without self-interest and with emotional neutrality
- A belief in self-regulation and collegial maintenance of standards (that is, a belief that fellow professionals are best qualified to judge and police one another)

Members of a profession vary on these dimensions. Those relatively high on most or all are highly professional by this definition.

The characteristics of professions and professionals may conflict with the characteristics of large bureaucratic organizations. Belief in autonomy may conflict with organizational rules and hierarchies. Emphasis on altruistic service to clients can conflict with organizational emphases on cost savings and standardized treatment of clients. Identification with the profession and desire for recognition from fellow professionals may dilute the impact of organizational rewards, such as financial incentives and organizational career patterns. Professionals might prefer an enhanced professional reputation to salary increases and prefer their professional work to moving "up" into management. Without moving up, however, they hit ceilings that limit pay, promotion, and prestige. Studies have found higher organizational formalization associated with higher alienation among professionals (Hall, 1996).

Conflicts between professionals and organizations do not appear to be as inevitable as once supposed, however. Certain bureaucratic values, such as emphasis on technical qualifications of personnel, are compatible with professional values (Hall, 1996). For example, professionals may approve of organizational rules on qualifications for jobs. Professionals in large organizations may be isolated in certain subunits, such as laboratories, where they are relatively free from organizational rules and hierarchical controls (Larson, 1977; Bozeman and Loveless, 1987; Crow and Bozeman, 1987). Certain professionals, such as engineers and accountants, may want to move up in organizations in nonprofessional roles (Schott, 1978; Larson, 1977). Some empirical studies indicate that, for some professionals, professional commitment is positively correlated with organizational commitment (Bartol, 1979).

Management writers offer some useful suggestions about the management of professionals. They prescribe *dual career ladders,* which add to the standard career path for managers another for professionals, so that professionals can stay in their specialty (research, legal work, social work) but move up to higher levels of pay and responsibility. This relieves the tension over deciding whether one must give up one's profession and go into management. Some organizations rotate professionals in and out of management positions. The U.S. Geological Survey has a policy of rotating geologists in administrative positions back into professional research positions after several years. Some organizations also allow professionals to take credit for their accomplishments. For example, they allow them to claim authorship of professional research reports rather than requiring that they publish them anonymously in the name of the agency or company. Organizations can also pay for travel to professional conferences and in other ways support professionals in their desire to remain excellent in their profession.

Researchers have not reported much research comparing professionals in the public and private sectors. Typically they treat issues involving professionals as very generic, crossing the sectors. Government agencies have many professional employees, however, and a particular profession dominates many government agencies (Mosher, [1968] 1982), so the issues figure importantly in public management. Recently, the Volcker Commission (1989) reported that the federal government faces grave difficulties in attracting highly qualified professionals because the private sector offers them so much higher salaries. On the other hand, work settings for some professionals in government appear to offer equal or superior intrinsic incentives. As noted earlier, Bozeman and Loveless (1987) found that public sector R&D labs have more positive work climates than private labs. Many public managers face a challenge in providing intrinsic incentives that can compete with the superior salaries available to some professionals in the private sector (Romzek, 1990).

Motivation-Related Variables in Public Organizations

Researchers have made comparisons on a number of these variables between public and private samples, shedding some light on how the two categories compare.

Role Ambiguity, Role Conflict, and Organizational Goal Clarity. For some work-related attitudes, researchers have found few differences between managers in public and private organizations. This has been the case with the most frequent observation in all the literature on the distinctive character of public management: public managers confront greater multiplicity, vagueness, and conflict of goals and performance criteria than managers in private organizations do (Rainey, 1989). As noted in Chapter Six, executives often mention this distinction, and researchers refer to it in interpreting their findings. These observations about vague, multiple goals in the public sector bear on classic questions about social control through politics or through markets (Lindblom, 1977); there is a fascinating divergence between political economists and organization theorists on the observations' validity. Political scientists and economists tend to regard this goal complexity as an obvious consequence or determinant of governmental (nonmarket) controls, while many organization theorists tend to regard it as a generic problem facing all organizations.

Beyond the observations of experienced executives, however, strikingly little comparative research directly addresses this issue. Rainey (1983) compared middle managers in government and business organizations concerning the role conflict and role ambiguity items described earlier, asking questions about the clarity of the respondents' goals in work, conflicting demands, and related matters. The government and business managers showed no differences on these questions nor on questions about whether they regarded the goals of their organization as clear and easy to measure. More recent surveys have confirmed these results (Rainey, Facer, and Bozeman, 1995). One explanation for these results may be that public managers clarify their roles and objectives by reference to standard operating procedures, whether or not the overall goals of the organization are clear and consistent (Perry and Porter, 1982). In addition, when researchers ask managers to describe their decision-making criteria, private managers mention financial performance criteria much more frequently than public managers do (Solomon, 1986; Schwenk, 1990).

The real issue, then, may not be whether managers perceive that goals are clear but rather what criteria and processes they use to clarify their goals, as well as just how valid those criteria are as sound measures of performance. Whatever the explanation, these limited findings point to important challenges for both researchers and practitioners in further analyzing such issues as how managers in various settings (public, private, and hybrid organizations) perceive objectives and performance criteria; how these objectives and criteria are communicated and validated, if they are; and whether these objectives and criteria do in fact coincide with the sorts of distinctions between public and private settings that are assumed to exist in our political economy.

Work Satisfaction. Many studies have found differences between respondents from the public and private sectors concerning other work-related attitudes and perceptions. Public employees and managers express high levels of general work satisfaction, usually comparable to that reported by their private sector counterparts (Kilpatrick, Cummings, and Jennings, 1964; U.S. Office of Personnel Management, 1979). Large-scale surveys have shown that younger members of the public sector work force show higher levels of general work satisfaction than younger private sector workers do (Steel and Warner, 1990) and that persons entering the public sector work force are higher on certain measures of quality than entry-level private sector employees (Crewson, 1995a).

However, numerous studies comparing the work satisfaction of public and private sector employees, especially at managerial levels, have reported somewhat lower satisfaction among public sector workers in various more specific facets of work (Paine, Carroll, and Leete, 1966; Rhinehart and others, 1969; Buchanan,

1974; Hayward, 1978; Rainey, 1983; Lachman, 1985; Solomon, 1986; Kovach and Patrick, 1989). These studies used different measures of satisfaction and varied samples, and this makes it hard to generalize about them. For example, Paine, Carroll, and Leete (1966) and Rhinehart and his colleagues (1969) found that groups of federal managers showed lower satisfaction than business managers on all categories of the Porter scale. Smith and Nock (1980), analyzing results of a large social survey, found that public sector blue-collar workers show more satisfaction with most aspects of their work than their private sector counterparts, but public sector white-collar workers show less satisfaction with co-workers, supervision, and intrinsic aspects of their work. Hayward (1978) compared employees and managers in a diverse group of public and private organizations and found satisfaction ratings generally high among both groups. The public sector respondents, however, gave somewhat more unfavorable ratings concerning their job overall, their ability to make necessary decisions, the adequacy of the supplies in their organization, the amount of duplication they have to contend with, and the amount of work they are expected to do. Rainey (1983) found that state agency managers scored lower than business managers on their satisfaction with promotion opportunities and with co-workers.

The findings of these studies vary a great deal and are not easily summarized. The public and private respondents often did not differ greatly, yet one finds it hard to dismiss as accidental the consistent tendency of the public managers and employees to score lower on various satisfaction scales. Taken together, these studies reveal a somewhat lower satisfaction with various intrinsic and extrinsic aspects of work in many public organizations than exists in many private ones. Some of the findings appear to reflect the sorts of administrative constraints described earlier—personnel system constraints (promotion) and purchasing constraints (supplies). Others appear to reflect related frustrations with administrative complexities and complex political and policymaking processes, public sector realities that diminish some intrinsic rewards. Administrative duplication and lack of authority, for example, result in lower satisfaction of managers' higher-order needs (Rhinehart and others, 1969).

Organizational Commitment and Job Involvement. As mentioned earlier, there has been an interesting stream of research related to the topic of organizational commitment and job involvement in public organizations, much of it based on comparisons of public and private managers and employees. The research has produced some indications of particular frustrations in the public service. As with other topics, such as motivation and work satisfaction, however, the evidence is somewhat conflicting and complicated and leads us back to the conclusion that public organizations and managers may face particular challenges, but the situation in the public sector is not necessarily dire. The research further provides suggestions of approaches for public managers to take and indications that public organizations and managers can take them effectively.

The stream of research began with studies by Buchanan (1974, 1975), who found that groups of federal executives expressed lower organizational commitment and job involvement than executives from private firms. He concluded that the public managers felt less commitment because they did not feel as strong a sense of having a personal impact on the organization, because the organization did not expect as much commitment, and because their work groups were more diverse and less of a source of attachment to the organization. Buchanan also suggested that the lower involvement scores indicated a frustrated service ethic and expressed concern that it reflected weak public service motivation on the part of the public managers. His evidence showed that the involvement responses resulted from a sense of holding a less challenging job, of working in less cohesive groups, and of having more disappointing experiences in the organization than the managers had expected when they joined it. These disappointments, he thought, might arise when idealistic, service-oriented entrants confront the realities of large government agencies, where they feel they have little impact.

More recently, Flynn and Tannenbaum (1993) also reported a study in which a sample of public managers expressed lower organizational commitment than a sample of private sector managers. The public managers were lower on their ratings of the clarity, autonomy, and challenge of their jobs. Their lower scores on clarity and autonomy appeared to be the strongest influences on their lower commitment scores.

Though they have not measured organizational commitment directly, other studies and observations have indicated similar general characteristics of the public sector work context. Boyatzis (1982) draws a conclusion similar to Buchanan's from his comparisons of public and private managers. And Chubb and Moe (1990) find a generally lower perceived sense of control and commitment among staff members and teachers in public schools than among their private school counterparts.

Case observations paint a similar picture. Michelson (1980) describes examples of hardworking bureaucrats in nonworking bureaucracies. They work hard, he observes, but the diffuse goals and haphazard designs of some programs make their efforts futile. Cherniss (1980) observes that many public service professionals experience stress and burnout as a result of their frustrated motivation to help their clients and the bureaucratic systems that aggravate their frustrations. Downs's observations about discouraged statesmen and increasing conservatism (1967) and Warwick's description of the State Department (1975) have similar implications.

The large federal surveys mentioned earlier have also found a combination of positive attitudes and frustration or discouragement among public employees.

The overwhelming majority of respondents to the federal employee attitude survey (U.S. Office of Personnel Management, 1979) said that they feel that they do meaningful work, that what happens in their organization is important, and that their organization performs effectively. Yet high percentages of these employees (more than 45 percent), managers (35 percent), and executives (25 percent) expressed concern that employees feel that they cannot trust the organization. Many employees expressed a sense of powerlessness and a lack of influence and participation in decision making (U.S. Office of Personnel Management, 1979, p. 36). In another large survey, only a limited number of respondents felt that the opportunity to have an impact on public affairs represents an important reason to stay in public service (U.S. Merit Systems Protection Board, 1987).

These research findings and observations support Buchanan's interpretation. But other studies have found that public employees were not necessarily lower on organizational commitment (Balfour and Wechsler, 1990, 1991). Steinhaus and Perry (1996) analyzed data from a major national survey, the 1991 General Social Survey, and found that public sector employees showed no significant difference from private sector employees on a measure of organizational commitment. They found that the industry in which a person was employed predicted organizational commitment better than whether the person worked in the public or private sector. They concluded that a public versus private dichotomy is too simple a distinction for analyzing organizational commitment.

These mixed results raise some important challenges for public sector managers and researchers alike. First, they emphasize the intriguing and important question of whether all the assertions about the context of public organizations reviewed in earlier chapters influence an important variable like organizational commitment. The studies that found a public-private difference concentrated on managers, whereas those that did not, such as the Steinhaus and Perry study, looked at all levels together or mostly at nonmanagerial employees. This suggests that the constraints and interventions that impinge on public organizations may have their greatest influence at managerial levels. The pattern of evidence also raise doubts about Buchanan's concerns about weakened motivation in government agencies. As noted in the discussion of the public service motive in Chapter Nine, it is not the same as organizational commitment and job involvement. Public managers and employees may show lower scores on organizational commitment, for example, because they feel strongly committed to serving clients and do not regard the organization itself as an important object of pride and loyalty (Romzek and Hendricks, 1982). Low scores on commitment questions may reflect problems but not necessarily weak public service motives or low levels of general motivation and effort.

The evidence leaves us in a situation like the case of work satisfaction discussed earlier. There are suggestions of problems in the public sector, but public sector managers and employees do not show sharply lower levels of organizational commitment, work satisfaction, or other important attitudes. Where public managers and employees do show lower scores on organizational commitment, the responses appear to be linked to aspects of the public sector environment discussed in earlier chapters, such as constraining rules, complex goals, political intervention, turnover, and uncertainty. Surveys that find lower levels of organizational commitment and other important attitudes among people in the public sector also tend to find very positive attitudes as well, such as high ratings of the importance of the work, of serving clients, and of working hard. In addition, when people in public organizations express higher levels of organizational commitment, their responses tend to be based on very desirable factors—as opposed, for example, to whether the organization provides generous material benefits—such as a sense of meaningful public service or the opportunity to participate in important decisions.

The mixed results in studies of organizational commitment in the public and private sectors actually move us toward suggestions for both managers and researchers. Balfour and Wechsler (1996) reported complex findings about variables related to their three dimensions of commitment described earlier. Generally, however, they found that four factors appeared to increase all three dimensions of commitment: more participation in decision making, lower political penetration (less external political influence on hiring, promotion, and treatment of clients), more respectful and supportive supervision, and more opportunity for advancement. In a similar vein, based on her own research and that of others, Romzek (1990) concludes that highly committed employees in government feel that their jobs are compatible with their ethics, values, and professional standards and that their families and friends support their affiliation with the organization they work for (Romzek, 1990). Although the studies reviewed above indicate difficulties in bringing about such conditions in some public organizations—probably in very complex, controversial, and highly politicized ones with diffuse mandates—public managers can often overcome those problems. As the research also shows, the problems in the public sector may not be more severe than those in the private sector but rather simply different (Golembiewski, 1985).

The Challenge of Motivation in the Public Sector

Like the topics before it, the topic of organizational commitment dramatizes the challenge for everyone concerned with effective public management. The research indicates frustrations, constraints, and problems of working and managing in the public sector. It also reflects, however, a strong current of motivation, effort, and constructive attitudes in public organizations. The challenge for leaders and managers involves dealing effectively with the complex environment of public organizations so as to support and make the most of the valuable human resources and potential. For all of us, the challenge is intensified by the absence of a conclusive, scientific solution to these problems in the research and theory in organizational behavior and related fields. Yet as the review and the examples here have shown, that body of knowledge does offer ideas, concepts, and methods that provide valuable support for those of us determined to pursue those challenges.

CHAPTER ELEVEN

LEADERSHIP, MANAGERIAL ROLES, AND ORGANIZATIONAL CULTURE

Figures 1.1 and 1.2 in Chapter One suggest the essential role of leadership in organizations and show its relationship to all the other parts of organizational management. This chapter is placed here because it discusses the many challenges of organizational leadership addressed in the preceding chapters. It focuses directly on the topic of leadership, reviewing theories of leadership and managerial roles from the generic literature and assessing the research on leadership in public organizations.

In the last two decades, organizational culture has also become a very important topic in management thought, both in research and practice. Much of the discussion of organizational culture in this chapter concerns the way effective executives influence it. Important developments in our thinking about leadership, such as the concept of transformational leadership, are important to the management of organizational culture. This chapter raises important points about how and when public managers can use such approaches. Also, champions of reforms and new approaches, such as Total Quality Management (described in Chapter Fourteen), empowerment, and "learning organization" initiatives, insist that such efforts require the support of an effective organizational culture. This chapter will discuss the meaning and assessment of organizational culture and the roles of leaders in communicating and transforming it.

Previous chapters have repeatedly raised the challenges of leading in the public sector. Civil service systems, other institutional controls, and the political environment weaken the authority of public sector leaders. Experts differ as to how much of this picture is a mere stereotype and how much is attributable to valid observations. Recently, a countertrend has begun to emphasize the prevalence of effective and entrepreneurial public leadership; this chapter will describe those developments.

Leadership Theories in Management and Organizational Behavior

An immense body of research has examined leadership in organizational settings. By *leadership*, most people mean the capacity of someone to direct and energize the willingness of people in social units to take actions to achieve goals. The issues raised in the discussion of power and authority in earlier chapters make up part of the discussion of leadership. Leadership in one sense can draw mainly on blunt power, but usually the term implies legitimate authority. Some people interpret leadership as a function of management; others treat management as a subordinate function of leadership. In the latter usage, *leadership* implies the crucial functions of championing goals and values, setting directions, and providing inspiration, while *management* implies housekeeping functions such as watching the budget and making sure that the work gets done. Faced with the challenge of understanding this paradoxical topic, how have management researchers attacked the problem?

Trait Theories

First, researchers have tried to determine those characteristics, or traits, that make a person an effective leader. Midcentury leadership researchers concentrated on this approach. They tried to identify the traits of effective leaders—physical characteristics such as height, intellectual characteristics such as intelligence and foresight, personality characteristics such as enthusiasm and persistence. They identified many important traits such as these, often demonstrating a relationship between them and effective leadership, and leadership characteristics of various sorts have remained an important element of leadership research. No one, however, has ever identified a common set of traits for excellent leaders. Leaders come in a variety of sizes, shapes, talents, and dispositions. The quest for universal traits has been replaced by other approaches.

The Ohio State Leadership Studies

The social sciences developed rapidly during the middle of this century. More and more studies used new techniques such as questionnaires and computer analysis, and there was an increasing emphasis on systematic observations of human behavior. Drawing on samples from the military, schools, and other organizations, researchers at Ohio State University developed questionnaires that asked people to report on the behaviors of their superiors. After repeated analyses of the questionnaire results, they found that observations about leaders fell into two dimensions—consideration and initiating structure. These would become central issues, under various names, in much of the subsequent work on leadership. *Consideration* refers to a leader's concern for his or her relationships with subordinates. Questionnaire items pertaining to consideration ask whether the leader is friendly and approachable, listens to subordinates' ideas and makes use of them, cares about the morale of the group, and otherwise deals with subordinates in an open, communicative, concerned fashion. *Initiating structure* refers to a leader's emphasis on setting standards, assigning roles, and pressing for productivity and performance. The two dimensions tend to be related to each other, but only to a limited extent.

This research played a pivotal role in moving the field into empirical research on leadership. It drove the trait approach into disrepute by showing that effective leaders vary on these dimensions and do not display a uniform set of traits. It also set the dimensions in place in the literature as two key aspects of leader behavior. Yet reviewers raised questions about the adequacy of the questionnaire measures of the two major dimensions and noted that two dimensions do not make for a complete picture of leadership practice and effectiveness. Researchers have since moved off in search of more complete models.

The Blake and Mouton Managerial Grid

The Ohio State leadership studies had a significant impact on Blake and Mouton's "managerial grid" approach to improving management practices (1984). Blake and Mouton characterized organizations according to two dimensions with clear roots in the Ohio State studies—*concern for people* and *concern for production*. Organizations low on the former and high on the latter have "authority-obedience" management. Those high on concern for people and low on concern for production have "country club management." Those low on both have "impoverished management." This approach sought to move organizations toward high levels of both factors, or to "team management," through open communication, participative problem solving and goal setting, confrontation of differences, and teamwork. This framework supported Blake and Mouton's popular organization development consulting method, which they applied in a broad range of government, business, and third-sector organizations.

Fiedler's Contingency Theory of Leadership

Researchers still sought more complete theories, especially theories that would better address the numerous situations that leaders face. Fiedler's contingency theory (1967) received a lot of attention because at the time it offered one of the best frameworks for examining the relationship between leadership style and organizational setting and how it affects a leader's effectiveness. Fiedler used a "least preferred co-worker" (LPC) scale to distinguish between types of leadership styles. The LPC scale asked a leader to think of the person with whom that leader could work least well and then to rate that person on about twenty numerical scales of personal characteristics, such as pleasant or unpleasant, tense or relaxed, boring or interesting, and nasty or nice. After repeated studies, Fiedler and his associates felt that the responses indicated two basic types of leaders: high-LPC leaders give relatively favorable ratings to this least preferred associate, and low-LPC leaders rate the associate much more unfavorably. The responses of high-LPC leaders show that they have more favorable dispositions toward co-workers and thus are *relationship-oriented*. Low-LPC leaders are *task-oriented;* they concentrate on task accomplishment over relationships with co-workers and find less desirable co-workers more irritating because they hinder successful work.

Fiedler's theory holds that either type of leadership style can be effective, depending on whether it properly matches the contingencies facing the leader. According to the theory, the key contingencies, in order of their importance in determining effective leadership, are *leader-member relations,* marked by the degree of friendliness, trust, initiative, and cooperativeness of the leader and the subordinates; *task structure,* shaped by the clarity and specificity of what must be done; and *position power of the leader,* determined by the amount of formal power the leader has.

Leadership situations vary on each of these dimensions, from good to bad. Obviously, a leader enjoys the most favorable setting when all three are good and the least favorable when all three are bad. Moderately favorable settings have a mixture of good and bad conditions, such as good leader-member relations but an unstructured task setting and weak position power. Fiedler contends that low-LPC (task-oriented) leaders perform most effectively in the very favorable or very unfavorable settings, while high-LPC (relationship-oriented) leaders do best in the intermediate settings.

Fiedler's rationale for this conclusion evades easy explanation, but the logic appears to go like this: low-LPC leaders do well in the best situations because everything is in place and the subordinates simply need to be given direction (and they accept the leader as authorized to give such direction). The leader of an airplane crew who has the benefits of clear power, a strong task structure, and good relations with subordinates does best if he or she concentrates on giving orders to best accomplish the task. The low-LPC type also does well in very bad situations that have so much potential disorder and disaffection anyway that worrying about establishing good personal relations simply wastes time. In such settings, the leader might as well go ahead and press for structure, order, and output.

High-LPC leaders do best in the intermediate situations because an emphasis on good relations can overcome the one or two bad dimensions and take advantage of other favorable aspects of the setting. For example, a weakly empowered chair of a newly formed, poorly structured interdepartmental committee who has good relations with the committee members can take advantage of those good relations, encouraging participation and opinion sharing, to overcome the committee's other problems.

Fiedler argued that his theory showed that, rather than trying to train leaders to fit a particular setting, organizations must alter the setting to fit the leader. He and his colleagues developed a "leader match" procedure, in which leaders use questionnaires to assess their own style and their leadership situation and then consider ways of changing the situation to make it better fit their style.

Fiedler has continued to report on studies supporting the theory, but critics question the adequacy of the evidence and the methods used. Clearly, the theory includes a very limited picture of the possible situational factors and variations in leadership styles. Still, it raises key issues about leadership processes and has advanced the effort to develop more complete theories.

The Path-Goal Theory of Leadership

The most comprehensive theory to date, the path-goal theory, draws on the expectancy theory of motivation (described in Chapter Ten). Expectancy theory treats motivation as arising from expectations about the results of actions and the value of those results. Similarly, path-goal theory holds that effective leaders increase motivation and satisfaction among subordinates when they help them pursue important goals—that is, when they help them see the goals, the paths to them, and how to follow those paths effectively. Leaders must do this by showing subordinates the value of outcomes over which the leader has some control, by finding ways to increase the value to subordinates of those outcomes, by using appropriate coaching and direction to clarify the paths to those outcomes, and by removing barriers and frustrations to those paths.

The theory also considers a variety of leadership styles, characteristics of subordinates, and situational factors that affect the proper approach to a leader's path-goal work (House, 1971; House and Mitchell, 1974; Filley, House, and Kerr, 1976). House and Mitchell considered four leadership styles: *directive*, where the leader gives specific directions and expectations; *supportive*, marked by encouraging, sympathetic relations with subordinates; *achievement-oriented*, where the leader sets high goals and high expectations for subordinates' performance and responsibility; and *participative*, where the leader encourages subordinates to express opinions and suggestions.

Which style is best depends on various situational factors, such as whether the task is structured and provides clear goals, whether subordinates have well-developed skills and a sense of personal control over their environment ("locus of control"), how much formal authority the leader has, and whether the work group has strong norms and social relationships. When factors such as these provide weak path-goal indications and incentives, the proper leadership style can enhance them. The leader must avoid behaviors that impose redundancies and aggravations, however.

Researchers have predicted and tested relationships such as these:

- Directive leadership enhances satisfaction and expectancies if the task is ambiguous but hurts them if the task is well structured and clear.
- Clear tasks already provide clear paths to goals, and subordinates may see more directions from a leader as redundant and irritating.
- Supportive leadership enhances satisfaction when tasks are frustrating and stressful but can be inappropriate when the task, the work group, and the organization provide plenty of encouragement. In such situations the leader need only clarify directions as needed and set high standards.
- Achievement-oriented leadership increases performance for ambiguous tasks, either because those conditions more often allow (or require) ambitious goals than simple tasks do or because achievement-oriented subordinates tend to select such tasks.
- Participative leadership works best for ambiguous tasks in which subordinates feel that their self-esteem is at stake, since participation allows them to influence decisions and to work out solutions to the ambiguity. For clear tasks, however, participative leadership is effective only if subordinates value self-control and independence.

As these examples show, the theory weaves together leadership styles and situational factors to make sufficiently subtle predictions to capture some of the complex variations in real leadership settings. A lot of research has produced mixed results and much debate concerning this theory, however. Some research continues to find support for some variant of the theory, although it has not received much attention recently.

The Vroom-Yetton Normative Model

Vroom and Yetton (1973; Vroom and Jago, 1974) propose an elaborate framework for leaders to use in deciding how and how much to involve subordinates or subordinate groups in decisions. The framework takes the form of a decision tree that guides the leader through a series of questions about how important the quality of the decision will be, whether the leader has the necessary information to make a high-quality decision, whether the problem is well structured, whether acceptance of the decision by subordinates is important, and whether conflict among them is likely. The decision-making process guides the leader in selecting from various ways of handling the decision, such as delegating it or making it after consulting subordinates.

Attribution Models

Social psychologists have developed a body of theory about how people make attributions about one another, or how they attribute characteristics to others. Some leadership researchers have applied this perspective to leadership and produced useful insights. They look at how leaders draw conclusions about how and why their subordinates are behaving and performing and how subordinates form impressions about leaders. Leaders interpret the apparent causes of subordinate behavior and performance in deciding how to respond. They take into account how unique to a particular task the performance happens to be, the consistency of the behaviors, and how they compare to those of other subordinates. Some of the research shows that when a subordinate performs poorly, leaders tend to attribute the problems to the subordinate if he or she has a bad record. If the person has a good record of past performance, however, leaders often conclude that the problems result from the situation surrounding the person and are not his or her fault. For their part, subordinates often attribute the lion's share of credit or blame for the group's performance and characteristics to their leader. If the group has performed well in the past, they tend more readily to give the leader credit for current successes, even rating him or her more highly on certain leader behaviors and interpreting these as causes.

Attribution theories obviously offer a partial approach that does not cover the full topic of leadership, but they clearly point to important processes for leaders to keep in mind. Leaders always face the challenge of managing others' impressions of them and of trying to form valid impressions themselves of their colleagues and subordinates. These attribution processes pertain especially to problems in public management, where political appointees come in at the tops of agencies and must establish relations with career civil servants. Frequently the political appointees anticipate resistance and poor performance from the careerists, and the careerists anticipate amateurishness from the political appointee. When problems come up, the two types tend to interpret them according to their preconceptions about each other, aggravating the problem of developing effective working relationships. The careerists and appointees often come to respect each other, but attribution processes often slow this process (Heclo, 1978; Light, 1987; Ingraham, 1988).

Life-Cycle Theory

Hersey and Blanchard (1982) offer another form of contingency theory. Their life-cycle theory suggests that leadership styles must fit the level of maturity of the group being led. Mature groups have a higher capacity for accepting responsibility because they are well educated, experienced, and capable at accomplishing group tasks and have well developed relationships with one another and the leader. With groups that are very low on these dimensions, however, leaders must engage in *telling*, emphasizing task directions over developing relationships with the group, to move the group toward better task capabilities. As the group moves higher on some dimensions of maturity but remains at a low level of maturity overall, the leader must do more *selling*, or heavily emphasizing both tasks and relationships. As the group moves to moderately high maturity, *participating* becomes the most effective style. The leader relaxes the emphasis on task direction but still attends to relationships. Finally, for a very mature group, *delegating* becomes the effective approach. The leader deemphasizes his or her own role in directing tasks and maintaining relationships and shifts responsibility to group members.

Loosely defined concepts plague the theory, but they make important points. Leaders often face the challenge of assessing just how much the group can accept delegation (how much it needs someone to take charge and set directions) and determining how to move the group toward a greater capacity for handling tasks and relationships independently.

Operant Conditioning and Social Learning Theory Models

The operant conditioning and behavior modification perspectives described in Chapter Ten have found their way into the search for leadership theories. Some early behavior modification approaches emphasized reinforcement of outcomes over concern with internal mental states. Proponents argued that these approaches offered significant improvements for leadership techniques, for several reasons. They stressed observations of behavior rather than dubious inferences about what happens in a person's head. For example, they said that managers should look at behaviors and performance outcomes rather than whether a person has a "good attitude." They called for close attention to the consequences of behavior, saying that leaders must attend to the behaviors that they reinforce or extinguish by associating consequences with those behaviors. They emphasized positive reinforcement as being most effective.

Later approaches began to take into account developments in social learning theory. Albert Bandura (1978) and other psychologists demonstrated that operant conditioning models needed to expand to include forms of learning and behavioral change that are not tied tightly to some reinforcement. People learn by watching others, through modeling and vicarious learning. They use mental symbols, rehearsal, and memorization techniques to develop their behaviors. Taking these insights into account, social learning theory models of leadership have added analysis of internal mental states and social learning to their assessments of leadership (Kreitner and Luthans, 1987). This has led to additional suggestions about leadership practices. Since internal mental states and social learning also affect behavior (in addition to feedback and after-the-fact reinforcement), leaders can use "feedforward" techniques to influence behavior. They can anticipate problems and actively avoid them by clarifying goals. They can enhance employees' acceptance of goals by having them participate in their development and through social cues (by acting as a good role model). They can also emphasize self-management, both for themselves and for their subordinates. This involves managing one's own environment by recognizing how environmental factors influence one's behavior and through personal goal setting, rehearsal, and self-instruction.

Cognitive Resource Utilization Theory

Researchers continue to work on additional theories. Among recent ones, Fiedler's cognitive resource utilization theory has received the most validation from supporting studies (Fiedler and Garcia, 1987). It extends the Fiedler contingency theory, specifying when directive (low-LPC) behaviors affect group performance but also drawing in the effects of the leader's intelligence, competence, and stress level. Fiedler and Garcia reported the unexpected finding that considerate (high-LPC) leader behavior has little effect on group performance. For such leaders, if the group supports them and the task requires cognitive abilities, then the cognitive abilities of the group determine its performance. If the group does not support them, then external factors, such as task difficulty, determine performance.

For directive leaders with much control over the situation, performance depends on whether the leader is free of stress, whether the task requires cognitive abilities, and whether the group supports the leader. If these conditions hold, the leader's intelligence strongly predicts performance. If the leader is under stress, however, the leader's experience becomes the best predictor of performance, because stress prevents the effective use of intelligence and brings experience more strongly into play. Also, if the task does not require cognitive skill or the group does not support the leader, then the leader's intelligence has little or no effect on performance. As the authors state, their theory and research suggest the "not surprising conclusion that directive leaders who are stupid give stupid directions, and if the group follows these directions, the consequences will be bad" (Fiedler and Garcia, 1987, p. 199). Directive leader behaviors result in good performance only if coupled with high leader intelligence and a supportive, stress-free setting. The theory offers useful new insights into such variables in the leadership process as stress, which leaders can strive to manage (House and Singh, 1987).

Other theories, such as social information processing theory and dyadic linkage theory, have also received attention, but probably the most striking departure in recent leadership research concerns transformational leadership. Before covering that approach, however, it is useful to review a body of research on managerial roles and behaviors to which the transformational leadership research reacts.

The Nature of Managerial Work and Roles

As the research on leadership developed, there also emerged a body of work on the characteristics of managerial work, roles, and skills. This literature actually involves something of a trait approach. It seeks to develop general conceptions of managerial activities and competencies. Ever since the classical theorists began trying to define the role of the administrator, the approach of "planning, organizing, staffing, directing, coordinating, reporting, and budgeting" (POSDCORB) or some variant of it has served as a guiding conception of what managers must do. Often coupled with this view is the constantly repeated view that managers in all settings must do pretty much the same general types of work. Allison (1983) illustrated the prevalence of the POSDCORB conception of managerial responsibilities when he used a form of it in one of the most widely reprinted and circulated articles ever written on public management (see Table 11.1).

Not so preoccupied with what managers must do as with what they actually do, Henry Mintzberg (1972) produced *The Nature of Managerial Work*, which now stands as a classic in the field. He did something that, remarkably, was considered quite original at the time. He closely observed the work of five managers who headed organizations by following them around and having them keep notebooks. He concluded that their work falls into the set of roles listed in Table 11.1.

Mintzberg also reported that when one actually watches what managers do, one sees the inaccuracy of some popular beliefs about their work. Managers do not play the role of systematic, rational planners but rather emphasize action over reflection. Their activities are characterized by brevity, variety, and discontinuity. While top-level managers are often told to plan and delegate and avoid regular duties, in reality they handle regular duties such as ceremonies, negotiations,

TABLE 11.1. MANAGERIAL ROLES AND SKILLS.

Allison (1983): Functions of General Management

Strategy
> Establishing objectives and priorities
> Devising operational plans

Managing internal components
> Organizing and staffing
> Directing personnel and the personnel management system
> Controlling performance

Managing external constituencies
> Dealing with external units subject to some common authority
> Dealing with independent organizations
> Dealing with the press and the public

Mintzberg (1972): Executive Roles

Interpersonal	*Informational*	*Decisional*
Figurehead	Monitor	Entrepreneur
Leader	Disseminator	Disturbance handler
Liaison	Spokesperson	Resource allocator
		Negotiator

Cameron and Whetten (1983): Management Skill Topics

Self-awareness	Effective delegation and joint decision making
Managing personal stress	Gaining power and influence
Creative problem solving	Establishing supportive communication
Managing conflict	Improving group decision making
Improving employee performance, motivating others	

The Benchmarks Scales (McCauley, Lombardo, and Usher, 1989)

1a. Resourcefulness
1b. Doing whatever it takes
1c. Being a quick study
2a. Building and mending relationships
2b. Leading subordinates
2c. Compassion and sensitivity
3. Straightforwardness and composure
4. Setting a developmental climate
5. Confronting problem subordinates
6. Team orientation
7. Balance between personal life and work
8. Decisiveness
9. Self-awareness
10. Hiring talented staff
11. Putting people at ease
12. Acting with flexibility

and relations with the environment, such as meeting visitors and getting information from outside sources (to which they have the best access of anyone in the organization). They meet visiting dignitaries, give out gold watches, talk with managers and officials from outside the organization, hobnob at charitable events, and preside over the annual banquet. While managers are sometimes told that they need aggregate, systematically analyzed information, they actually favor direct and interactive sources, such as telephone calls and face-to-face talks and meetings. While management increasingly has scientific supports and processes, managers still rely a great deal on intuition and judgment. A good deal of research now supports Mintzberg's observations about management and his typology of managerial roles (Kurke and Aldrich, 1983). Generally, the research finds his typology widely applicable to managers in many settings. Yet Mintzberg also found some characteristics unique to the public sector setting, and these, too, have been supported in recent research, as discussed later.

Transformational Leadership

Interest in transformational leadership has burgeoned recently. During the 1970s, researchers in the field expressed increasing concern about the inadequacy of their theories. Leadership theorists began to argue that research had concentrated too narrowly on the exchanges between leaders and their subordinates in task situations and on highly quantified models and analyses. Some researchers called for more attention to larger issues and other sources of leadership thought, such as political and historical analyses and more qualitative research using interviews and case studies. A political scientist, James MacGregor Burns (1978), exerted a seminal influence on leadership thought in the management field. Concerned with major political and social leaders such as presidents and prime figures in social movements, Burns distinguished between *transactional* leadership and *transformational* leadership.

Transactional leaders motivate followers by recognizing their needs and providing rewards to fulfill those needs in exchange for their performance and support. Transformational leaders raise followers' goals to higher planes, to a focus on transcendental, higher-level goals akin to the self-actualization needs defined by Maslow. In addition, they motivate followers to transcend their own narrow self-interest in pursuit of these goals, for the benefit of the community or the polity. Martin Luther King provides an example of a leader who did not simply offer to exchange benefits for support but called for a new order of existence—a society of greater justice—and he inspired many people to work for this vision. Many others refrained from opposing it because of its moral rightness.

Management experts found these ideas provocative. Uncharitably, Bennis and Nanus (1985, p. 4) say of the body of research on leadership, "Never have so many labored so long to say so little." They argue that our institutions and their leaders face increasing complexity and challenges to their credibility, requiring new conceptions of "transformative" leadership. This type of leadership relies on power, but not in a controlling, centralized way. These leaders possess an extraordinary talent for coupling visions of success (and of the road to their attainment) to empowerment and motivation among their followers.

Bennis and Nanus report on their interviews with ninety outstanding leaders from business and the "public sector" (for example, a federal agency director, an orchestra leader, and a football coach). They draw a sharp distinction between leading and managing. The latter, they say, involves conducting, taking charge, accomplishing goals with efficiency, and "doing things right" (p. 21). Leading involves guiding directions, actions, opinions, or, as they put it, "doing the right thing" (p. 21). Excellent leaders, they conclude, lead others largely by carefully managing *themselves,* through such strategies as the following:

- *Attention through vision.* They effectively create visions of successful futures, which focus their attention and that of their followers. They achieve this in part through transactions with followers that bring out the best in both leader and followers (Tichy and Ulrich, 1984).
- *Meaning through communication.* They effectively transmit this vision to others in ways that give meaning to their work and their quest. Bennis and Nanus describe examples of even very taciturn leaders who get their point across and communicate their purposes through symbols and drawings. The communication transmits not simply facts but, more importantly, reasons for and ways of learning and problem solving.
- *Trust through positioning.* Outstanding leaders show particular skill at choosing the best course, at knowing what is right and necessary. They choose directions and themes and adhere to them with constancy in ways that induce trust in their identity and integrity.
- *The deployment of self through positive self-regard.* They have high regard for their own skills and utilize them effectively. Yet they also remain aware of their own limitations and work to overcome them, often by attracting people who compensate for those limitations. They work with those people with respect, courteous attention, and trust, and they have the ability to do without constant approval from them.
- *The Wallenda factor.* Bennis and Nanus describe one way leaders pursue this deployment of self by pointing to the example of the famous tightrope walker Karl Wallenda. Wallenda put great energy and focus into his work; he did

not obsess himself with past problems or prospects of failure. Wallenda finally lost his life in a major appearance before which he had been utterly preoccupied with not falling. The outstanding leaders encourage in themselves and others a spirit of development, experimentation, reasonable risk taking and adventure, and even tolerance for well-intentioned mistakes that lead to learning. They concentrate on succeeding and do not become obsessed with the possibility of failure.

• *Empowerment.* Successful leaders also expand their own capacity by empowering others, making them feel a sense of significance, community, competence, and even fun. Thus, the others strive to contribute not because of close direction and control by the leader but through empowerment.

Bass (1985) presents a much more systematic analysis of transformational leadership, which adds too many additional points to be covered here. Like Burns, he sharply distinguishes transactional from transformational leadership. Burns, however, sees transformational leadership as uplifting. It shifts followers' focus from lower- to higher-order needs. It motivates them to sacrifice their own self-interest by showing followers that their self-interests are fulfilled or linked to community or higher-order needs. Bass agrees that there must be a shift in needs, but he points out that major leaders—Hitler, for instance—can have a transforming influence through a *negative* shift. Bass argues that the wrong kind of transformational leadership can damage followers and other groups.

Bass's analysis of transformational leadership is so careful and elaborate that any summary does injustice to it. Generally, he points out that this form of leadership involves an emotional and intellectual component. The emotional component involves charisma, an inspiring influence on followers. The intellectual component involves careful attention to individual followers, often of a benevolent, developmental, mentoring nature, as well as intellectual stimulation. The intellectual aspects can take various forms, such as manipulating symbols, using rational discourse, or evoking ideals, and involve cognitive stimulation as much as intellectual teaching. Bass emphasizes that leadership research has often underrated the importance of leaders' technical competence for their influence and effectiveness. Followers often admire and follow leaders primarily because they are very good at what they do.

While Burns treats transactional and transformational leadership as two polar extremes, Bass argues that transformational leaders also engage in varying degrees of transactional interaction with followers. They have to provide rewards and reasonably clear goals and directions. But overemphasis on exchanges with followers, especially negative or punishing ones, can be harmful. The significance of transformational leadership derives from its capacity to lift and expand the goals of individuals, not by overemphasizing direct, extrinsic satisfaction of self-interest but rather by inspiring new, higher aspirations. Hence comes the emphasis on relatively intangible, idealized influences through vision, empowerment, charisma, inspiration, individual consideration, and intellectual stimulation. Transformational leaders do not directly control their subordinates but rather seek to influence the climate in which they work. Thus, this view of leadership has connections with another recent trend, the emphasis on managing organizational culture.

Leadership and Organizational Culture

Transformational leaders avoid closely "managing" their subordinates and organizations. Rather, they exert their influence through "social architecture," by working with the basic symbols and core values, or *culture,* of their organization. Writers on organizational culture describe the key roles leaders play in forming, maintaining, and changing those cultures (Schein, 1992). Organizational analysts have been interested in similar themes for a long time, as suggested by the work of Chester Barnard and Philip Selznick described in Chapter Two. The topic really came alive in the management literature, however, when management experts began to find that leaders in excellent corporations in the United States and other countries placed heavy emphasis on managing the cultural dimensions of their firms (Peters and Waterman, 1982; Ouchi, 1981). In addition, researchers who study organizational cultures often use methods similar to those used by anthropologists to study the cultures of different societies. They argue that these methods provide deeper, more sensitive understanding of the realities of organizational life than do methods used by other researchers (Ott, 1989; Schein, 1992). Researchers have proposed various definitions of culture and undertaken studies of basic values, symbols, myths, norms of behavior, and other elements of culture in organizations.

Some of these studies have focused on public organizations, and certainly the topic applies to them. For example, Maynard-Moody, Stull, and Mitchell (1986) provide a rich description of the development and transformation of culture in the Kansas Department of Health and Environment. Early in the century, an influential secretary of the department instituted a culture that emphasized professional expertise in the defense of public health, relative autonomy from political intrusion, strict rules, and adherence to the budget. Through slogans, pamphlets, symbolic political actions, and publicity campaigns, he led the development of a well-established culture that predominated for decades. Much later, the governor and legislators, to bring the department under stronger political control, brought in an outsider as secretary. He and his followers led a reorganization that reduced the status of the adherents of the old culture and their beliefs and values, in part through constant denunciations of the old ways of doing things. The new culture, which emphasized different basic beliefs, such as the importance of political responsiveness and adherence to strict operating procedures, clashed with and eventually supplanted the older culture.

Previous chapters and later ones also provide illustrations of organizational culture in public organizations. The development of strategies and mission statements often draws on ideas about culture, and it seeks to shape culture in turn (see Chapter Seven and Table 7.1). Chapter Seven described the efforts of an executive trying to manage aspects of the culture of a law enforcement agency, including its basic assumptions about communicative leadership and decision making. Chapters Thirteen and Fourteen provide further examples of leaders' efforts to influence culture in changing, revitalizing, and building excellence in public and private organizations. These examples force the question of what we mean by culture. Scholars use the term in diffuse ways, and journalists and managers often use it very loosely. If it takes very careful, long-term observations to understand it, will that not make it difficult for managers to understand it? If it is a strong determinant of what happens in organizations, will it not be hard to change?

The literature provides some guidance for confronting these challenges. One succinct definition, for example, says that organizational culture is the pattern of shared meaning in an organization (Trice and Beyer, 1993). In what sense, however, do shared meanings exist? Schein's conception of culture (1992), illustrated in Table 11.2, provides some clarification. He contends that culture exists on various levels. The most basic and least observable level, often overlooked in other conceptions of culture, includes the *basic assumptions* on which the organization operates. Often invisible and unconscious, these concern the organization's relationship with its environment; the nature of reality, time, and space; and the nature of humans and their activities and relationships. The next level involves more overtly expressed *values* about how things ought to be and how one ought to respond in general. Finally, the most observable level includes *artifacts and creations*, such as actual technological processes (purposely designed work processes and administrative procedures and instructions), art (symbols, logos, and creations), and behaviors (words used, communication patterns, significant outbursts, and rituals and ceremonies).

A policy about uniforms in a military unit illustrates Schein's three levels (Lewis, 1987). Admiral Hyman Rickover discouraged the wearing of uniforms in the project teams working in the U.S. Navy's nuclear program. Lower-ranking officers with more recent training often had the best knowledge. Uniforms carry symbols of hierarchical rank and authority (representing the first, most observable

TABLE 11.2. CONCEPTIONS AND DIMENSIONS OF CULTURE.

Levels and Basic Assumptions of Organizational Culture (Schein, 1992)

Levels of Organizational Culture

1. Artifacts and creations (the most observable level). Examples: the design of work processes and administrative procedures, art (logos and symbols), overt behaviors (words used, rituals, ceremonies, significant outbursts—such as something a top executive gets openly mad or happy about).

2. Basic values (a less observable level). Examples: values about how things ought to be and how one ought to respond and behave in general (for example, always help younger employees develop their skills and careers, always have strong relationships with key officials in the legislative branch).

3. Basic assumptions (the most basic, least observable level). Examples: basic assumptions on which people in the organization operate (for example, decisions should be made by people with the best brains, not the highest rank).

Key Dimensions of the Basic Assumptions

1. The organization's relation to its environment. Example: whether members see the organization as dominant or dominated.

2. The nature of reality and truth, and the basis for decisions. Example: whether decisions are based on tradition or on a scientific test. Subdimensions: the nature of time (for example, the length of cycles) and space (for example, perceived availability or constraints).

3. The nature of human nature. Examples: humans as bad or good, mutable or fixed.

4. The nature of human activity. Example: proactive versus reactive.

Dimensions of Organizational Culture (Hofstede, Neuijen, Ohayv, and Sanders, 1990; Robbins, 1996)

Member identity: The degree to which individuals identify with the organization as a whole rather than some subgroup or specialization.

Group emphasis: The degree to which work is organized around groups rather than individuals.

People focus: The extent to which management considers the effects of their decisions on people in the organization.

Unit integration: The amount of encouragement of coordinated, interdependent activity among units.

Control: The degree to which rules and supervision are used to control employees.

Risk tolerance: The encouragement of risk and innovation.

Reward criteria: The extent to which rewards are based on performance rather seniority or favoritism.

Conflict tolerance: The degree to which open airing of conflict is encouraged.

Means-ends orientation: The extent of managerial focus on outcomes and results rather than processes.

Open-systems focus: The amount of monitoring of external developments.

Source: Adapted from Perry, 1996b.

level of organizational culture). The absence of uniforms reduces the value of hierarchical rank and promotes the value of individuals' technical knowledge (the second level). At the third, most basic level, the underlying assumption is that those with the "best brains, not the highest rank" make the best decisions (Lewis, 1987, p. 107).

Other researchers have developed more elaborate sets of dimensions of organizational culture. Table 11.2 also summarizes the dimensions of organizational culture that Hofstede, Neuijen, Ohayv, and Sanders (1990) used in their study of twenty organizations. Leaders and teams working on the development of organizational culture can make pragmatic use of such dimensions as well as the measures of them described below. Researchers can work on further developing and confirming the role of such dimensions in public organizations.

Variations Among Cultures

Analysts also emphasize variations among cultures. One such distinction points out that organizations can vary between *strong* and *weak* cultures. In organizations with strong cultures, the members share and strongly adhere to the organization's basic values and assumptions. In weaker cultures, members feel less consensus and commitment. DiIulio (1994) describes how some employees of the U.S. Bureau of Prisons feel a very strong commitment to the mission and values of the bureau, to the point that some retirees will rush to the scene of a crisis in the prison system to volunteer their services.

There may be *multiple cultures and subcultures* within an organization (Trice and Beyer, 1993, chaps. 5 and 6). Subcultures can form around occupational specializations, subunits or locations, hierarchical levels, labor unions, and countercultural groups such as rebellious units. Public agencies often have a single dominant occupational or professional specialization (Mosher, [1968] 1982; Warwick, 1975). Strong differences between cultures or subcultures obviously complicate the challenge of forging consensus on cultural changes and priorities.

Another source of variation comes from the role of *external societal cultures* and their influences on an organization. Research has not provided a great deal of systematic, well-validated evidence of external cultural influences. The interest in the successes of Japanese management has led to analyses of their more consensual decision-making processes, their group-oriented norms, and other characteristics of Japanese corporations that reflect their distinctive external societal culture (Ouchi, 1981). There is not a great deal of well-developed knowledge about variations among societal cultures, however, nor about variations in subcultures within them.

Assessing the Culture

As suggested earlier, the task of developing an understanding of an organization's culture imposes a major challenge on managers and researchers alike. The concepts and dimensions in Table 11.2 can serve as focal points for such an assessment. Researchers use elaborate procedures for measuring and assessing culture. Table 11.3 suggests references and sources for this undertaking.

The Communication of Culture

Various forms that transmit an organization's culture serve as "sense-making mechanisms" for people in the organization as they interpret what goes on around them (Trice and Beyer, 1993, p. 80). The forms transmit information about the organization's basic values and assumptions. In the course of the assessment described above, leaders and teams must assess the current roles of these forms and the ways they need to be transformed.

Symbols. Physical objects, settings, and certain roles within an organization convey information about its values and basic assumptions. The uniforms in the example about Rickover above provide one example. Goodsell (1977) studied 122

TABLE 11.3. BACKGROUND REFERENCES FOR ASSESSING ORGANIZATIONAL CULTURE.

Schein (1992, chap. 5). Procedures and interview questions for assessing culture, including the dimensions of culture that his analysis emphasizes). *Methods:* Interviews focusing on surprises and critical incidents, and group interviews about the basic dimensions.

Wilkins (1989). Suggestions and interview questions for assessing "corporate character." Corporate character emphasizes "motivational faith" along two dimensions, fairness and ability. *Methods:* Interview and self-assessment questions for use in assessing faith in leaders' and their own fairness and in the organization's and their own abilities.

Hofstede, Neuijen, Ohayv, and Sanders (1990). Description of the measures of the cultural dimensions described in Table 11.2. *Method:* Survey research questionnaires.

Kotter and Heskett (1992). Survey instrument and interview questions used in their study of the relations between corporate culture and performance in numerous business firms. *Method:* Organizational questionnaire survey and interviews.

Ott (1989, chap. 5). General review of methods of studying organizational culture.

Source: Perry: 1996b. Reprinted with permission.

government agencies and found various physical conditions that symbolized either authority or service to clients. For example, flags, official seals, and physical distance between employees and clients symbolized authority. Symbols of a client service orientation included comfortable furniture and descriptions of services available.

Employees use symbols, too. In a large service center of the Social Security Administration, members of a problem-ridden subunit held a funeral for the subunit, complete with black balloons, a small black coffin, and the singing of hymns. Later, when the director had effectively resolved their concerns, the members gave him the coffin with the balloons deflated inside it, as a symbol that the problems were over.

Physical settings can have potent symbolic effects. Zalesny and Farace (1987), in a study of a public agency in a Midwestern state, found that a change to a more open office design—with no interior walls or partitions—had significant psychological effects on employees. Lower-level employees saw the change as promoting more democratic values. Managers felt they had lost status.

Language. Slang, songs, slogans, jargon, and jokes can all carry the messages of a culture. Maynard-Moody, Stull, and Mitchell (1986) describe the transformation of the culture of the Kansas Department of Health and Environment. One way they instituted cultural changes involved derogatory references to "the old way of doing things" that debunked the assumptions and values of the former culture.

Narratives. The people in an organization often repeat stories, legends, sagas, and myths that convey information about the organization's history and practices. Bennis and Nanus (1985) report that in a large computer company, a manager lost a lot of money on an aggressive project. When he offered his resignation, his superior asked, "How can we fire you when we have just spent ten million dollars educating you?" Repeated around the organization, such a story can send a powerful message about the organization's support of reasonable risk taking and aggressiveness.

Practices and Events. Repeated practices and special events, including recurrent or memorable one-time incidents, can transmit important assumptions and values. They may include rites and ceremonies such as graduation ceremonies, induction and initiation ceremonies, annual meetings, annual banquets or holiday parties, and homecomings. Rites promote changes and goals such as passage, renewal, elevation, or degradation of individuals, conflict reduction, and integration of the group. Leaders' actions at times of crisis, memorable and widely noted speeches, and outbursts can all have such influences. Organizations have taken particular steps to support employees or customers during times of crisis or hardship, leading to legends and stories that symbolize and communicate organizational values.

Leading Cultural Development

Experts on organizational culture heavily emphasize the crucial role of leadership in creating and upholding culture (Schein, 1992; Trice and Beyer, 1993). Leaders create culture in new organizations and embody and transmit it in existing organizations. They can integrate cultures in organizations with multiple cultures by forging consensus. These different roles are important, because different types of leaders may play them. A long-term member of the organization, for example, often plays the strongest role in embodying and transmitting existing cultures. Nevertheless, while some leaders may embody existing cultures, leaders of high-performance organizations typically strive for an improved culture, even if the organization performs well already (Kotter and Heskett, 1992).

The concepts and points discussed earlier present challenges for leadership. Enhancing culture involves understanding its nature, assessing the particular culture of one's organization, dealing with multiple subcultures as necessary, understanding the different cultural forms in the organization, and using those forms to facilitate change. Leaders and leadership teams can use a variety of methods and strategies to lead the development of effective culture:

1. *Make clear what leaders will monitor, ignore, measure, or control.* For example, a leadership team can announce that a significant proportion of each manager's evaluation and bonus will be based on an assessment of how well the manager performed in developing subordinates' skills.

2. *React to critical incidents and organizational crises in ways that send appropriate cultural messages.* Crises provide opportunities for leaders to demonstrate fortitude, commitment to organizational members, and other values and basic assumptions. The computer firm manager who got the expensive "education," described earlier, provides an example. The Social Security Administration center director described earlier, when confronted with the funeral in the troubled subunit, reacted not punitively but communicatively. He thus sent a message about the value he placed on communication and participation.

3. *Practice deliberate role modeling, teaching, and coaching.* Leaders can show, tell, and encourage values and behaviors they want employees to adopt. Chapter Thirteen describes a director of a state human services agency who led a transformation of the agency from a troubled, control-oriented organization to a more

participative, quality-oriented one (Stephens, 1988). She led a participative process in which project teams developed a "blueprint for the future" aimed at improving organizational policies, designs, and procedures. She faithfully attended team meetings and made it clear she would commit her time and the needed resources to them. Her actions demonstrated her commitment to change and to the value of participation, teamwork, and new ideas and approaches. She presented herself as a role model as well as a teacher.

4. *Establish effective criteria for granting rewards and status, for selection and promotion of employees, and for dismissal or punishment.* The example above about introducing the development of subordinates as a criterion for managers' performance evaluations and bonuses shows that what an organization rewards its members for sends a powerful message about values and basic assumptions. Punishments send equally strong messages.

5. *Coordinate organizational designs and structures with cultural messages.* Without appropriate structural redesign, a leader's modeling and coaching about new approaches and values can evaporate into empty rhetoric and posturing (Golembiewski, 1985). If the leader's criteria for rewards conflict with features of the organization that impede the behaviors the leader wants to reward, role conflict and stress for members will surely result. Chapter Thirteen describes how, in the 1970s, large Social Security Administration service centers redesigned their structures and work processes. They changed from large units composed of specialists who worked on only one specific part of a case to work modules made up of different specialists who together handled each case as a whole. The change embodied very strong messages about the values of teamwork, communication, and the removal of status differences among co-workers.

6. *Coordinate organizational systems and procedures with cultural messages.* Systems and procedures, such as technological systems, routine reporting requirements, performance evaluations, and group meetings, provide important messages about important values and basic beliefs. Bourgault, Dion, and Lemay (1993) describe how a performance appraisal system for Canadian government executives has a team-building effect, in part because of its basis in shared values. On the other hand, studies of pay-for-performance systems, including the Performance Management and Recognition System for middle managers in the U.S. federal government, often illustrate how such systems fail to communicate useful information about important values (Perry, 1986; Perry, Petrakis, and Miller, 1989).

7. *Design physical spaces, including facades and buildings, to communicate the culture.* The study by Goodsell (1977), described earlier, suggests some of the aspects of physical setting and space that can communicate cultural information about public agencies.

8. *Employ stories about events and people.* Leaders can also make use of stories and accounts of past events and people as a way of promoting values and assumptions. Cooper (1987) describes Gifford Pinchot's effective efforts to build support for the Forest Service and strong commitment among forest rangers, in part by taking wilderness treks with foresters. These served to build his image as a person committed to his mission and richly appreciative of forest resources.

9. *Develop formal statements of the organizational philosophy or creed.* Formal credos and value statements promote an organization's values and generally commit the organization to them. Table 7.1 provides examples. Denhardt (1993) provides numerous examples of such statements in public agencies in several different nations.

10. *Approach cultural leadership as comprehensive organizational change.* Leadership teams must approach the development of an effective organizational culture as they would any major, influential initiative. Chapter Thirteen covers successful organizational change, discussing how leadership teams can marshall resources, commitment, and consensus in a sustained, comprehensive fashion.

As indicated earlier, Chapter Fourteen includes further examples of the importance of effective culture in public organizations. A major issue for public managers and researchers concerns the context of leadership in the public sector and how leaders have to work with it in developing culture and carrying out other management responsibilities.

Leadership and Management in Public Organizations

A review of the management literature shows that researchers have treated leadership and management in the public sector as being essentially the same as they are in other settings, including business. Many major contributions to the field, such as the Ohio State leadership studies and Fiedler's theories, were developed in part from research on military officers or government managers. Bennis and Nanus (1985) included public sector leaders, such as the head of the Securities and Exchange Commission and the city manager of Cincinnati, in their research and emphasized the similarities they discovered among all the leaders they studied. Mintzberg's study (1972) included a public manager (a school system superintendent) and a quasi-public manager (a hospital administrator). Additional studies have found that Mintzberg's role categories apply to managers in government agencies (Lau, Pavett, and Newman, 1980). While Mintzberg and later researchers (Kurke and Aldrich, 1983) noted some special features of public managers' work, still others found that even these few distinctions do not always hold for all types of public managers (Ammons and Newell, 1989). Small wonder that leadership researchers typically regard a public-versus-private distinction as rather inconsequential. Leaders in all settings face the challenges and general tasks suggested by the theories we have reviewed.

Generalizations About the Distinctive Context of Public Service

Although virtually everyone accepts the premise that all executives and managers face very similar tasks and challenges, a strong and growing body of evidence suggests that public managers operate within contexts that require rather distinctive skills and knowledge. For years, political scientists writing about public bureaucracies argued that the political processes and government institutions in which government managers work make their jobs very different from those of business executives. Those writers did not, however, do as much empirical research on leadership as the organizational behavior and management researchers did. Clear evidence of differences remained rather scarce, and many management scholars noted the evidence of similarities among all managerial roles and rejected such notions as crude stereotypes.

More recently, however, greater attention to the topic of public management has brought out additional evidence concerning the distinctive nature of public management. Some of this evidence comes from executives who served in both business and government and wrote about the differences they saw between the two roles (Allison, 1983; Blumenthal, 1983; Chase and Reveal, 1983; Rumsfeld, 1983). Although their experiences and opinions were diverse, the executives agreed that constraints, controls, and processes weighed heavily on their managerial behaviors. Though these have been discussed in earlier chapters, it may be useful here to review a number of these aspects of the context of leadership in the public sector:

- Jurisdiction-wide rules for personnel, purchasing, budgeting, and other administrative functions, usually with an oversight agency administering them, which limit executive authority
- Legislature and interest-group alliances with subgroups and individuals within the organization, which dilute executives' authority over those groups or individuals
- Control by legislatures and chief executives over resource and policy decisions, and strong demands from legislators for strict accountability on the part of the agency head for all matters pertaining to the agency
- The influence of the press and the imperative that executives concern themselves with media coverage

- The short tenure of many top executives, which limits their time to accomplish goals and weakens their influence over careerists
- The absence of clear and accepted performance measures for their organizations and the activities within them

Federal executives report from a very special perspective, of course. Although we have more than a dozen such reports (Allison, 1983), this still includes only a small sample. Yet more structured academic research paints a similar picture. Various studies of public managers show a general tendency for their roles to reflect the context of political interventions and administrative constraints.

Much of this evidence comes not from studies of leadership practices but from analyses of managerial roles. In his seminal study, Mintzberg (1972) found that the work of all the managers fell into his now well-known role categories. Yet the public manager in the sample (a school administrator) and the quasi-public manager (a hospital administrator) spent more time in contacts and formal meetings with external interest groups and governing boards and received more external status requests than did the private managers. More recently, Kurke and Aldrich (1983) replicated the study, including its findings about public management; they point to public-versus-private comparisons as an important direction for future research on managerial roles. Lau, Pavett, and Newman (1980), also using a technique based on Mintzberg's, found the roles of civilian managers in the U.S. Navy comparable to those of private manufacturing and service firm managers. Yet they also add the role of "technical expert" to the role categories for the navy managers and note that they spend more time in crisis management and "fire drills" than private managers. Ammons and Newell (1989), on the other hand, conducted a survey of mayors and city managers using Mintzberg's categories and found somewhat different results. Comparing their sample of mayors and city managers to private sector samples from previous studies, they found that these city officials spent no more time in formally scheduled meetings than did the private sector managers. This contradicts the findings of Mintzberg and of Kurke and Aldrich in general. Yet a closer look shows that the mayors and city managers did spend more time making phone calls and conducting tours than did the private sector managers. Ammons and Newell note that they cannot really say what the phone calls involved, and they may well represent contacts with external groups and political actors.

A study by Porter and Van Maanen (1983) supports this interpretation. They compared city government administrators to industrial managers and found that the city administrators felt less control over how they allocate their own time, felt more pressed for time, and regarded demands from people outside the organization as a much stronger influence on how they manage their time. At the level of state government, Weinberg (1977) reported on a case study of the management of New Jersey state agencies by the governor, concluding that "crisis management" plays a central role in shaping public executives' decisions and priorities.

In an observational study of six bureau chiefs of large federal bureaus, Kaufman (1979) found that they spend much of their time in classic, generic management functions such as motivating employees, communicating, and decision making. The political environment figures crucially in their roles, however. Relations with Congress outweigh relations with the higher executives of their departments. Clearly, they operate within a web of institutional constraints on organizational structure, personnel administration, and other matters. Aberbach, Putnam, and Rockman's study of legislators and administrators in six countries (1981), described in Chapter Three, supports this depiction of congressional influence as stronger than that of agency heads.

Boyatzis (1982) conducted a study of managerial competencies that compared managers in four federal agencies and twelve large firms. He found that private managers were higher on "goal and action" competencies; he attributed this to clearer performance measures, such as profits, in the private sector. The private managers also scored higher on competencies in "conceptualization" and "use of oral presentations." Boyatzis suggests that more strategic decision making in the private firms and more openness and standard procedures in the public sector account for this. Interestingly, Boyatzis's findings correspond to those of earlier studies. Like Guyot (1960), he finds that public managers show higher levels of need for achievement and need for power. Yet their lower scores on goal and action competencies reflected less ability to fulfill such needs. Boyatzis's interpretation agrees with that of Buchanan (1975). They both regard this as evidence that fairly ambitious and idealistic people come to managerial work in government but appear to experience constraints within complex government agencies and policy-making processes.

Chase and Reveal (1983) discuss the challenges of public management on the basis of Chase's extensive experience in government, especially in large urban agencies. Their depiction of the key challenges in managing a public agency concentrates on those posed by the external political and institutional environment—dealing with elected chief executives who have shorter-term, more election-oriented priorities and competing for a place on their agenda; coping with overhead agencies such as civil service commissions, budget bureaus, and general service agencies (for travel, purchasing, space allocation); dealing with legislators (including city councils); and managing relations with special-interest groups and the media.

While these studies differ in their findings, types of managers studied, and other important ways, they confirm the general observations that public managers carry out their work under conditions marked by constraints and interventions from the political and administrative environment. The form of influence or constraint may vary between mayors, public school superintendents, governors, and middle managers in federal agencies, but it shows up consistently in one form or another. Formal meetings with controlling groups, fire drills, crisis management, phone calls, external demands on time and priorities, the power of legislators, media, and interest groups—all are indications of the exposure of the public sector manager's role to the political process and to the administrative structures of government.

Does the Context Affect Performance and Behavior?

Clearly, the executives who reported on their experiences in both sectors in the above-mentioned studies do not regard themselves as inferior managers. They agree that managing in the public sector is harder (Allison, 1983), and in this sense they acknowledge that a public executive has more trouble exerting a great impact.

Yet sharper critiques raise crucial questions about whether the public sector context penalizes excellence in leadership or actually prevents it. From his case study of the U.S. State Department, Warwick (1975) concluded that federal executives and middle managers face strict constraints on their authority. Goals are vague. Congress and other elements of the federal system—including many politically appointed executives themselves—adhere to an "administrative orthodoxy" akin to the old principles of administration. They hold top executives accountable for all that happens in their agency and expect agencies to show clear lines of authority and accountability through their ranks and narrow spans of control. The executives and middle managers have little control over career civil servants, yet they feel intense pressure to control them to avoid bad publicity or political miscues. Because of vague performance criteria, they try to control behavior rather than outcomes through a profusion of rules and clearance requirements. Paradoxically, this fails to exert real control on the lower levels and further complicates the bureaucratic system. Warwick refers to this drawing upward of authority as "escalation to the top"; he says that an "abdication at the bottom" mirrors it at lower levels, where careerists emphasize security and accept the rules. When they disagree, they simply "wait out" the executives' short tenure. Top executives also preoccupy themselves with external politics and public policy issues, abdicating any role in developing human resources or organizational support systems and processes and otherwise developing the organization itself. Warwick cites Downs (1967) pointedly, and his view accords with Downs's and Niskanen's views described in Chapter Nine.

Lynn (1981) and Allison (1983) display much less pessimism but nevertheless express a similar concern about a performance deficit. Lynn laments the tendency of many federal executives to emphasize political showmanship over substantive management. He refers to the problem of "inevitable bureaucracy," in which higher levels try to control lower levels by disseminating new rules and directives, which simply add to the existing array of rules without exerting any real influence. Similarly, the report of the National Academy of Public Administration (1986) laments the complex web of controls and rules over managerial decisions in federal agencies and their adverse effect on federal managers' capacity and motivation to manage.

In addition, the Volcker Commission (1989) reported a quiet crisis at the higher levels of the career federal service. The poor image of the federal service, pay constraints and higher pay levels in the private sector, and pressures from political executives and appointees have damaged morale among these executives and increased their likelihood of leaving the federal service. Recruitment to replace them is hampered by the same factors that discourage these individuals. The loss and demoralization of experienced executives and difficulties in finding high-quality replacements will likely diminish effective leadership practices in the future.

Surveys Concerning Leadership Practices

Several surveys of employees' ratings of their supervisors provide mixed evidence about the quality of leadership in government organizations. The large survey by the U.S. Merit Systems Protection Board (1987) found that only 49 percent of the respondents agreed that "my supervisor has good leadership qualities." Also, bare majorities agreed that they have trust and confidence in their supervisor and that the supervisor does well at organizing the work group and encouraging suggestions. Just over 60 percent agreed that the supervisor is fair, communicative, and technically skillful. The even larger Federal Employee Attitude Survey (U.S. Office of Personnel Management, 1979) found more favorable ratings. Sixty to 75 percent of the respondents agreed that their supervisor deals well with subordinates, handles the technical and administrative parts of his or her job well, encourages subordinates' help in developing work methods, and asks for employees' opinions about work-related matters. Yet sizable percentages did not feel that their supervisor encouraged their participation in making important decisions. Managers and executives were asked a series of questions about whether top executives get their appointments through skill and merit, whether they express dissenting views and try new ideas, and whether there are good provisions in their organization for developing executives. Sizable percentages (20 to 40 percent) gave unfavorable responses to these questions.

Responses such as these admit to no easy interpretation. Should we rejoice that 60 percent respond favorably about some aspect of leadership, or should we worry that 40 percent disagree or say that they are undecided? In addition, a comparison with the private sector might reveal that government experiences no greater problems than other domains. We do have some comparative evidence. The National Center for Productivity and Quality of Working Life (1978) analyzed a large data set compiled from surveys taken in ten public and eleven private organizations, where thousands of employees responded to the same questionnaire. The public organizations included state and city governments and federal agencies, and the private organizations included private manufacturing, food service, and banking firms. The private respondents generally gave more favorable ratings about their organizations, work, and supervision. The private sector managers and employees were 10 to 15 percent more likely to agree that their supervisors do a good job and show technical competence and that their supervisors' supervisors do a good job. The public managers gave slightly higher ratings of their supervisors' human relations skills. Ten percent more of the public employees, however, disagreed with a statement that their supervisors had good human relations skills.

The most reasonable conclusion from these surveys resembles the general conclusion about the differences between the sectors in satisfaction ratings. In general, with the exception of possible problems at the higher levels of the federal career service, the public sector does not show problems of crisis proportions or of markedly greater severity than the private sector. Generally, public sector employees and managers express favorable impressions of the leadership practices in their agencies. Yet the evidence also indicates some public sector problems and a degree of private sector superiority in developing leaders, participativeness of leaders, and some other leadership practices and conditions. These results coincide generally with some of the concerns expressed by the authors cited above about constraints on leadership in government. Yet they also place those concerns in perspective by showing the inaccuracy of overstatements of the problem. While governments probably do face constraints in encouraging and developing excellent leadership practices, many excellent leaders and managers serve in government.

Attention to Management and Leadership

Although many observers claim that public managers pay scant attention to leading and managing their organizations, the evidence clearly shows otherwise, at least in many specific cases. Critics say that public managers show too little attention to long-range objectives and internal development of their organization and human resources. But critics of business management, especially in recent years, complain that similar problems plague industry in the United States and that firms place too much emphasis on short-term profit. Critics also accuse business leaders of concentrating on achieving huge financial returns for themselves, even when the firm's performance lags. These criticisms of businesses and executives make it hard to depict government as inferior.

Moreover, abundant evidence shows that many government managers work very hard. Ammons and Newell (1989) report that mayors, city managers, and their immediate executive assistants say that they work about sixty to sixty-six hours per week. Executives from the private sector who have served in Washington regularly report their impressions of how hard the staff members and executives in the federal government work (Volcker Commission, 1989).

Do they spend much of this time on political gamesmanship, as some critics of federal executives suggest? At the city level, several surveys have asked city officials to report on the time they spend in managerial roles (staffing, budgeting, evaluating, directing, and so on), policymaking roles (forming policy about the future of the city, meeting with other city officials, and so on), and political roles (dealing with external political groups and authorities, such as state and federal officials and active community groups, and engaging in public relations activities such as speeches and ceremonies). Ammons and Newell (1989) found that the mayors, city managers, and executive assistants in their survey reported, on average, devoting 55 percent of their time to managerial roles, 28 percent to policy roles, and 17 percent to political roles. As might be expected, mayors ranged above these averages in their concentration on political activities, and assistants paid more attention to management tasks.

Ammons and Newell asked questions about the importance of the various roles to the officials' success. Most mayors placed the greatest importance on the political role, although 23 percent emphasized the managerial role as most important. The city managers emphasized the policy role more frequently than other roles, but they also heavily emphasized management; about 40 percent rated the managerial role as most important. The executive assistants overwhelmingly rated the managerial role as most important. In sum, city officials see themselves as devoting substantial amounts of time to managerial roles.

Similarly, the small sample of federal bureau chiefs in the Kaufman study noted earlier (1979) indicated that they spent much of their time in typical managerial activities, such as motivating the people in their bureaus. This orientation does not square with the complaints that public managers do not manage very conscientiously. What explains this distance between various observers and researchers on a key point such as this?

Contingencies and Variations

Obviously, many variations in context and in the individual officials surveyed account for these different views. The bureau chiefs that Kaufman studied tended to be longer-term career civil servants, at levels lower than the short-tenure political appointees that commonly head government agencies. The level of the manager and the institutional context make a lot of difference. As pointed out earlier, officials vary by elected versus appointed status, level in the agency hierarchy, distance from the political center (such as Washington, D.C., versus a district office, or the state capitol versus a state district office), political and institutional setting of the agency (such as executive and legislative authority in the jurisdiction; weak-mayor, strong-mayor, and council-manager structures at the local level), level of government, and other factors.

These variations have great significance. At virtually all levels and in virtually all settings, public managers must to some degree balance managerial tasks with policymaking and with handling the political and institutional environment (oversight agencies, legislative and other executive authorities, clients and constituents, and the media). Yet some managers in public agencies (and many private non-profit agencies) face intense challenges of the latter sort, while others operate in virtual isolation from political intrusions. At present, however, the field lacks a coherent model of all these variations. Development of better conceptions of such variations represents a challenge for practitioners and scholars in the field.

Despite these deficiencies, there is a good deal of relevant research and thinking available, including the previously described studies by Aberbach, Putnam, and Rockman (1981), Abney and Lauth (1986), and Brudney and Hebert (1987). Meyer (1979) concludes from a large study of heads of state and local finance agencies that those in stronger positions politically—those who are elected or are career civil servants, rather than political appointees—show more ability to defend their agency against pressures for change in structure and against the loss of units to other agencies, apparently because of their greater ability to draw on support from political networks.

Even more research and thinking have focused on officials in cities, probably because city management has developed into one of the more professionalized areas of public management and has inspired more systematic research and theory as a result. Kotter and Lawrence (1974) reported one of the most elaborate analyses, in which they argued that effective mayors must effectively "coalign" major components of their context. These include the mayor's own personal characteristics (cognitive and interpersonal skills, needs, and values), their agendas (tasks and objectives in the short and long run), their networks (the resources and expectations of city government members and their relationship to the mayor), and characteristics of the city itself (such as size and rate of change). For example, they argue that the mayor's cognitive style must align with the variety and variability of information about the city that must be processed. A *technician* orientation, emphasizing the analysis of discrete amounts of information, best aligns with a small, homogeneous, stable city, where information varies little and can be analyzed relatively easily. A *professional* orientation fits a large, heterogeneous city with unstable, hard-to-analyze information. The professional mayor emphasizes using his or her professional judgment and applying professional guidelines and knowledge. Between these extremes, an *engineering* mayor works best in a large, diverse, stable city where information is highly varied but analyzable. A *craftsman* most effectively deals with the less varied but less analyzable information in a small but unstable city. This typology draws on Perrow's ideas about information contingencies of tasks (see Chapter Eight). Kotter and Lawrence also discuss ways in which the mayor's network must coincide with the city's agenda and the agenda with the city's characteristics.

Anderson, Newland, and Stillman (1983) also propose a typology, one based more on a framework akin to Blake and Mouton's managerial grid (1984), described earlier in this chapter. They argue that cities have varied levels of demand for their officials to display a people orientation versus a technical orientation. *Growth communities* create high demand for both orientations and for a chief executive–type manager who works for change within regular organizational structures. *Caretaker communities* demand maintenance of existing services and an administrative caretaker, a leader with a technical orientation. *Arbiter communities* require much conflict resolution and therefore more of a people orientation than a technical one; a community leader mode of management best satisfies these requirements. A *consumption community* demands the most public services for the least cost and hence needs an administrative innovator who will follow the direction set by elected council members and seek innovations for the sake of efficiency and service delivery (that is, less emphasis on people, more on technical skill).

Entrepreneurship in Government

Recent studies of entrepreneurial leaders and policy innovators in government also break away from overgeneralizations about ineffectual managers struggling with an overwhelming political and administrative system (Roberts and King, 1996). Much of this work consists of case studies about major executives, but it suggests some general conclusions.

For example, Lewis (1980) studied Hyman Rickover's development of the "unclear navy," J. Edgar Hoover's impact on the FBI, and Robert Moses's transformation of the New York Port Authority. He observed a common developmental pattern in these three cases. In each case he found an organization that was ineffective at achieving the major goals for which it presumably existed until it experienced a process of mentoring by an effective superior. In this process, the superiors developed appropriate goals and learned how to get things done. They then engaged in an "entrepreneurial leap" that changed the organization and its resource allocation in unforeseen ways, and they created an "apolitical shield" that defended their work from political intervention by casting it as nonpolitical and objectively necessary. Later phases involved struggling for autonomy, reducing environmental uncertainty, expanding the organization's domain, and fully institutionalizing the new organization (with consequent problems of "ultra stability").

Lewis's subjects stand as controversial titans who, through exceptional ambition, energy, and political and technical skill, took advantage of key political and technological developments to build effective organizations. Other writers have described executives who played major roles in the development of the National Aeronautics and Space Administration, the Tennessee Valley Authority, major Department of Defense policies, the Social Security Administration, and the Forest Service. Doig and Hargrove (1987) conclude from a set of such studies that entrepreneurial leaders in the public sector display general patterns. They identify new missions and programs for their agencies. They develop external and internal constituencies for these new initiatives, identify areas of vulnerability, and neutralize opposition. For their new missions, they enhance the technical expertise of the agency and provide motivation and training for organizational members. The leaders tend to follow some mixture of rhetorical strategy, involving evocative symbols and language, and coalition-building strategy, emphasizing the development of political support from many groups. Some leaders rely on both strategies; some emphasize one over the other.

External conditions set the stage for these activities, according to Doig and Hargrove. The entrepreneurs actually take advantage of the diverse and fragmented governance structures often cited as reasons why public managers accomplish little. The difficulties of strong central control in such a system provide the entrepreneurs opportunities to forge their own direction. They also take advantage of patterns of potential public support (for example, changing public attitudes during the 1930s supported a more active role for the federal government) and new technologies and alliances with elected political officials.

In their personalities and skills, the leaders display an "uncommon rationality," a remarkable ability to perceive effective means to ends. They are able to see the political logic in an emerging historical situation and link their initiatives to broader political and social trends. Doig and Hargrove also stress the individual's motivation to "make a difference," coupled with a sustained determination and optimism. Success depends, however, on the association of personal skills with organizational tasks and with favorable historical conditions, such as public and political support and timely technological possibilities.

Another important point about the ability of public managers to influence important developments is revealed in studies of policy entrepreneurs (Roberts and King, 1996). This conception of entrepreneurship focuses on people who influence policy, often from outside formal positions, by pressing for innovations in policies and programs. Some develop public support for the innovations, press legislators and administrators for support, and otherwise move the system by taking on a sustained role as a policy champion. Others may play the role of "policy intellectual," providing innovative ideas. As described above, public executives and managers can play such roles, but they sometimes face constraints on their independence to do so. They can also act as catalysts and sponsors, however, providing support, listening, and responding when policy champions with good ideas press for a hearing.

All these studies of entrepreneurship suggest ways we might reconcile the broad observations about indifferent public management with the evidence that many public managers have hammered out so much change that they raise concerns about their proper role in a democratic republic (Lewis, 1980). Marmor and Fellman (1986; Marmor, 1987), for example, offer a typology of public executives that is akin to many previous typologies, such as that of Downs. It concentrates more directly on the issue of internal program management and program accomplishment, however, and therefore suggests key distinctions in leaders' motivation and objectives. They argue that public executives vary in managerial skills and commitment to program goals. Among those with low managerial skills are the *administrative survivors*, who also have low commitment to program goals and provide little effective leadership. *Program zealots* have high programmatic commitments but weak skills and also tend to be unsuccessful administrators. The Reagan administration provided numerous examples of this pattern, since political ideology often served as a major criterion for executive appointments. As for those with high managerial skills, *generalist managers* show low commitment to program goals. The executive elite at the federal level has included highly respected executives such as Eliot Richardson and Donald Ruckleshaus who developed excellent reputations for effective management in a variety of agencies. Yet Marmor and Fellman suggest that this dilutes their commitment to the long-term care and feeding of particular programs.

Program loyalists, highly skilled managers with strong programmatic commitments, serve as the most likely candidates for having entrepreneurial impact. Their commitment focuses on programs as their personal business and concern, with deemphasis of personal fame, recognition, and influence. Thus they tend to have the longevity and sustained commitment to hammer out substantial, long-term, original changes. Marmor and Fellman point to Robert Ball, an influential leader in the development of the Social Security Administration, as a prime example of a program loyalist. Interestingly, they indicate that Ball himself suggested that they missed an important category—the dedicated career administrators at the second, third, and fourth hierarchical levels, the midlevel managers at the central office or the heads of district offices. Marmor and Fellman label these "competent loyalists" and locate them between program zealots and program loyalists, because they competently manage only one part of a general program. Ball's remembering these people and emphasizing their significance reflects their sustained commitment to competent management in general, however, as well as to the management of particular programs.

Later chapters continue the discussion of effective public leadership and management, so efforts to summarize this topic are better left until later. The theories and studies reviewed here provide valuable contributions to the analysis of organizational leadership and to the long-term challenge of developing a conception of public management that recognizes the skills and practices of the many effective managers of public organizations.

CHAPTER TWELVE

TEAMWORK

Understanding Communication and Conflict in Groups

Although the framework at the beginning of this book places groups and communications in different locations, these elements of organizations have an important relationship. As indicated in Figures 1.1 and 1.2 in Chapter One, like the other factors, they interrelate with most of the other aspects of organization and management. And although the figures did not mention conflict, it is an extremely important process in organizations, also intertwined with communication and group processes.

The human group served as one of the founding topics in the social and administrative sciences. Teams, committees, task forces, staffs, work units, and other groupings make up the structure and activity of organizations (Hackman, 1989). Many organizational change and improvement efforts revolve around group processes, such as quality circles, and organizational development interventions, such as team-building exercises, problem-solving groups, and sensitivity sessions. Social scientists studied groups so intensively for so many years that, as with other important topics, such as motivation, the research discovered more and more complexities. So many kinds of groups operate under so many different conditions that researchers must strain to understand all the variations. Yet group processes have never lost their significance for managers. If anything, they have become more significant recently. A recent trend toward "team-based organization" and "team-based management" has swept through many organizations, including public agencies (Katzenbach and Smith, 1994; Mohrman, Cohen, and Mohrman, 1995). In some agencies, such as the Social Security Administration, district managers have received directives to move toward team management.

Organizational communications and conflict do not have to occur in and between groups. As suggested in Chapter Five in the discussion of managing relations with the media, public managers' communication responsibilities involve managing a complex range of channels and targets (Garnett, 1992). Yet much of the research on groups came about because people realized that groups influence communication and conflict among their members and between themselves and other groups. In addition, communication and conflict often intertwine. For example, suppose members of the department of human services of a large state communicate to members of the state's department of labor that the labor department's opposition to a program to aid migrant laborers simply reflects its subservience to certain wealthy fruit growers. The labor department officials communicate back that the human services department is proposing an incompetently designed program just to build its own empire. Any skillful, highly trained social scientist may detect the presence of conflict in this situation! Conflict may cause or result from bad communication, and the way out of conflict usually emphasizes the establishment of effective communication.

Researchers have examined many dimensions of communication and conflict in organizations. This chapter concentrates on certain fundamental points that figure importantly in discussions of organizational change and improvement. In addition, as usual, the discussion will cover the application of these topics to public organizations.

Groups in Organizations

Research has demonstrated that while groups often create strong pressures on their members to conform with others in their group, they also represent arenas for sharing and communicating. They affect the way we view ourselves and others, in and out of our groups, and the way we behave toward people. They influence our attitudes, including acceptance or rejection of new ideas. Chapter Two describes some of the classic research on groups, by Lewin, the Hawthorne researchers, Coch and French, and others, and how group processes have been a central topic in organizational development over the years. These and many other researchers have developed a number of important and lasting insights about groups. They have shown how groups can influence work habits and productivity, and they have shed light on the attitudes group members maintain and how changes in those attitudes affect their behaviors. They have found that cohesion and commitment in groups can enforce attitudes and norms within the group and increase or decrease group performance and productivity, depending on the direction of group consensus. Group participation in decision making can enhance the quality of decisions and acceptance of change within an organization. Yet very cohesive groups can also clash with other groups, and groups can censor each other in harmful ways. Developing effective groups, then, involves a careful process of taking advantage of their potential without falling prey to their pitfalls. The literature now contains abundant guidance for the design and operation of groups and teams (Hackman, 1989; Katzenbach and Smith, 1994; Mohrman, Cohen, and Mohrman, 1995; Zander, 1994), so the discussion here will concentrate on some basic topics about the nature of groups and their advantages and disadvantages.

Group Formation, Norms, and Roles

The question of why and how groups form invites simple answers, such as "The assistant secretary appointed a representative of each major division in the agency." Yet in every group, unique informal patterns emerge that belie these simple answers. Groups may form through official appointments by leaders or under official rules or as a result of task imperatives such as the need for certain specializations. Some groups form entirely voluntarily, and even in formally established groups, members may decide how much to contribute or hold back, how much to cooperate or conflict, and so on. Groups vary in their attraction for members and their influence over them. Members move into roles and levels of influence that may correspond little to those that are formally designated.

Earlier chapters discussed some of the reasons for these variations, including French and Raven's typology of power (1968)—reward power, coercive power, expert power, referent power, and legitimate power. French and Raven were group theorists and intended their typology for analyses of why groups vary in power and in attractiveness to their members and power over them. Psychological experiments have shown that people often have fundamental impulses to group together with others. Psychologists interested in *social comparison processes* have pointed out that people often lack clear information about how they are doing and what they should do and thus draw on others as referents for their own behavior. Groups have a strong influence on people in this respect. Also, groups gain power and attractiveness as referents partly by dint of their other bases of power, such as their control of rewards, their expertness, and so on.

The controls groups exert over their members have received much attention because of their obvious importance. As groups form, group norms and values develop. Some researchers find the concept of norms, or standards of behavior and attitudes shared by group members, to be elusive and vague. But whether or not the concept of norms perfectly captures the phenomena, groups clearly display patterns of conformity to certain behaviors and beliefs.

Researchers have also analyzed the elaboration of various roles in groups, especially the psychological and social roles that may not follow formal assignments. Leadership obviously figures very importantly, and much of the work reviewed in Chapter Eleven, such as Fiedler's theory, pertains to group leadership. While leadership in groups obviously may follow from formal assignments and rank, informal leaders often emerge as well. Researchers who have intensively studied the development of leadership in newly formed groups report such findings as the importance of participation: those who participate most actively most often become the leader in the eyes of other members. Researchers have also discovered, however, that although long-winded, assertive types sometimes come to be regarded as leaders early on, groups later turn more and more to less outspoken, more competent persons. In fact, multiple roles can emerge, with one or several people taking the lead in social and emotional matters, such as maintaining morale and harmony, and another pressing for effective group structure and task accomplishment.

Group Contexts, Structures, and Outcomes

Generalizations about groups, particularly from research on experimental groups, provide insights, but very diffuse ones. Researchers have worked on the implications of variations in group settings and characteristics to try to understand the effects of such contingencies as group size, tasks, communication patterns, and composition. Groups often have advantages over individuals (and larger groups over smaller groups) because of the availability of more talents, ideas, viewpoints, and other resources. Groups often outperform individuals at certain decision-making and problem-solving tasks. Yet larger groups can often suffer problems related to unwieldiness, diffusion of responsibility, and the presence of "free riders." Some research has also suggested that social relations tend to become more formal in larger groups and that their members tend to tolerate more impersonal, task-oriented behaviors by leaders.

Researchers have also intensively examined variations in group tasks, such as variations between individual and collaborative tasks and structured and unstructured tasks. Some researchers have produced evidence of the social facilitation of individual tasks, where the mere presence of another person enhances performance on familiar tasks. For more collaborative or group tasks, researchers and theorists have woven a complex array of concepts and relationships among group size and such task characteristics as homogeneity or heterogeneity and disjunctiveness or conjunctiveness. The material on contingency theories of organization provides some of the most important implications for managers in relation to this topic, such as the need for subunits with more complex and variable tasks to have more flexible, interactive processes.

The structure and composition of groups also influence their processes, of course. Highly diverse groups whose members represent many different backgrounds and goals face particularly severe challenges in establishing smooth working relations. Examples include groups with an appointed member from each department in an organization or each of a set of interest groups (such as a community advisory group for a government agency) and groups formed to carry out negotiations between labor and management. The communication structure imposed on a group can also determine many important outcomes. For example, Leavitt (1951) conducted research on communication networks in groups, comparing communication processes and outcomes in groups required to communicate in different patterns. In one pattern, the circle, members communicated only with two members (those adjacent to them), so that information had to move around the group in a circle. In a chain pattern, members were arranged in a line, along which communication had to flow back and forth. In a wheel pattern, all communication had to flow through one member occupying the center, hub position. Other patterns included a fully interconnected group with all members able to communicate directly with all the others. The patterns determined numerous outcomes for the groups. The wheel produced the fastest transmission of information and good accuracy but low overall satisfaction, except for the person in the middle, who had a great time, usually emerging as the leader of a centralized process. The chain and circle produced slower communication, with less accuracy; nobody liked the chain very much, but members expressed high satisfaction with the circle. In both the circle and the completely interconnected group, communication was often slow, but everyone got the word more effectively than with the other forms, and members felt higher satisfaction. The research thus dramatizes a trade-off faced by managers and groups that is also suggested by contingency theory. Many of the human relations–oriented models prescribe participation, and these experiments demonstrate that when people more actively participate, they understand more and feel better about the process. Yet the research also shows that such processes often move slowly, and a more centralized structure has some advantages in speed, accuracy, and leadership impact. Managers and groups have to choose the most important outcome.

Advantages and Disadvantages of Groups

These sorts of findings from research and experience have made it clear that groups can serve as media for good or bad outcomes, depending on many factors.

Managers must consider when and how groups can operate with the most value. Maier (1967) provided a list of pros and cons of using groups for problem solving, to which people often refer. Groups can often bring in more knowledge, information, approaches, and alternatives. The participation of more people in group settings increases organization members' understanding and acceptance of decisions; members have a better idea of what the group decided and why, and they can carry this information back to others in the other units or groups to which they belong. But the social pressures in groups can bolster majority opinions regardless of their quality. Aggressive individuals or subgroups may stifle more capable members. As indicated by research described above, groups may press for conformity and move toward solutions too rapidly by stifling dissent. Some members may concentrate simply on winning, from their own or their unit's point of view.

Maier also points out that other factors can be good or bad, depending on the skill of the leader. Effective leaders can manage conflict and disagreement constructively and turn the relative slowness of group decision making to advantage, achieving good outcomes such as conflict resolution and more carefully discussed decisions. Groups may also make riskier decisions. While exerting pressures for conformity, they often paradoxically create a dispersion of responsibility, where individuals shirk or evade responsibility for the group's actions or take social cues from others in the group that lead them to mistakenly underestimate the significance of a problem. Individuals may outperform groups where creativity and efficiency are paramount, acceptance of the decision is less crucial, the most qualified person is easy to identify, individuals are very unlikely to cooperate, or little time is available (Gordon, 1993).

Groupthink

Irving Janis's work on groupthink (1971) reflects many of the elements of this body of research that have particular significance for managers, especially managers and leaders in government ('t Hart, 1990). Janis says that he has discovered groupthink not just in many organizational decision-making processes but also in relation to some of the most immensely significant decisions, such as major strategic decisions by firms and public policy decisions such as the bombing of North Vietnam during the Johnson administration and John Kennedy's decision to carry out the Bay of Pigs invasion. Janis argues that groups under the stress of making major decisions often exhibit the symptoms of groupthink. They need consensus and commitment to the course of action they choose, and the pressures for conformity lead members to see the group as invulnerable to opponents, to develop rationales to explain away or avoid serious consideration of apparent problems and threats, and to see themselves as morally right and to stereotype their opponents as incapable or immoral. Pressure for agreement and unanimity falls on members who dissent, as others press them to agree and to support the group and its leader. Members sometimes adopt the role of "mind guards," withholding information that might shake the group consensus, and engage in self-censorship, stifling their own impulse to disagree.

Janis describes instances of groupthink primarily at lofty levels of authority, but managers encounter it in many settings. At the annual meeting of the county commissioners' association of a large state, for example, when the association's governing council convened, council members expressed outrage over new environmental protection regulations that the state legislature was imposing on the state's counties. Certain council members fulminated against the regulations, charging that they usurped the counties' rightful authority. As the discussion continued, members increasingly characterized the state legislators and agency executives behind the changes as tyrants and empire builders and depicted themselves as noble defenders of their constituents' right to govern themselves. They boldly proclaimed their intention to write a strong letter of protest to the legislators and agency officials (a step likely to prove very ineffectual). These members reacted fairly scornfully to suggestions that a more reasonable and moderate discussion of the situation would be more productive, as if those making such suggestions lacked courage. They thus displayed groupthink symptoms, such as stereotyping the opposition, overestimating one's own position, and stifling dissent.

Janis prescribes a number of steps leaders can take to help groups avoid groupthink:

- Encourage members to act as critical evaluators and impartial decision makers.
- Accept criticisms of your own actions.
- Invite outside experts to join the discussion.
- Require members to discuss the matter with others outside the group.
- Assign two or more groups to work on the problem separately.
- Assign a member to play devil's advocate.
- Break the group into two subgroups at key points.
- Set aside time to review threats to the group's decision and any possible weaknesses in it.
- At major decision points, hold "last chance" sessions in which members can air their reservations.

Later in this chapter we will consider an abundance of additional advice and procedures for managing groups. Before turning to those, however, it is useful to cover some basic ideas about communication and conflict.

Communication in Organizations

Besides communication in and between groups, other forms and channels of communication play crucial roles in organizations. The ideas about power, strategy, structure, and leadership considered earlier are relevant here as well, since communication can occur through organizational rules and structures themselves, through formal written documents, in one-on-one exchanges with superiors, and so on.

Discussions of organizational communication typically begin with a very general model of the communication process. According to such models, communication begins with the source from which a message originates. A transmitter encodes the message and sends it to a receiver, who decodes it and moves it to a destination. Noise influences the accuracy of the transmission. Other general conceptions depict a person as both a sender of messages, through particular channels, to another person and a receiver of messages, back through the same or other channels, from that other person. Both people also communicate with other recipients and senders concomitantly. These fairly obvious models show what the research and theory emphasize—the nature of sources, senders, and recipients; the channels along which messages flow; and, in particular, the problem of noise or distortion that impedes the accurate transmission of information (Downs, 1988).

Typical discussions also distinguish among horizontal communication, vertical (upward and downward) communication, and external (outward) communication with environmental components. Horizontal communications encounter difficulties as a result of conflict, competition, or other differences between subunits and groups. Vertical communications encounter difficulties as a result of hierarchical filtering and superior-subordinate relationships, including resistance, inattentiveness, misunderstanding, and reticence or withholding of information by lower levels. The distinction between formal and informal communications processes, already familiar by now, receives due notice, as does the research on communication networks described above.

Communication Roles

Analysts of organizational communication have drawn on concepts from other areas of the social sciences to distinguish roles in the communication process (Rogers and Argawala-Rogers, 1976). *Gatekeepers* occupy positions where they can control the flow of information between units and groups. Others around them look to *opinion leaders* for information about the form that their own opinions should take. People in *liaison* roles transmit information between two or more units or groups. *Cosmopolites* have many contacts outside the organization and bring a lot of external information into the organization.

Communication Assessments and Audits

Beyond these generalizations, obviously, myriad dimensions of communication receive attention from researchers, as illustrated by the now numerous survey instruments and other procedures for assessing communication in organizations (Downs, 1988). Most of these ask individuals for their perceptions and evaluations of the information they receive in their organization and its communication process. For example, the communications audit questionnaire of the International Communications Association asks about the amount of information the respondent sends and receives on an array of topics—job performance, pay and benefits, relationship of his or her own work to the overall organization, new procedures, organizational problems and policies, and so on. It also asks about the amount of information the respondent *needs* to send and receive. It asks similar questions about the amount of information sent to and received from various sources, such as top management, middle management, immediate supervisors, co-workers, and the grapevine. Other questions ask about respondents' satisfaction with the information they receive, the organization and extent of their organization's communication processes, how much follow-up on communications they need and receive, and the quality of the organizational and work climate. Other communication assessment procedures track specific messages through the organization and map the dissemination of information. Still others map actual communication networks in organizations, analyzing who communicates with whom and about what.

Communication Problems

Obviously, the main issue in communications is getting it right, so the discussion often turns rapidly to what goes wrong. Table 12.1 provides a description of two representative lists of communication difficulties. The table first presents a list that represents a typical treatment of such problems in the general management and organizational behavior literature. Then it presents a list of categories that apply more directly to some of the problems typically regarded as most serious in public bureaucracies, such as jargon, inflated prose, and the manipulation of information for political or bureaucratic purposes.

Some of the greatest literary and journalistic figures of the last two centuries have poured their talents into ridiculing and decrying these tendencies in

TABLE 12.1. COMMUNICATIONS PROBLEMS AND DISTORTIONS.

Barriers to Effective Communication

Lack of feedback: One-way communication, in which the receiver provides no return of information about whether and with what effect the information came across

Noise in communication: Interference with the message during its transmission, ranging from actual physical noise or distortion to distractions or interference from the presence of others, personal biases, or past experiences

Misuse of language: Excessively vague, inaccurate, inflammatory, emotional, positive, or negative language

Listening deficiencies: Receivers' listening inattentively, passively, or not at all

Barriers to Effective Communication Between Groups

When two groups define a conflict between them as a win-or-lose conflict

When one or both groups seek to aggrandize their own power and emphasize only their own goals and needs

When they use threats

When they disguise their true positions and actively distort information

When they seek to exploit or isolate the other group

When they emphasize only differences and the superiority of their own position

Communication Distortions in Public Bureaus

Distorted perceptions: Inaccurate perceptions of information that result from preconceived ideas or priorities or from striving to maintain self-esteem or cognitive consistency

Erroneous translation: Interpretation of information by receivers in ways not intended by the senders

Errors of abstraction and differentiation: Transmission of excessively abstract or selective information; underemphasis of differences in favor of similarities or excessive polarization of fairly similar positions

Lack of congruence: Ambiguity or inconsistency between elements of a message or between the particular message and other sources of information, such as conflicts between verbal and nonverbal cues or between officially communicated values and policies and other communications indicating that these policies and values do not hold

Distrusted source: Failure to accept an accurate message because of suspicions about bias or lack of credibility of the source

Jargon: Communications difficulties that result from highly specialized professional or technical language that confuses those outside the specialization (and often those within it). Some jargon has value, but officials may use inflated and pretentious language to appear knowledgeable or important, to intimidate or impede clients, to distort true intentions, or to evade accountability and scrutiny.

Manipulating and withholding information: Senders' actively distorting or withholding information in line with their own interests and related influences that they seek to impose on the receiver

Sources: Johnson and Johnson (1994); Gortner, Mahler, and Nicholson (1987).

government bureaucracies. Some of these critiques have become embodied in academic theories that posit that public bureaucracies and bureaucrats distort and manipulate information more aggressively than their counterparts in business. Before examining these and some other theories and evidence about communication in public organizations, it is useful to cover the concept of conflict in organizations, which often intermingles with communication processes.

Conflict in Organizations

Although conflict obviously presents major challenges for managers, the literature on organizational conflict is not as elaborately developed as the body of research and theory on many other topics in organizational studies. Conflict receives attention in work on other major topics, however. Frederick Taylor said that he pursued the principles of scientific management in part because he wanted to diminish conflicts between workers and managers by providing scientific solutions to the questions they regularly disputed. Lawrence and Lorsch (1967), in their seminal study of organizational design processes, found high levels of conflict in very effective organizations and very high investments in managing rather than avoiding conflict. Some of the most recent developments in organizational design, such as matrix designs and ideas about fluid and duplicating structures, intentionally design conflict into organizational structures. Research shows that well-managed conflict often improves decision making in organizations. Research also shows, however, that managers, especially in business organizations, tend to dislike conflict and seek to avoid it, even though such conflict avoidance may lead to less effective decision making (Schwenk, 1990).

In public and nonprofit organizations, one expects and even hopes for intense conflicts, although preferably not destructive ones. As noted earlier, public organizations often embody the unceasing political competition and public policy dilemmas of the nation. Government agencies and their subunits and managers compete for resources, executive and legislative attention, and turf. They share responsibilities for programs and policies but often have differing points of view and priorities. New administrations and newly elected and appointed officials enter the picture regularly and rapidly, claiming new mandates, attempting to forget or freeze programs that people have poured their working lives into, or setting out to do things differently and better. Ombudsmen, examiners, auditors, oversight agencies, and legislative committees and hearings have a duty to take a sharply questioning and often conflicting view of an agency's operations. Often at issue are the very lives or major life conditions of many people, and massive amounts of money, power, and influence. The separation of powers designed into the U.S. government actually calls for conflicting interests and authority as checks against one another. Yates (1985) observes that "Madisonian systems" with built-in contentions and divided authority abound in public and private organizations. Schwenk (1990) found that executives in nonprofit organizations see a positive relationship between conflict in the decision-making process and the quality of the resultant decisions, while executives in for-profit organizations regard conflict as damaging to the quality and clarity of decisions. The nonprofit executives, which included executives from government agencies, had to consider the needs of diverse constituents and groups. They found conflict unpleasant, but they regarded it as useful in clarifying the needs and goals of diverse groups.

One must expect conflict, then, and try to make a healthy form of it flow in government and its agencies. Keeping it healthy represents the key challenge. Research on organizations has focused on what types of conflict occur, what brings it about, how it proceeds, and, as this chapter covers somewhat later, how to manage it constructively.

Types of Conflict

Experts on organizational conflict point out that numerous types and forms of conflict occur in organizations. Conflict can exist within a person (as the concepts of role conflict and role ambiguity emphasize), between people, and within and between groups and organizational departments or divisions. Conflict can range horizontally, across levels of an organization. It can occur vertically, between higher and lower levels (the classic example is a dispute between management and labor; another common example is a battle within a geographically dispersed government agency or business firm between the people at headquarters and field or district personnel).

Bases of Conflict

All types of conflict can originate in or be aggravated by organizational or subunit culture, values, goals, structures, tasks and functions, authority and leadership processes, and environmental pressures, as well as by the demographics and individual personalities of organizational or group members. You name it and it can cause a flare-up.

Researchers provide useful lists of some of the most frequent sources of strife; these can help us sort through some of this complexity. They cite differences in goals, values, cultures, and priorities, of course. The sociologists who began emphasizing dysfunctional bureaucracies around midcentury pointed out that the specialization of work and responsibility that bureaucracy involves, with its emphasis on reliable adherence to the rules and goals of specialized units, virtually ensures conflicts among units (for example, see the entry on Merton in Table 2.1 in Chapter Two). Differences in power, status, rewards, and resources among people and groups can lead to feelings of inequity, or the simple need to compete with others can cause conflict. Where two groups' tasks or decision-making processes overlap, are intensely interdependent, or naturally compete, tensions can boil over. Not always mentioned in the research, but quite obvious, are the surprisingly frequent instances of very significant conflict among high-level officials based simply on clashes of personal style and ego.

Conflict Stages and Modes

Analysts of conflict also note what they call the phases of conflict episodes. Pondy's frequently cited classification (1967), for example, includes five stages:

1. *Latent* conflict exists when conditions have set the stage for conflict, but it has not yet simmered to the surface.
2. *Perceived* conflict begins when the people involved begin to sense that conflict exists, even though they may attempt to downplay or deny it.
3. *Felt* conflict emerges when individuals begin to feel its effects—tension, anxiety, anger, or practical problems resulting from the conflict.
4. *Manifest conflict,* figuratively or actually, involves open warfare. People or groups try to frustrate, harm, or defeat one another. Either one group must win or lose; the conflict must continue, with destructive effects; or managers and members must effectively channel and manage the conflict toward constructive ends.
5. The *conflict aftermath* is the stage after the outbreak of conflict when some alternative and its results become evident.

As people and groups respond to the onset of conflict, their responses can take various forms. Thomas (1983) points out that people can respond through *avoidance* (trying to ignore or withdraw from the conflict). They can try *accommodation,* in which they cooperate and make concessions to the other party's demands or needs. *Compromise* involves an exchange of concessions and cooperative responses (without one side's being more accommodating than the other). *Competing* involves simply trying to force, outdo, or defeat the other party without any appreciable accommodation or concern for its goals and needs. *Collaborating* occurs when two parties work together to meet both parties' needs mutually; it differs from compromise in that the two parties do not simply give up on certain goals and values but rather work to find ways to maximize returns for both.

Yates (1985) also offers useful suggestions for developing strategies and tactics for managing conflict. He describes methods of fostering a competitive debate among conflicting parties, using neutral language to avoid escalating hostilities, and behaving with civility and mutual respect. He suggests approaches that involve identifying mutual problems and avoiding enmity, win-or-lose situations, and long-term resentments. One does this partly through including all affected parties, providing complete information, and keeping communication channels open. Yates proposes a process of conflict management that has many similarities to the management of culture and transformational leadership described in Chapter Eleven. The conflict manager must understand the people involved, establish a sense of shared mission to give the parties an incentive to resolve the conflict, and adopt an incremental approach, focusing on winning concrete issues.

Conflict Outcomes, Suppression, and Escalation

Experts on conflict have also detailed its outcomes and effects, though these are fairly obvious in much of the rest of the organizational behavior literature. Excessive conflict can induce stress, frustration, dissatisfaction, high turnover, absenteeism, and poor performance among employees. When poorly managed, it can damage organizations. The preceding discussion of types and modes of conflict provides a useful reminder that suppressed or poorly handled conflict can hurt an organization, in part because it can escalate more easily. Researchers point out that conflict can feed on itself, aggravating the sorts of barriers to communication described earlier—the use of charged language, bias in sending and receiving information, a tendency to interpret neutral statements from the other party as negative or aggressive, reduction of communication, and formation of we-they, win-lose perceptions of relationships. Severely entrenched, intense conflict can make an organization sick, like a mentally disturbed person who does irrational, self-destructive things.

Sometimes managers have to work with organizations facing severe challenges to effective communication and deal with people and groups that have many reasons to come into conflict. Researchers and consultants have developed a fairly rich fund of prescriptions for managing and improving group processes, communication, and conflict resolution processes in such organizations. After we look at these, the discussion will return to special considerations about public organizations.

Managing Groups, Communication, and Conflict in Organizations

Earlier chapters covered many topics relevant to managing groups, communication, and conflict, and the following chapters will cover still more. The discussion of leadership in Chapter Eleven described propositions from Fiedler's contingency theory, path-goal theory, life-cycle theory, and other approaches to understanding how leaders should and do behave toward the groups they lead. These theories emphasize the many variations in leadership settings and styles among organizations and the need for setting and style to mesh. Keeping these many variations in mind, group theorists have suggested numerous general prescriptions for managing groups. The prescriptions for avoiding groupthink provide one example. Leaders also have to try to enhance the attractiveness of group membership to increase group harmony, cohesiveness, and motivation (Zander, 1994). The typology of power offered by French and Raven—reward, coercive, expert, referent, and legitimate power—serves as a guide to some of the types of incentives that leaders can enhance and draw on to make groups effective. That typology implies additional incentives for group membership and motivation, such as prestige, a sense of having an impact or being important, conviviality, specialness of membership, and so on, that group theorists advise leaders to utilize. Many group theorists have a greater human relations orientation than leadership theorists. Prominent group theorists have typically argued that, in general, effective work groups require participative leaders who respect the dignity of group members and maintain harmony in groups (Zander, 1994).

This human relations emphasis probably comes from the close connections between group theory and the field of organization development (OD). Chapter Thirteen describes OD and some of the specific group techniques used to improve organizations, such as *team building* and *T-group* procedures, and to enhance effectiveness, communication, and conflict resolution in work groups. OD consultants also use a variety of techniques to enhance communication and resolve conflicts between different groups (Gordon, 1993). For example, they might use an *organizational mirror* procedure, in which other groups in the organization report their views of a particular group or unit to that group so that it can better assess its impact on and relations with others. A *confrontation meeting* brings two or more warring groups together to analyze and resolve the conflicts between them. *Third-party interventions* and *interpersonal facilitator* approaches have a person from outside the groups, and often outside the organization, come in to help with the conflict-resolution process. The latter involves a more central role for the facilitator in transmitting communications between the two groups (Blake and Mouton, 1984).

Most of these techniques involve ways of controlling the expression of hostility and aggression to prevent conflict from escalating. They usually try to provide a systematic way to uncover the nature of the conflict and discover a base for resolving it, through such procedures as *image exchanges,* in which members of the groups relate their views of the other group; *sharing appreciation* procedures, which call on group members to express appreciation of good things about the other group; and having the members list their expectations about the outcomes of the process. Management consultants may propose the use of a *dialectical inquiry* technique for managing and encouraging conflict in strategic decision-making processes. In this technique, the development of a strategic plan is followed by the development of a counterplan that questions the assumptions of the original plan. A *devil's advocacy* approach involves a critique of the basic assumptions of the strategic plan but does not propose a specific alternative (Schwenk, 1990).

Numerous other group procedures and techniques, not necessarily connected to OD practices, abound in organizations. The success of *quality circles* in Japan has led to their proliferation among organizations in the United States and other countries. As noted in Chapter Ten, a quality circle brings the members of a work group or organizational unit together for special group sessions on how to improve the quality of the unit's work and products. Organizations also typically employ special task forces, venture groups, policy committees, and other group-based approaches that explicitly seek to take advantage of group capacities. Several group decision-making procedures, such as the *nominal group technique, brainstorming,* and the *Delphi technique,* can facilitate communication and management of potential conflict within and among groups (Gordon, 1993). In the nominal group technique, each group member makes a list of responses to a focal question or issue—for example, what are the organization's most important goals? One by one, each group member reads aloud the first item on his or her list; then each reads the second item, and so on. As the lists are read, the items are recorded and displayed for the group to see. The group then discusses the set of items—goals, in this example—to clarify them, discuss disagreements, and combine similar ones. They then follow any of several possible methods for coming to agreement on the final set of goals. The procedure thus allows each person to contribute, minimizes digression, and channels conflict into constructive patterns. Brainstorming sessions invite members to suggest all alternatives or possibilities about an issue or problem that they can think of. The group records all suggestions and then evaluates them and works toward a conclusion. In the Delphi technique, a smaller group prepares a questionnaire about a topic, circulates it to a larger group, and then uses the latter's responses to prepare a revised questionnaire. This second questionnaire is circulated along with information about the results of the first, and the process is repeated until a consensus develops within the larger group.

In addition, communications experts commonly stress the usefulness of conducting organization-wide communications audits of the sort described above. They point to the crucial role of the climate or culture of an organization in fostering or stifling communication and in determining whether and how well people manage conflicts.

Special Considerations for Public Organizations

The preceding review demonstrates that researchers have treated these topics as being generally applicable across all organizations, with no need for any particular distinction among public, private, and nonprofit organizations. The review also indicates why they have taken this posture. They state the models and propositions at a high level of generality to make them applicable across groups and organizations. They see that managers in government, business, and nonprofit settings face common challenges in dealing with these dimensions of their work and can apply many of the proposed responses just as well in any of the sectors.

Still, some of the time-honored observations about government bureaucracies claim sharp distinctions between that domain and business firms in matters pertaining to groups, communication, and conflict. Many of these virtually classic views echo throughout some of the most prominent recent theoretical efforts. In many governmental settings, for example, an elaborate, diverse configuration of groups and authorities contests over organizational policies and decisions. As noted earlier, inside and outside government organizations, "Madisonian systems" operate (the product of laws that formally establish multiple authorities) or arise as a result of the activities of groups and individuals seeking to influence government policies—the pluralistic governmental processes long discussed by political scientists. Complex groups and interests outside an organization often mirror a corresponding complexity within, according to many people who write about government organizations. Interest groups, congressional committees, and elements of the executive branch form alliances with units and individuals inside a particular agency and jealously defend these relationships. Consequently, many large government agencies become highly diverse confederations of groups and units whose relative independence weakens the authority of the politically appointed executives at the top (Warwick, 1975; Seidman and Gilmour, 1986).

Observers also say that the fact that the goals of public agencies are multiple, hard to specify and measure, and conflicting adds to this complexity. Often, two government agencies or two bureaus within a particular agency pursue diametrically opposed goals—stop smoking but support tobacco farmers, enhance international trade but prevent the sale of sensitive technology—or have sharply differing priorities for a program for which they share responsibility.

For all these reasons, government often involves a particularly high frequency of power-sharing situations (Bryson and Einsweiller, 1991; Kettl, 1993). Many commentators note that government managers need a particularly high level of tolerance for ambiguity and diversity and must deal frequently with conflicts among diverse groups.

Public managers must also deal with particularly diverse work groups in many cases. Buchanan (1974, 1975) felt that his findings of lower organizational commitment among public managers resulted in part from his concurrent finding that they felt less encouragement from their work group to perform well and to form a strong commitment to the organization. He noted the sources of diversity mentioned above. He added, however, that government has proceeded more rapidly than industry in employing minorities and women. Buchanan suggested that these trends have led to more diversity within working groups and organizations in government. They simply employ more different types of people from different backgrounds and perspectives, which in turn leads to more diversity of perspective within these organizations and groups.

People who know government well also point out that the diversity plays a role in a paradox. Government heavily emphasizes control and accountability, but it does so within a context in which clear performance measures such as profits and sales are not available to aid in assessing accountability and performance. The greater diversity in public organizations, they say, aggravates their tendency to emphasize reporting, record keeping, and requests for clearances from higher hierarchical levels. Even smaller units in government face intense requirements to report to higher levels as a result of the federal system of grants and contracts, requirements imposed by larger agencies and jurisdictions, and so on. The system has become an elaborate array of "centrifugal and centripetal" forces (Warwick, 1975) and "inevitable bureaucracy" (Lynn, 1981). More and more diversity, coupled with pressures for accountability but few clear performance measures, breeds a profusion of rules, regulations, clearances, and reporting requirements.

While media commentators and the general public typically interpret these conditions as the result of bureaucratic bungling and officiousness, careful examinations show that there is a reasonable rationale behind a great many of these forms of red tape (Kaufman, 1976), and thus intense efforts to reduce federal paperwork and red tape have not made a great deal of headway. All this implies that public management typically involves great information intensity and information traffic. The tasks that public organizations carry out, of course, tend to be service-oriented and information-intensive. Careful studies of information handling in the public and private sectors have shown that public organizations do in fact involve greater information intensity, with private service organizations such as banks and insurance companies coming close to resembling them but actually falling in an intermediate range between industrial firms and public agencies (Bretschneider, 1990).

Tullock (1965) developed theoretical arguments that foreshadowed these observations about the paradox in public organizations of many efforts at control coupled with weak controls. He argued that the size and complexity of government bureaus create information leakage as lower-level officials communicate up the hierarchy. The officials must summarize the information that they report upward and screen the information that they receive from lower levels before transmitting it upward. This process deletes much of the information. And in addition to simply boiling the information down, they report the information that is most favorable to them and screen out unfavorable information. This leads to substantial distortions in upward communications in public bureaucracies, according to Tullock. He argued that private firms are better able to avoid such problems because their higher levels use such measures as sales and profits to prevent the lower levels from inaccurately reporting favorable information about their activities.

Downs (1967) elaborated Tullock's observations into a more complex set of hypotheses. According to Downs, most communication in bureaus is "subformal." Subformal communication increases with greater interdependence among activities, with uncertainty, and with time pressure but decreases between subunits in sharp conflict with one another. Newer, fast-growing, changing bureaus have less effective communication networks than older, more stable ones. Information moving up the hierarchy becomes distorted for the reasons that Tullock described, and successful high-level officials use various strategies to counteract this distortion. They develop informal channels of information outside the bureau and set up overlapping responsibilities inside the bureau to create redundant internal channels. They employ "counterbiasing," which means that they adjust their own reactions to information from lower levels in ways that counter the biases that they know the reports contain. For example, they reduce reliance on information about future events or qualitative factors. In agencies with many crises and much specialization, they bypass levels to get the "straight scoop" from lower levels. They seek to develop distortion-proof information systems, especially when precise accuracy and rapid transmission are very important and when there is a "tall" hierarchy and important variables are quantifiable. This characterization of the public sector setting, together with preceding ones, if correct, means that communications in the public sector are more intensive and difficult, with conflicts more likely to occur and more difficult to manage.

Yet little explicit comparative research has assessed this view. While researchers have examined communications in public agencies (Warwick, 1975), such studies cannot resolve the question of whether large private firms would show the same characteristics and processes. Besides the Buchanan studies mentioned above, searches for this book located few public-private comparative studies explicitly dealing with groups, communication, and conflict. In one, Boyatzis (1982) found that a sample of public managers showed lower levels of skill at managing group processes than private sector managers did. In another, Baum and James (1984) compared the responses of 2,300 employees from nine "clearly public" and five "clearly private" organizations to the International Communications Association

(ICA) communications audit survey questionnaire. On most of these questions, the respondents in the public organizations scored less favorably than the private sector employees. On almost every item about information received and sent, they felt that they received and sent less and needed to send and receive more than the private sector respondents. They also scored lower on each of thirty-two questions about organizational climate (concerning relations with co-workers, supervisors, and subordinates; satisfaction with work, pay, communication, and other factors; and quality of products and services). As with the satisfaction studies discussed in Chapter Ten, the public sector respondents expressed reasonably high satisfaction on many of these items but scored lower than private sector respondents. Baum and James concluded that public managers face greater challenges in establishing effective communications and must work harder at it.

Schwenk (1990) compared the perceptions of forty executives from for-profit (FP) and not-for-profit (NFP) organizations regarding conflict surrounding decision making in their organizations. All the executives found conflict unpleasant, but the FP executives felt that conflict diminished the quality and clarity of decisions, and they found it more unpleasant than the NFP executives. The NFP executives reported a positive association between conflict and the quality and clarity of decisions. In describing their decisions, the FP executives much more frequently mentioned criteria related to financial performance—a finding consistent with that of Solomon (1986)—while the NFP managers more often mentioned the needs of constituents and the speed and effectiveness of service delivery.

Schwenk (1990) also analyzed the executives' descriptions of their decisions using the decision framework developed by Mintzberg, Raisinghani, and Theoret (1976), described in Chapter Seven. He found that conflict in the NFP organizations more often occurred in the early phases of the decision-making process (the phases concerned with problem recognition and diagnosis) and that NFP decision-making processes involved more steps and more "recycles," in which the decision process cycles back to an earlier phase. In the FP decision-making processes, conflict tended to occur later, in the phase involving evaluation and choice of alternatives. The NFP executives apparently regarded conflict as useful in clarifying diverse criteria and the demands of diverse interests and constituencies, particularly in the recognition and diagnosis of problems. While the sample for the Schwenk study was not large, the findings tend to reflect the organizational context of public organizations described earlier in this and in other chapters. They also tend to concur with other researchers' findings about decision-making processes in public organizations as compared to private ones (Hickson and others, 1986; Solomon, 1986).

In sum, much theory and some expert observation hold that public organizations face greater complexity and more potential problems in group relations, communication, and conflict resolution. Little direct comparative evidence supports these observations, but the few studies that provide evidence about them tend to show greater complexity and problems. This conclusion should not be overstated and overgeneralized, however. The interpretation that the private sector performs better on these dimensions is too simple and easy. Previous chapters, and Chapters Thirteen and Fourteen, show numerous examples of effective public management involving strong and productive communication. The public sector may face greater challenges precisely because of the nature of government as an arena for the complex policymaking decisions and political choices of an advanced political economy. Yet, as the review in this chapter has shown, the literature phrases the issues and prescriptions at a high level of generality, making them applicable to public, private, and nonprofit organizations. Public managers may not need significantly different knowledge and skills from those covered here, but they do need particularly well-developed knowledge and skills in this area. For effective communication in public agencies, there are now well-developed frameworks, guidelines, and advice for public managers (Garnett, 1992).

PART THREE

STRATEGIES FOR MANAGING AND IMPROVING PUBLIC ORGANIZATIONS

CHAPTER THIRTEEN

MANAGING ORGANIZATIONAL CHANGE AND DEVELOPMENT

If, as Chapter Six asserts, organizational effectiveness is the fundamental issue in organizational analysis, then the challenge of changing organizations is a strong candidate for second place. A sprawling literature addresses organizational change and innovation, with much of it, including the elaborate subfield of organization development, focused on how to change organizations for the better. As we have pointed out, controversy simmers over whether public organizations and their employees resist change. As with all other topics taken up in this book, careful research uncovers many more dimensions and issues than popular discussions and some economic theories consider.

In fact, researchers and experts note a paradoxical aspect of change in public organizations. Far from being isolated bastions of resistance to change, they change constantly (Meyer, 1979). This pattern may impede substantial long-term change, however. In many public organizations, the politically appointed top executives and their own appointees come and go fairly rapidly. In federal agencies, the agency heads stay less than two years on average. Shifts in the political climate cause rapid shifts in program and policy priorities. This can make it hard to sustain implementation of major changes. This chapter also shows examples of successful change in public organizations, however.

Relatively Natural Change: Organizational Life Cycles

Members of organizations plan and carry out some changes very purposefully. Other changes occur more spontaneously or naturally as organizations pass through phases of development or respond to major shifts in their environment. The two types of change intermingle, of course, as managers and other members respond to shifting circumstances. In the last two decades, scholars have turned more attention to externally imposed and naturally evolving change processes in writing and research on organizational life cycles, birth, and decline (Kimberly, Miles, and Associates, 1980; Cameron, Sutton, and Whetten, 1988).

Much of this work concentrates on business firms but applies to public organizations as well (for example, Van de Ven, 1980; Quinn and Cameron, 1983). Years ago, Simon, Smithburg, and Thompson (1950) noted that public organizations become distinct by the nature of their birth. An influential set of interests must support the establishment of a public organization as a means of meeting a need that those interests perceive, and they must express that need politically. Public agencies are born of and live by satisfying interests that are sufficiently influential to maintain the agencies' political legitimacy and the resources that come with it.

Downs (1967) later suggested a number of more elaborate ways in which public bureaus form. For one of these, Max Weber coined the term *routinization of charisma*. People devoted to a charismatic leader can press for an organization that pursues the leader's goals. Alternatively, as Simon, Smithburg, and Thompson (1950) pointed out, interested groups press for the formation of a bureau to carry out a function for which they see a need. A new bureau can split off from an existing one, as did the Department of Education from what used to be the Department of Health, Education, and Welfare (Radin and Hawley, 1988). Also, entrepreneurs may gain enough support to form a new bureau. Admiral Hyman Rickover became a virtual legend by building an almost autonomous program for the development of nuclear propulsion in the nuclear power branch of the navy's Bureau of Ships and the nuclear reactor branch of the Atomic Energy Commission (Lewis, 1987).

The Stages of Organizational Life

Downs also said that bureaus have a three-stage life cycle. The earliest stage involves a struggle for autonomy. "Zealots" and "advocates" dominate young bureaus and struggle to build political support for its legitimacy and resource requests. Once a bureau has established itself and ensured its survival, it enters a stage of rapid expansion, in which its members emphasize innovation. Ultimately, it enters a deceleration phase, in which the administrators concentrate on elaborating rules and ensuring coordination and accountability. Downs associated this process with what he called the rigidity cycle for bureaus. He said that as bureaus grow older and larger and enter the deceleration stage, the zealots and advocates either depart for more active, promising programs or settle into the role of "conservers." Conservers come to dominate the bureau, and it ossifies. Others have pointed out that over time, many bureaus form strong alliances with interest groups and legislators—especially legislators on the committees that oversee them. These allies guard the bureaus' access and influence and stave off many change attempts (Warwick, 1975; Seidman and Gilmour, 1986).

Yet Downs oversimplifies about the foot-dragging bureaucracy. Large, old organizations change markedly, as has been recognized in recent life-cycle models. Quinn and Cameron (1983) developed a framework based on similarities among models others have proposed. Their framework conceives four stages of organizational development—the entrepreneurial, collectivity, formalization, and elaboration stages.

In the *entrepreneurial* stage, members of the new organization concentrate on marshaling resources and establishing the organization as a viable entity. An entrepreneurial head or group usually plays a strong leading role, pressing for innovation and new opportunities and placing less emphasis on planning and coordination. Quinn and Cameron illustrate this stage by describing a newly created developmental center for the mentally disabled in a state department of mental health (DMH). The energetic center director led a push for new treatment methods that involved deinstitutionalizing clients and developing their self-reliance. The center began to receive expanded support from federal grants, the DMH, and the legislature. In this stage, the center emphasized the open-systems model of organization.

Out of the first stage develops the second, or *collectivity* stage. In this stage the members of the center developed high cohesion and commitment. They operated in a flexible, team-based mode, exhibiting high levels of effort and zeal for the center's mission. This type of shift represents an expanded emphasis on teamwork, marked by adherence to the human relations model as well as the open-systems component of the competing values framework described in Chapter Six.

The research on life cycles points out that crises sometimes push organizations into new stages. About six years after the formation of the center, a major newspaper ran articles attacking the DMH for inefficiency, poor treatment of clients, and loose administrative practices. The articles cited critical reports from oversight agencies concerning inadequacies in such control mechanisms as organizational charts, records, job descriptions, policy manuals, and master plans. The

DMH conducted a special investigation and instructed the center director to move toward a more traditional organizational structure and more traditional controls. The director left, and the new director emphasized clear lines of authority, rules, and accountability. Staff commitment fell, and many staff members left. The center had clearly moved into the *formalization and control* stage. In competing values terms, the rational control model predominated, and the importance of open systems and human relations criteria declined.

The case ended at this point, but the life-cycle framework includes a fourth stage, involving *structural elaboration and adaptation*. Confronting the problems of extensive control and bureaucracy that develop during the third stage, the organization moves toward a more elaborate structure to allow more decentralization but also corresponding coordination processes (Lawrence and Lorsch, 1967). The organization seeks new ways to adapt, renew itself, and expand its domain. A large corporation may become more of a conglomerate, multiplying its profit centers, or it may adopt a matrix design (Mintzberg, 1979). It appears to be difficult for public agencies to decentralize in these ways, however (Mintzberg, 1989). They have no sales and profit indicators to use in establishing profit centers, and they face stronger external accountability pressures. Note that in the DMH case, the press and the oversight agencies both pressed for traditional bureaucratic structures—charts, manuals, job descriptions. Some public agencies, however, also reconfigure in later stages, as described below.

Organizational Decline and Death

Many older, supposedly entrenched organizations face intense pressure to renew themselves. During the 1970s and 1980s, such pressures rose to particular intensity in the United States. Businesses faced surging international competition and swings in the price of oil and other resources. Government agencies faced tax revolts and skepticism about government. This bolstered the Reagan administration's efforts to cut the federal budget, including funding for many agencies and for federal support to state and local governments, many of which also faced state and local initiatives to force tax cuts (Levine, 1980a).

Organizational researchers realized that while such pressures may have intensified during the period, they actually reflected ongoing processes of decline and demise that had received little attention in organizational research (Kimberly, Miles, and Associates, 1980; Cameron, Sutton, and Whetten, 1988). Bankruptcy rates among business firms have always been very high, and all organizations, including public ones, tend to have low survival rates (Starbuck and Nystrom, 1981). Organizations may decline at various rates and in various patterns, for a number of reasons (Levine, 1980b). They may atrophy, their performance declining due to internal deterioration. They may become rigid, inefficient, and plagued with overstaffing and ineffective structures and communications. As described below, the Social Security Administration once became so backlogged in processing client requests that everyone involved agreed that something had to be done.

Vulnerability and Loss of Legitimacy. Organizations, especially new ones, can also be quite vulnerable to the loss of resources or support from their environment. Shifts in consumer preferences can undercut businesses. Government organizations face an analogous problem when voters resist taxes. This is related to another reason for decline, the loss of legitimacy. Private firms, such as tobacco companies, can suffer when the public or public officials question the legitimacy of their products or activities. Legitimacy figures even more crucially for public organizations. Public and oversight authorities often impose stricter criteria on public organizations for honest, legitimate behaviors, as in the example of the HUD scandal described in Chapter Seven.

Environmental Entropy. An organization's environment can simply deteriorate in its capacity to support the organization. Resources may dry up. Political support may wane. Public organizations often lose support because of the waning of the social need that they address (Levine, 1980a).

Responses to Decline. Organizations respond to decline with greater or lesser aggressiveness and more or less acceptance of the need for change. Whetten (1988) characterizes several patterns for response. Some organizations take a *negative, resistant disposition* toward the pressures for change. They may aggressively strike a *preventive* posture or more passively react in a *defensive* mode. They may try to prevent pressures for change by manipulating the environment. Public agencies may try to develop or maintain legislation that rules out competition from other agencies or private providers of similar services. Public employee unions aggressively attack privatization proposals because they threaten public employees. On the other hand, organizations may adopt a less proactive defense against cuts, citing statistics showing the need for their programs and working to persuade legislators that their programs meet important social needs.

Other organizations take a more *receptive* approach to the need for change, either *reactively* or by *generating* change and adaptation. Many public agencies react with across-the-board cuts in subunit budgets, layoffs, or other reductions in their work force. On the other hand, a growing literature discusses ways organizations seek to adapt through very flexible, self-designing structures and processes. They allow lower-level managers and employees to redesign their units when they feel the need. The work on this topic concentrates on private firms and usually treats public organizations as less capable of making independent, aggressive responses to pressures for change (Whetten, 1988).

The pressures for reduced government taxing and spending have led to a rich discussion of tactics for responding to funding cutbacks. Table 13.1 summarizes Charles Levine's description of some of those tactics (1980b). Rubin (1985) analyzed the Reagan administration's cutbacks in five federal agencies. She found that the agencies' responses in some ways matched what one would expect from the public administration literature and in some ways differed markedly. The president was fairly successful in achieving cutbacks in the agencies. His strong popular support blunted interest-group opposition to the cuts in the early phases. Still, agencies with interest-group support more effectively resisted the cutbacks. Interest groups and congressional supporters do fight for their programs. Yet Rubin found no evidence of strong "iron triangles" protecting the agencies. Sometimes agencies worked with congressional supporters, or Congress with interest groups, or agencies with interest groups, but not usually in a well-developed iron triangle.

The agencies were not nearly so self-directed and uncontrollable as is sometimes claimed. Agency heads tended to comply with the president's cutback initiatives and usually did *not* work aggressively to mobilize interest-group support. Career personnel carried out many of the cuts as part of their responsibility to serve the president. Rubin even suggests that one of the agencies self-destructed, refusing to fight for itself. Some of the agencies, particularly central administrative and regulatory agencies, had no strong interest-group support and were more vulnerable to cuts. In fact, such agencies are sometimes cut back even if they are effective, because they have no natural group support (or they may even have made enemies of some interest groups).

Because of congressional and interest-group opposition to some of the Reagan administration cuts, the president relied on internal reorganizations and personnel cuts that did not require congressional approval. This damaged management and reduced productivity in some of the agencies. In the short term, the agencies suffered bad morale, lower productivity, bad decision making, and general disruption. The cutback process increased polarization among blacks and whites, labor and management, and career civil servants and political appointees. The cuts reduced the attractiveness of federal employment and increased political influence over the federal agencies. Rubin's appraisal of these effects was made during the middle of the Reagan administration, and their duration remains to be seen. The analysis, however, does make some important points: agency responses to decline are more complex and perhaps less politically resistant than depicted in the general literature—agencies *do* change, and they do not necessarily resist change as forcefully as stereotypes and some theories suggest. Still, politics figures very importantly in change and cutback attempts and can severely impede them. Understanding when and how one can effect change becomes the major challenge, to which we return below.

TABLE 13.1. ORGANIZATIONAL DECLINE AND CUTBACK MANAGEMENT: TACTICS FOR RESPONDING TO DECLINE AND FUNDING CUTS.

	Tactics to Resist Decline	Tactics to Smooth Decline
External political (problem depletion)	1. Diversify programs, clients, and constituents 2. Improve legislative liaison 3. Educate the public about the agency's mission 4. Mobilize dependent clients 5. Become "captured" by a powerful interest group or legislator 6. Threaten to cut vital or popular programs 7. Cut a visible and widespread service a little to demonstrate client dependence	1. Make peace with competing agencies 2. Cut low-prestige programs 3. Cut programs to politically weak clients 4. Sell and lend expertise to other agencies 5. Share problems with other agencies
External economic/ technical (environmental entropy)	1. Find a wider and richer revenue base (for example, metropolitan reorganization) 2. Develop incentives to prevent disinvestment 3. Seek foundation support 4. Lure new public- and private-sector investment 5. Adopt user charges for services where possible	1. Improve targeting on problems 2. Plan with preservative objectives 3. Cut losses by distinguishing between capital investments and sunk costs 4. Yield concessions to taxpayers and employers to retain them
Internal political (political vulnerability)	1. Issue symbolic responses, such as forming study commissions and task forces 2. "Circle the wagons"—develop a siege mentality to retain esprit de corps 3. Strengthen expertise	1. Change leadership at each stage in the decline process 2. Reorganize at each stage 3. Cut programs run by weak subunits 4. Shift programs to another agency 5. Get temporary exemptions from personnel and budgetary regulations that limit discretion
Internal economic/ technical (organizational atrophy)	1. Increase hierarchical control 2. Improve productivity 3. Experiment with less costly service-delivery systems 4. Automate 5. Stockpile and ration resources	1. Renegotiate long term contracts to regain flexibility 2. Install rational choice techniques such as zero-based budgeting and evaluation research 3. Mortgage the future by deferring maintenance and downscaling personnel quality 4. Ask employees to make voluntary sacrifices such as taking early retirements and deferring raises 5. Improve forecasting capacity to anticipate future cuts 6. Reassign surplus facilities to other users 7. Sell surplus property, lease back when needed 8. Exploit the exploitable

Source: Levine (1980b). Reproduced by permission of Chatham House Publishers, Inc.

The Ultimate Decline: Organizational Death. A conclusion similar to Rubin's comes from a debate over whether public agencies can "die." Kaufman (1976) investigated the question of whether government organizations are immortal, in view of the many assertions about their staunch political support and their intransigence against pressures for change, reduction, or elimination. He noted many threats to an agency's survival. They face competition from other agencies, loss of political support, and the constant reorganization movements that keep officials continuously hunting for ways to reshape government, especially ways that appear more efficient. He reviewed statistics on the death rates of federal agencies and concluded that such rates are not negligible. Generally, however, federal agencies have a very strong tendency to endure. Of the agencies existing in 1923, he said, 94 percent had lineal descendants in 1974.

Later, Starbuck and Nystrom (1981) mounted a fascinating challenge to this conclusion. They pointed out that Kaufman had classified agencies as lineal descendants even if they had changed organizational locations, names, or personnel or had substantially different functions. When agencies merged, he treated the new agency as a descendant of both of the former ones. Starbuck and Nystrom pointed out that studies of death rates of industrial organizations typically treat mergers between corporations as resulting in only one existing organization. When a corporation goes bankrupt and employees start a very similar new one, analysts do not count this as a continuation. Difficult issues exist, then, in defining organizational death. Starbuck and Nystrom reanalyzed Kaufman's data, using criteria more akin to those used in studies of industry; they found that government agencies and industrial corporations have very similar death and survival rates. A large proportion of both government agencies and business firms do not survive very long. The analysis turns on whether one uses criteria biased toward organizational change or against it.

Peters and Hogwood (1988) also report finding a great deal of organizational change in the U.S. federal bureaucracy. Their analysis shows, however, what other organization theorists have seen when they study public organizations (Meyer, 1979): public organizations may be quite change-resistant and intransigent in some ways, and steering them in new and innovative directions can be a major challenge for society. Yet they do, in fact, change a great deal, including undergoing the ultimate change of passing out of existence. As described in later sections, they can also revitalize themselves after periods of decline.

Innovation and Organizations

Innovations in society figure so importantly in social progress that a body of research focused specifically on such processes has developed in the last several decades. Some of it addresses the broad topic of diffusion of innovations in societies and across levels and units of government. Numerous studies have analyzed such topics as the adoption of birth control methods in overpopulated countries, new agricultural methods in less developed countries, and different ways of providing firefighting, garbage-collection, and teaching services in governments across the United States. Some studies have also analyzed general measures of innovativeness in a certain type of organization, such as the number of health-related innovations adopted by county health departments. According to Rogers and Kim (1985), the vast majority of these innovation studies have focused on public organizations or public programs, and their application to business organizations remains open to question. They also point out that many of these studies followed what they called the classical diffusion model, which includes the following components: characteristics of the innovation itself (see Table 13.2), communication channels in the social system being studied, time (for example, rate of adoption of innovations), and members of the social system (the characteristics of its individuals and groups and how those characteristics influence their response to innovation).

TABLE 13.2. ATTRIBUTES OF INNOVATIONS THAT AFFECT THEIR IMPLEMENTATION.

1. Cost—initial and continuing; financial and social
2. Returns on investment
3. Efficiency—improvements in efficiency offered by innovation
4. Risk and uncertainty
5. Communicability—clarity of the innovation and its results
6. Compatibility—similarity to existing product or process
7. Complexity
8. Scientific status
9. Perceived relative advantage—whether potential advantages can be demonstrated or made visible
10. Point of origin—from inside or outside the organization; from what person, unit, or institution
11. Terminality—whether the innovation has a specific end point
12. Reversibility and divisibility—whether the innovation can be reversed or divided into steps or components so that the organization can return to the status quo if necessary
13. Commitment—the degree of behavioral and attitudinal commitment required for success
14. Interpersonal relations—how the innovation influences personal relations
15. Public- versus private-good attributes—whether the innovation provides public benefits or restricts benefits to a smaller set of individuals
16. Gatekeepers—how the innovation is related to various influential persons or groups that can block or initiate the innovation
17. Adaptability—whether users can modify and refine the innovation
18. Successive innovations—prospects for leading to additional innovations

Source: Adapted from Zaltman, Duncan, and Holbek (1973).

This work provides useful insights. Analyses of the attributes of innovations (Table 13.2), for example, provide useful guides for thinking through the prospects for a particular innovation. Yet studies following this general model have been criticized for concentrating too much on the relationships between such factors. Researchers have argued the need for greater attention to the processes involved in the development of innovations, from their initiation to their implementation, and to how particular organizations respond to particular innovations. Rogers and Kim argue that this orientation moves researchers toward a newer model of innovation, composed of these components:

I. Initiation process
    A. *Agenda setting.* Members of the organization perceive a performance gap or deficit (Zaltman, Duncan, and Holbek, 1973) that requires attention. This perception leads to an agreement on the need for innovation.
    B. *Matching.* A solution—the innovation—is matched to the problem.
II. Implementation process
    A. *Redefinition.* The members of the organization modify the innovation to fit their organization. This involves some "reinvention" of the original innovation.
    B. *Structuring.* Members modify the organization's structure to accommodate the innovation.
    C. *Interconnecting.* Also called *institutionalization* or *routinization,* this phase involves establishing permanent relationships between the innovation and other elements of the organization.

Planned Change

Innovations in organizations commonly involve purposeful, planned changes, initiated by organization members. External or internal pressures usually press them into it, but managers and other members must come together to plan them and carry them out.

Resistance to Change

From the beginning, management and organization theorists have recognized the problem of resistance to change in organizations. Many authors have argued that traditional bureaucratic forms of organization inhibit change. They assign people to positions and departments on the basis of rules and job descriptions, require people to adhere to them, and reward them for doing so. This aggravates the normal human tendency to resist change for all the reasons implied by Zaltman, Duncan, and Holbek's analysis (1973) of the characteristics of innovations (Table 13.2): change can be costly, troublesome, unfamiliar, threatening, and difficult to understand and accomplish.

Good Reasons to Resist Change

Human resistance to change can be one of the most destructive, dangerous tendencies in life, but managers and researchers often appear to forget that people have good reasons to resist change. Fairly typically, a new manager enters an organization with a desire to have an impact and not simply to serve as a caretaker. Employees sometimes throw objections and obstacles in the way of the new manager's proposals. Quite often, the new manager expresses frustration with longtime employees' commitment to the status quo.

Certainly, the new manager may have good reason to complain, but he or she may also cripple effective change by too readily assuming that resistance means laziness, selfishness, or stupidity. People may have well-justified reasons to resist. Some ideas are simply bad ideas, and the people with the most experience realize it. The *New Yorker* magazine once ran a cartoon in which two employees of a fast-food restaurant watched a family stopped in their car at the drive-through window of the restaurant. The family members were leaning out of the car with tongs in hand, struggling to serve themselves out of a large salad bowl perched on the windowsill of the drive-through window. Cherry tomatoes bounced like Ping-Pong balls on the pavement. Lettuce floated in the wind. One employee was saying to the other, "Well, it looks as if the drive-through salad bar is an idea whose time has not yet come." Some ideas are bad ideas. They deserve to be resisted.

Unsuccessful ideas abound in government and industry. As one prominent example, Lyndon Johnson directed that the planning and program budgeting system (PPBS) be adopted in all federal agencies. Within a few years, the directive was withdrawn. Many elected officials and politically appointed executives at all levels of government initiate new programs, reforms, or legislation but show a disinclination to become too deeply involved in implementing them. Often they feel that their duty involves setting policy and directing the bureaucracy rather than closely following its management. Many of them do not stay very long in their positions. Often their mandate is far from clear, however much they claim that it is. This can deprive the change process of essential support and leadership.

The point is not to defend the prerogative of the public bureaucracy to resist change but rather to emphasize a dilemma about organizational change in government. As described below, successful organizational change requires sustained support from higher levels, participative planning, and flexible implementation.

Government managers achieve these conditions more often than many people suppose, but much of the literature nevertheless suggests their scarcity in the public sector. What we learn from the management literature on change makes the point that, in the example just above, the reason for the failure of PPBS was not necessarily that it was a bad idea. It was a well-intentioned innovation advocated by many experts on public administration. Good ideas are not simply born, however; they are made—developed and nurtured—through appropriate change processes. Too negative a view of resistance to new initiatives and ideas can cloud the message that people may have reasonable objections that can make a dubious idea into a better one. The challenge for public managers is to find ways to overcome obstacles to such participation and flexibility amid the political complexities and accountability pressures in government.

Types of Change

Many types, levels, and degrees of change complicate the discussion of the change process. Researchers have not incorporated these variations into their models very thoroughly; instead, they have moved to highly general frameworks that broadly cover many types of change. Still, the variations bear noting and have implications taken up in later sections. Daft (1995) points out that organizations undergo at least four types of change:

- Technology changes occur in production processes and equipment, as in the installation of computerized client information systems or word processing systems.
- Administrative changes include new performance-appraisal systems, such as the Performance Management and Recognition System for all middle managers in the federal civil service; pay-for-performance systems, such as those that state and local agencies have tried to implement; and affirmative action programs.
- Changes in products and services abound in all types of organizations. As described below, the Social Security Administration has struggled for the last several decades with steady increases in the number and nature of Social Security services mandated by Congress.
- Human resources changes occur as a result of training, development, and recruitment efforts aimed at improving leadership and human relations practices or upgrading employee skills.

While each of these different domains may undergo limited change relatively independently, they frequently intertwine. In fact, for major changes, the challenge is to coordinate them. Tichy (1983) argues that most approaches to organizational change have concentrated on one of three primary dimensions: the political, technical, or cultural aspects of change. Strategic change, as Tichy calls it, involves moving beyond these more fragmented approaches, coordinating these three dimensions to effect large-scale transformations in an organization's relationship to its environment.

Golembiewski (1986) introduces further complexities by arguing that at least three types of change can occur in individual responses in organizations. *Alpha* change involves the change from one level to another along a measure of some dimension, such as job satisfaction. *Beta* change involves a similar change in degree, except that the significance that people attach to intervals on the measure may change as well. *Gamma* change, however, involves a general change in state rather than just a change in degree. A person may shift to a redefinition or new conception of reality such that the meaning of the dimension fundamentally changes for that person. In their research, Golembiewski and his colleagues found that virtually all the people in the most advanced stages of "burnout" fall at a point on a measure of work satisfaction that is almost the exact opposite of the point at which virtually all of those in the earliest phases fall. This suggests that once a person moves into the more serious phases of burnout, he or she also moves to a fundamentally different state, in which the meaning and nature of job satisfaction change radically. Differences in responses to job satisfaction measures do not fully capture this shift. This raises major issues for both research and practice pertaining to organizational change, since it complicates the measurement and assessment of change in very challenging ways.

As noted, research and theory have not yet accounted for these complexities and variations. The organizational literature does, nevertheless, provide useful, meaningful insights about change in organizations.

Organizational Development

A well-established subfield of organization theory concentrates on changing organizations for the better. Writers and practitioners in organization development (OD) work to improve the functioning of organizations, especially along human relations and social dimensions, by applying social scientific theory and techniques. OD consultants or "change agents" work with people in organizations to improve communication, problem solving, renewal and change, conflict airing and resolution, decision making, and trust and openness. They often go into organizations to help them diagnose and overcome problems that they have in these areas. Ideally, they seek to leave the organization better able to manage such processes effectively. A mountain of books, articles, and professional journals, as well as a number of professional associations, deliberate about OD, and large corporations or government agencies sometimes have OD offices or bureaus that minister to the other parts of the organization.

As this description suggests, OD has firm roots in the human relations orientation in organizational studies and in the group dynamics movement. It also draws on various elements of social science and organizational behavior, such as theories of motivation, leadership and systems, and techniques such as survey research. OD theory and practice vary widely, but they tend to have common basic values and assumptions about organizations and the people in them. French and Bell (1990) point out that OD involves common assumptions about people, groups, and organizations:

- People have a drive to grow and develop, especially if they are provided with an encouraging environment. They want to make a greater contribution to their organization than most organizational settings permit.
- For most people, the work group is a very important factor. People value acceptance and cooperation in it. Leaders cannot provide for all leadership needs, so members of groups must assist one another.
- Suppressed feelings are detrimental to satisfaction, trust, and cooperation. Most groups and organizations induce suppressed feelings more than they should. Solutions to most problems in groups must be transactional, involving changes in people's relationships.
- The leadership style and culture at higher levels tend to pervade the organization, shaping levels of trust and teamwork throughout.
- Win-lose conflict management strategies usually do harm in the long run.
- Collaborative effort has value. The welfare of all members of the system is important and should be valued by those most powerful in the system.

OD practitioners tend to value personal growth for people in organizations; a richer, more meaningful, more enjoyable, more effective life for people in organizations, especially through allowing their feelings and sentiments to have a legitimate value; a commitment to both action and research; and democratization and power equalization in organizations. One can begin to guess some of the controversies that these assumptions and values engender among management experts. Before looking at those, however, it is useful to consider how OD interventions in organizations tend to proceed.

OD Interventions and Change Processes

OD consultants take a variety of approaches, but the action-research model shown in Table 13.3 illustrates a typical pattern. Key executives perceive a problem or

TABLE 13.3. PHASES OF AN ACTION RESEARCH MODEL FOR ORGANIZATIONAL DEVELOPMENT.

1. Performance gap: Key executives perceive problems.
2. Executives confer with an organizational consultant.
3. Diagnosis: The consultant begins a process of diagnosing and data gathering.
4. Feedback: The consultant communicates the results to key clients and client groups.
5. Joint action planning: The consultant works with client groups in planning the objectives and procedures (such as team building) for the OD program.
6. Further data gathering. The consultant continues to monitor perceptions and attitudes.
7. Further feedback. In team-building sessions or other settings, the organizational members address the problems identified in the diagnostic work.
8. The client groups discuss and work on the data from the diagnosis and earlier sessions. New attitudes emerge.
9. Action planning. The groups set objectives for further development and develop plans for getting there.
10. Action. The plans are carried out, and new behaviors develop.
11. Further data gathering.
12. Further feedback.
13. Further action planning.
14. Continuation and consultant departure. The cycle of diagnosis, feedback, planning, and action continues until the appropriate point for the departure of the consultant.

Sources: Burke (1982); French and Bell (1990).

performance gap. They bring in a consultant, who conducts a diagnosis on the organization and the problem, often using interviews, surveys, and group meetings. The consultant feeds the results back to the clients and works with them in interpreting the results and developing plans for the OD program, including objectives, problems to be addressed, and techniques to be used. The consultant continues gathering information for use in the activities, using such tools as group problem-solving and team-building sessions. Further planning takes place as new ideas arise from the activities, and the consultant continues to gather information to assess the newly planned activities and their effects. The consultant continues this developmental process for a period of time, until eventually he or she leaves it to the people in the organization to continue it on their own. Similar models include an ultimate phase, consisting of institutionalizing the changes that the OD project has developed and terminating the relationship with the consultant (Burke, 1982).

OD Intervention Techniques

OD consultants can draw from an array of responses to the problems they help an organization identify. The literature in the field provides a variety of models, typologies, and tables suggesting the type and level of intervention that the people in the organization and the consultant might select (Burke, 1982). For example, if the organization wants to focus on problems at the level of individual organizational members, it might work on new approaches to recruitment and selection, training and development, counseling, and job design. At the broader organizational level, OD may involve organization-wide survey-feedback processes, grid OD projects, quality-of-work-life programs, management by objectives projects, intergroup conflict-management procedures, and so on.

For the development of group processes, an OD project might employ team-building techniques that work groups can use to develop more effective relationships. Team-building exercises typically focus on setting goals for the group, analyzing members' roles and responsibilities and the work processes of the team, and examining the relationships among the members. The OD consultant might draw on various techniques to support these efforts, such as a role negotiation process in which members list the things they feel each other member should do more or less of in the group. Then the members negotiate agreements about the changes and confirm these agreements with a written contract (Burke, 1982).

OD consultants also employ a technique they call *process consultation*. The consultant observes the work groups and other activities, gathers observations and information about key processes such as communication, teamwork, and interpersonal conflict handling, and consults with the members on interpreting and improving these processes.

OD projects in the past often employed T-groups, encounter groups, or sensitivity sessions. All are group sessions intended to develop communication and understanding among the members of the group and enhance each member's sensitivity to the feelings and viewpoints of the other members. These approaches grew out of the work of Kurt Lewin and his colleagues described in Chapter Two. Such groups engage in intensive discussions aimed at helping participants learn more about how other people see them and respond to them and how they perceive others. The sessions follow a diverse array of approaches, often involving such exercises as having members take turns expressing perceptions of other members. In some versions, these techniques become highly confrontational and emotional, and participants often find the experience exhilarating. These techniques were very widely used during the 1960s, but their use has dwindled, apparently because of controversy about whether they had much long-term impact and evidence that when they did have an impact, it often appeared to be damaging to some participants (Back, 1972).

OD Effects and Controversies

Just how a consultant selects, combines, and uses all these procedures depends on his or her experience and skill. No organizing theory links the aspects of OD or systematically guides its practice. OD consultants play a role much like that of clinicians in psychology or psychiatry in that they have no clear, uncontested theory or guide for practice. They operate on the basis of their experience and intuition, choosing from an array of loosely defined procedures. The complexity of organizations and their problems makes it hard for them to establish and prove clear successes. Critics sometimes attack OD for this lack of substantive theory and theory-based research. They say that OD's concentration on human relations issues can lead to misdiagnosing an organization's problems when they involve other dimensions, such as the accounting system or production processes. Tichy (1983), for example, argues that OD concentrates on human resources issues in organizations when large-scale strategic change requires coordinating those issues with strategies for improving the organization's technical and political dimensions. OD adherents respond that they know that their efforts are often valuable, even if they cannot always produce simple, clear evidence of marked improvements in profits or other performance criteria. They also argue that other areas of organization theory hardly provide managers with beautifully crafted guides to changing and improving their organization and that they are justified in trying to go out and do what they can to apply behavioral science knowledge to the problems that organizations face.

OD in the Public Sector

Despite these controversies, OD remains a widely used approach for improving and changing public and nonprofit organizations. OD experts who work with public sector organizations regularly discuss the issue of whether public and private organizations differ in ways that affect the application of OD. That discussion has an interesting history.

In the leading article in this debate, Golembiewski (1969) cited greater challenges in the public sector as a result of factors much like those discussed in earlier chapters. He said that five primary structural constraints complicate the application of OD in government. First, multiple actors have access to multiple authorities, thus presenting a complex array of possible supporters or resisters for an OD project. For example, the State Department began Project ACORD (Action for Organizational Development) after a career official with strong ties to key members of Congress pushed for it. Yet the project stalled when other prominent actors—the department head and officials in the budget and personnel bureaus—attacked it. The newspapers even got into the act, Golembiewski reports, with editorials calling for the State Department to leave its long-term civil servants alone and not pester them with a dubious program. Second, different interests and reward structures complicate the problem. Different congressional committees, legislators, and administrators may respond to different incentives. For example, some actors may press for improved organizational operations, while others may seek to defend political alliances. Third, the administrative hierarchy is fragmented and weakened by these competing affiliations, thus making it harder to sustain the implementation of OD projects. Administrative officials may have stronger ties to congressional allies and stronger commitment to their programs than to the top executives in their department or the president. Fourth, weak relationships between career civil servants and politically appointed executives produce a similar problem of diffuse authority. Fifth, Golembiewski agrees with Kaufman (1969) that the political system continually shifts its emphasis among several goals for the executive branch—representativeness, executive leadership, and politically neutral competence. During a period of emphasis on the first two, such as President Reagan's drive to master and reduce the federal bureaucracy, the climate for OD deteriorates.

Golembiewski argues that these factors interact with managerial "habits" in government in ways that hinder OD. Higher-level executives tend to avoid delegating authority and tend to establish multiple layers of review and approval because of their tenuous authority over lower levels. Legislative and legal strictures constrain many dimensions that OD often seeks to reform, such as reward systems and job classifications. Government agencies, more often than business firms, have secrecy and security requirements. People in government show more "procedural regularity and caution." The role of the professional manager is poorly developed in government as compared to business, according to Golembiewski. He suggests that this results in part from the difficulty of enhancing public managers' sense of ownership of organizational objectives and values, a result of the public nature of the organizations they lead. This in turn poses greater challenges in enhancing managers' commitment to their agency.

Golembiewski concludes that these conditions create differences in the culture that predominates in public agencies. They place more constraints on managers and offer fewer supports and rewards for inventiveness, risk taking, and effort. Not surprisingly, some public managers are cautious about supporting initiatives in their organization.

Most other authors who have examined this issue agree with Golembiewski in general but make variations in his analysis. Davis (1983), for example, offers a very similar analysis of the effects of the external political environment on the use of OD in the public sector. Yet he more heavily emphasizes the problem of public agencies' pursuing multiple goals with vague programs and performance criteria (perhaps because he draws on an OD project in a human services agency, the area of government where these problems are probably severest).

Fascinatingly, however, these writers emerge from these discussions with the conclusion that OD certainly can succeed in the public sector. While their depictions of the public sector environment make some common notions of bureaucratic rigidity sound positively optimistic, these OD experts treat the public sector context as perhaps more challenging but ultimately manageable, as presenting a set of conditions for which one can be prepared. Golembiewski (1985) reports evidence that OD projects in the public sector enjoy a relatively impressive success rate, apparently in line with that of projects in the private sector. First, he and his colleagues reviewed numerous published reports of OD initiatives in public organizations and classified the difficulties they apparently encountered. They found that in 270 reports of OD applications, the writers frequently mentioned the sort of constraints that Golembiewski had described. They mentioned external constraints such as procedural rigidity (mentioned in 124 cases), diversity of interests and values (111), public scrutiny (87), and the "volatile political/administrative interface"—the rocky relationship between legislative and administrative units and between career officials and political officials (62). They also mentioned internal constraints such as lack of professionalism (78), weak chains of command (70), complex objectives (61), and short time frames (52). Also, the reports for city governments were generally similar to those for other levels of government. While the reports cited these complications, Golembiewski noted that the large number of initiatives reported—especially considering that agencies carry out many efforts that are not reported in the professional literature—suggests that "the constraints may be tougher in the public sector, but they are not *that* tough" (p. 67).

To add to the evidence, Golembiewski reports on studies that have sought to assess the effectiveness of OD applications in both sectors. One of his students assessed the success of the 270 OD initiatives mentioned above, using procedures similar to those used in previous studies of OD success rates, and found that most of the reports indicated either positive effects (43 percent) or highly positive effects (41 percent), with only 7 percent indicating no effect and 9 percent reporting negative effects (p. 82). The results also suggested that the public sector initiatives included a healthy percentage of the most demanding OD applications; furthermore, they did not indicate that the success rate in public agencies resulted from a tendency to try more limited forms of OD interventions in government. Golembiewski also had independent observers do similar ratings of forty-four OD applications in city governments and found even higher success rates. These success rates are very similar to those reported for the private sector, Golembiewski concluded, and indicate that despite the apparent constraints of the government context, OD practitioners do fairly well at adapting to them.

Gortner, Mahler, and Nicholson (1987) raise some challenging issues about Golembiewski's conclusions. They argue that his methodology has weaknesses because people report the successful cases but not the unsuccessful ones. When they write articles, they describe the project in the best possible light. In addition, the OD application may fade over time.

Very recently, however, Robertson and Seneviratne (1995) reported on a study that generally supported Golembiewski's conclusions. Robertson and Seneviratne performed a general analysis (a "meta-analysis") of about fifty studies of planned change interventions in public and private organizations. They found that OD interventions in public and private organizations showed similar rates of success in such areas as work setting and organizational outcomes. They found some differences in more specific areas, however. The evidence indicated that change efforts in the private organizations led to positive changes in four components of work settings—organizing arrangements, social factors, technology, and physical setting. In the public organizations, however, the change efforts appeared to have a positive effect only on organizing arrangements and social factors, not on technology and physical setting. In addition, even though change efforts showed positive effects on organizing arrangements in both sectors, these effects were significantly stronger in the private sector. Also, change efforts in both sectors showed positive influences on a general measure of organizational outcomes, with no significant difference between the sectors. Change interventions in the public organizations, however, showed a significantly stronger relationship to one dimension of the organizational outcomes measure—improved organizational performance—than change efforts in the private organizations. These results support many of the observations about public and private organizations cited in previous chapters—such as the greater constraints on organizational structures in public organizations. They also generally support Golembiewski and his colleagues' conclusion that public agencies may face certain particular challenges. Generally, however, planned change initiatives appear to succeed about as often in public organizations as they do in private organizations. In spite of stereotypes and some academic assertions based more on simplistic theory than on systematic evidence, organizational change initiatives occur with frequency and apparent success throughout government.

Success and Failure in Large-Scale, Planned Organizational Change

The evidence of successful change initiatives in public organizations suggests the importance of how the members of an organization manage and implement change. Organizations have always periodically undertaken large-scale planned change processes that are well beyond the scope of OD initiatives. In recent decades, challenges from international competition and other pressures have caused many U.S. corporations to undergo thorough overhauls. The management literature began to resound with terms such as *transformation, reinvention,* and *reengineering,* all referring to strategies for large-scale planned change in organizations. Under the pressures described earlier and in previous chapters, governments have followed suit (Gore, 1993). The literature on large-scale organizational change is quite diverse and difficult to summarize succinctly. Two articles, however, in which the authors summarize patterns of organizational change and transformation, provide particularly valuable observations about analyzing and managing successful initiatives. Although they were published some thirty years apart, they show some interesting similarities.

About three decades ago, Greiner (1967) analyzed eighteen major organizational change attempts and drew conclusions about the patterns of successful change. He noted that some frequently used approaches to change often seem to founder. Examples include unilateral actions, such as top-down decrees or commands for structural changes, limited attempts at power sharing through group decision making, and efforts to encourage delegation of authority through T-group training. The successful change efforts that Greiner observed involved much more comprehensive approaches, as illustrated in Table 13.4.

TABLE 13.4. PATTERNS OF SUCCESSFUL ORGANIZATIONAL CHANGE.

Phase I: Pressure and Arousal

1. *There is significant external and internal pressure for change.* There is a widespread perception of performance gaps and of a need for change, placing pressure on top management.

Phase II: Intervention and Reorientation

2. *A new person enters as change leader.* The person has a record as a successful change agent and enters as a leader of the organization or as a consultant working with the leader.
3. *The new person leads a reexamination of past practices and current problems.* The newcomer uses his or her objective, external perspective to encourage examination of old views and rationalizations and attention to "real" problems.
4. *Top management becomes heavily involved in the reexamination.* The head of the organization and his or her immediate subordinates assume a direct, heavily involved role in the reexamination.

Phase III: Diagnosis and Recognition

5. *The change leader engages multiple levels in diagnosis.* The change leader involves multiple levels and units in collaborative, fact-finding, problem-solving discussions to identify and diagnose current problems. The diagnosis involves significant power sharing.

Phase IV: Invention and Commitment

6. *The change leader stimulates a widespread search for creative solutions, involving many levels.*

Phase V: Experimentation and Search

7. *Solutions are developed, tested, and proven on a small scale.* Problems are worked out and solved. Experimentation is encouraged.

Phase VI: Reinforcement and Acceptance

8. *Successes are reinforced and disseminated and breed further success.* People are rewarded. Successes become accepted and institutionalized.

Source: Adapted from Greiner (1967).

As the table suggests, Greiner's observations about successful patterns of change emphasize the following conditions and steps:

- Pressure for improvement is felt widely among people within the organization and among relevant actors outside it.
- A new person is brought in as head of the organization or as a consultant to lead the change effort.
- Top executives involve themselves very heavily in beginning and sustaining the change process.
- The change agent (the new head or consultant), with the involvement of top executives, initiates a general diagnosis.
- The change agent leads this diagnostic process, using multilevel, collaborative fact-finding and problem-solving sessions to identify and diagnose the key problems. Representatives of many units and levels participate. The human resources unit is heavily involved.
- Participants develop solutions. The solutions are tested first on a small scale, then on a wider scale, and finally implemented.
- Participants use successes to reinforce results, and the results become widely accepted.

As indicated in step 5 (Phase III) of Table 13.4, and implied in other phases, Greiner emphasizes the key role of power sharing in successful patterns of change. He concludes that success requires it and that it must occur through a developmental process. The failures that he observed involved more unilateral pressures for change, with an illogical sequence of steps.

About thirty years later, Kotter (1995), a prominent author on leadership, organizational change, and other topics, published an article on organizational change in the same journal in which Greiner's had appeared, the *Harvard Business Review*. In the article, Kotter presented a number of reasons for the failure of organizational "transformations" (a currently fashionable term for large-scale, comprehensive change efforts). Table 13.5 turns Kotter's reasons for failure around, transposing them into requirements for success. Kotter's observations about organizational change differ from Greiner's in important ways. Kotter refers to "vision," a contemporary and much discussed topic in management theory today. He also emphasizes the role of a "guiding coalition," in contrast to Greiner's focus on a change leader who comes in from the outside (a later section in this chapter describes a successful change in the Social Security Administration that did not involve a change leader from the outside). Kotter's phrasing is consistent with other recent research on large-scale change in organizations. Very recent studies (Huber and Glick, 1993) emphasize the essential role of "shared values" (which can equate

TABLE 13.5. STEPS FOR SUCCESSFUL ORGANIZATIONAL TRANSFORMATIONS.

1. *Establish a sense of urgency.*
   - Examine market and competitive realities.
   - Identify crises and opportunities.
2. *Form a powerful guiding coalition.*
   - Assemble a group with enough power to lead the change effort.
   - Encourage the group to work as a team.
3. *Create a vision.*
   - Create a vision to help direct the change effort.
   - Develop strategies for achieving that vision.
4. *Communicate the vision.*
   - Use all available means to communicate the new vision and strategy.
   - Have the guiding coalition teach the necessary new behaviors by example.
5. *Empower others to act on the vision.*
   - Remove obstacles to change.
   - Change systems or structures that present obstacles.
6. *Create short-term wins.*
   - Plan for visible performance improvements.
   - Create those improvements.
   - Recognize and reward employees involved in those improvements.
7. *Consolidate Improvements and produce further change.*
   - Use increased credibility to change systems, structures, and policies to pursue the vision.
   - Hire and develop employees who can implement the vision.
8. *Institutionalize the new approach.*
   - Articulate the connection between the new behaviors and organizational success.
   - Ensure leadership development and succession.

Source: Adapted from Kotter (1995).

to "vision" in important ways) and leadership teams rather than individual, heroic leaders.

The similarities between the two views, thirty years apart, are striking and provide a simple but deceptively demanding framework for large-scale organizational change:

- Widespread belief in the need for change
- Clear, sustained leadership, including support from top executives
- Broad participation in diagnosing problems and planning the change
- Flexible, incremental implementation, involving experimentation, feedback, adaptation, and building on prior success to institutionalize change

These elements appear luxurious to public sector managers, since so many public organizations face frequent turnover of top executives, interventions and constraints from external authorities, and other conditions that might block some of these steps. Nevertheless, the following sections note examples of the effective adoption of many of these elements of successful change in public agencies.

Successful Revitalization in Public Agencies

Many of these conditions and steps, together with an emphasis on transforming organizational culture, characterize successful revitalization efforts in public organizations that had declined. Poister (1988b) provides a compilation of case studies of such efforts. In one of these, Holzer (1988) describes a marked enhancement in the productivity of the New York City Department of Sanitation, with improved labor-management cooperation and teamwork, enhanced productivity and information management, technical innovations in refuse collection, and upgrading of managerial talent and organization (which involved contending with stringent civil service regulations and trying to modify them).

Decker and Paulson (1988) describe how a multifaceted performance-improvement system vastly improved the performance of the Jacksonville Electric Authority. The system included efforts to improve work planning and information management and to transform the organizational culture to place more emphasis on consultative team management, strategic planning and identification of corporate goals, and well-developed management systems to achieve them.

Stephens (1988) describes how a new director of the Alabama Division of Rehabilitation and Crippled Children Service led the division through a transformation from a troubled, control-oriented organization to a more quality-oriented, participative one. She led a widely participative process to develop the division's "Blueprint for the Future" and to improve agency policies, performance evaluation, quality assurance, and organization. The process also aimed to make supervisors more oriented to coaching and consultation and to involve project teams in reviewing agency policies. The director used aspects of managing culture similar to those described in Chapter Seven (see Table 7.1). She faithfully met and spoke with the teams. She posted the "Blueprint for the Future" on her office wall. She redesigned the organization chart, placing Alabama's disabled children and adults at the top of the chart, to dramatize her emphasis on client service.

Poister and Larson (1988) describe the revitalization of the Pennsylvania Department of Transportation, which involved a reorganization to make the agency less top-heavy and a greater emphasis on merit selection to improve the professional capabilities and management capacity of the agency's personnel. The agency's leaders also mounted a campaign to build political support. They worked to improve financial and programmatic control and to develop the organization through quality circles, participative management, and the identification of guiding values.

Poister (1988a) points out that all these efforts reflect multifaceted processes of strategic change, involving many policy, managerial, technological, and political initiatives and a series of strategies that developed over time. While diverse, they all emphasize developing a shared vision and mission, strategic planning, and developing the organization's leadership and culture. They involve redistributions of power toward more active involvement of the agency's members. Yet they also emphasize enhancements of management systems, such as financial, productivity-measurement, and information-management systems. Effective revitalization campaigns also required the agency managers to develop and maintain effective political support, to provide resources and a mandate for the changes. Thus successful revitalizations occur in different types of public organizations, often in patterns very similar to those in private firms. Yet success requires more than skillful employment of generic principles of organizational change—it requires skill in dealing with the political context and administrative features of public organizations. These skillful applications and the conditions supporting them can be further clarified by a comparison between a successful and an unsuccessful attempt at large-scale change in public agencies.

Two Contrasting Cases

Reviewing two cases of large-scale change in government agencies helps to clarify the applicability of Greiner's and Golembiewski's observations. Warwick (1975) reports on a failed attempt in the U.S. State Department to do what everyone would love to do—reduce bureaucracy. The Social Security Administration (SSA), on the other hand, succeeded in a similar effort. When the SSA faced extreme problems with administrative foul-ups and delays in processing claims, the people in the agency responded with a successful redesign of the organization and its claims processing system and improved performance. These cases illustrate the validity of the many observations about the ways in which the political and institutional context of government and the internal cultures of public agencies can impede change. Yet they also support the claim that, under the right circumstances, applying sound principles of change, skillful public managers and employees can carry out major changes very effectively.

The "O Area" Reforms in the Department of State. Warwick (1975) describes a fascinating case in which a well-intentioned undersecretary in the State Department initiated an unsuccessful effort to decentralize decision making and eliminate levels of hierarchy. An administrative area known as the O Area had become a complex array of hierarchical layers and diverse offices. The undersecretary's reforms eliminated six hierarchical levels (including 125 administrative positions) and started a process of "management by objectives and programs." According

to the undersecretary's plan, the program managers at the levels below the eliminated layers would manage more autonomously—without so many administrators above them and with more direct lines to the deputy undersecretary. They
would also follow a management by objectives program in which they would specify objectives, target dates, and needed resources.

Although the undersecretary's ideas for reform were heavily influenced by
McGregor's concept of Theory Y management (1960), other managers com-
mented that he sought to apply Theory Y using Theory X methods. The undersecretary made the changes fairly unilaterally and then called together a large
group of managers and employees to announce them. Rumors had gone around
about the reforms, but the nature of them, according to Warwick (1975, p. 37),
caught "even the most reorganized veterans off guard."

Yet Warwick devotes most of his analysis to the factors hindering change in
the State Department, which he tends to generalize to all government agencies.
Externally, congressional relations and related politics played a major role. Some
of the administrators whose positions were targeted for elimination had strong allies in Congress and among interest groups that opposed the changes. The State
Department had several different personnel systems (foreign service officers and
others), which complicated the change process. A bill that would have unified the
systems, however, did not pass in Congress. A civil service union opposed it, a powerful senator felt that it would dilute the foreign service, and the chair of the Senate
Foreign Relations Committee gave it little support because he wanted better cooperation from the secretary of state on matters pertaining to the war in Vietnam.
The secretary of state became concerned about the wide span of control that the
reduction in the hierarchy created (with many program managers reporting to the
undersecretary).

Warwick argues that an "administrative orthodoxy" prevails in Washington
and elsewhere in government. Legislators and political executives expect traditional chains of command and hierarchical arrangements and worry that their
absence means disorganization. The secretary of state faced a great deal of political pressure from Congress and the public over decisions about the Vietnam
War and did not want to waste political capital on any controversy over the administration of the State Department.

Warwick argues that career civil servants are accustomed to turnover among
top political executives every two or three years. Motivated by caution and security, they can easily build defenses against the repetitive cycles of reform and
change that the political executives attempt during their short stays in public agencies. The careerists can simply wait out the top executives by doing nothing, or
they can mobilize opposition in Congress and among interest groups. Like many
public agencies, the State Department also had internal conflicts among units and

specialists, including a tradition of rivalry between foreign service officers and other types and between units organized by function versus units organized by geographical regions of the world. These internal conflicts complicate change efforts, especially because the participants often have external political allies.

The undersecretary implemented his changes with some good effect. The changes appeared to have beneficial effects on the autonomy, willingness to experiment, and motivation of some of the units and managers. Yet coordination appeared to suffer, and internal and external resistance mounted. Not long after attempting the changes, the undersecretary left the State Department. His successor derided the reforms, and within about nine months he eliminated most of them. Some useful remnants endured, according to Warwick, and some of the lessons learned proved valuable in later change efforts. Yet he concludes that the reforms clearly failed.

More generally, Warwick suggests that the conditions he found in the State Department tend to sustain complex bureaucracy in all government agencies. Congress and interest groups often resist change because they develop alliances with agencies and their subunits. They jealously guard against reorganizations that threaten those arrangements. Rapid turnover at the tops of agencies has the effects noted already. The diversity and interrelations of government agencies complicate change efforts. Any one public policy arena tends to involve many different agencies (for example, the Departments of Agriculture and Commerce and many other agencies are involved in foreign affairs). Since legislation and policymaking decisions may involve many agencies, consensus and support become more elusive. Statutes and "systemwide rules" govern many aspects of organization and procedure, sometimes dictating the actual agency structure and placing constraints on job descriptions, purchasing, space procurement, personnel decisions, and many other processes. Administrative orthodoxy, coupled with diffuse agency goals, reinforces the tendency to impose classic bureaucratic control.

Warwick notes conditions particular to the State Department that had a lot to do with the outcome of the reforms—the problems of the Vietnam War during this period, a history of complex political influences on the department, internal rivalries, the particularly great need for secure communications, and the worldwide scope of operations. Still, he moves toward very gloomy conclusions about prospects for changing public bureaucracies. Almost as if he is determined not to end on such a note, however, Warwick offers suggestions about reducing and changing bureaucracy that echo those of Greiner and the OD experts. He points out that facile prescriptions for participative management in public agencies face some sharp challenges. Many of the conditions described above weigh against prospects for highly participative processes, but for successful change, government managers must deal with these conditions. Warwick argues that one cannot eliminate bureaucracy by decimation—by firing people or merging or cutting units—or by top-down demands for reform. Effective debureaucratization, he concludes, must have strong roots within the agency. The people in the agency must see the changes as important and useful to them. All significant internal constituencies must participate in considering the problem. There must be a careful, collaborative diagnosis, followed by broad-based discussions about concrete alternatives for change. Then proponents of the change must seek support from external controllers and allies. To avoid the problems of rapid turnover among top executives, a coordinating body should monitor and sustain the change, and this body should include more than one senior political appointee.

Modularization of Claims Processing in the Social Security Administration.

While the very words *modularization of claims processing* summon up the impulse to doze off, this example represents an effective attempt to do something similar to what the State Department reforms failed to do—to reform bureaucracy in the direction of decentralized control over the work and an enriched work environment. In the 1960s, the Social Security Administration became overloaded and backlogged in processing claims for Retirement and Survivors' Insurance (that is, Social Security payments). Clients complained to the SSA and to members of Congress, who passed the heat along to the agency. At one point, the SSA struggled with a backlog of one million claims. Something had to be done.

The problem had developed largely because Congress had added new programs and new forms of coverage to the original Social Security program, such as extending coverage to dependents, farmers, the self-employed, and the disabled. Together with population growth, this continually expanded the number of claims to be processed. In addition, with the different programs and the complications of individual cases, some of the claims could raise confounding difficulties. A claimant might have worked under multiple aliases, for example, and have a degenerative brain disease and no memory of his or her original name and birth date.

The organizational system for handling the claims proved more and more ineffective at responding to the load. The SSA had several major functional bureaus—for the Retirement and Survivors' Insurance (RSI) program, for disability insurance, for data processing and records, and for supervising the district offices. The district offices, located around the country, took in claims from clients applying for their benefits. For the RSI program, they then forwarded the claims to one of six program service centers (PSCs). These were located in six regions of the country. Each had around two thousand employees. When a claim arrived at a PSC from the district office, a clerical support unit would prepare a folder for the claimant and forward it to a claims unit. There, a claims authorizer would determine the type and degree of eligibility for Social Security payments. Then the folder would be forwarded to a payments unit, where a benefit authorizer would compute the amount of the benefit payment and do some paperwork necessary to begin processing the payments through the computer. Then the folder would go to an accounts unit, which assembled and coded information about the case, then to another unit for entry into the computer, then to a records maintenance unit for storage. In some of these units, hundreds of people worked at desks in long rows, receiving deliveries of stacks of folders from shopping carts, with coffee and lunch breaks announced by the ringing of bells. Control clerks and supervisors, emphasizing the technical issues and production rates of their unit, spot-checked the work for accuracy.

Any incomplete information or disagreements among the technical specialists would delay a claim, because it would have to be sent back to the earlier point in the process for clarification or correction. Communication about the problem usually had to be in writing. There was no provision for getting a problem claim back to the same person who had done the earlier work. The increasing numbers of claims and the complications of many of the claims increasingly clogged the system. The system created incentives for employees to "cream" the cases by avoiding the very difficult ones or even slipping them by to the next phase to get them off their desk. Problem cases piled up.

Robert Ball, the long-term, highly respected commissioner of the Social Security Administration, appointed an experienced SSA official, Hugh McKenna, as director of the RSI bureau, with a mandate to correct the problems. McKenna initiated an open-ended process of change, with some four years of research, development, experimentation, and morale building. Several task forces with internal and external representation studied management processes, case handling, and labor relations. A consulting firm analyzed the case-management process. Large team-building and morale-boosting meetings were held between managers and staff from the PSCs, district offices, and the RSI central office. The office staff worked with the PSCs to develop training courses on participatory management. Interestingly, some made a comment about McKenna similar to the one made about the State Department undersecretary—that he "*ordered* participatory management." He did, but obviously with a crucial difference in the way that order was imposed.

Out of these efforts emerged the concept of modular claims-processing units. The planning staff in the central office suggested setting up smaller units—composed of fifty employees—containing all the technical specialists needed to process a claim and let them handle claims from beginning to end. Claiming to draw on the ideas of McGregor, Herzberg, Likert, and Maslow (described in Chapters Two and Ten), the proponents of the module concept argued that it would provide job enrichment and participatory management. Individuals would identify with their tasks more and see their clients as individuals, they would have easier access to supervisors and managers, and they would have more control over the process and their part in it.

One of the PSCs tried out one such unit on an experimental basis and then created a total of six modules. Problems arose. At one point, productivity had dropped in the modules, and termination of the experiment was seriously considered. However, the staff decided that the problems could be corrected. Managers apparently had some trouble adjusting to the new system. In one instance, two module managers tried to merge their modules to create combined functional units for files, accounts, claims, and so on. The central staff had to urge them back to the original concept. The blending of clerical staff and technical specialists in the modules caused some racial and status conflicts. Relations with other agencies, such as the Civil Service Commission (now the Office of Personnel Management), required skillful handling to obtain new space and to receive approval of new personnel structures. Ultimately other PSCs adopted the modules, with some modifications. In one, the specialists involved in processing a claim sat around a desk together, working through individual cases in direct contact with one another. The modular approach was also adopted by the Disability Insurance Bureau, although with more employees per module.

The modular concept became widely accepted in the agency as a success. At one point, processing time for new claims in the PSCs had dropped by 50 percent, to an average of twenty days, and it later dropped further, to an average of fifteen days, with very few long-delayed cases. Some employee surveys showed increased job satisfaction in the modules. The picture was not all rosy, however. Some long-standing employees disliked the change. Problems with computer systems complicated matters. Morale later suffered very badly when the agency began a process of eliminating seventeen thousand employees in the 1980s, which apparently made it difficult to properly staff some of the modules. Nevertheless, many people in the agency regarded the modular concept as successful. Today, the Program Service Centers are all organized into modules, and the employees regard the modules not as an innovation but as a standard feature of the centers. Recent developments, such as computerization of claims processing, are causing some problems for the modular design. Some of the centers are experimenting with new forms of organizing the claims-processing work. As they do so, managers and employees frequently express concern about moving away from the modular design. It has been such a successful change that members of the organization now express anxiety about moving away from it.

The success may simply reflect the proper application of some of the generic principles of change. The change was widely recognized as necessary, it had support from the top, and there was flexible implementation, with adaptation, feedback, and experimentation, and a realistic strategy for achieving the agency's objectives. The change did, in a sense, have a top-down character, but in this case, this appears to illustrate what the experts mean by "support from the top." There must be sponsors and champions of the change with sufficient authority and resources to see it through.

Some particulars about the SSA case distinguish it from the State Department case; these are summarized in Table 13.6. SSA had as chief executive a long-term career civil servant who had enjoyed trust and support from key congressional figures and thus could gain a grant of authority to solve the agency's problems without interference. SSA has strong support from a large clientele receiving a specific service, and the agency's tasks tend to be clear and mechanistic. The people in the agency were able to "encapsulate" their work processes and management methods and seal them off from political intervention.

While such factors may have provided SSA with advantages, the case suggests some key additional considerations about successful change in public organizations (G. W. Rainey, 1990). SSA had a durable, skillful power center, committed to successful change. Ironically, for all the stereotypes about career bureaucrats resisting change, in this case the long-term civil servants were the champions of change. In one instance, they even had to outwit a conservative political appointee who sought to undercut the reforms because he thought that they would result in "grade creep"—employees might get higher salary grade classifications because

TABLE 13.6. CONDITIONS FOR A SUCCESSFUL CHANGE IN A FEDERAL AGENCY.

1. *A durable power center, committed to successful change*
   - Strong, stable leadership by career civil servants
   - An internal change agent (career agency executive) with sufficient authority and resources
   - Active, creative bureau staff
2. *Appropriate timing for collective support*
   - A political "window of opportunity"
   - Political overseers (congressional committee heads) who are supportive but not interventionist
   - Political sophistication of agency leaders and staff—effective management of relations with Congress and oversight agencies (OPM, GSA)
   - Strategies that blend sincere employee involvement with decisive exercise of authority
3. *A comprehensive, clear, realistic alternative process*
   - A long-term change strategy, using group processes to develop new structures
   - A major structural reform, focused on measurable outputs, that decentralizes operational responsibility
   - Reasonable clarity about the nature and objectives of the new structure and process

Source: Rainey and Rainey (1986).

of increased responsibilities in the modules. The leaders of the change effort hurried through an approval of the new personnel structure by the Civil Service Commission to prevent any blockage of the reforms. In this and many other ways, they utilized their knowledge of the political and administrative system to sustain the change. Also, they were not leaving soon. They had the career commitment to the agency to want the changes to succeed, and they and others knew that they would be there for the duration.

In addition, the SSA change took place at the appropriate time for it to garner collective support. (See the section on the agenda-setting process in Chapter Five for a discussion of the concept of "windows of opportunity" in the political process.) As noted above, the reform at the State Department was hindered by the Vietnam War and other problems with the timing of the change. Of course, the SSA enjoys no inherent immunity from political interference; many agencies that do mechanistic work with clear outputs get buffeted by external political forces. The timing was right for this change at the SSA, however, in that no distracting crises or controversies weighed against it. The need for change was widely recognized inside and outside the SSA. In part this reflects luck. In part it reflects the skill of experienced public managers and staff members who knew when and how to work for better alternatives.

Indeed, they did develop a better alternative, one that was comprehensive, clear, and realistic. Rather vague, prepackaged models, such as management by objectives, will fail if they are not adapted to fit the particular structural and cultural conditions within the organization. The sponsors and champions of the change in the SSA applied relatively firm, consistent pressure for a reasonably clear, realistic idea, while allowing a degree of experimentation and variation in its implementation.

Other aspects of the Social Security program and related policies can be debated at length. Nevertheless, in this case, experienced career civil servants in the Social Security Administration brought about an effective improvement in a process essential to one of the largest single categories of disbursement from the federal budget of the United States, and that very directly affects the lives of at least sixty million Americans. The public has heard little about this. News reporters have overlooked it. But perhaps it should not receive heroic treatment—it represents only one of many instances of skillful change and management that go on in government continually.

CHAPTER FOURTEEN

MANAGING FOR EXCELLENCE IN THE PUBLIC SECTOR

This final chapter returns to the component of the framework for organizational analysis concerned with performance and effectiveness. Chapter Six described concepts and models for analyzing organizational goals and effectiveness and examined whether certain traits of public organizations, such as their purportedly diffuse, multiple, and conflicting goals, make them distinctive. All the other previous chapters have in some way described possibilities for effective management of public organizations. This chapter covers some more summative approaches to the topic, including general issues about the performance of public organizations, and reviews profiles in the literature of excellent organizations in both the private and public sectors. Then it reviews some recent trends in management reform and the pursuit of excellence that have had a major influence on public management, including Total Quality Management and Osborne and Gaebler's *Reinventing Government* (and the National Performance Review in the federal government with which it is associated). Finally, the chapter discusses two alternative strategies for pursuing excellence in public organizations—privatization and volunteer programs—that despite their long history in government are widely proposed today as innovative solutions for public organizations. This section illustrates ways in which topics and ideas from the framework for organizational analysis and from previous chapters can be brought to bear in pursuing new (or renewed) alternatives in public management.

The Performance of Public Organizations

The history and culture of the United States in many ways reflect the fundamental assumption that public organizations are beset with performance problems such as red tape and inefficiency while private business firms perform more efficiently and effectively. This assumption is widespread but not universal: surveys show that a majority of Americans share it, but not all. Surveys have also found that some Americans are suspicious of private business but have a strong, deep-seated support for—if not confidence in—their government's institutions (Lipset and Schneider, 1987). Still, many governmental reform efforts in the United States and other nations have assumed that government agencies need to improve by adopting techniques from private firms (Gore, 1993; Peters and Savoie, 1994). This section examines the evidence and debate on the topic of the performance of public organizations versus the private sector, leading to the conclusion that in spite of the assumption to the contrary, many public organizations and managers perform very well.

Chapter Two described how the management literature has increasingly emphasized the complexity and turbulence confronting organizations. If anything, that theme has grown in very recent years, with the management literature now discussing the paradoxes, conflicting values, and even chaos facing all organizations (Kiel, 1994; Peters, 1987; Quinn, 1988). The mounting complexity organizations face leads some authors to question whether they can manage to avoid crisis and failure (Lindblom, 1977). For public organizations, the pressures include public and political hostility and funding reductions that have created what many experts depict as a crisis at all levels of government (Gore, 1993; Thompson, 1993; Volcker Commission, 1989).

Somewhat paradoxically, during the same recent years, a growing literature has concentrated on successful organizations. Peters and Waterman's *In Search of Excellence* (1982), which describes many excellent corporations, became one of the best-selling popular books about management in history. It led to a profusion of similar books about successful corporate management. The success of Japanese corporations has also attracted much attention (Ouchi, 1981), and many American corporations emerged from the problems of the 1970s and 1980s as strong international competitors in the 1990s.

Similarly, pressures on the public sector during the 1970s and 1980s prompted many authors and officials to defend the record of public organizations (Milward and Rainey, 1983). In the leading book in this genre, Goodsell (1994) mounts a strong case that public organizations and employees frequently perform well and defy many of the negative stereotypes that echo in the media, popular opinion, and political and academic discourse. Many others have described effective public managers and organizations as well (Ban, 1995; Behn, 1991; Cohen and Eimicke, 1995; Denhardt, 1993; DiIulio, 1989, 1994; Doig and Hargrove, 1987; Gold, 1982; Hargrove and Glidewell, 1990; Kelman, 1987; Poister, 1988b; Porter, Sargent, and Stupak, 1986; Riccucci, 1995; Tierney, 1988; Wilson, 1989).

The debate over whether public organizations perform well—or as well as private firms—has many complexities. Previous chapters have discussed the many constraints on public organizations that can hamper their performance—complex sets of goals and difficulties in measuring performance, political interventions and turnover, externally imposed rules, inadequate resources and funding, policies and programs that are poorly designed by policymakers in the executive and legislative branches, and many others. Research fairly commonly finds that when public services are directly compared to privately delivered forms of the same service, the private sector displays more efficiency (Savas, 1987)—but not always (Donahue, 1990). In fact, Downs and Larkey (1986) describe one national study that found that federal agencies showed higher rates of increase on productivity measures during the late 1960s than did a large sample of private firms. Individual agencies provide further examples. Studies have found that the U.S. Postal Service, the target of criticism and brunt of jokes for decades, shows a much higher level of productivity per worker than any other postal service in the world, coupled with lower first-class mail rates than all but two other nations in the world—Belgium and Switzerland—in spite of contending with greater geographic distances and other complexities. In addition, as Chapter Thirteen illustrated, there are many examples of innovative behaviors in public organizations and of studies that have found receptivity to change among public employees (U.S. Office of Personnel Management, 1979; Raincy, 1983) and no difference between the public and private sectors in general innovativeness (Roessner, 1983).

In fact, the population of private and nonprofit organizations displays abundant weaknesses in many ways. Scholarly analyses and media reports regularly detail failures and bankruptcies, massively expensive blunders, and patterns of fraud and abuse in many of these organizations, sometimes in the most prestigious and reputable of them. At times the litany of problems is so long that one wonders whether these sectors serve as useful guiding models for the public sector. On the other hand, just as with the public sector, the list of successes by business and nonprofit organizations is long and impressive, often involving accomplishments that would have seemed miraculous to people living even a few decades ago.

The point, then, is not to belabor invidious questions about whether one sector is better than another but to underscore the challenge of pursuing excellence in all managerial settings. Many public and private organizations perform very well. What can we learn from studies of them?

Profiles of Corporate Excellence

Peters and Waterman's *In Search of Excellence* (1982) apparently became so popular because it forged beyond complicated debates about organizational effectiveness and put forth stimulating observations about management in excellent firms (although their conclusions actually echo much of the earlier literature on human relations in organizations and organizational responses to complexity). They used a set of performance and reputation indicators to choose the sixty-two best-managed American companies. From their observations of these companies and from interviews with their managers, they found that these organizations place a heavy emphasis on "productivity through people" (p. 14). They do not merely mouth that value, they "live their commitment to people" (p. 16), and they "achieve extraordinary results with ordinary people" (p. xxv). They definitely try to attract and reward excellent performers, and they also emphasize both autonomy and teamwork. According to Peters and Waterman, these companies reject a heavy emphasis on big raises for top performers and on weeding out the poorest performers.

The firms devote careful attention to managing their organizational culture. They develop coherent philosophies concerning product quality, business integrity, and fair treatment of employees and customers. Together with the stories and slogans that flourish in these companies, these philosophies emphasize shared values that guide major decisions and motivate and guide performance. The firms nurture the philosophies through heavy investments in training and socialization, including out-and-out hoopla. "Without exception," the authors note, "the dominance and coherence of culture proved to be an essential quality of the excellent companies" (p. 75). The firms behaved as if they accepted the principle that "soft is hard"; that is, that the intangible issues of culture, values, human relations— matters that many managers regard as fuzzy and unmanageable—can and must be skillfully managed.

The successful firms strive for coherence in their approach to management, with the shared values of the culture guiding the relationships between staff characteristics, skills, strategies, structure, and management systems. In so doing, they accept ambiguity and paradox as part of the challenge. Organizing involves paradoxes, where one tries to do conflicting things at the same time, under conditions that often provide little clarity. The paradoxical aspects are evident in some of their approaches to management, which Peters and Waterman describe in these terms:

- *A bias for action.* These companies tend toward an approach that one executive described as "ready, fire, aim." They avoid analyzing decisions to death and take action aggressively.

- *Staying close to the customer.* Deeply concerned about the quality of their products and services, people in these companies seek both to stay in close touch with their customers and to be aware of their reactions.
- *Valuing autonomy and entrepreneurship.* Many of these companies try to provide autonomy in work and encourage people to engage in entrepreneurial behaviors. They often tolerate the failure of well-intended, aggressive initiatives.
- *Enhancing productivity through people.* As noted above, the companies emphasize motivating and stimulating their people through respect, participation, and encouragement. They often use imagery, language, symbols, events, and ceremonies to do this.
- *A hands-on, value-driven approach.* The people in these firms devote much attention to clarifying and stating the primary beliefs and values that guide the organization, to clarify what the company "stands for."
- *Sticking to the knitting.* While often very complex, the companies stay focused on the things that they can do well and avoid ill-advised forays into activities that dilute their efforts and goals.
- *A simple form and lean staff.* The companies often have relatively simple structures and small central staffs. Some massive corporations achieve this by decentralizing into fairly autonomous business units, each like a smaller company in itself.
- *Simultaneous loose and tight properties.* The companies balance the need for direction and control with the need for flexibility and initiative. They might have "tight" general guidelines and commitments to certain values, but they allow considerable flexibility within those general values and guidelines. The approach that the Social Security Administration took when it adopted its modular work units (described in Chapter Thirteen) appears to fit this pattern. The change followed a clear general concept—modularization—with firm commitment from the top, yet units could adopt the concept experimentally and flexibly. They could make reasonable adaptations but not radically depart from the basic idea. This example suggests the ways in which many of these approaches mesh together. A relatively clear idea for a change, coupled with relatively clear and appealing values expressed as part of that idea, provides both a source of motivation and direction and a reasonable framework that higher levels can firmly insist on, without being rigid or dictatorial.

At about the same time as Peters and Waterman's book appeared, Americans became increasingly interested in the success of Japanese firms, which had competed so effectively against American companies in many key industries. Observations of these firms reveal similarities to the particularly successful American companies. In one prominent book on the topic, Ouchi (1981) says that many

Japanese firms offer lifetime employment and seek to avoid layoffs in hard times. They express a holistic concern for employees. They move slowly in evaluating and promoting personnel. They use more implicit control mechanisms, such as social influences on employees. They practice collective decision making and collective responsibility and develop relatively nonspecialized career paths.

The Japanese companies strive for trust on the part of their employees so that they will have the confidence to contribute to the organization in many ways. They emphasize work groups as the basis for collective decisions and responsibilities. Through these collective activities, slow evaluations, and nonspecialized career paths involving reassignments and varied experiences, the Japanese system achieves subtlety and intimacy by encouraging detailed knowledge of the company and its employees. The companies emphasize the development of philosophies or styles that guide organizational objectives, operating procedures, and major decisions such as new product lines. They support these philosophies through extensive training programs. Ouchi notes that some successful American corporations, such as IBM, Procter & Gamble, Hewlett Packard, and Eastman Kodak (which were included in Peters and Waterman's study), have orientations similar to some of these aspects of Japanese management.

The appearance of books such as these, especially the Peters and Waterman book and several sequels and television programs on the same theme, produced a movement within management circles in the United States. Numerous similar books appeared, and many corporations took steps to emulate the purported patterns of excellence. More and more annual reports proclaimed a company philosophy, typically including sonorous expressions of devotion to employees, customers, and high-quality products. The annual report of one high-tech firm described the company as a "closely knit family" of forty thousand!

Predictably, controversy has followed this material on corporate excellence and Japanese management. The very generalized observations about the characteristics of successful firms leave some questions concerning just how valid they are and how closely they apply to any particular organization. It is not always clear how one carries out some of the prescriptions these books offer—especially how one weaves them all together. Some of the excellent companies that Peters and Waterman studied encountered some difficulties later. Peters and Waterman themselves noted that some managers told them that culture is only one of many important aspects of their organization. Other features, such as sound technical and production systems, can figure just as crucially. Ouchi notes that a very strong culture and familial orientation in an organization could imply that those who do not fit in need to leave or not apply in the first place. Still, the organizational excellence trend raises some valuable and fascinating points, including the importance of people, human relations, and organizational culture; the inevitability of paradox and ambiguity and the necessity to manage them; and the feasibility of managing complex organizations successfully.

There is also the question of whether this trend applies to public organizations. Certainly, some of the approaches and suggestions do apply. Many public agencies used the films Peters produced in training sessions. Robert Dempsey, director of the Florida Department of Law Enforcement, found the Peters and Waterman material very attractive and successfully used his own version of many of the ideas. He adopted an open-door policy and encouraged the managers below him to do so as well. He moved around the organization and visited and talked with employees. He conducted surveys and invited employees to write to him about what they did and did not like. He initiated many events aimed at stimulating the atmosphere of the department and making it an enjoyable place to work, including picnics, a five-kilometer run for charity, and a fitness program. He worked to ensure that contractors responsible for keeping the offices painted kept up with their contracts, and he generally emphasized cleanliness and pride in the appearance of the organization. He sought to encourage and develop his immediate staff by giving them more responsibility. He sought higher pay for department employees but openly pointed out that he could not control such factors, since the legislature had the ultimate authority. He would do what he could about pay, he told them, and they could all try to make the organization a better place in which to work in as many other ways as possible. Of course, he and others in the department also worked hard on technical and policy-related issues, but it was primarily the more general and cultural innovations that gained the organization a well-deserved reputation as a well-managed and increasingly effective organization.

This example clearly shows that a dedicated public manager can make effective use of the excellence literature. The trend set in motion by the Peters and Waterman book has become outmoded in some ways and been superseded by other trends (or fads and fashions, perhaps), such as the wave of interest in Total Quality Management, described below. Yet this general orientation toward locating and describing excellence has continued to play out in very important ways in the public sector, and it has heavily influenced management, as the sections below describe.

Effective Public Organizations

Strikingly, the corporate excellence literature turns on their heads some previous observations about the problems of public organizations. The Civil Service Reform Act of 1978 institutionalized the belief that weak links between pay, firing, and performance cause public organizations to perform poorly. Yet the writers on corporate excellence say that the best profit-oriented firms do not worry too much about such tight linkages. They try very hard to recognize and reward excellent performers, but not in a harshly competitive way. They emphasize a culture of communication, shared values, and mutual loyalty and support between the organization and its employees. They also emphasize decentralization, flexibility, and adaptiveness. Can this strategy apply to the public sector, given the context and constraints it faces? As with virtually all the issues taken up heretofore, the answer is yes, but with special considerations and with a degree of inconclusiveness, demonstrated by the research and thinking on the topic. Examples of public organizations' achieving these conditions do exist and are even fairly common. Yet these examples also suggest some particular difficulties that public organizations face in achieving them, and they leave questions about whether the good examples are relatively exceptional.

Gold (1982) studied ten successful organizations, five public and five private. He chose healthy organizations with well-respected products or services that appeared to be good places to work. The public organizations included the U.S. Forest Service, the U.S. Customs Service, the U.S. Passport Office, and the city governments of Sunnyvale, California, and Charlotte, North Carolina. The private organizations included a regional theater organization, the Dana Corporation (an automobile parts manufacturer), Hewlett Packard, L. L. Bean, and Time, Inc. He found that the ten organizations had certain common characteristics:

- They emphasize clear missions and objectives, and these are widely communicated and understood throughout the organization.
- The people in the organization see it as special because of its products or services and take pride in this.
- Management places great value on the people in the organization, on treating them fairly and respectfully, and on open, honest, informal communication with them.
- The managers do not see their organization as particularly innovative, but they emphasize innovative ways of managing people.
- Management emphasizes delegation of responsibility and authority as widely and as far down in the organization as possible. They strive to involve as many people as possible in decision making and other activities.
- Job tasks and goals are clear, and employees receive much feedback. Good performance earns recognition and rewards.
- The handling of jobs, participation, and the personnel function is aimed at challenging people and encouraging their enthusiasm and development.

Gold did find some distinctions between the public and private organizations, however. The public organizations did not articulate their mission as clearly and consistently as the private ones. Apparently the private organizations' focus on profit as an element of their objectives helped in this regard. The studies described above cite Hewlett Packard as a pioneer in issuing statements of corporate philosophy that express a commitment to employees and customers. Yet Gold found that in that same corporation, the managers and the policy statements consistently cite profit as an indispensable objective. The managers in the public organizations, however, talked about excellence in the professionalism of the staff and smoothly run operations and processes. The public organizations also had a harder time promoting from within, an approach that the private firms emphasized as a way of building experience, knowledge, and commitment among their employees.

Porter, Sargent, and Stupak (1986) identified a set of federal agencies with a reputation for excellence, as well as some that had lost such a reputation. For example, the Federal Executive Institute (FEI) developed a reputation for excellent training and development programs for federal executives. The FEI follows such principles as "intraprencurship" (internal entrepreneurial activities), an emphasis on process as much as product, and the value of interaction among executives as part of their development. The Treasury Executive Institute within the Department of the Treasury also emphasizes interaction among participants and close attention to the needs of executives, and it reputedly provides sophisticated executive training programs. The Naval Weapons Center at China Lake, California, encourages intrapreneurialism, team building, risk taking, and mentoring and has earned a reputation as an innovative, effective research and development laboratory. The Office of the Comptroller in the Environmental Protection Agency initiated an ambitious and effective program for human resource development in the agency. The Office of Fusion Energy in the Department of Energy adopted a successful program for developing the skills of its scientists and technicians for working in teams and dealing with counterparts in other countries.

Porter, Sargent, and Stupak (1986) found that a number of agencies, including the Internal Revenue Service, have fallen from a former highly effective status. The IRS once had an excellent reputation for client service and employee development, but it appears to have lost its emphasis on client service. NASA once had a strong reputation for participative management, for encouraging openness and honesty, and for collegial and highly professional relations with contractors, but it appears to have moved to more operational, money-making objectives. The Federal Aviation Administration lost a reputation for effectiveness in the wake of President Reagan's firing of striking flight controllers early in his administration. The Social Security Administration lost some of its reputation when its mission became diffused by the requirement that it administer the Supplementary Social Insurance program, which made it a welfare agency as well as a client service agency and severely overburdened its computer system and other management systems.

Whether or not these evaluations are correct, they do raise important questions about influences on the effectiveness of public agencies. They echo the fairly common observations about why it is harder to develop excellence in the federal government—the sheer size and complexity of the system, a fuzzy bottom line, greater difficulty in establishing a clear mission, vulnerability to the political environment, multiple participants in decision making, political scrutiny of managers' decisions, micromanagement by oversight bodies, and difficulties between career and politically appointed officials. Porter, Sargent, and Stupak argue, however, that excellence can prevail when agencies establish a clear vision and mission, have effective top leadership, encourage idea champions and entrepreneurial behaviors, establish close involvement with employees and clients, develop the managerial capacities of the professional and technical experts who serve in management positions, and emphasize culture over structure and process over product.

These types of studies have continued in recent years, with many relatively similar findings (for example, see Denhardt, 1993). Hale (1996) summarizes the conclusions of some of the most recent studies of high-performance public agencies, as illustrated in Table 14.1.

Hale concludes that in high-performance organizations, leaders define their key role as providing conditions that support employee productivity and support employees in providing the organizations' customers with what they want and need from the organization. These organizations, and their leaders, typically emphasize the following values:

- *Learning.* The organizations emphasize and support learning, risk taking, training, communication, and work measurement.
- *A focused mission.* They emphasize clarifying their mission and communicating it to the members of the organization, its customers, and other stakeholders.
- *A nurturing community.* Hale says that high-performance organizations provide a supportive culture, with an emphasis on teamwork, participation, flexible authority, and effective reward and recognition processes.
- *Enabling leadership.* Leaders in high-performance public organizations emphasize learning, communication, flexibility, sharing, and the development of a vision and commitment to it.

TABLE 14.1. COMPARISON OF HIGH-PERFORMANCE CHARACTERISTICS ACROSS TEN YEARS.

Principle	How Three Groups Defined the Characteristics		
	STEP (1985)	Denhardt (1993)	Alliance (1994)
Mission and customer orientation	• Closer contact with the customer for a better understanding of the customer's needs	• Dedication to public service • Commitment to values • Serving the public	• Mission clarity and understanding
Employee empowerment, including the provision of tools and use of performance measurement	• Tapping the knowledge, skills, and commitment of all state workers • Increasing discretionary authority to give managers and employees control over and accountability for a bottom line • State-of-the-art productivity improvement techniques • Partnerships to allow the sharing of knowledge, expertise, and other resources • Improved work measurement to provide a base for planning and implementing service improvements and giving workers information about their performance	•Empowerment and shared leadership • Pragmatic incrementalism (a free-flowing process of seizing opportunities)	• Restructured work processes to meet customer needs • Flexible adaptability, ability to adjust when conditions change • Open and productive communications among stakeholders • Employee empowerment • New processes to motivate and inspire people to succeed • Defined outcomes and focus on results • Competitive in terms of performance

Source: Hale (1996, p. 139). Reprinted by permission.

These studies of excellent public organizations are stimulating and encouraging. They continue the stream of work that has followed the Peters and Waterman book in certain ways (including the Reinventing Government movement, described below). They further support the conclusions that there are many effective public organizations and that these are often similar to effective private ones. This in turn suggests that many of them can be managed as well as or better than private ones and that many public managers perform very effectively. Yet the conclusions from these studies often have an idealized, very general character. Questions remain about how one actually implements the changes they propose. The challenge is to continue to develop our knowledge of how public organizations change for the better; the sections to follow argue that the ideas and topics covered in earlier chapters can help with this challenge.

Total Quality Management

Before covering some additional developments in the stream of ideas about excellence in public management, it is useful to examine one major trend that has heavily influenced some of those ideas. In the last ten or fifteen years, organizations throughout the public and private sectors have undertaken Total Quality Management (TQM) programs. The widespread implementation of these programs in itself makes it important for public managers and students of public management to be aware of TQM. As we will see, the topic also raises challenging alternatives for management. It has clearly influenced the objectives of current government reform efforts described later in this chapter (for example, focusing on the customer, the use of teams, and continuous improvement). It also provides an interesting and useful example of the dissemination of ideas and techniques in public and private management (Berman and West, 1995).

The term *Total Quality Management* refers more to a general movement or philosophy of management than to a very specific set of management procedures. Different authors take different approaches to TQM. W. Edwards Deming, one of the founders of this movement who developed many of the original ideas behind it, did not refer to his approach as Total Quality Management. In fact, he disapproved of this label. Yet a review of some of Deming's seminal ideas provides a useful introduction to TQM (Dean and Evans, 1994; Deming, 1986).

Deming was an industrial statistician. Writing in the 1950s, he advocated using statistical measures of the quality of a product during all the phases of its production. He called for this approach to replace the quality-control procedures often used in industry, which assessed the product only at the end of the production process. Deming included this commitment to statistical quality control in his general philosophy of management. He put together fourteen tenets of his approach. These tenets, frequently quoted in the TQM literature, include the following:

- Publish a statement of company aims and purposes for all employees to see, and demonstrate commitment to the statement on the part of management.
- Have everyone in the company learn and adopt the new philosophy.
- Constantly improve the production system.
- Institute training, teach leadership skills, and encourage self-improvement.
- Drive out fear and create trust and a climate of innovation.
- Use teams to pursue optimal achievement of company goals.
- Eliminate numerical production quotas and management by objectives, and concentrate on improving processes and on methods of improvement.
- Remove barriers to pride of workmanship.

Although some of these sound simple, many have profound implications for an organization's basic approach to organizing and managing. For example, these principles led Deming to oppose individualized performance appraisals because they damage teamwork, fail to focus on serving the customer, and usually emphasize short-term results. Compare his orientation to the themes in civil service reforms and government pay reforms described in Chapter Ten (for example, pay-for-performance plans based on individual performance appraisals, and the streamlining of procedures for firing and disciplining employees).

Deming argued that his approach to management represented a general philosophy that must receive total commitment from the organization. Measures of quality should be used at all phases of production and should be the basis for continuous efforts to improve quality. The organization should strive to improve against its own past quality measures as well as those of comparable organizations. The quality measures should be based on the preferences and point of view of the organization's customers.

To make this continuous commitment to improving quality work, people have to feel free to contribute their ideas about problems and improvements. Hence, the leaders of the organization must "drive out fear." Deming advocated doing away with individual performance evaluations, since they focus the attention of the individual on her or his own performance and can reduce employees' incentive to help those around them. Performance evaluation must be based on group and organizational performance so that people will have the incentive to share their ideas and efforts and to support one another.

When Deming first began to advance his ideas, they received little attention from managers in the United States. The Japanese, however, embraced his ideas enthusiastically. Today, the Deming Award is a very prestigious award in Japan for excellence in management. As the Japanese economy boomed, and as Japanese firms joined the list of the most successful firms in the world and began outcompeting U.S. firms in many markets, managers in the United States decided that they needed to pay some attention to what this fellow Deming had to say. For example, Deming was instrumental in Ford Motor Company's adoption of a corporate strategy and philosophy based on a commitment to quality (Dean and Evans, 1994). The general acceptance and adoption of these programs became so widespread that by 1987 Congress passed legislation establishing the Malcolm Baldrige National Quality Award Program (named for a former U.S. secretary of commerce), which annually recognizes organizations with excellent quality management programs and achievements.

Other authors, such as Joseph Juran (1992), have also advanced influential ideas about quality improvement, advocating a number of different approaches to it. In general, however, the principles put forward by Deming, Juran, and others are general, and these authors provide no precise guidance concerning their implementation in specific situations. Organizations adapt them to their own circumstances.

Well-developed TQM programs tend to involve such conditions and principles as the following (Dean and Evans, 1994; Cohen and Brand, 1993):

- An emphasis on defining quality in terms of customer needs and responses.
- Working with suppliers to improve their relationship to the quality of the organization's production processes and products.
- Measurement and assessment of quality at all phases of production, with commitment to continuous improvement in quality. Quality measures are often "benchmarked" against similar measures for similar organizations as a way of assessing improvement and general level of performance.
- Teamwork, trust, and communication in improving quality. Use of decision-making and quality improvement teams involving participants from many areas and levels of the organization that are involved in the production process.
- Well-developed training programs to support teamwork and quality assessment and improvement.
- A broad organizational commitment to the process, from the top-executive ranks on down, that encompasses strategy, cultural development, communication, and other major aspects of the organization.

Very well developed programs, such as the one at Allied-Signal Corporation, involve comprehensive commitments. Top executives demonstrate commitment and leadership. Symbols, language, communication, and training are coordinated around the quality program. In some of the companies, for example, every employee receives sixty days of quality training within two weeks of joining the organization, and everyone, including the CEO, takes the training. The training often involves coverage of a fairly standard set of analytical procedures, including such techniques as cause-and-effect diagrams ("fishbone" diagrams), flowcharts, and procedures for counting and tabulating data related to production quality and for analyzing causes and interpretations. In some organizations the training and procedures involve standard practices for team meetings and decision-making processes, with standard roles such as timekeepers and scribes and standard formats for discussion and problem solving.

Though the TQM movement originally focused on industry, it has swept through government as well, with applications in many different types of agencies and at all levels of government (Council of State Governments, 1994). Applications in government face constraints of the sort described in earlier chapters—problems in securing sustained commitment in the context of political turnover at executive levels, problems in identifying customers, problems in measuring outputs and products, personnel and procurement systems that limit empowerment and the use of teams. Nevertheless, the professional literature provides numerous examples of successful TQM efforts in government (Cohen and Brand, 1993).

Consistent with the theme of this book, the basic principles of TQM emphasize that successful total quality efforts depend heavily on commitment and strategic implementation (Cohen and Brand, 1993). The principles of TQM are often general, stressing leadership, culture, incentives and motivation, groups and teams, and many of the other topics covered in previous chapters. Failed TQM efforts often display the opposite of these qualities—insufficient leadership, weak culture, weak management of the change process, poor provisions for motivation and teamwork. For example, in one class discussion of TQM, a student familiar with the program at Allied-Signal Corporation described its elaborate and comprehensive provisions, including the provision mentioned above for sixty days of training for every employee. Another student, an employee in a federal agency, smiled wryly and described how the TQM program for her bureau involved having two different members of the unit go for two days of TQM training every month. At that rate, it would take two years for every member of the unit to receive two days of TQM training. As pointed out in Chapter Thirteen, such piecemeal efforts at any innovation, whatever its attributes, will fail.

TQM has its detractors, who criticize it as one more management fad that will soon be supplanted by another. It obviously has very challenging and interesting features, however, especially for government. It proposes a management philosophy quite opposed to the one that has prevailed in many government reforms in recent years (Peters and Savoie, 1994). Its history also illustrates the need for comprehensive, strategic approaches to many innovations in management—approaches that apply many of the ideas covered in previous chapters.

Reinventing Government

Osborne and Gaebler's book *Reinventing Government* (1992) became a best-seller during the early 1990s and has shaped many government reforms in the years since its publication. Like the other studies of excellence in public management described earlier, it provides provocative and challenging ideas about approaches to public management and the delivery of government services. Interestingly, however, its perspective on the state of performance in the public sector was mixed. The authors introduced the book with the claim that in many ways, government is failing and breaking down. Yet they also argued that government plays an essential role in society and has to define and carry out that role effectively—hence the need for reinvention. In particular, the authors attacked the old-fashioned, centralized, bureaucratic model that dominated many government agencies and programs. They called for more entrepreneurial activities to supplant that approach.

Interestingly, however, to support their call for a more entrepreneurial approach in government, they cited many government practices they had observed around the country that were already quite effective. They described many activities that involved decentralizing, encouraging privatization, encouraging control of programs at the community level, increasing attention to the "customers" of government programs, finding ways for government to make money on its operations ("enterprising government"), and increasing competition among government programs and between government and the private sector. Table 14.2 summarizes their strategies for more entrepreneurial government. They illustrated the use of these strategies through numerous examples from government programs.

Their proposals had a rapid, major impact, including the establishment of the Clinton administration's National Performance Review, described below. "REGO" (reinventing government) became a widely used term in the federal government and other government circles. The REGO trend heavily influenced a broad array of developments, including such examples as the "reinvention" of the civil service system of the state of Florida and an entrepreneurial effort at getting a hotel built in downtown Visalia, California. These two examples are quite significant, because according to some observers they were unsuccessful. Wechsler (1994) concludes that the civil service reform efforts in Florida had little important effect. Gurwitt (1994) reports that the Visalia episode had bad results. There, government officials wanted a hotel built downtown to support economic development efforts. Pursuing entrepreneurial strategies, they tried to avoid spending government funds to subsidize the development of the hotel. They bought land and worked out an arrangement with a developer to lease the land from the city and build a hotel on it. This way, the city would make money on the arrangement

TABLE 14.2. OSBORNE AND GAEBLER'S STRATEGIES FOR REINVENTING GOVERNMENT.

Catalytic Government

"Leverage" government authority and resources by using private- and nonprofit-sector resources and energies, through such strategies as privatization of public services and public-private partnerships.

Government should "steer" rather than "row," by emphasizing directions and priorities but letting private and nonprofit organizations deliver services and carry out projects.

Community-Owned Government

Empower local communities and groups. Allow more local control through such strategies as community policing and resident control of public housing.

Competitive Government

Introduce more competition between government and private organizations, within government, and between private organizations through such strategies as competitive contracting, private competition with public services, and school choice and voucher programs.

Mission-Driven Government

Focus government programs on their missions rather than bureaucratic rules and procedures, through such strategies as flexible budgeting procedures (such as expenditure control budgets) and more flexible personnel rules and procedures (such as broader, more flexible pay categories, as studied in the China Lake Experiments).

Results-Oriented Government

Place more emphasis on outcomes rather than inputs, through greater investment in performance measures, including using them in budgeting and evaluation systems.

Customer-Driven Government

Give customers of public programs and services more influence over them. Pay more attention to customers through procedures such as customer surveys, toll-free numbers, TQM programs, and complaint tracking. Give customers more choice through voucher systems and competition among service providers.

Enterprising Government

Find ways to earn money through user fees, profitable uses of government resources and programs, and innovative cost-saving and privatization projects.

Anticipatory Government

Prevent problems before they occur rather than curing them after they do, through strategic planning, futures commissions, long-range budgeting, interdepartmental planning and budgeting, and innovative prevention programs in environmental protection, crime, fire, and other service areas.

Decentralized Government

Decentralize government activities through such approaches as relaxing rules and hierarchical controls, participatory management, innovative management, employee development, and labor-management partnerships.

Market-Oriented Government

Use economic market mechanisms to achieve public policy goals and deliver public services, through such techniques as pollution taxes, deposit fees on bottles, user fees, tax credits, and vouchers.

Source: Adapted from Osborne and Gaebler (1992).

through the lease payments. Unfortunately, the developer folded, and rather than give up on the project and take a loss, the city assumed over $20 million of the developer's debts.

These examples are presented not to attack or belittle the REGO ideas but because they have been controversial. For example, some critics have raised concerns about thinking of citizens as "customers" of public organizations. Yet, like many new approaches, the proposals are stimulating and challenging. The examples are presented to underscore a main theme of this book: challenging new ideas require effective implementation, and in government that means public management, even in cases where government seeks to devolve its services to the private sector.

The National Performance Review

The REGO movement influenced the Clinton administration's National Performance Review (NPR). As with the other recent developments described above, NPR deserves attention as a major recent reform effort in public management. Some experts regard the NPR as unprecedented in terms of the activity it generated and the attention it has received (Kettl, 1993). The NPR involved a review of federal operations by a staff in Washington under the leadership of Vice-President Gore. Among other activities, Gore conducted meetings with employees in federal agencies, ostensibly to gather ideas about problems and solutions but also with the obvious intent of making a symbolic statement.

In many ways, the NPR's tenor was similar to that of the reinventing government movement. The first report (Gore, 1993) argued that the federal government needed a drastic overhaul to improve its operations, a reinvention similar to that in many corporations that had reformed themselves in the face of international competition in the 1980s. Yet the report—and Vice-President Gore, in his public statements and actions (such as his meetings with agency employees)—took the position that federal employees were not to blame for the problems in government. The structures and systems were the problems, the report said, and it emphasized the importance of listening to federal employees' ideas and observations.

The report announced numerous initiatives to reform the structure and operations of the federal government, as well as many change efforts within federal agencies. Table 14.3 summarizes some of the major priorities and initiatives announced in the first report of the NPR.

As the table suggests, the NPR emphasized the need to reform many of the constraints on federal agencies discussed in this book. The reforms would decentralize and relax personnel and procurement regulations, for example.

TABLE 14.3. THE NATIONAL PERFORMANCE REVIEW: MAJOR PRIORITIES AND INITIATIVES.

1. Cut Red Tape
   - *Streamline the budget-making process.* Use biennial budgeting; relax OMB categories and ceilings; allow agencies to roll over 50 percent of funds not spent.
   - *Decentralize personnel policy.* Eliminate the *Federal Personnel Manual;* allow departments to conduct their own recruiting, examining, evaluation, and reward systems; simplify the classification system; reduce the time to terminate employees and managers for cause and to deal with poor performers.
   - *Streamline procurement.* Simplify procurement regulations; decentralize GSA authority for buying information technology; allow agencies to buy where they want, rely on the commercial marketplace.
   - *Reorient the inspectors general.* Reorient them from strict compliance auditing to evaluating management control systems.
   - *Eliminate regulatory overkill.* Eliminate 50 percent of internal agency regulations; improve interagency coordination of regulations; allow agencies to obtain waivers from regulations.
   - *Empower state and local governments.* Establish an enterprise board for new initiatives in community empowerment; limit the use of unfunded mandates; consolidate grant programs into more flexible categories; allow agency heads to grant states and localities selective waivers from regulations and mandates; give control of public housing to local housing authorities with good records.

2. Put Customers First
   - *Give customers "voice" and "choice."*
   - *Make service organizations compete.*
   - *Create market dynamics and use market mechanisms.*

3. Empower Employees to Get Results
   - *Decentralize decision making.*
   - *Hold federal employees accountable for results.*
   - *Give federal workers the tools they need.*
   - *Enhance the quality of work life.*

4. Cut Back to Basics
   - *Eliminate what we don't need.*
   - *Collect more.*
   - *Invest in productivity and reengineer to cut costs.*

Source: Adapted from Gore (1993).

Many of the NPR reforms also reflect the management trends described in this book—including the prescriptions of Peters and Waterman, TQM, REGO, and others—with an emphasis on serving the customer, decentralization, empowerment, and relaxed controls. The report thus provides an interesting example of the infusion into government reform of trends and ideas in business management.

Predictably, the NPR has been controversial in public administration circles, in terms of whether it is well conceived and whether it will have lasting and beneficial effects. Its ultimate effects remain to be seen, but without question it has caused a lot of activity in federal agencies. Among other steps, the NPR announced a reduction of about 11 percent of the federal work force, or over two hundred thousand employees. This gave rise to questions about whether such cuts were really the result of an ulterior motive behind the glowing discourse about reforms, and whether the NPR was simply part of the recent trend of presidents' attacking the bureaucracy for political effect (Arnold, 1995). In addition, many of the NPR initiatives were implemented by executive orders, including one instructing federal agencies to reduce their internal regulations by 50 percent and one eliminating the elaborate federal personnel manual. Whether such measures will have substantial and lasting effects is unclear at present.

Subsequent NPR reports have announced additional reforms. An executive order directed federal agencies to publish customer service standards, and a great many have (Clinton and Gore, 1995). Follow-up reports have announced indications of progress, such as reductions in regulations, cost savings of $58 billion, and a variety of steps in different agencies to improve operations and services (Gore, n.d.). One of the efforts under the NPR involved a presidential directive ordering federal agencies to set up "reinvention laboratories" to work on improving their procedures. Some of these reinvention labs have reported successes in finding improved and innovative ways of carrying out their agency's business, although they have also encountered many obstacles to change (Sanders and Thompson, 1996).

Whether or not the NPR achieves significant long-term reform depends in large part on political developments, such as whether the Clinton administration remains in office and continues to emphasize the program. Controversy over the sincerity, design, and effects of the initiative will continue for years. The NPR is nevertheless a major development in the effort to enhance excellence in public management. It has revealed many of the obstacles to reform. At the same time, though, it has also documented many examples of effective public management. While critics may be right about various problems with the NPR, it represents an application of some of the principles of effective large-scale change discussed in Chapter Thirteen. It has received relatively strong support from top executives (the president and vice-president); it has made an effort to involve organizational members (the federal employees) in change and to enlist their support; it has advanced measures for decentralized diagnosis and incremental improvement of performance problems (the reinvention labs); and it has been marked by other features that characterize successful change. Significantly, it has clearly exerted far more influence on federal agencies than did Reagan-era reform efforts like the Grace Commission. And returning to the theme of this book, the NPR, despite its problems, has demonstrated the importance of excellent public management in translating attractive generalizations into effective change.

Managing Major Initiatives and Priorities: Privatization and Volunteer Programs

We can further illustrate this theme—that the need for effective public management is inescapable and that this need becomes especially apparent when we observe the implementation (or failed implementation) of new initiatives in government. We can do so by examining two very recent trends in public management, the increasing emphasis on privatization of public services and on using volunteers to deliver public services. Although they have a long history in the United States and other nations, these approaches have received greater emphasis lately as strategies for dealing with tightened budgets in the public sector (and the consequent need for reducing costs and increasing efficiency) and for escaping alleged weakness of government through innovative and flexible ways of delivering public services. Yet careful attention to these approaches shows that they *increase* the imperative for effective public management rather than relax or ease it.

In addition, discussing these two trends illustrates another major theme. As mentioned at the beginning of this book, effective management and leadership require sustained, careful, comprehensive approaches to the challenges of organizing and managing. The discussions to follow suggest how the conceptual frameworks presented at the outset, together with the concepts and ideas from the preceding chapters, can support the development of such an approach to these two topics.

Managing Privatization

Earlier chapters have mentioned the increased use of privatization as a means of delivering public services. Government contracts with private providers are nothing new in the United States, but privatization has increased a great deal in the last several decades, with governments at all levels sharply increasing their contracts with the private sector (Chi, 1994; Council of State Governments, 1993). In addition, privatization has increased in service areas where it has been rare in the past, such as the operation of prisons. As Chapters Five and Six mentioned, the expansion of privatization has raised issues concerning the "hollow state," third-party government, and the changing nature of government and public management (Kettl, 1993; Milward, 1996; Moe, 1996; National Academy of Public Administration, 1989; Smith and Lipsky, 1993). Privatization, then, is a widely and increasingly utilized mode of service delivery that imposes problems on public managers but also offers them strategic options. Managing privatization effectively thus represents one aspect of excellence in public management. This section discusses privatization as a management challenge for public managers and offers suggestions for utilizing it effectively.

During the 1980s a wave of privatization initiatives swept the globe, with nations on all continents trying to transfer government activities to private operators. Most nations have many more government-owned enterprises than the United States, and in most of these countries the privatization issue concerned how to sell or transfer such enterprises to private owners and operators. In the United States, by contrast, privatization primarily involves government contracts with private or nonprofit organizations to deliver public services and carry out public policies. Actually, privatization of public services can take many forms besides selling the operation or contracting it out. These forms include the following:

- Granting a franchise to private operators.
- Providing vouchers to service recipients to purchase services from private providers.
- Using volunteers (for staff support or service delivery, for example).
- Providing subsidies and financial incentives to private operators, such as tax incentives, grants, and subsidization of startup costs.
- Initiating self-help or coproduction programs, where citizens perform services for their own benefit or share in providing them.
- Selling off or shedding activities. Governments can sell activities to private operators, or they can simply cease them so that private operators can take them over.

For the most part, however, privatization in the United States involves contracts with nongovernmental organizations. As mentioned above, contracts and similar arrangements such as grants and franchises have been part of government for a long time. Eli Whitney, the famous inventor, received a contract from the government in 1798 to provide ten thousand muskets in two years. It took him ten years to finish the project (Dean and Evans, 1994, p. 5).

Privatization Pitfalls and Ironies

The example of Whitney's overrun suggests one of the many pitfalls of privatization. In recent years, proponents of privatization, some of whom show an obvious ideological bias toward private business and against government activity, have promoted privatization as a bold new initiative. Yet the Whitney example and thousands of similar ones remind us that privatization is as old as the republic and that, while it has produced many benefits, its history has been fraught with scandals and problems. In addition, rather than offering a private sector alternative to government, privatization can lead to a "governmentalization" of the private sector, in which government increasingly draws segments of the private sector into its sphere of activity (Moe, 1996). Private contractors and service providers can then become just one more interest group, lobbying for government policies favorable to themselves and their industry or service area (Smith and Lipsky, 1993). The greatest irony of privatization, however, is that it increases demands for excellence in public management rather than alleviating them. *The chief irony of privatization is that proponents tout it as a cure for bad government, but it takes excellent government to make it work.* The discussions of third-party government in earlier chapters point out that contracting out and other forms of privatization, grant programs, and operation of government services by nongovernmental organizations strain the lines of management and accountability. Public managers become increasingly responsible for programs and services over which they have less control. They can influence the outcomes of such programs and services only through the vehicles spelled out in their contracts with private service providers, rather than through direct administrative control. Major issues, such as the legal liability of government and public managers, can become more complex and uncertain. As the history of privatization has shown, private service providers may perform poorly or even illegally. Armed only with relatively loose lines of control and accountability, government officials nevertheless share responsibility for such failures. On the other hand, privatization persists as an option in part because it can offer a valuable alternative for government managers. It can produce savings and efficiencies, flexibility in management, and other strategic advantages. Thus, to avoid the problems and take advantages of the promise, successful privatization requires skillful public management (Gill, 1996).

What does successful management of privatization involve? We now have a well-developed literature on privatization and contracting out that considers its pros and cons and what needs to happen for such strategies to work well (Chi, 1994; Council of State Governments, 1993; Donahue, 1990; Savas, 1987; Rehfuss, 1989). Table 14.4 presents some of the conditions that should be in place for successful privatization and contracting out, according to the professional literature. As noted, its proponents make very strong claims for privatization as a panacea for the alleged ills of government. They point to a fairly consistent set of research findings that indicate that private organizations often provide services at lower costs per unit of output compared to government agencies. Other authors, however, point to some problems with many of these studies and to the complication introduced by the fact that government organizations often have to pursue different goals and values than private organizations, even in the same service areas (for example, see the sections in Table 14.4 on goals and values and on performance and effectiveness).

TABLE 14.4. CONDITIONS FOR SUCCESSFUL PRIVATIZATION AND CONTRACTING OUT.

The conditions necessary for successful privatization, especially through contracting out, organized by the components in Figure 1.1:

1. Environment

Bidders. There must be a set of competitive bids for the contract. Bidders need to be experienced in the service area, have a good record, and be qualified on such criteria as having the capacity to operate in the geographic area where the service is needed and in the manner required by the size and scope of the required operation.

Political environment. The environment should be free of inappropriate political pressure for privatization, especially pressure to select a particular provider.

Resource support. Authorities should be willing to provide resources to support the provisions for privatization listed in the sections below.

Legal and institutional environment. The privatization initiative must conform to federal and state government mandates. Examples: federal statutes may require payment of prevailing wages; state laws may limit contracts to the present fiscal year.
Liability issues should be carefully reviewed.

2. Goals/Values

The privatization initiative should support the agency's mission and its primary goals and values. Governments should usually avoid contracting out certain core functions, such as those involving public safety and security, deadly force, and the handling of public funds.

The goals and values of the privatized activity should be clear (see Performance and Effectiveness, below).

3. Leadership/Strategy/Culture

Agency leaders should be carefully involved with privatization policies and activities, including their coordination with agency strategies and culture.

4. Structure

Specialization and responsibility. Responsibility for privatization and contracting out should be clearly defined. Qualified personnel need to be hired, trained, and otherwise set in place to supervise and run the process. Examples: agencies need expertise in contracting processes, in legal issues related to contracting out (or vouchers, franchising, or other modes), and in accounting and financial issues, such as cost accounting and comparisons of the cost of in-house service provision versus contracting out—all coordinated with expertise in the policy or service area involved. Responsibilities for contract development and monitoring need clear definition.

Departmentalization or subunits. Agencies should have effective organizational structures for contracting out, with effective locations of offices and units with expertise and responsibility. Example: small agencies may have a central contracting office as well as contracting officers in an administrative services unit; larger agencies may have contracting and privatization units in larger subunits. Departments may place subunits in charge of monitoring contracts.

Agencies may need to maintain the capacity to take over the activity if the contractor goes bankrupt or the contracting process otherwise encounters problems. The responsible units need to be clearly designated and provided with appropriate resources (for example, to maintain the necessary equipment and personnel).

TABLE 14.4. CONDITIONS FOR SUCCESSFUL PRIVATIZATION AND CONTRACTING OUT, cont'd.

Hierarchy and centralization. Accountability, reporting, and authority relationships should be effectively designed, with clear arrangements for reporting and review of contracts and contracting-out processes and for involvement and awareness of appropriate managers and executives.

Rules and regulations. Appropriate rules and procedures should be in place for the provisions mentioned above (reporting, review, taking back the contracted activity) and below (precontracting procedures, monitoring).

5. Process

Power relationships. Authority and power relationships related to issues of contracting out should be clarified. Authority and accountability relationships with the contractor, and the responsibilities of the contractor, should be clear and carefully reviewed and specified. (For example, details such as the responsibility for maintaining equipment and machinery should be clarified. Required approvals, such as agency authority to approve the contractor's decision to raise user fees, should be clear. Quality control and review procedures should be clarified). Incentives for effective performance and sanctions for poor performance should be clear and effective.

Decision-making processes. Precontracting and contract selection and supervision processes should be well developed. Precontracting processes should involve careful specification of needs and requirements and of the pros and cons of contracting out, including cost comparisons. Meetings and communications with potential bidders about RFP details and goals should be carefully planned. Processes for monitoring and evaluation, and for related evaluative decisions and actions (sanctions and incentives), should be clear and well developed.

Communications. As suggested above, communications with potential bidders and contractors and among responsible agency personnel should be well planned, with responsibilities and procedures well clarified.

Change and innovation. The role of contracting out and privatization in relation to change and innovation should be carefully developed, to make use of the advantages of these strategies for gaining access to new flexibility, technologies, personnel, and other opportunities.

People. The effects on agency personnel should be assessed. Often new contracting-out initiatives should not go forward if there is sharp employee resistance, without effective plans for responding to the resistance.

Effective plans for existing employees should include provisions for supportive discharge of those employees as necessary (that is, effective management of downsizing). Contractors can sometimes offer existing employees attractive alternatives, and contracts can sometimes include provisions that the contractor will hire some existing employees. Analysis of the costs of contracting out should include consideration of the costs to the jurisdiction of layoffs or reduced employment.

6. Performance and Effectiveness

Privatization initiatives should have performance measures associated with them that are monitored and used in evaluation, with incentives and sanctions attached, as feasible.

These measures should include public sector performance criteria, such as equity, representativeness, responsiveness, and community and social goals (see Goals/Values above).

In addition to not focusing on the many examples of problems with private sector contracts and how to avoid them, these studies, frequently conducted by economists, tend to overlook the issue of management.

A growing body of experience and research has increasingly documented the problems that can occur and conditions that need to be in place for effective contracting out. These authors implicitly present a contingency theory of privatization, in that they suggest the contingencies that managers have to deal with in successful privatization initiatives. As suggested in Table 14.4, they tend to emphasize such contingencies as the following:

- Having a range of contractors submit competitive bids for the contract, to avoid monopolistic bidding situations.
- Effective management of strong employee or union opposition to the contract (see People on Table 14.4).
- Effective precontract planning and analysis, including such precautions as well-developed cost comparisons and meetings with potential bidders.
- Effective contracts, with clear stipulation of goals and performance criteria and provisions for monitoring, evaluation, incentives, and sanctions. The goals and performance criteria must include consideration of equity, effects on the community, social goals, and other typical public sector issues.

The professional literature emphasizes contingencies such as these and the others indicated in Table 14.4. Not all of them apply in all situations. For example, there may be situations in which effective relations with a single long-term contractor provide better results than soliciting competitive bids from many providers. Still, we now have a growing consensus on a set of contingencies to be managed in successful contracting out.

Recognizing and managing such contingencies thus becomes one part of excellence in public management. As suggested earlier, however, a more general objective of Table 14.4 is to illustrate an approach to privatization that involves a comprehensive and well-developed approach to organizing for the challenge and managing it. The suggestions in the table are limited by space and time and could be richly expanded with ideas from the earlier chapters. For example, one could approach privatization initiatives as matters of change management, drawing on the ideas in Chapter Thirteen about managing successful change. One could combine change management with a strategic planning process that focuses on privatization and contracting out specifically, or one could draw those topics into a broader strategic plan to coordinate privatization with the overall organizational strategy. In dealing with how privatization affects the culture of one's organization, one can draw on the discussion in Chapter Eleven about leadership and culture, with its ideas about how leaders can influence such matters as employee concerns about privatization initiatives and how they mesh with their agency's mission and values. In these and many other ways, the framework for the book, and the deeper treatment of its components, illustrate another view of privatization (perhaps a limited one that managers and researchers will revise or even discard in favor of a better one): a challenge to excellence in organizing and managing in the public sector.

Managing Volunteer Programs

Another alternative for innovative, cost-saving programs in public agencies involves the use of volunteers (Brudney, 1990). In the United States, a large segment of the population volunteers their time and services to charitable, community, and public service activities. The use of volunteers in government programs is a long-standing tradition in some service areas, and it is an increasingly utilized option. Among many others, parks and recreation services, small business advisory services, and various human service activities regularly use volunteers for support and service delivery. As with privatization and the other trends mentioned previously, volunteer programs in public agencies require excellent public management.

Also as with privatization, the professional literature suggests contingencies for effective volunteer programs. Brudney (1990), for example, describes potential advantages and disadvantages of such programs that suggest the conditions managers must try to establish or avoid. The potential advantages include the following:

- *Cost savings to the agency or program.* Volunteers, obviously, do not draw salaries.
- *Expansion of government activity.* Volunteers make it possible to provide new services that an agency could not otherwise offer. The agency can provide more service with the same or fewer resources.
- *Better community relations.* Volunteer participation can enhance community relations by increasing public support for agencies and increasing awareness of agency issues and constraints. Volunteers can gain skills and experience as well as provide advice and guidance to the agency that benefits community relations.
- *Enhancements in service quality.* Volunteers can bring specialized skills, can help improve the quality of service, and can devote more detailed attention to clients.

Brudney also points out potential challenges and disadvantages:

- *Funding needs.* Even though volunteers do not draw salaries, volunteer programs are not free. They require funding for liability insurance for volunteers, for volunteers' expenses, for support needs (such as training, equipment, office space), and for agency staff to train and supervise the volunteers and run the volunteer program.

- *Work relations.* The agency has to recruit a good supply of volunteers. Some volunteers have problems with absenteeism, poor work, unreliability, and turnover. Agencies need to develop effective incentives and positive control and accountability processes for volunteers.
- *Political and labor difficulties.* Agency executives and supervisors and elected officials may not support volunteer programs. Unions may object to the programs. Permanent employees may mistrust the volunteers or have poor working relations with them.

One can review Brudney's observations about the potential advantages and disadvantages of volunteer programs and see applications of many of the topics in organizing and managing from previous chapters and the framework in Figures 1.1 and 1.2. Certainly, knowledge of volunteer programs and their specific topics and issues is crucial. As with privatization, however, one can also approach volunteer programs as another challenge in organizing and managing a component of an agency, as well as an important part of organizing and managing the agency overall. Without going into as elaborate an examination as that on privatization above, one can suggest a number of examples of applications of the framework to managing volunteers:

- Concerning the environment, managing a volunteer program requires obtaining resources to support the program. The program's leader (or, preferably, leadership team) must cultivate political support for the program from officials and top executives that can be translated into resources for the program. This includes managing publicity and public relations for the program, including media relations. Also essential is a supply of good volunteers; these have to be either located or developed.
- Concerning goals and values, leadership and strategy, and organizational culture, the program leader must clarify the program's goals and dominant values, possibly through a strategic planning process. The leader should develop an effective culture for the program and work with other leaders in the organization on defining how the program fits into the culture and strategy of the overall organization.
- Concerning structure, there must be clear decisions about the location of the program as a subunit within the organization, its relationship to other organizational units, and its responsibilities. Lines of authority and accountability need to be clarified. Specialization needs attention, in that the special skills of the volunteers need to be assessed and assigned effectively.
- Concerning processes, the program will need effective evaluation procedures for individual volunteers as well as for assessing the program's progress toward achieving its goals and toward furthering the agency's overall goals and values.

Process for effective communication with volunteers, between volunteers and the rest of the agency, and with other stakeholders should be designed, using newsletters, mailings, meetings, and other media (which require both financial resources and political support).

- The leadership team needs to design incentives for the volunteers—possibly including recognition programs, certificates, and enjoyable or commemorative events—and this requires coordination with agency communication processes, cultural leaders, and resource providers.

These examples represent only a portion of the suggestions and considerations triggered by approaching a volunteer program as an organizational and management challenge. A useful exercise for students would be to flesh out this example and the previous one on privatization with a design for a well-organized and well-managed program.

In Conclusion

The foregoing discussions of the management of privatization and volunteer programs emphasize the general point that while the concepts, theories, and ideas covered in this book do not offer a scientific solution, they can certainly support the development of a well-conceived, well-informed orientation toward excellence in public organization and management.

It is consistent with the theme repeatedly stated in this book that its conclusion should be brief. Effective understanding and management of public organizations do not sum up neatly into a set of snappy aphorisms. The preceding examples are intended to illustrate ideas and topics developed in earlier chapters of the book, applied as comprehensively as possible to management initiatives. The framework offered in this book may need some improvements for some people and for various situations, but knowledge of the ideas and materials in this book should still be valuable to those with a sustained commitment to excellence in public management. Ultimately, it is that general determination to maintain and improve public management that remains essential.

The government of the United States, including all its levels and adjoining private activities, amounts to one of the great achievements in human history. Like private and nonprofit organizations, public organizations routinely provide beneficial services that would have been considered miracles a century ago. Yet they also have the capacity to do great harm and impose severe injustice. The viability and value of government depend on legions of managers, employees, supporters—and critics—who share a determination that this great institution will perform well and that, through its performance, the nation will prosper.

REFERENCES

Aberbach, J. D., Putnam, R. D., and Rockman, B. A. *Bureaucrats and Politicians in Western Democracies.* Cambridge, Mass.: Harvard University Press, 1981.

Abney, G., and Lauth, T. *The Politics of State and City Administration.* Albany: State University of New York Press, 1986.

Adams, J. S. "Inequity in Social Exchange." In L. Berkowitz (ed.), *Advances in Experimental and Social Psychology.* Orlando, Fla.: Academic Press, 1965.

Aharoni, Y. *The Evolution and Management of State-Owned Enterprises.* New York: Ballinger, 1986.

Alderfer, C. P. *Existence, Relatedness, and Growth: Human Needs in Organizational Settings.* New York: Free Press, 1972.

Aldrich, H. E. *Organizations and Environments.* Upper Saddle River, N.J.: Prentice Hall, 1979.

Alimard, A. *Management Policy in State Government: The Commonwealth of Virginia.* Richmond: Center for Public Affairs, Virginia Commonwealth University, 1987.

Allison, G. T. "Public and Private Management: Are They Fundamentally Alike in All Unimportant Respects?" In J. L. Perry and K. L. Kraemer (eds.), *Public Management.* Mountain View, Calif.: Mayfield, 1983.

Ammons, D. N., and Newell, C. *City Executives: Leadership Roles, Work Characteristics, and Time Management.* Albany: State University of New York Press, 1989.

Anderson, W. F., Newland, C., and Stillman, R. *The Effective Local Government Manager.* Washington, D.C.: International City Management Association, 1983.

Angle, H., and Perry, J. L. "An Empirical Assessment of Organizational Commitment and Organizational Effectiveness." *Administrative Science Quarterly,* 1981, *26,* 1–13.

Argyris, C. "The Individual and Organization: Some Problems of Mutual Adjustment." *Administrative Science Quarterly,* 1957, *2,* 1–24.

Argyris, C. *The Applicability of Organizational Sociology.* London: Cambridge University Press, 1972.

Arnold, P. E. "Reform's Changing Role." *Public Administration Review,* 1995, *55,* 407–417.

Atkinson, S. E., and Halversen, R. "The Relative Efficiency of Public and Private Firms in a Regulated Environment: The Case of U.S. Electric Utilities." *Journal of Public Economics,* 1986, *29,* 281–294.

Back, K. *Beyond Words.* New York: Russell Sage Foundation, 1972.

Baldwin, J. N. "Perceptions of Public Versus Private Sector Personnel and Informal Red Tape: Their Impact on Motivation." *American Review of Public Administration,* 1990, *20,* 7–28.

Balfour, D. L., and Wechsler, B. "Organizational Commitment: A Reconceptualization and Empirical Test of Public-Private Differences." *Review of Public Personnel Administration,* 1990, *10,* 23–40.

Balfour, D. L., and Wechsler, B. "Commitment, Performance, and Productivity in Public Organizations." *Public Productivity and Management Review,* 1991, *14,* 355–367.

Balfour, D. L., and Wechsler, B. "Organizational Commitment: Antecedents and Outcomes in Public Organizations." *Public Productivity and Management Review,* 1996, *19,* 256–277.

Ban, C. "The Crisis of Morale and Federal Senior Executives." *Public Productivity Review,* 1987, *11,* 31–49.

Ban, C. *How Do Public Managers Manage? Bureaucratic Constraints, Organizational Culture, and the Potential for Reform.* San Francisco: Jossey-Bass, 1995.

Bandura, A. *Principles of Behavior Modification.* Austin, Tex.: Holt, Rinehart and Winston, 1969.

Bandura, A. *Social Learning Theory.* Upper Saddle River, N.J.: Prentice Hall, 1978.

Bandura, A. *Social Foundations of Thought and Action: A Social Cognitive Theory.* Upper Saddle River, N.J.: Prentice Hall, 1986.

Bandura, A. "Self-Regulation of Motivation and Action Through Internal Standards and Goal Systems." In L. A. Pervin (ed.), *Goal Concepts in Personality and Social Psychology.* Hillsdale, N.J.: Erlbaum, 1989.

Barnard, C. I. *The Functions of the Executive.* Cambridge, Mass.: Harvard University Press, 1938.

Bartol, K. M. "Professionalism as a Predictor of Organizational Commitment, Role Stress, and Turnover: A Multidimensional Approach." *Academy of Management Journal,* 1979, *22,* 815–826.

Barton, A. H. "A Diagnosis of Bureaucratic Maladies." In C. H. Weiss and A. H. Barton (eds.), *Making Bureaucracies Work.* Thousand Oaks, Calif.: Sage, 1980.

Barzelay, M. *Breaking Through Bureaucracy.* Berkeley: University of California Press, 1992.

Bass, B. M. *Leadership and Performance Beyond Expectations.* New York: Free Press, 1985.

Baum, E., and James, A. C. "Communication in Public and Private Sector Organizations." Paper presented at the annual meeting of the Academy of Management, Boston, 1984.

Beck, P. A., Rainey, H. G., and Traut, C. "Disadvantage, Disaffection, and Race as Divergent Bases for Citizen Fiscal Policy Preferences." *Journal of Politics,* 1990, *52,* 71–93.

Bellante, D., and Link, A. N. "Are Public Sector Workers More Risk Averse Than Private Sector Workers?" *Industrial and Labor Relations Review,* 1981, *34,* 408–412.

Behn, R. D. *Leadership Counts.* Cambridge: Harvard University Press, 1991.

Behn, R. D. "The Big Questions of Public Management." *Public Administration Review,* 1995, *55,* 313–324.

Bendor, J., and Moe, T. M. "An Adaptive Model of Bureaucratic Politics." *American Political Science Review,* 1985, *79,* 755–774.

Benn, S. I., and Gaus, G. F. *Public and Private in Social Life.* New York: St. Martin's Press, 1983.

Bennis, W., and Nanus, B. *Leaders: The Strategies for Taking Charge.* New York: HarperCollins, 1985.

Berman, E. M., and West, J. P. "Municipal Commitment to Total Quality Management: A Survey of Recent Progress." *Public Administration Review,* 1995, *55,* 57–66.

Beyer, J. M., and Trice, H. M. "A Reexamination of the Relations Between Size and Various Components of Organizational Complexity." *Administrative Science Quarterly*, 1979, *24*, 48–64.

Blais, A., and Dion, S. (eds.). *The Budget-Maximizing Bureaucrat*. Pittsburgh: University of Pittsburgh Press, 1991.

Blake, R. R., and Mouton, J. S. "Overcoming Group Warfare." *Harvard Business Review*, 1984, *62*, 98–108.

Blau, P. M., and Schoenherr, R. A. *The Structure of Organizations*. New York: Basic Books, 1971.

Blau, P. M., and Scott, W. R. *Formal Organizations*. Novato, Calif.: Chandler & Sharp, 1962.

Block, P. *The Empowered Manager: Positive Political Skills at Work*. San Francisco: Jossey-Bass, 1987.

Blumenthal, J. M. "Candid Reflections of a Businesswoman in Washington." In J. L. Perry and K. L. Kraemer (eds.), *Public Management*. Mountain View, Calif.: Mayfield, 1983.

Boschken, H. L. *Strategic Design and Organizational Change: Pacific Rim Seaports in Transition*. University: University of Alabama Press, 1988.

Bourgault, J., Dion, S., and Lemay, M. "Creating a Corporate Culture: Lessons from the Canadian Federal Government." *Public Administration Review*, 1993, *53*, 73–80.

Bowsher, C. A. "OMB Management Leadership." Testimony before the Committee on Governmental Affairs, U.S. Senate, Oct. 31, 1990. U.S. General Accounting Office/T GGD 91-1.

Boyatzis, R. E. *The Competent Manager*. New York: Wiley, 1982.

Bozeman, B. *All Organizations Are Public: Bridging Public and Private Organizational Theories*. San Francisco: Jossey-Bass, 1987.

Bozeman, B. (ed.). *Public Management: State of the Art*. San Francisco: Jossey-Bass, 1993.

Bozeman, B., and Bretschneider, S. "The 'Publicness Puzzle' in Organization Theory: A Test of Alternative Explanations of Differences Between Public and Private Organizations." *Journal of Public Administration Research and Theory*, 1994, *4*, 197–223.

Bozeman, B., and Loveless, S. "Sector Context and Performance: A Comparison of Industrial and Government Research Units." *Administration and Society*, 1987, *19*, 197–235.

Breton, A., and Wintrobe, R. *The Logic of Bureaucratic Conduct*. Cambridge: Cambridge University Press, 1982.

Bretschneider, S. "Management Information Systems in Public and Private Organizations: An Empirical Test." *Public Administration Review*, 1990, *50*, 536–545.

Brock, J. *Managing People in Public Agencies*. New York: Little, Brown, 1984.

Brudney, J. L. *Fostering Volunteer Programs in the Public Sector: Planning, Initiating, and Managing Voluntary Activities*. San Francisco: Jossey-Bass, 1990.

Brudney, J. L., and Hebert, F. T. "State Agencies and Their Environments: Examining the Influence of Important External Actors." *Journal of Politics*, 1987, *49*, 186–206.

Bryant, A. "Business Advice from the Sidelines." *New York Times*, Mar. 6, 1996, p. C1.

Bryson, J. M. *Strategic Planning for Public and Nonprofit Organizations: A Guide to Strengthening and Sustaining Organizational Achievements*. San Francisco: Jossey-Bass, 1995.

Bryson, J. M., and Roering, W. D. "Strategic Planning Options for the Public Sector." In J. L. Perry (ed.), *Handbook of Public Administration*. (2nd ed.) San Francisco: Jossey-Bass, 1996.

Bryson, J. M., and Einsweiller, R. C. (eds.). *Shared Power*. Lanham, Md.: University Press of America, 1995.

Buchanan, B. "Government Managers, Business Executives, and Organizational Commitment." *Public Administration Review*, 1974, *35*, 339–347.

Buchanan, B. "Red Tape and the Service Ethic: Some Unexpected Differences Between Public and Private Managers." *Administration and Society*, 1975, *6*, 423–438.

Burke, W. W. *Organization Development*. Glenview, Ill.: Scott, Foresman, 1982.

Burns, J. M. *Leadership*. New York: HarperCollins, 1978.

Burns, T., and Stalker, G. M. *The Management of Innovation*. London: Tavistock, 1961.

Burrell, G., and Morgan, G. *Sociological Paradigms and Organizational Analysis*. London: Heinemann, 1980.

Cameron, K. "Measuring Organizational Effectiveness in Institutions of Higher Education." *Administrative Science Quarterly*, 1978, *23*, 604–632.

Cameron, K., Sutton, R. I., and Whetten, D. A. (eds.). *Readings in Organizational Decline*. New York: Ballinger, 1988.

Cameron, K., and Whetten, D. A. (eds.). *Organizational Effectiveness: A Comparison of Multiple Models*. Orlando, Fla.: Academic Press, 1983.

Campbell, J. P. "On the Nature of Organizational Effectiveness." In P. S. Goodman, J. M. Pennings, and Associates, *New Perspectives on Organizational Effectiveness*. San Francisco: Jossey-Bass, 1977.

Campbell, J. P., and Pritchard, R. D. "Motivation Theory in Industrial and Organizational Psychology." In M. D. Dunnette (ed.), *Handbook of Industrial and Organizational Psychology*. New York: Wiley, 1983.

Carroll, G. R., Delacroix, J., and Goodstein, J. "The Political Environments of Organizations: An Ecological View." In B. M. Staw and L. L. Cummings (eds.), *Research in Organizational Behavior*, Vol. 10. Greenwich, Conn.: JAI Press, 1988.

Chackerian, R., and Abcarian, G. *Bureaucratic Power in Society*. Chicago: Nelson-Hall, 1984.

Chase, G., and Reveal, E. C. *How to Manage in the Public Sector*. Reading, Mass.: Addison-Wesley, 1983.

Cherniss, G. *Professional Burnout in Human Service Organizations*. New York: Praeger, 1980.

Chi, K. "Privatization in State Government: Trends and Issues." Paper presented at the National Conference of the American Society for Public Administration, Kansas City, July 23–27, 1994.

Child, J. "Organizational Structure, Environment, and Performance: The Role of Strategic Choice." *Sociology*, 1972, *6*, 1–22.

Chubb, J. E., and Moe, T. M. "Politics, Markets, and the Organization of Schools." *American Political Science Review*, 1988, *82*, 1065–1088.

Chubb, J. E., and Moe, T. M. *Politics, Markets, and America's Schools*. Washington, D.C.: Brookings Institution, 1990.

Clark, P. B., and Wilson, J. Q. "Incentive Systems: A Theory of Organizations." *Administrative Science Quarterly*, 1961, *6*, 129–166.

Clausewitz, C. V. *On War* (M. Howard and P. Paret, eds. and trans.). Princeton, N.J.: Princeton University Press, 1986.

Clinton, B., and Gore, A. *Putting Customers First '95: Standards for Serving the American People*. Washington, D.C.: U.S. Government Printing Office, 1995.

Coch, L., and French, J.R.P. "Overcoming Resistance to Change." *Human Relations*, 1948, *1*, 512–532.

Cohen, M. D., March, J. G., and Olsen, J. P. "A Garbage Can Model of Organizational Choice." *Administrative Science Quarterly*, 1972, *17*, 1–25.

Cohen, S., and Brand, R. *Total Quality Management in Government: A Practical Guide for the Real World*. San Francisco: Jossey-Bass, 1993.

Cohen, S., and Eimicke, W. *The New Effective Public Manager: Achieving Success in a Changing Government*. San Francisco: Jossey-Bass, 1995.

Contino, R., and Lorusso, R. M. "The Theory Z Turnaround of a Public Agency." *Public Administration Review*, 1982, *42*, 66–72.

Cook, J. D., Hepworth, S. J., Wall, T. D., and Warr, P. B. *The Experience of Work*. London: Academic Press, 1981.

Cooper, J. M. "Gifford Pinchot Creates a Forest Service." In J. W. Doig and E. C. Hargrove (eds.), *Leadership and Innovation*. Baltimore: Johns Hopkins University Press, 1987.

Cooper, P. J. "Understanding What the Law Says About Administrative Responsibility." In J. L. Perry (ed.), *Handbook of Public Administration*. (2nd ed.) San Francisco: Jossey-Bass, 1996.

Cooper, T. L., and Wright, N. D. *Exemplary Public Administrators: Character and Leadership in Government*. San Francisco: Jossey-Bass, 1992.

Council of State Governments. "Privatization." *State Trends and Forecasts*, 1993, *2*, 1–36.

Council of State Governments. "Total Quality Management." *State Trends and Forecasts*, 1994, *3*, 1–35.

Coursey, D., and Bozeman, B. "Decision-Making in Public and Private Organizations: A Test of Alternative Concepts of 'Publicness.'" *Public Administration Review*, 1990, *50*, 525–535.

Coursey, D., and Rainey, H. G. "Perceptions of Personnel System Constraints in Public, Private, and Hybrid Organizations." *Review of Public Personnel Administration*, 1990, *10*, 54–71.

Crane, D. P., and Jones, W. A. *The Public Manager's Guide*. Washington, D.C.: Bureau of National Affairs, 1982.

Cranny, C. J. (ed.). *Job Satisfaction*. San Francisco: New Lexington Books, 1992.

Crewson, P. E. "A Comparative Analysis of Public and Private Sector Entrant Quality." *American Journal of Political Science*, 1995a, *39*, 628–639.

Crewson, P. E. "The Public Service Ethic." Unpublished doctoral dissertation, American University, Washington, D.C., 1995b.

Crow, M., and Bozeman, B. "R&D Laboratory Classification and Public Policy: The Effects of Environmental Context on Laboratory Behavior." *Research Policy*, 1907, *16*, 229–250.

Cyert, R. M., and March, J. G. *A Behavioral Theory of the Firm*. Upper Saddle River, N.J.: Prentice Hall, 1963.

Daft, R. L. *Organization Theory and Design*. St. Paul, Minn.: West, 1995.

Dahl, R. A., and Lindblom, C. E. *Politics, Economics, and Welfare*. New York: HarperCollins, 1953.

Davis, S. M., and Lawrence, P. R. *Matrix*. Reading, Mass.: Addison-Wesley, 1977.

Davis, T.R.V. "OD in the Public Sector: Intervening in Ambiguous Performance Environments." In J. L. Perry and K. L. Kraemer (eds.), *Public Management*. Mountain View, Calif.: Mayfield, 1983.

Dean, J. W., and Evans, J. R. *Total Quality*. St. Paul, Minn · West, 1994.

Decker, J. E., and Paulson, S. K. "Performance Improvement in a Public Utility." *Public Productivity Review*, 1988, *11*, 52–66.

Demerath, N., Marwell, G., and Aiken, M. *Dynamics of Idealism*. San Francisco: Jossey-Bass, 1971.

Deming, W. E. *Out of Crisis*. Cambridge, Mass.: MIT Center for Advanced Engineering Study, 1986.

Denhardt, R. B. *Theories of Public Organizations*. Pacific Grove, Calif.: Brooks/Cole, 1984.

Denhardt, R. B. *The Pursuit of Significance*. Belmont, Calif.: Wadsworth, 1993.

Denhardt, R. B., and Jennings, E. T. *The Revitalization of the Public Service*. Columbia: Extension Publications, University of Missouri, 1987.

Dess, G. G., and Beard, D. W. "Dimensions of Organizational Task Environment." *Administrative Science Quarterly*, 1984, *29*, 52–73.

Dewey, J. *The Public and Its Problems*. Chicago: Swallow Press, 1927.

DiIulio, J. J. "Recovering the Public Management Variable: Lessons from Schools, Prisons, and Armies." *Public Administration Review*, 1989, *49*, 127–133.

DiIulio, J. J. "Managing a Barbed-Wire Bureaucracy: The Impossible Job of Corrections Commissioner." In E. C. Hargrove and J. C. Glidewell (eds.), *Impossible Jobs in Public Management.* Lawrence: University Press of Kansas, 1990.

DiIulio, J. J. "Principled Agents: The Cultural Bases of Behavior in a Federal Government Bureaucracy." *Journal of Public Administration Research and Theory,* 1994, *4,* 277–320.

DiMaggio, P. J., and Powell, W. R. "The Iron Cage Revisited: Institutional Isomorphism and Collective Rationality in Organizational Fields." *American Sociological Review,* 1983, *48,* 147–160.

Dobbin, F. R., and others. "The Expansion of Due Process in Organizations." In L. G. Zucker (ed.), *Institutional Patterns and Organizations.* New York: Ballinger, 1988.

Doig, J. W., and Hargrove, E. C. (eds.). *Leadership and Innovation.* Baltimore: Johns Hopkins University Press, 1987.

Dominick, J. "Business Coverage in Network Newscasts." *Journalism Quarterly,* 1981, *58,* 184.

Donahue, J. D. *The Privatization Decision.* New York: Basic Books, 1990.

Downs, A. *Inside Bureaucracy.* New York: Little, Brown, 1967.

Downs, C. W. *Communication Audits.* Glenview, Ill.: Scott, Foresman, 1988.

Downs, G. W., and Larkey, P. *The Search for Government Efficiency: From Hubris to Helplessness.* New York: Random House, 1986.

Drake, A. W. "Quantitative Models in Public Administration: Some Educational Needs." In A. W. Drake, L. Keeney, and P. M. Morse (eds.), *Analysis of Public Systems.* Cambridge, Mass.: MIT Press, 1972.

Durant, R. F. *The Administrative Presidency Revisited.* Albany: State University of New York Press, 1992.

Eadie, D. C. "Leading and Managing Strategic Change." In J. L. Perry (ed.), *Handbook of Public Administration.* (2nd ed.) San Francisco: Jossey-Bass, 1996.

Earley, P. C., and Lituchy, T. R. "Delineating Goal and Efficacy Effects: A Test of Three Models." *Journal of Applied Psychology,* 1991, *76,* 81–98.

Elling, R. C. "The Relationships Among Bureau Chiefs, Legislative Committees, and Interest Groups: A Multistate Study." Paper presented at the annual meeting of the American Political Science Association, Washington, D.C., 1983.

Elling, R. C. "Civil Service, Collective Bargaining, and Personnel-Related Impediments to Effective State Management: A Comparative Assessment." *Review of Public Personnel Administration,* 1986, *6,* 73–93.

Emery, F. E., and Trist, E. L. "The Causal Texture of Organizational Environments." *Human Relations,* 1965, *18,* 21–32.

Emmert, M. A., and Crow, M. M. "Public-Private Cooperation and Hybrid Organizations." *Journal of Management,* 1987, *13,* 55–67.

Emmert, M. A., and Crow, M. M. "Public, Private, and Hybrid Organizations: An Empirical Examination of the Role of Publicness." *Administration and Society,* 1988, *20,* 216–244.

Etzioni, A. "Mixed Scanning: A 'Third' Approach to Decision Making." *Public Administration Review,* 1967, *27,* 385–392.

Etzioni, A. *A Comparative Analysis of Complex Organizations.* New York: Free Press, 1975.

Etzioni, A. "Mixed Scanning Revisited." *Public Administration Review,* 1986, *46,* 8–14.

Evans, M. G. "Organizational Behavior: The Central Role of Motivation." *Journal of Management,* 1986, *12,* 203–223.

Federal Executive Institute Alumni Association. "Quality of Federal Work Force and Morale Down." (Press release.) Great Falls, Va., Mar. 14, 1991.

Fiedler, F. E. *A Theory of Leadership Effectiveness.* New York: McGraw-Hill, 1967.

Fiedler, F. E., and Garcia, J. E. *New Approaches to Leadership: Cognitive Resources and Organizational Performance.* New York: Wiley, 1987.

Filley, A. C., House, R. J., and Kerr, S. *Managerial Process and Organizational Behavior.* Glenview, Ill.: Scott, Foresman, 1976.

Flynn, D. M., and Tannenbaum, S. I. "Correlates of Organizational Commitment: Differences in the Public and Private Sector." *Journal of Business and Psychology,* 1993, *8,* 103–116.

Follett, M. P. "The Giving of Orders." In J. S. Ott (ed.), *Classic Readings in Organizational Behavior.* Pacific Grove, Calif.: Brooks/Cole, 1989.

Fottler, M. D. "Management: Is It Really Generic?" *Academy of Management Review,* 1981, *6,* 1–12.

Frederickson, H. G., and Hart, D. K. "The Public Service and the Patriotism of Benevolence." *Public Administration Review,* 1985, *45,* 547–553.

French, J.R.P., and Raven, B. "The Bases of Social Power." In D. Cartwright and A. Zander (eds.), *Group Dynamics.* New York: HarperCollins, 1968.

French, W. L., and Bell, C. H. *Organization Development: Behavioral Science Interventions for Organization Improvement.* (4th ed.) Upper Saddle River, N.J.: Prentice Hall, 1990.

Fried, R. C. *Performance in American Bureaucracy.* New York: Little, Brown, 1976.

Fry, B. R. *Mastering Public Administration.* Chatham, N.J.: Chatham House, 1989.

Gabris, G. T. (ed.). "Why Merit Pay Plans Are Not Working: A Search for Alternative Pay Plans in the Public Sector—A Symposium." *Review of Public Personnel Administration,* 1987, *7,* 9–90.

Galbraith, J. R. *Organizational Design.* Reading, Mass.: Addison-Wesley, 1977.

Galbraith, J. R. *Designing Organizations: An Executive Briefing on Strategy, Structure, and Process.* San Francisco: Jossey-Bass, 1995.

Garnett, J. L. *Communicating for Results in Government: A Strategic Approach for Public Managers.* San Francisco: Jossey-Bass, 1992.

Garson, G. D., and Overman, E. S. *Public Management Research Directory,* Vols. 1 and 2. Washington, D.C.: National Association of Schools of Public Affairs and Administration, 1981, 1982.

Gawthorp, L. C. *Bureaucratic Behavior in the Executive Branch.* New York: Free Press, 1969.

Georgiou, P. "The Goal Paradigm and Notes Towards a Counter Paradigm." *Administrative Science Quarterly,* 1973, *18,* 291–310.

Gerth, H., and Mills, C. W. *From Max Weber: Essays in Sociology.* New York: Oxford University Press, 1946.

Gill, J. M. "Perspectives on Privatization." Working paper, University of Georgia, Department of Political Science, Athens, 1996.

Goggin, M. L., Bowman, A. O., Lester, J. P., and O'Toole, L. J. *Implementation Theory and Practice.* Glenview, Ill.: Scott, Foresman, 1990.

Gold, K. A. "Managing for Success: A Comparison of the Public and Private Sectors." *Public Administration Review,* 1982, *42,* 568–575.

Gold, S. D., and Ritchie, S. "Compensation of State and Local Employees: Sorting Out the Issues." In F. J. Thompson (ed.), *Revitalizing State and Local Public Service: Strengthening Performance, Accountability, and Citizen Confidence.* San Francisco: Jossey-Bass, 1993.

Golembiewski, R. T. "Civil Service and Managing Work." *American Political Science Review,* 1962, *56,* 964–969.

Golembiewski, R. T. "Organization Development in Public Agencies: Perspectives on Theory and Practice." *Public Administration Review,* 1969, *29,* 367–368.

Golembiewski, R. T. "Organizing Public Work, Round Three: Toward a New Balance Between Political Agendas and Management Perspectives." In R. T. Golembiewski and A. Wildavsky (eds.), *The Costs of Federalism.* New Brunswick, N.J.: Transaction, 1984.

Golembiewski, R. T. *Humanizing Public Organizations.* Mount Airy, Md.: Lomond, 1985.

Golembiewski, R. T. "Contours in Social Change: Elemental Graphics and a Surrogate Variable for Gamma Change." *Academy of Management Review,* 1986, *11,* 550–566.

Golembiewski, R. T. "Public-Sector Organization: Why Theory and Practice Should Emphasize Purpose, and How to Do So." In R. C. Chandler (ed.), *A Centennial History of the American Administrative State.* New York: Free Press, 1987.

Golembiewski, R. T. "Differences in Burnout, by Sector: Public vs. Business Estimates Using Phases." *International Journal of Public Administration,* 1990, *13,* 545–560.

Golembiewski, R. T. *Practical Public Management.* New York: Dekker, 1995.

Golembiewski, R. T., Proehl, C. T., and Sink, D. "Success of OD Applications in the Public Sector: Totting Up the Score for a Decade, More or Less." *Public Administration Review,* 1981, *41,* 679–682.

Goodman, P. S., Pennings, J. M., and Associates. *New Perspectives on Organizational Effectiveness.* San Francisco: Jossey-Bass, 1977.

Goodsell, C. T. "Bureaucratic Manipulation of Physical Symbols: An Empirical Study." *American Journal of Political Science,* 1977, *21,* 79–91.

Goodsell, C. T. *The Case for Bureaucracy.* Chatham, N.J.: Chatham House, 1994.

Gordon, J. R. *Organizational Behavior.* Needham Heights, Mass.: Allyn & Bacon, 1993.

Gore, A. *Common Sense Government: Works Better and Costs Less. Third Report of the National Performance Review.* Washington, D.C.: U.S. Government Printing Office, n.d.

Gore, A. *From Red Tape to Results: Creating a Government That Works Better and Costs Less. Report of the National Performance Review.* Washington, D.C.: U.S. Government Printing Office, 1993.

Gortner, H. F., Mahler, J., and Nicholson, J. B. *Organization Theory: A Public Perspective.* Florence, Ky.: Dorsey Press, 1987.

Greiner, L. E. "Patterns of Organizational Change." *Harvard Business Review,* 1967, *45,* 119–128.

Gross, B. M. "What Are Your Organization's Objectives?" In W. R. Nord (ed.), *Concepts and Controversy in Organizational Behavior.* Pacific Palisades, Calif.: Goodyear, 1976.

Gruneberg, M. M. *Understanding Job Satisfaction.* London: Macmillan, 1979.

Guion, R. M., and Landy, F. J. "The Meaning of Work and Motivation to Work." *Organizational Behavior and Human Performance,* 1972, *7,* 308–339.

Gulick, L. "Notes on the Theory of Organization." In L. Gulick and L. Urwick (eds.), *Papers on the Science of Administration.* New York: Institute of Public Administration, 1937.

Guralnick, D. B. (ed.). *Webster's New World Dictionary of the American Language.* New York: Simon & Schuster, 1980.

Gurwitt, R. "The Entrepreneurial Gamble." *Governing,* 1994, *7,* 34–40.

Guy, M. E. "Productivity and Gender." *Public Productivity and Management Review,* 1995, *19,* 125–127.

Guyot, J. F. "Government Bureaucrats Are Different." *Public Administration Review,* 1960, *20,* 195–202.

Haas, J. E., Hall, R. H., and Johnson, N. J. "Toward an Empirically Derived Taxonomy of Organizations." In R. V. Bowers (ed.), *Studies of Behavior in Organizations.* Athens: University of Georgia Press, 1966.

Hackman, J. R. (ed.). *Groups That Work (and Those That Don't): Creating Conditions for Effective Teamwork.* San Francisco: Jossey-Bass, 1989.

Hackman, J. R., and Oldham, G. R. *Work Redesign.* Reading, Mass.: Addison-Wesley, 1980.

Hage, J., and Aiken, M. "Routine Technology, Social Structure, and Organizational Goals." *Administrative Science Quarterly,* 1969, *14,* 366–376.

Hale, S. J. "Achieving High Performance in Public Organizations." In J. L. Perry (ed.), *Handbook of Public Administration.* (2nd ed.) San Francisco: Jossey-Bass, 1996.

Hall, R. H. *Organizations: Structure and Process.* (6th ed.) Upper Saddle River, N.J.: Prentice Hall, 1996.

Hammond, T. H. "In Defence of Luther Gulick's 'Notes on the Theory of Organizations.'" *Public Administration,* 1990, *68,* 143–173.

Hannan, M. T., and Freeman, J. *Organizational Ecology.* Cambridge, Mass.: Harvard University Press, 1989.

Hargrove, E. C., and Glidewell, J. C. (eds.). *Impossible Jobs in Public Management.* Lawrence: University Press of Kansas, 1990.

Hartman, R., and Weber, A. *The Rewards of Public Service.* Washington, D.C.: Brookings Institution, 1980.

Hayward, N. *Employee Attitudes and Productivity Differences Between the Public and Private Sectors.* Washington, D.C.: Productivity Information Center, National Technical Information Center, U.S. Department of Commerce, 1978.

Heclo, H. "Issue Networks and the Executive Establishment." In A. King (ed.), *The New American Political System.* Washington, D.C.: American Enterprise Institute, 1978.

Hellriegel, D., Slocum, J. W., and Woodman, R. W. *Organizational Behavior.* St. Paul, Minn.: West, 1995.

Hersey, P., and Blanchard, K. H. *Management of Organizational Behavior.* Upper Saddle River, N.J.: Prentice Hall, 1982.

Herzberg, F. "One More Time: How Do You Motivate Employees?" *Harvard Business Review,* 1968, *46,* 36–44.

Herzberg, F., Mausner, B., Peterson, R. O., and Capwell, D. F. *Job Attitudes: Review of Research and Opinion.* Pittsburgh: Psychological Service of Pittsburgh, 1957.

Hickson, D. J., and others. "A 'Strategic Contingencies' Theory of Interorganizational Power." *Administrative Science Quarterly,* 1971, *16,* 216–229.

Hickson, D. J., and others. *Top Decisions: Strategic Decision Making in Organizations.* San Francisco: Jossey-Bass, 1986.

Hill, L. B. (ed.). *The State of Public Bureaucracy.* Armonk, N.Y.: Sharpe, 1992.

Hirschman, A. O. *Shifting Involvements.* Princeton, N.J.: Princeton University Press, 1982.

Hjern, B., and Porter, D. O. "Implementation Structures: A New Unit of Administrative Analysis." *Organization Studies,* 1981, *2,* 211–227.

Hofstede, G., Neuijen, B., Ohayv, D. D., and Sanders, G. "Measuring Organizational Cultures: A Qualitative and Quantitative Study Across Twenty Cases." *Administrative Science Quarterly,* 1990, *35,* 286–316.

Holdaway, E., Newberry, J. F., Hickson, D. J., and Heron, R. P. "Dimensions of Organizations in Complex Societies: The Educational Sector." *Administrative Science Quarterly,* 1975, *20,* 37–58.

Holzer, M. "Productivity In, Garbage Out: Sanitation Gains in New York." *Public Productivity Review,* 1988, *11,* 37–50.

Hood, C. *The Tools of Government.* London: Macmillan, 1983.

Hood, C., and Dunsire, A. *Bureaumetrics: The Quantitative Comparison of British Central Government Agencies.* University, Ala.: University of Alabama Press, 1981.

House, R. J. "A Path-Goal Theory of Leader Effectiveness." *Administrative Science Quarterly,* 1971, *16,* 321–338.

House, R. J., and Mitchell, T. R. "Path-Goal Theory of Leadership." *Journal of Contemporary Business,* 1974, *3,* 81–97.

House, R. J., and Rizzo, J. R. "Role Conflict and Ambiguity as Critical Variables in a Model of Organizational Behavior." *Organizational Behavior and Human Performance*, 1972, *7*, 467–505.

House, R. J., and Singh, J. V. "Organizational Behavior: Some New Directions in I/O Psychology." *Annual Review of Psychology*, 1987, *38*, 619–718.

Huber, G. P., and Glick, W. H. (eds.). *Organizational Change and Redesign*. New York: Oxford University Press, 1993.

Hult, K. M. "Feminist Organization Theories and Government Organizations: The Promise of Diverse Structural Forms." *Public Productivity and Management Review*, 1995, *19*, 128–142.

Hummel, R. *The Bureaucratic Experience*. New York: St. Martin's Press, 1994.

Ingraham, P. W. "Transition and Policy Change in Washington." *Public Productivity Review*, 1988, *12*, 61–72.

Ingraham, P. W. "Of Pigs in Pokes and Policy Diffusion: Another Look at Pay-for-Performance." *Public Administration Review*, 1993, *53*, 348–356.

Janis, I. L. "Groupthink." *Psychology Today*, Nov. 1971, p. 43.

Johnson, D. W., and Johnson, F. P. *Joining Together: Group Theory and Group Skills*. Needham Heights, Mass.: Allyn & Bacon, 1994.

Juran, J. M. *Juran on Quality by Design: The New Steps for Planning Quality into Goods and Services*. New York: Free Press, 1992.

Kahn, R. F., and others. *Organizational Stress: Studies in Role Conflict and Ambiguity*. New York: Wiley, 1964.

Kalleberg, A. L., Knoke, D., Marsden, P. V., and Spaeth, J. L. "The National Organizations Study: An Introduction and Overview." *American Behavioral Scientist*, 1994, *37*, 860–871.

Kanter, R. M. "Power Failure in Management Circuits." In J. M. Shafritz and J. S. Ott (eds.), *Classics of Organization Theory*. Florence, Ky.: Dorsey Press, 1987.

Kast, F. E., and Rosenzweig, J. E. (eds.). *Contingency Views of Organization and Management*. Chicago: Science Research Associates, 1973.

Katz, D., Gutek, B. A., Kahn, R. L., and Barton, E. *Bureaucratic Encounters: A Pilot Study in the Evaluation of Government Services*. Ann Arbor: Survey Research Center, Institute for Social Research, University of Michigan, 1975.

Katz, D., and Kahn, R. L. *The Social Psychology of Organizations*. New York: Wiley, 1966.

Katzell, R. A., and Thompson, D. E. "Work Motivation: Theory and Practice." *American Psychologist*, 1990, *45*, 144–153.

Katzenbach, J. R., and Smith, D. K. *The Wisdom of Teams*. New York: HarperCollins, 1994.

Kaufman, H. *The Forest Ranger*. Baltimore: Johns Hopkins University Press, 1960.

Kaufman, H. "Administrative Decentralization and Political Power." *Public Administration Review*, 1969, *29*, 3.

Kaufman, H. *Are Government Organizations Immortal?* Washington, D.C.: Brookings Institution, 1976.

Kaufman, H. *The Administrative Behavior of Federal Bureau Chiefs*. Washington, D.C.: Brookings Institution, 1979.

Keeley, M. "Impartiality and Participant-Interest Theories of Organizational Effectiveness." *Administrative Science Quarterly*, 1984, *29*, 1–12.

Kellough, J. E., and Lu, H. "The Paradox of Merit Pay in the Public Sector." *Review of Public Personnel Administration*, 1993, *13*, 45–64.

Kelman, S. "The Grace Commission: How Much Waste in Government?" *Public Interest*, 1985, *78*, 62–82.

Kelman, S. *Making Public Policy.* New York: Basic Books, 1987.

Kelman, S. "The Making of Government Good Guys." *New York Times,* July 2, 1989, Business Section, p. 1.

Kenny, G. K., and others. "Strategic Decision Making: Influence Patterns in Public and Private Sector Organizations." *Human Relations,* 1987, *40,* 613–631.

Kerr, S. "On the Folly of Rewarding A, While Hoping for B." In J. S. Ott (ed.), *Classic Readings in Organizational Behavior.* Pacific Grove, Calif.: Brooks/Cole, 1989.

Kettl, D. F. *Government by Proxy.* Washington, D.C.: CQ Press, 1988.

Kettl, D. F. "The Image of the Public Service in the Media." In Volcker Commission, *Leadership for America: Rebuilding the Public Service.* Lexington, Mass.: Heath, 1989.

Kettl, D. F. *Sharing Power.* Washington, D.C.: Brookings Institution, 1993.

Khojasteh, M. "Motivating the Private vs. Public Sector Managers." *Public Personnel Management,* 1993, *22,* 391–399.

Kiel, L. D. *Managing Chaos and Complexity in Government: A New Paradigm for Managing Change, Innovation, and Organizational Renewal.* San Francisco: Jossey-Bass, 1994.

Kilpatrick, F. P., Cummings, M. C., and Jennings, M. K. *The Image of the Federal Service.* Washington, D.C.: Brookings Institution, 1964.

Kimberly, J. R. "Organizational Size and the Structuralist Perspective: A Review, Critique, and Proposal." *Administrative Science Quarterly,* 1976, *21,* 577–597.

Kimberly, J. R., Miles, R. H., and Associates. *The Organizational Life Cycle: Issues in the Creation, Transformation, and Decline of Organizations.* San Francisco: Jossey-Bass, 1980.

Kingdon, J. W. *Agendas, Alternatives, and Public Policies.* New York: Little, Brown, 1984.

Kingsley, G. A., and Reed, P. N. "Decision Process Models and Organizational Context: Level and Sector Make a Difference." *Public Productivity and Management Review,* 1991, *14,* 397–414.

Klein, H. J. "An Integrated Control Theory Model of Work Motivation." *Academy of Management Review,* 1989, *14,* 150–172.

Klein, J. I. "Feasibility Theory: A Resource-Munificence Model of Work Motivation and Behavior." *Academy of Management Review,* 1990, *15,* 646–665.

Kleinbeck, U., Quast, H. H., Thierry, H., and Harmut, H. (eds.). *Work Motivation.* Hillsdale, N.J.: Erlbaum, 1990.

Knott, J. H., and Miller, G. J. *Reforming Bureaucracy.* Upper Saddle River, N.J.: Prentice Hall, 1987.

Koenig, H., and O'Leary, R. "Eight Supreme Court Cases That Have Changed the Face of Public Administration." *International Journal of Public Administration,* 1996, *19,* 5–22.

Kotter, J. P. "Leading Change: Why Transformation Efforts Fail." *Harvard Business Review,* Mar.–Apr. 1995, pp. 59–67.

Kotter, J. P., and Heskett, J. L. *Corporate Culture and Performance.* New York: Macmillan, 1992.

Kotter, J. P., and Lawrence, P. R. *Mayors in Action.* Somerset, N.J.: Wiley-Interscience, 1974.

Kovach, K. A., and Patrick, S. L. "Comparisons of Public and Private Subjects on Reported Economic Measures and on Facet Satisfaction Items for Each of Three Organizational Levels." Paper presented at the annual meeting of the Academy of Management, Washington, D.C., 1989.

Kraemer, K. L., and Perry, J. L. "Institutional Requirements for Research in Public Administration." *Public Administration Review,* 1989, *49,* 9–16.

Kreitner, R., and Luthans, F. "A Social Learning Approach to Behavioral Management." In J. R. Gordon (ed.), *Organizational Behavior.* (2nd ed.) Needham Heights, Mass.: Allyn & Bacon, 1987.

Kurke, L. E., and Aldrich, H. E. "Mintzberg Was Right! A Replication and Extension of the Nature of Managerial Work." *Management Science*, 1983, *29*, 975–984.

Lachman, R. "Public and Private Sector Differences: CEOs' Perceptions of Their Role Environments." *Academy of Management Journal*, 1985, *28*, 671–679.

Ladd, E. C. "What the Voters Really Want." In J. L. Perry and K. L. Kraemer (eds.), *Public Management*. Mountain View, Calif.: Mayfield, 1983.

Landy, F. J., and Becker, W. S. "Motivation Theory Reconsidered." In L. L. Cummings and B. M. Staw (eds.), *Research in Organizational Behavior*, Vol. 9. Greenwich, Conn.: JAI Press, 1987.

Landy, F. J., and Guion, R. M. "Development of Scales for the Measurement of Work Motivation." *Organizational Behavior and Human Performance*, 1970, *5*, 93–103.

Larkin, J. "Spreading the Word: Improving Government/Media Relations Means a Better Image for Public Service." *PA Times*, 1992, *15*, 3.

Larson, M. *The Rise of Professionalism*. Berkeley: University of California Press, 1977.

Lasko, W. "Executive Accountability: Will SES Make a Difference?" *Bureaucrat*, 1980, *9*, 6–7.

Lau, A. W., Pavett, C. M., and Newman, A. R. "The Nature of Managerial Work: A Comparison of Public and Private Sector Jobs." *Academy of Management Proceedings*, 1980, 339–343.

Lawler, E. E., III. *Pay and Organizational Effectiveness*. New York: McGraw-Hill, 1971.

Lawler, E. E., III. *Strategic Pay: Aligning Organizational Strategies and Pay Systems*. San Francisco: Jossey-Bass, 1990.

Lawler, E. E., III, and Hall, D. T. "Relationship of Job Characteristics to Job Involvement, Satisfaction, and Intrinsic Motivation." *Journal of Applied Psychology*, 1970, *54*, 305–312.

Lawrence, P. R., and Lorsch, J. W. *Organization and Environment*. Cambridge, Mass.: Harvard University Press, 1967.

Leavitt, H. J. "Some Effects of Certain Communication Patterns on Group Performance." *Journal of Abnormal and Social Psychology*, 1951, *46*, 38–50.

Lerner, A. W., and Wanat, J. "Fuzziness and Bureaucracy." *Public Administration Review*, 1983, *43*, 500–509.

Lester, J. P., Bowman, A. O., Giggin, M. L., and O'Toole, L. J. "Public Policy Implementation: Evolution of the Field and Agenda for Future Research." *Policy Studies Review*, 1987, *7*, 200–216.

Levine, C. H. (ed.). *Managing Fiscal Stress*. Chatham, N.J.: Chatham House, 1980a.

Levine, C. H. "Organizational Decline and Cutback Management." In C. H. Levine (ed.), *Managing Fiscal Stress*. Chatham, N.J.: Chatham House, 1980b.

Lewis, E. B. *Public Entrepreneurship*. Bloomington: Indiana University Press, 1980.

Lewis, E. B. "Admiral Hyman Rickover: Technological Entrepreneurship in the U.S. Navy." In J. W. Doig and E. C. Hargrove (eds.), *Leadership and Innovation*. Baltimore: Johns Hopkins University Press, 1987.

Lewis, G. B. "Turnover and the Quiet Crisis in the Federal Service." *Public Administration Review*, 1991, *50*, 145–155.

Lichter, R. S., Rothman, S., and Lichter, L. *The Media Elite*. Bethesda, Md.: Adler and Adler, 1986.

Light, P. C. "When Worlds Collide: The Political-Career Nexus." In G. C. Mackenzie (ed.), *The In-and-Outers*. Baltimore: Johns Hopkins University Press, 1987.

Likert, R. *The Human Organization*. New York: McGraw-Hill, 1967.

Lindblom, C. E. "The Science of Muddling Through." *Public Administration Review*, 1959, *19*, 79–88.

Lindblom, C. E. *Politics and Markets*. New York: Basic Books, 1977.

Linsky, M. *Impact: How the Press Affects Federal Policymaking*. New York: Norton, 1986.

Lipset, S. M., and Schneider, W. *The Confidence Gap: Business, Labor, and Government in the Public Mind.* Baltimore: Johns Hopkins University Press, 1987.

Lipsky, M. *Street-Level Bureaucracy.* New York: Russell Sage Foundation, 1980.

Locke, E. A. "What Is Job Satisfaction?" *Organizational Behavior and Human Performance,* 1969, *4,* 309–336.

Locke, E. A. "The Nature and Causes of Job Satisfaction." In M. D. Dunnette (ed.), *Handbook of Industrial and Organizational Psychology.* New York: Wiley, 1983.

Locke, E. A. "The Myth of Behavior Modification in Organizations." *Academy of Management Review,* 1977, *2,* 543–553.

Locke, E. A., and Henne, D. "Work Motivation Theories." In C. L. Cooper and I. Robertson (eds.), *International Review of Industrial and Organizational Psychology.* New York: Wiley, 1986.

Locke, E. A., and Latham, G. P. *A Theory of Goal Setting and Task Performance.* Upper Saddle River, N.J.: Prentice Hall, 1990a.

Locke, E. A. and Latham, G. P. "Work Motivation: The High Performance Cycle." In U. Kleinbeck and others (eds.), *Work Motivation.* Hillsdale, N.J.: Erlbaum, 1990b.

Lodahl, T. M., and Kejner, M. "The Definition and Measurement of Job Involvement." *Journal of Applied Psychology,* 1965, *49,* 24–33.

Long, N. E. "Power and Administration." *Public Administration Review,* 1949, *9,* 257–264.

Lowi, T. *The End of Liberalism.* New York: Norton, 1979.

Luthans, F., and Kreitner, R. *Organizational Behavior Modification: An Operant and Social Learning Approach.* Glenview, Ill.: Scott, Foresman, 1985.

Lynn, L. E. *Managing the Public's Business.* New York: Basic Books, 1981.

Lynn, L. E. *Managing Public Policy.* New York: Little, Brown, 1987.

Lynn, L. E. *Public Management as Art, Science, and Profession.* Chatham, N.J.: Chatham House, 1996.

MacAvoy, P. W., and McIssac, G. S. "The Performance and Management of United States Federal Government Enterprises." In P. W. MacAvoy, W. T. Stanbury, G. Yarrow, and R. J. Zeckhauser (eds.), *Privatization and State-Owned Enterprises.* Boston: Kluwer, 1989.

MacDonald, F. "Economic Freedom and the Constitution." *Florida Policy Review,* 1987, *3,* 38–44.

Macy, J. W. *Public Service: The Human Side of Government.* New York: HarperCollins, 1971.

Maier, N.R.F. "Assets and Liabilities in Group Problem Solving: The Need for an Integrative Function." *Psychological Review,* 1967, *74,* 239–249.

Mainzer, L. C. *Political Bureaucracy.* Glenview, Ill.: Scott, Foresman, 1973.

Maitland, L. "Focus of H.U.D. Inquiry: An Obscure and Influential Woman." *New York Times,* May 31, 1989, p. 11.

Manz, C. C., and Neck, C. P. "Inner Leadership: Creating Productive Thought Patterns." *Academy of Management Executive,* 1991, *5,* 87–95.

March, J. G. "The Business Firm as a Political Coalition." *Journal of Politics,* 1962, *24,* 662–678.

March, J. G., and Olsen, J. P. (eds.) *Ambiguity and Choice in Organizations.* Bergen, Norway: Universitetsforlaget, 1976.

March, J. G., and Olsen, J. P. "Garbage Can Models of Decision Making in Organizations." In J. G. March and R. Weissinger-Baylon (eds.), *Ambiguity and Command.* White Plains, N.Y.: Pitman, 1986.

March, J. G., and Simon, H. A. *Organizations.* New York: Wiley, 1958.

Marmor, T. R. "Entrepreneurship in Public Management: Wilbur Cohen and Robert Ball."

In J. W. Doig and E. C. Hargrove (eds.), *Leadership and Innovation*. Baltimore: Johns Hopkins University Press, 1987.

Marmor, T. R., and Fellman, P. "Policy Entrepreneurship in Government: An American Study." *Journal of Public Policy*, 1986, *6*, 225–253.

Marsden, P. V., Cook, C. R., and Kalleberg, A. L. "Organizational Structures: Coordination and Control." *American Behavioral Scientist*, 1994, *37*, 911–929.

Marsden, P. V., Cook, C. R., and Knoke, D. "Measuring Organizational Structures and Environments." *American Behavioral Scientist*, 1994, *37*, 891–910.

Mascarenhas, B. "Domains of State-Owned, Privately Held, and Publicly Traded Firms in International Competition." *Administrative Science Quarterly*, 1989, *34*, 582–597.

Mashaw, J. L. *Bureaucratic Justice*. New Haven, Conn.: Yale University Press, 1983.

Maslow, A. H. *Motivations and Personality*. New York: HarperCollins, 1954.

Maslow, A. *Eupsychian Management*. Burr Ridge, Ill.: Irwin, 1965.

Maynard-Moody, S., Stull, D. D., and Mitchell, J. "Reorganization as Status Drama: Building, Maintaining, and Displacing Dominant Subcultures." *Public Administration Review*, 1986, *46*, 301–310.

Mazmanian, D. A., and Sabatier, P. A. (eds.). *Effective Policy Implementation*. Lexington, Mass.: Heath, 1981.

McCauley, C. D., Lombardo, M. M., and Usher, C. H. "Diagnosing Management Development Needs: An Instrument Based on How Managers Develop." *Journal of Management*, 1989, *15*, 389–404.

McClelland, D. C. *The Achieving Society*. New York: Free Press, 1961.

McClelland, D. C. *Power: The Inner Experience*. New York: Irvington, 1975.

McClelland, D. C., and Winter, D. G. *Motivating Economic Achievement*. New York: Free Press, 1969.

McCurdy, H. E., and Cleary, R. "Why Can't We Resolve the Research Issue in Public Administration?" *Public Administration Review*, 1984, *44*, 49–55.

McGregor, D. *The Human Side of Enterprise*. New York: McGraw-Hill, 1960.

McGregor, E. B. "Administration's Many Instruments: Mining, Refining, and Applying Charles Lindblom's *Politics and Markets*." *Administration and Society*, 1981, *13*, 347–375.

McKelvey, B. *Organizational Systematics*. Berkeley: University of California Press, 1982.

Meier, K. J. *Politics and the Bureaucracy*. Pacific Grove, Calif.: Brooks/Cole, 1993.

Merton, R. K. "Bureaucratic Structure and Personality." *Social Forces*, 1940, *18*, 560–568.

Meyer, J. W., and Rowan, B. "Institutionalized Organizations: Formal Structure as Myth and Ceremony." In J. W. Meyer and W. R. Scott (eds.), *Organizational Environments: Ritual and Rationality*. Thousand Oaks, Calif.: Sage, 1983.

Meyer, M. W. *Change in Public Bureaucracies*. Cambridge: Cambridge University Press, 1979.

Meyer, M. W. "'Bureaucratic' vs. 'Profit' Organization." In B. L. Staw and L. L. Cummings (eds.), *Research in Organizational Behavior*. Greenwich, Conn.: JAI Press, 1982.

Michelson, S. "The Working Bureaucrat in the Nonworking Bureaucracy." In C. H. Weiss and A. H. Barton (eds.), *Making Bureaucracies Work*. Thousand Oaks, Calif.: Sage, 1980.

Miles, R. E., and Snow, C. C. *Organizational Strategy, Structure, and Process*. New York: McGraw-Hill, 1978.

Miles, R. H. "A Comparison of the Relative Impacts of Role Perceptions of Ambiguity and Conflict by Role." *Academy of Management Journal*, 1976, *19*, 25–35.

Miles, R. H. *Macro Organization Behavior*. Glenview, Ill.: Scott, Foresman, 1980.

Miles, R. H., and Petty, M. M. "Relationships Between Role Clarity, Need for Clarity, and Job Tension and Satisfaction for Supervisory Roles." *Academy of Management Journal*, 1975, *18*, 877–883.

Miller, J. C. "A Presidential Veto for Pork Spending." *Wall Street Journal,* Jan. 30, 1990, p. A18.

Milward, H. B. "The Changing Character of the Public Sector." In J. L. Perry (ed.), *Handbook of Public Administration.* (2nd ed.) San Francisco: Jossey-Bass, 1996.

Milward, H. B., Provan, K. G., and Else, B. A. "What Does the 'Hollow State' Look Like?" In B. Bozeman (ed.), *Public Management: State of the Art.* San Francisco: Jossey-Bass, 1993.

Milward, H. B., and Rainey, H. G. "Don't Blame the Bureaucracy." *Journal of Public Policy,* 1983, *3,* 149–168.

Milward, H. B., and Wamsley, G. "Interorganizational Policy Systems and Research on Public Organizations." *Administration and Society,* 1982, *13,* 457–478.

Miner, J. B. *Theories of Organizational Behavior.* Orlando, Fla.: Dryden, 1980.

Mintzberg, H. *The Nature of Managerial Work.* New York: HarperCollins, 1972.

Mintzberg, H. *The Structuring of Organizations.* Upper Saddle River, N.J.: Prentice Hall, 1979.

Mintzberg, H. *Power in and Around Organizations.* Upper Saddle River, N.J.: Prentice Hall, 1983.

Mintzberg, H. *Mintzberg on Management.* New York: Free Press, 1989.

Mintzberg, H., Raisinghani, D., and Theoret, A. "The Structure of Unstructured Decisions Processes." *Administrative Science Quarterly,* 1976, *21,* 266–273.

Mitnick, B. M. *The Political Economy of Regulation.* New York: Columbia University Press, 1980.

Moe, R. C. "Managing Privatization: A New Challenge to Public Administration." In B. G. Peters and B. A. Rockman (eds.), *Agenda for Excellence 2: Administering the State.* Chatham, N.J.: Chatham House, 1996.

Mohrman, S. A., Cohen, S. G., and Mohrman, A. M. *Designing Team-Based Organizations: New Forms for Knowledge Work.* San Francisco: Jossey-Bass, 1995.

Molnar, J. J., and Rogers, D. L. "Organizational Effectiveness: An Empirical Comparison of the Goal and System Resource Approaches." *Sociological Quarterly,* 1976, *17,* 401–413.

Mooney, J. D. "The Scalar Principle." In J. D. Mooney and A. C. Reiley (eds.), *The Principles of Organization.* New York: HarperCollins, 1930.

Moore, M. H. "Police Leadership: The Impossible Dream." In E. C. Hargrove and J. C. Glidewell (eds.), *Impossible Jobs in Public Management.* Lawrence: University Press of Kansas, 1990.

Morgan, G. *Riding the Waves of Change: Developing Managerial Competencies for a Turbulent World.* San Francisco: Jossey-Bass, 1988.

Morrisey, G. L. *Management by Objectives and Results in the Public Sector.* Reading, Mass.: Addison-Wesley, 1976.

Morse, P. M., and Bacon, L. W. (eds.). *Operations Research for Public Systems.* Cambridge, Mass.: MIT Press, 1967.

Mosher, F. *Democracy and the Public Service.* New York: Oxford University Press, 1982. (Originally published 1968.)

Mott, P. E. *The Characteristics of Effective Organizations.* New York: HarperCollins, 1972.

Mowday, R. T., Porter, L. W., and Steers, R. M. *Employee-Organization Linkages.* Orlando, Fla.: Academic Press, 1982.

Murray, H. A. *Explorations in Personality.* New York: Oxford University Press, 1938.

Murray, M. A. "Comparing Public and Private Management: An Exploratory Essay." *Public Administration Review,* 1975, *35,* 364–371.

Musolf, L., and Seidman, H. "The Blurred Boundaries of Public Administration." *Public Administration Review,* 1980, *40,* 124–130.

National Academy of Public Administration. *Revitalizing Federal Management.* Washington, D.C.: National Academy of Public Administration, 1986.

National Academy of Public Administration. *Privatization: The Challenge to Public Management.* Washington, D.C.: National Academy of Public Administration, 1989.

National Center for Productivity and Quality of Working Life. *Employee Attitudes and Productivity Differences Between the Public and Private Sectors.* Washington, D.C.: National Center for Productivity and Quality of Working Life, 1978.

National Commission on the Public Service. *Leadership for America: Rebuilding the Public Service.* Washington, D.C.: National Commission on the Public Service, 1989.

Niskanen, W. A. *Bureaucracy and Representative Government.* Hawthorne, N.Y.: Aldine de Gruyter, 1971.

Nutt, P. C., and Backoff, R. W. *Strategic Management of Public and Third-Sector Organizations: A Handbook for Leaders.* San Francisco: Jossey-Bass, 1992.

O'Leary, R. "The Expanding Partnership Between Personnel Management and the Courts." In P. W. Ingraham and B. S. Romzek (eds.), *New Paradigms for Government: Issues for the Changing Public Service.* San Francisco: Jossey-Bass, 1994.

O'Leary, R., and Straussman, J. D. "The Impact of Courts on Public Management." In B. Bozeman (ed.), *Public Management: State of the Art.* San Francisco: Jossey-Bass, 1993.

Olshfski, D. F. "Critical-Incident Analysis of the Individual and Organizational Environment of Public-Sector Executives." In J. Rabin, G. Miller, and W. B. Hildreth (eds.), *Handbook of Strategic Management.* New York: Dekker, 1989.

Olshfski, D. F. "Politics and Leadership Political Executives at Work." *Public Productivity and Management Review,* 1990, *13,* 225–244.

Osborne, D., and Gaebler, T. *Reinventing Government.* Reading, Mass.: Addison-Wesley, 1992.

Ospina, S. M. "Realizing the Promise of Diversity." In J. L. Perry (ed.), *Handbook of Public Administration.* (2nd ed.) San Francisco: Jossey-Bass, 1996.

O'Toole, L. J. "Treating Networks Seriously: Practical and Research-Based Agendas in Public Administration." *Public Administration Review,* forthcoming.

Ott, J. S. *The Organizational Culture Perspective.* Pacific Grove, Calif.: Brooks/Cole, 1989.

Ouchi, W. *Theory Z: How American Business Can Meet the Japanese Challenge.* Reading, Mass.: Addison-Wesley, 1981.

Paine, F. T., Carroll, S. J., and Leete, B. A. "Need Satisfactions of Managerial Level Personnel in a Government Agency." *Journal of Applied Psychology,* 1966, *50,* 247–249.

Parkinson, C. N. *Parkinson's Law.* Boston: Houghton Mifflin, 1957.

Patchen, M., Pelz, D., and Allen, C. *Some Questionnaire Measures of Employee Motivation and Morale.* Ann Arbor: Survey Research Center, Institute for Social Research, University of Michigan, 1965.

Patterson, T. E. *Out of Order.* New York: Vintage Books, 1994.

Patterson, T. E. *The American Democracy.* New York: McGraw-Hill, 1996.

Perrow, C. "The Analysis of Goals in Complex Organizations." *American Sociological Review,* 1961, *26,* 688–699.

Perrow, C. "Departmental Power and Perspective in Industrial Firms." In M. N. Zald (ed.), *Power in Organizations.* Nashville, Tenn.: Vanderbilt University Press, 1970a.

Perrow, C. *Organizational Analysis.* Belmont, Calif.: Wadsworth, 1970b.

Perrow, C. "A Framework for Comparative Analysis of Organizations." In F. E. Kast and J. E. Rosenzweig (eds.), *Contingency Views of Organization and Management.* Chicago: Science Research Associates, 1973.

Perry, J. L. "Merit Pay in the Public Sector: The Case for a Failure of Theory." *Review of Public Personnel Administration,* 1986, *7,* 57–69.

Perry, J. L. "Measuring Public Service Motivation: An Assessment of Construct Reliability and Validity." *Journal of Public Administration Research and Theory*, 1996a, *6*, 5–24.

Perry, J. L. (ed.). *Handbook of Public Administration*. (2nd ed.) San Francisco: Jossey-Bass, 1996b.

Perry, J. L., and Kraemer, K. L. (eds.). *Public Management*. Mountain View, Calif.: Mayfield, 1983.

Perry, J. L., and Miller, T. K. "The Senior Executive Service: Has It Worked?" Paper presented at the annual meeting of the American Political Science Association, San Francisco, Aug. 1990.

Perry, J. L., Petrakis, B. A., and Miller, T. K. "Federal Merit Pay, Round II: An Analysis of the Performance Management and Recognition System." *Public Administration Review*, 1989, *49*, 29–37.

Perry, J. L., and Porter, L. W. "Factors Affecting the Context for Motivation in Public Organizations." *Academy of Management Review*, 1982, *7*, 89–98.

Perry, J. L., and Rainey, H. G. "The Public-Private Distinction in Organization Theory: A Critique and Research Strategy." *Academy of Management Review*, 1988, *13*, 182–201.

Perry, J. L., and Wise, L. R. "The Motivational Bases of Public Service." *Public Administration Review*, 1990, *50*, 367–373.

Pervin, L. A. (ed.). *Goal Concepts in Personality and Social Psychology*. Hillsdale, N.J.: Erlbaum, 1989.

Peters, B. G., and Hogwood, B. W. "The Death of Immortality: Births, Deaths, and Metamorphoses in the U.S. Federal Bureaucracy, 1933–1982." *American Review of Public Administration*, 1988, *18*, 119–133.

Peters, B. G., and Savoie, D. J. "Civil Service Reform: Misdiagnosing the Patient." *Public Administration Review*, 1994, *54*, 418–425.

Peters, T. J. *Thriving on Chaos*. New York: Knopf, 1987.

Peters, T. J. "Restoring American Competitiveness: Looking for New Models of Organizations." *Academy of Management Executive*, 1988, *2*, 104–110.

Peters, T. J., and Waterman, R. H. *In Search of Excellence: Lessons from America's Best-Run Companies*. New York: HarperCollins, 1982.

Petty, M. M., McGee, G. W., and Cavender, J. W. "A Meta-Analysis of the Relationship Between Individual Job Satisfaction and Individual Performance." *Academy of Management Review*, 1984, *9*, 712–721.

Pfeffer, J. *Power in Organizations*. Boston: Pitman, 1981.

Pfeffer, J. *Organizations and Organization Theory*. Boston: Pitman, 1982.

Pfeffer, J., and Salancik, G. R. *The External Control of Organizations*. New York: HarperCollins, 1978.

Pinder, C. C. *Work Motivation*. Glenview, Ill.: Scott, Foresman, 1984.

Pitt, D. C., and Smith, B. C. *Government Departments: An Organizational Perspective*. London: Routledge, 1981.

Poister, T. H. "Crosscutting Themes in Public Sector Agency Revitalization." *Public Productivity Review*, 1988a, *11*, 29–35.

Poister, T. H. (ed.). "Success Stories in Revitalizing Public Agencies." *Public Productivity Review*, 1988b, *11*, 27–103.

Poister, T. H., and Larson, T. D. "The Revitalization of PennDOT." *Public Productivity Review*, 1988, *11*, 85–103.

Pondy, L. R. "Organizational Conflict: Concepts and Models." *Administrative Science Quarterly*, 1967, *12*, 296–320.

Porter, E. A., Sargent, A. G., and Stupak, R. J. "Managing for Excellence in the Federal Government." *New Management*, 1986, *4*, 24–32.

Porter, L. W. "Job Attitudes in Management: Perceived Deficiencies in Need Fulfillment as a Function of Job Level." *Journal of Applied Psychology,* 1962, *46,* 375–384.

Porter, L. W., and Lawler, E. E., III. *Managerial Attitudes and Performance.* Burr Ridge, Ill.: Irwin, 1968.

Porter, L. W., and Van Maanen, J. "Task Accomplishment and the Management of Time." In J. L. Perry and K. L. Kraemer (eds.), *Public Management.* Mountain View, Calif.: Mayfield, 1983.

Porter, M. E. *Competitive Advantage.* New York: Free Press, 1985.

Provan, K. G., and Milward, H. B. "A Preliminary Theory of Interorganizational Network Effectiveness: A Comparative Study of Four Community Mental Health Systems." *Administrative Science Quarterly,* 1995, *40,* 1–33.

Pugh, D. S., Hickson, D. J., and Hinings, C. R. "An Empirical Taxonomy of Work Organizations." *Administrative Science Quarterly,* 1969, *14,* 115–126.

Quinn, J. B. *Strategies for Change: Logical Incrementalism.* Homewood, Ill.: Irwin, 1990.

Quinn, R. E. *Beyond Rational Management: Mastering the Paradoxes and Competing Demands of High Performance.* San Francisco: Jossey-Bass, 1988.

Quinn, R. E., and Cameron, K. "Organizational Life Cycles and Shifting Criteria of Effectiveness: Some Preliminary Evidence." *Management Science,* 1983, *29,* 33–51.

Quinn, R. E., and Rohrbaugh, J. "A Spatial Model of Effectiveness Criteria: Towards a Competing Values Approach to Organizational Analysis." *Management Science,* 1983, *29,* 363–377.

Radin, B. A., and Hawley, W. D. *The Politics of Federal Reorganization: Creating the U.S. Department of Education.* New York: Pergamon Press, 1988.

Rainey, G. W. "Implementation and Managerial Creativity: A Study of the Development of Client-Centered Units in Human Service Programs." In D. J. Palumbo and D. J. Calista (eds.), *Implementation and the Policy Process.* Westport, Conn.: Greenwood Press, 1990.

Rainey, G. W., and Rainey, H. G. "Breaching the Hierarchical Imperative: The Modularization of the Social Security Claims Process." In D. J. Calista (ed.), *Bureaucratic and Governmental Reform.* (JAI Research Annual in Public Policy Analysis and Management.) Greenwich, Conn.: JAI Press, 1986.

Rainey, H. G. "Perceptions of Incentives in Business and Government: Implications for Civil Service Reform." *Public Administration Review,* 1979, *39,* 440–448.

Rainey, H. G. "Reward Preferences Among Public and Private Managers: In Search of the Service Ethic." *American Review of Public Administration,* 1982, *16,* 288–302.

Rainey, H. G. "Public Agencies and Private Firms: Incentive Structures, Goals, and Individual Roles." *Administration and Society,* 1983, *15,* 207–242.

Rainey, H. G. "Public Management: Recent Research on the Political Context and Managerial Roles, Structures, and Behaviors." *Yearly Review of Management of the Journal of Management,* 1989, *15,* 229–250.

Rainey, H. G. "Toward a Theory of Goal Ambiguity in Public Organizations." In J. L. Perry (ed.), *Research in Public Administration,* Vol. 2. Greenwich, Conn.: JAI Press, 1993a.

Rainey, H. G. "Work Motivation." In R. T. Golembiewski (ed.), *Handbook of Organizational Behavior.* New York: Dekker, 1993b.

Rainey, H. G., Backoff, R. W., and Levine, C. L. "Comparing Public and Private Organizations." *Public Administration Review,* 1976, *36,* 233–246.

Rainey, H. G., Facer, R., and Bozeman, B. "Repeated Findings of Sharp Differences Between Public and Private Managers' Perceptions of Personnel Rules." Paper presented at the 1995 Annual Meeting of the American Political Science Association, Chicago, Aug. 31–Sept. 3, 1995.

Rainey, H. G., and Milward, H. B. "Public Organizations: Policy Networks and Environments." In R. H. Hall and R. E. Quinn (eds.), *Organizational Theory and Public Policy.* Thousand Oaks, Calif.: Sage, 1983.

Rainey, H. G., Traut, C., and Blunt, B. "Reward Expectancies and Other Work-Related Attitudes in Public and Private Organizations: A Review and Extension." *Review of Public Personnel Administration,* 1986, *6,* 50–73.

Rawls, J. R., Ullrich, R. A., and Nelson, O. T. "A Comparison of Managers Entering or Reentering the Profit and Nonprofit Sectors." *Academy of Management Journal,* 1975, *18,* 616–622.

Rehfuss, J. *The Job of the Public Manager.* Florence, Ky.: Dorsey Press, 1989.

Rhinehart, J. B., and others. "Comparative Study of Need Satisfaction in Governmental and Business Hierarchies." *Journal of Applied Psychology,* 1969, *53,* 230–235.

Riccucci, N. M. *Unsung Heroes: Federal Executives Making a Difference.* Washington, D.C.: Georgetown University Press, 1995.

Ring, P. S. "Strategic Issues: What Are They and Where Do They Come From?" In J. M. Bryson and R. C. Einsweiller (eds.), *Strategic Planning.* Chicago: Planners Press, 1988.

Ring, P. S., and Perry, J. L. "Strategic Management in Public and Private Organizations: Implications of Distinctive Contexts and Constraints." *Academy of Management Review,* 1985, *10,* 276–286.

Ripley, R. B., and Franklin, G. A. *Bureaucracy and Policy Implementation.* Florence, Ky.: Dorsey Press, 1982.

Ripley, R. B., and Franklin, G. A. *Congress, the Bureaucracy, and Public Policy.* Florence, Ky.: Dorsey Press, 1984.

Rizzo, J. R., House, R. J., and Lirtzman, S. E. "Role Conflict and Ambiguity in Complex Organizations." *Administrative Science Quarterly,* 1970, *15,* 150–163.

Robbins, S. P. *Organizational Behavior.* Englewood Cliffs, N.J.: Prentice-Hall, 1996.

Roberts, N. C., and King, P. J. *Transforming Public Policy: Dynamics of Policy Entrepreneurship and Innovation.* San Francisco: Jossey-Bass, 1996.

Robertson, P. J., and Seneviratne, S. J. "Outcomes of Planned Organizational Change in the Public Sector: A Meta-Analytic Comparison to the Private Sector." *Public Administration Review,* 1995, *55,* 547–558.

Roessner, J. D. "Incentives to Innovate in Public and Private Organizations." In J. L. Perry and K. L. Kraemer (eds.), *Public Management.* Mountain View, Calif.: Mayfield, 1983.

Roethlisberger, F. J., and Dickson, W. J. *Management and the Worker.* Cambridge, Mass.: Harvard University Press, 1939.

Rogers, E. M., and Argawala-Rogers, R. *Communication in Organizations.* New York: Free Press, 1976.

Rogers, E. M., and Kim, J. "Diffusion of Innovations in Public Organizations." In R. L. Merrit (ed.), *Innovation in the Public Sector.* Thousand Oaks, Calif.: Sage, 1985.

Rohrbaugh, J. "Operationalizing the Competing Values Approach: Measuring Performance in the Employment Service." *Public Productivity Review,* 1981, *5,* 141–159.

Rokeach, M. *The Nature of Human Values.* New York: Free Press, 1973.

Romzek, B. S. "Employee Investment and Commitment: The Ties That Bind." *Public Administration Review,* 1990, *50,* 274–382.

Romzek, B. S., and Dubnick, M. J. "Accountability in the Public Sector: Lessons from the *Challenger* Tragedy." *Public Administration Review,* 1987, *47,* 227–239.

Romzek, B., and Hendricks, J. "Organizational Involvement and Representative Bureaucracy: Can We Have It Both Ways?" *American Political Science Review*, 1982, *76*, 75–82.

Rosen, B. *Holding Government Bureaucracies Accountable*. New York: Praeger, 1989.

Rosenbloom, D. H. *Public Administration and Law*. New York: Dekker, 1983.

Rosenbloom, D. H. *Public Administration*. New York: Random House, 1989.

Rourke, F. E. *Bureaucracy, Politics, and Public Policy*. New York: Little, Brown, 1984.

Rubin, I. S. *Shrinking the Federal Government: The Effect of Cutbacks on Five Federal Agencies*. White Plains, N.Y.: Longman, 1985.

Rubin, M. S. "Sagas, Ventures, Quests, and Parlays: A Typology of Strategies in the Public Sector." In J. M. Bryson and R. C. Einsweiller (eds.), *Strategic Planning*. Chicago: Planners Press, 1988.

Rumsfeld, D. "A Politician-Turned-Executive Surveys Both Worlds." In J. L. Perry and K. L. Kraemer (eds.), *Public Management*. Mountain View, Calif.: Mayfield, 1983.

Ruttenberg, S. H., and Gutchess, J. *Manpower Challenge of the 1970s: Institutions and Social Change*. Baltimore: Johns Hopkins University Press, 1970.

Salamon, L. M. (ed.). *Beyond Privatization: The Tools of Government Action*. Washington, D.C.: Urban Institute, 1989.

Saltzstein, G. H. "Explorations in Bureaucratic Responsiveness." In L. B. Hill (ed.), *The State of Public Bureaucracy*. Armonk, N.Y.: Sharpe, 1992.

Sandeep, P. "Why Government Can't Always Get the Best." *Government Executive*, Mar. 1989, p. 64.

Sanders, R. P. "The 'Best and Brightest': Can the Public Service Compete?" In Volcker Commission, *Leadership for America: Rebuilding the Public Service*. Lexington, Mass.: Heath, 1989.

Sanders, R. P., and Thompson, J. D. "The Reinvention Revolution." *Government Executive*. 1996, *28*, 1–12.

Savas, E. S. *Privatization: The Key to Better Government*. Chatham, N.J.: Chatham House, 1987.

Schay, B. W. "Effects of Performance-Contingent Pay on Employee Attitudes." *Public Personnel Management*, 1988, *17*, 237–250.

Schein, E. H. *Organizational Culture and Leadership: A Dynamic View*. San Francisco: Jossey-Bass, 1992.

Schott, R. L. "The Professions in Government: Engineering as a Case in Point." *Public Administration Review*, 1978, *38*, 126–132.

Schuler, R. S. "Role Perceptions, Satisfaction, and Performance Moderated by Organizational Level and Participation in Decision Making." *Academy of Management Level*, 1977, *20*, 159–165.

Schuster, J. R. "Management Compensation Policy and the Public Interest." *Public Personnel Management*, 1974, *3*, 510–523.

Schwartz, J. E. *America's Hidden Success: A Reassessment of Twenty Years of Public Policy*. New York: Norton, 1983.

Schwenk, C. R. "Conflict in Organizational Decision Making: An Exploratory Study of Its Effects in For-Profit and Not-for-Profit Organizations." *Management Science*, 1990, *36*, 436–448.

Scott, W. R. "The Adolescence of Institutional Theory." *Administrative Science Quarterly*, 1987, *32*, 493–511.

Seidman, H. "Public Enterprises in the United States." *Annals of Public and Cooperative Economy*, 1983, *54*, 3–18.

Seidman, H., and Gilmour, R. *Politics, Position, and Power*. New York: Little, Brown, 1986.

Selznick, P. *Leadership and Administration*. New York: HarperCollins, 1957.

Selznick, P. *TVA and the Grass Roots*. New York: HarperCollins, 1966.

Sharkansky, I. "The Overloaded State." *Public Administration Review*, 1989, *49*, 201–203.

Sherman, W. M. *Behavior Modification*. New York: HarperCollins, 1990.

Sherwood, F. P., and Rainey, H. G. "Management Policy in the State Government of Florida." In P. Downing (ed.), *Florida State University Policy Sciences Annual*. Tallahassee: Policy Sciences Program, Florida State University, 1983.

Siegel, G. B. "Who Is the Public Employee?" In W. B. Eddy (ed.), *Handbook of Organization Management*. New York: Dekker, 1983.

Sikula, A. F. "The Values and Value Systems of Governmental Executives." *Public Personnel Management*, 1973a, *2*, 16–22.

Sikula, A. F. "The Values and Value Systems of Industrial Personnel Managers." *Public Personnel Management*, 1973b, *2*, 305–309.

Simon, H. A. "The Proverbs of Administration." *Public Administration Review*, 1946, *6*, 53–67.

Simon, H. A. *Administrative Behavior*. New York: Free Press, 1948.

Simon, H. A. "On the Concept of Organizational Goal." In F. E. Kast and J. E. Rosenzweig (eds.), *Contingency Views of Organization and Management*. Chicago: Science Research Associates, 1973.

Simon, H. A. "Organizations and Markets." *Journal of Public Administration Research and Theory*, 1995, *5*, 273–294.

Simon, H. A., Smithburg, D. W., and Thompson, V. A. *Public Administration*. New York: Knopf, 1950.

Simon, M. E. "Matrix Management at the U.S. Consumer Product Safety Commission." *Public Administration Review*, 1983, *43*, 357–361.

Sims, H. P., and Lorenzi, P. *The New Leadership Paradigm*. Thousand Oaks, Calif.: Sage, 1992.

Skinner, B. F. *Science and Human Behavior*. New York: Free Press, 1953.

Smith, F. J. "Index of Organizational Reactions." *JSAS Catalogue of Selected Documents in Psychology*, 1976, *6*, 54.

Smith, M. P., and Nock, S. L. "Social Class and the Quality of Life in Public and Private Organizations." *Journal of Social Issues*, 1980, *36*, 59–75.

Smith, S. R., and Lipsky, M. *Nonprofits for Hire: The Welfare State in the Age of Contracting*. Cambridge, Mass.: Harvard University Press, 1993.

Solomon, E. E. "Private and Public Sector Managers: An Empirical Investigation of Job Characteristics and Organizational Climate." *Journal of Applied Psychology*, 1986, *71*, 247–259.

Starbuck, W. H. "Organizations and Their Environments." In M. D. Dunnette (ed.), *Handbook of Industrial and Organizational Psychology*. New York: Wiley, 1983.

Starbuck, W. H., and Nystrom, P. C. "Designing and Understanding Organizations." In P. C. Nystrom and W. H. Starbuck (eds.), *Handbook of Organizational Design*. New York: Oxford University Press, 1981.

Steel, B. S., and Warner, R. L. "Job Satisfaction Among Early Labor Force Participants: Unexpected Outcomes in Public and Private Sector Comparisons." *Review of Public Personnel Administration*, 1990, *10*, 4–22.

Steinhaus, C. S., and Perry, J. L. "Organizational Commitment: Does Sector Matter?" *Public Productivity and Management Review*, 1996, *19*, 278–288.

Stephens, J. E. "Turnaround at the Alabama Rehabilitation Agency." *Public Productivity Review*, 1988, *11*, 67–84.

Stevens, J. M., Wartick, S. L., and Bagby, J. *Business-Government Relations and Interdependence: A Managerial and Analytical Perspective*. New York: Praeger, 1988.

Stewart, R. B. "The Reformation of American Administrative Law." *Harvard Law Review,* 1975, *88,* 1667–1711.

Stillman, R. *The American Bureaucracy.* Chicago: Nelson-Hall, 1996.

Swiss, J. E. *Public Management Systems.* Upper Saddle River, N.J.: Prentice Hall, 1991.

Taylor, F. W. *The Principles of Scientific Management.* New York: HarperCollins, 1919.

Tehrani, M., Montanari, J. R., and Carson, K. R. "Technology as Determinant of Organization Structure: A Meta-Analytic Review." In L. R. Jauch and J. L. Wall (eds.), *Proceedings of the Annual Meeting of the Academy of Management, 1990.*

't Hart, P. *Groupthink in Government: A Study of Small Groups and Policy Failure.* Amsterdam: Swetz and Zeitlinger, 1990.

Thomas, K. W. "Conflict and Conflict Management." In M. D. Dunnette (ed.), *Handbook of Industrial and Organizational Psychology.* New York: Wiley, 1983.

Thompson, F., and Jones, L. R. *Reinventing the Pentagon: How the New Public Management Can Bring Institutional Renewal.* San Francisco: Jossey-Bass, 1994.

Thompson, F. J. *Personnel Policy in the City.* Berkeley: University of California Press, 1975.

Thompson, F. J. "Managing Within Civil Service Systems." In J. L. Perry (ed.), *Handbook of Public Administration.* San Francisco: Jossey-Bass, 1989.

Thompson, F. J. (ed.). *Revitalizing State and Local Public Service: Strengthening Performance, Accountability, and Citzen Confidence.* San Francisco: Jossey-Bass, 1993.

Thompson, J. D. "Common and Uncommon Elements in Administration." *Social Welfare Forum,* 1962, *89,* 181–201.

Thompson, J. D. *Organizations in Action.* New York: McGraw-Hill, 1967.

Tichy, N. M. *Managing Strategic Change.* New York: Wiley, 1983.

Tichy, N. M., and Ulrich, D. "The Leadership Challenge: A Call for the Transformational Leader." *Sloan Management Review,* 1984, *26,* 59–68.

Tierney, J. T. *The U.S. Postal Service.* Westport, Conn.: Auburn House, 1988.

Tolbert, P. S. "Resource Dependence and Institutional Environments: Sources of Administrative Structure in Institutions of Higher Education." *Administrative Science Quarterly,* 1985, *30,* 1–13.

Tolbert, P. S., and Zucker, L. G. "Institutional Sources of Change in the Formal Structure of Organizations: The Diffusion of Civil Service Reform, 1880–1935." *Administrative Science Quarterly,* 1983, *28,* 22–39.

Tolchin, M. "Sixteen States Failing to Pay Required Medicare Costs." *New York Times,* Mar. 9, 1989, p. 45.

Trice, H. M., and Beyer, J. M. *The Cultures of Work Organizations.* Upper Saddle River, N.J.: Prentice Hall, 1993.

Trist, E. L., and Bamforth, K. W. "Some Social and Psychological Consequences of the Longwall Method of Coal Getting." *Human Relations,* 1951, *4,* 3–38.

Tullock, G. *The Politics of Bureaucracy.* Washington, D.C.: Public Affairs Press, 1965.

U.S. Department of Health and Human Services, Social Security Administration, Office of Strategic Planning. *2000: A Strategic Plan.* (SSA Publication no. 01–001.) Washington, D.C.: U.S. Department of Health and Human Services, 1988.

U.S. Department of the Treasury, Internal Revenue Service. *Internal Revenue Service Strategic Plan.* (IRS Document no. 6941.) Washington, D.C.: U.S. Department of the Treasury, 1984.

U.S. General Accounting Office. *Social Security: Actions and Plans to Reduce Agency Staff.* (GAO/HRD-86-76BR.) Washington, D.C.: U.S. General Accounting Office, 1986.

U.S. General Accounting Office. *Federal Pay: Comparisons with the Private Sector by Job and Locality.* (GAO/GGD-90-81FS.) Washington, D.C.: U.S. General Accounting Office, 1990.

U.S. Merit Systems Protection Board. *Working for the Federal Government: Job Satisfaction and Federal Employees.* Washington, D.C.: U.S. Merit Systems Protection Board, 1987.

U.S. Office of Personnel Management. *Federal Employee Attitudes.* Washington, D.C.: U.S. Office of Personnel Management, 1979, 1980, 1983.

U.S. Social Security Administration. *General Business Plan.* (SSA Publication no. 01–008.) Washington, D.C.: U.S. Social Security Administration, 1995.

Van de Ven, A. H. "Review of H. E. Aldrich, *Organizations and Environments.*" *Administrative Science Quarterly,* 1979, *24,* 320–326.

Van de Ven, A. H. "Early Planning, Implementation, and Performance of New Organizations." In J. R. Kimberly, R. H. Miles, and Associates, *The Organizational Life Cycle: Issues in the Creation, Transformation, and Decline of Organizations.* San Francisco: Jossey-Bass, 1980.

Van de Ven, A. H., Delbecq, A. L., and Koenig, R. "Determinants of Coordination Modes Within Organizations." *American Sociological Review,* 1976, *41,* 322–338.

Van de Ven, A. H., and Ferry, D. L. *Measuring and Assessing Organizations.* New York: Wiley-Interscience, 1980.

Viteritti, J. P. "Public Organization Environments: Constituents, Clients, and Urban Governance." *Administration and Society,* 1990, *21,* 425–451.

Volcker Commission. *Leadership for America: Rebuilding the Public Service.* Lexington, Mass.: Heath, 1989.

Vroom, V. H. *Work and Motivation.* New York: Wiley, 1964.

Vroom, V. H., and Jago, A. J. "Decision Making as a Social Process: Normative and Descriptive Models of Leader Behavior." *Decision Sciences,* 1974, *5,* 743–769.

Vroom, V. H., and Yetton, P. W. *Leadership and Decision-Making.* Pittsburgh: University of Pittsburgh Press, 1973.

Waldman, S., Cohn, B., and Thomas, R. "The HUD Ripoff." *Newsweek,* Aug. 7, 1989, pp. 16–22.

Waldo, D. *The Administrative State.* New York: Holmes & Meier, 1984. (Originally published 1947.)

Walsh, A. H. *The Public's Business: The Politics and Practices of Government Corporations.* Cambridge, Mass.: MIT Press, 1978.

Walters, J. "Flattening Bureaucracy." *Governing,* 1996, *9,* 20–24.

Wamsley, G. L., and Zald, M. N. *The Political Economy of Public Organizations.* Lexington, Mass.: Heath, 1973.

Wamsley, G. L., and others. *Refounding Public Administration.* Thousand Oaks, Calif.: Sage, 1990.

Warwick, D. P. *A Theory of Public Bureaucracy.* Cambridge, Mass.: Harvard University Press, 1975.

Waste, R. J. *Power and Pluralism in American Cities.* Westport, Conn.: Greenwood Press, 1987.

Webber, R. A. "Staying Organized." *Wharton Magazine,* 1979, *3,* 16–23.

Wechsler, B. "Reinventing Florida's Civil Service System: The Failure of Reform." *Review of Public Personnel Administration,* 1994, *14,* 64–75.

Wechsler, B., and Backoff, R. W. "Policy Making and Administration in State Agencies: Strategic Management Approaches." *Public Administration Review,* 1986, *16,* 321–327.

Wechsler, B., and Backoff, R. W. "The Dynamics of Strategy in Public Organizations." In J. M. Bryson and R. C. Einsweiller (eds.), *Strategic Planning.* Chicago: Planners Press, 1988.

Weick, K. E. *The Social Psychology of Organizing.* Reading, Mass.: Addison-Wesley, 1979.

Weidenbaum, M. L. *The Modern Public Sector: New Ways of Doing the Government's Business.* New York: Basic Books, 1969.

Weinberg, M. W. *Managing the State.* Cambridge, Mass.: MIT Press, 1977.

Weiss, D. J., Dawis, R. V., England, G. W., and Lofquist, L. H. *Manual for the Minnesota Satisfaction Questionnaire.* Minneapolis: Industrial Relations Center, University of Minnesota, 1967.

Weiss, H. L. "Why Business and Government Exchange Executives." In J. L. Perry and K. L. Kraemer (eds.), *Public Management.* Mountain View, Calif.: Mayfield, 1983.

West, W. F. *Controlling the Bureaucracy.* Armonk, N.Y.: Sharpe, 1995.

Whetten, D. A. "Interorganizational Relations." In J. Lorsch (ed.), *Handbook of Organizational Behavior.* Upper Saddle River, N.J.: Prentice Hall, 1987.

Whetten, D. A. "Sources, Responses, and Effects of Organizational Decline." In K. Cameron, R. I. Sutton, and D. A. Whetten (eds.), *Readings in Organizational Decline.* New York: Ballinger, 1988.

White, J. D., and Adams, G. B. *Research in Public Administration: Reflections on Theory and Practice.* Thousand Oaks, Calif.: Sage, 1994.

Whorton, J. W., and Worthley, J. A. "A Perspective on the Challenge of Public Management: Environmental Paradox and Organizational Culture." *Academy of Management Review,* 1981, *6,* 357–361.

Wildavsky, A. *The New Politics of the Budgetary Process.* Glenview, Ill.: Scott, Foresman, 1988.

Wildavsky, A. *Speaking Truth to Power.* New York: Little, Brown, 1979.

Wilkins, A. L. *Developing Corporate Character: How to Successfully Change an Organization Without Destroying It.* San Francisco: Jossey-Bass, 1989.

Williamson, O. E. *Markets and Hierarchies.* New York: Free Press, 1975.

Williamson, O. E. "The Economics of Organizations: The Transaction Cost Approach." *American Journal of Sociology,* 1981, *87,* 548–577.

Williamson, O. E. (ed.). *Organization Theory: From Chester Barnard to the Present and Beyond.* New York: Oxford University Press, 1990.

Wilson, J. Q. *Political Organizations.* New York: Basic Books, 1973.

Wilson, J. Q. *Bureaucracy.* New York: Basic Books, 1989.

Wise, C. R. "Public Service Configurations and Public Organizations: Public Organization Design in the Post-Privatization Era." *Public Administration Review,* 1990, *50,* 141–155.

Wittmer, D. "Serving the People or Serving for Pay: Reward Preferences Among Government, Hybrid Sector, and Business Managers." *Public Productivity and Management Review,* 1991, *14,* 369–384.

Woll, P. *American Bureaucracy.* New York: Norton, 1977.

Wood, B. D., and Waterman, R. W. *Bureaucratic Dynamics.* Boulder, Colo.: Westview Press, 1994.

Woodward, J. *Industrial Organization: Theory and Practice.* Oxford: Oxford University Press, 1965.

Yates, D., Jr. *The Politics of Management: Exploring the Inner Workings of Public and Private Organizations.* San Francisco: Jossey-Bass, 1985.

Yuchtman, E., and Seashore, S. E. "A System Resource Approach to Organizational Effectiveness." *American Sociological Review,* 1967, *32,* 891–903.

Zalesny, M. D., and Farace, R. V. "Traditional Versus Open Offices: A Comparison of Sociotechnical, Social Relations, and Symbolic Meaning Perspectives." *Academy of Management Journal,* 1987, *30,* 240–259.

Zaltman, G., Duncan, R., and Holbek, J. *Innovations and Organizations.* New York: Wiley, 1973.

Zander, A. *Making Groups Effective.* (2nd ed.) San Francisco: Jossey-Bass, 1994.

NAME INDEX

A

Abcarian, G., 10
Aberbach, J. D., 115, 284, 289
Abney, G., 106, 109, 115, 192, 289
Adams, J. S., 222, 227–228
Adams, G. B., 9
Aharoni, Y., 70
Aiken, M., 50, 175, 217
Alderfer, C. P., 206, 207
Aldrich, F., 72, 270, 281, 283
Aldrich, H. E., 51, 72, 83, 270, 281, 283
Alimard, A., 136
Allen, C., 202, 203, 243
Allison, G. T., 9, 10, 103, 130, 144, 167, 238, 268, 269, 282, 283, 285, 286
Ammons, D. N., 281–282, 283, 288
Anderson, W. F., 290
Angle, H., 249
Argawala-Rogers, R., 301
Argyris, C., 43–44, 52, 175
Arnold, P. E., 34, 97, 368
Atkinson, S. E., 71

B

Back, K., 42, 332
Backoff, R. W., 9, 72, 73–74, 161, 164, 165
Bacon, L. W., 152
Bagby, J., 60
Baldrige, M., 362
Balfour, D. L., 249 250, 256, 257
Ball, R., 293, 345
Bamforth, K. W., 46
Ban, C., 10, 13, 84, 198, 199, 242, 351
Bandura, A., 233, 236, 237, 238, 267
Barnard, C., 25, 37–38, 39–40, 51, 145, 203–204, 208, 210, 273
Bartol, K. M., 251
Barton, A. H., 8, 129, 171, 200
Barton, E., 5, 101
Barzelay, M., 13, 70
Bass, B. M., 272
Baum, E., 312–313
Beard, D. W., 83
Beck, P. A., 100–101
Becker, W. S., 238

B

Behn, R. D., 13, 97, 130, 196, 238, 351
Bell, C. H., 330, 331
Bellante, D., 243–244
Bendor, J., 21, 153
Benn, S. I., 63
Bennis, W., 271 272, 278, 281
Berman, E. M., 360
Beyer, J. M., 52, 176, 274, 277, 279
Blais, A., 153, 213
Blake, R. R., 135, 261, 290, 308
Blanchard, K. H., 266
Blau, P. M., 27, 50, 52, 69, 175–176
Block, P., 144, 148, 224
Blumenthal, J. M., 71, 103, 130, 282
Blunt, B., 243
Boschken, H. L., 164, 165–166
Bourgault, J., 280
Bowman, A. O., 121, 193
Bowsher, C. A., 152
Boyatzis, R. E., 129, 255, 284, 312
Bozeman, B., 6, 9, 55, 58–59, 66–67, 68, 70, 71, 188, 189–190, 191, 198, 200, 203, 242, 243, 251, 252, 253

SUBJECT INDEX